EXPLORING SCIENCE IN EARLY CHILDHOOD: A DEVELOPMENTAL APPROACH

Second Edition

Delmar Publishers' Online Services

To access Delmar on the World Wide Web, point your browser to:

http://www.delmar.com/delmar.html

To access through Gopher: gopher://gopher.delmar.com

(Delmar Online is part of "thomson.com", an internet site with information on more than 30 publishers of the International Thomson Publishing organization.)

For information on our products and services:

email: info @ delmar.com

or call 800-347-7707

EXPLORING SCIENCE IN EARLY CHILDHOOD: A DEVELOPMENTAL APPROACH

Second Edition

Karen K. Lind

University of Louisville

Delmar Publishers

I (T) P An International Thomson Publishing Company

Albany • Bonn • Boston • Cincinnati • Detroit • London • Madrid • Melbourne
Mexico City • New York • Pacific Grove • Paris • San Francisco • Singapore
Tokyo • Toronto • Washington

NOTICE TO THE READER

Cover Design: Spiral Design

Delmar Staff
Senior Editor: Jay S. Whitney
Associate Editor: Erin J. O'Connor
Production Coordinator: Sandra Woods
Art and Design Coordinator: Timothy J. Conners
Editorial Assistant: Glenna Stanfield

COPYRIGHT © 1996
By Delmar Publishers
a division of International Thomson Publishing Inc.

The ITP logo is a trademark under license.

Printed in the United States of America

For more information, contact:

Delmar Publishers
3 Columbia Circle, Box 15015
Albany, New York 12212-5015

International Thomson Publishing Europe
Berkshire House 168-173
High Holborn
London, WC1V 7AA
England

Thomas Nelson Australia
102 Dodds Street
South Melbourne, 3205
Victoria, Australia

Nelson Canada
1120 Birchmont Road
Scarborough, Ontario
Canada, M1K 5G4

International Thomson Editores
Campos Eliseos 385, Piso 7
Col Polanco
11560 Mexico D F Mexico

International Thomson Publishing GmbH
Kônigswinterer Strasse 418
53227 Bonn
Germany

International Thomson Publishing Asia
221 Henderson Road
#05-10 Henderson Building
Singapore 0315

International Thomson Publishing—Japan
Hirakawacho Kyowa Building, 3F
2-2-1 Hirakawacho
Chiyoda-ku, Tokyo 102
Japan

2 3 4 5 6 7 8 9 10 XXX 01 00 99 98 97

Library of Congress Cataloging-in-Publication Data

Lind, Karen.
    Exploring science in early childhood : a developmental approach /
Karen Lind. — 2nd ed.
        p.   cm.
    Includes bibliographical references and index.
    ISBN 0-8273-7309-0
    1. Science—Study and teaching (Primary) I. Title.
LB1532.L47   1995
372.3'5044—dc20   95-35176
                                                            CIP

Contents

SECTION I CONCEPT DEVELOPMENT IN SCIENCE

SECTION II FUNDAMENTAL CONCEPTS, SKILLS, AND ACTIVITIES

SECTION III USING SKILLS, CONCEPTS, AND ATTITUDES FOR SCIENTIFIC INVESTIGATIONS IN THE PRIMARY GRADES

SECTION IV THE SCIENCE ENVIRONMENT

APPENDICES

Preface

Exploring Science in Early Childhood: A Developmental Approach, Second Edition, is designed to be used by students in training and teachers in service in early childhood education. To the student, it introduces the excitement and extensiveness of science experiences in programs for young children. For teachers in the field, it presents an organized, sequential approach to creating a developmentally appropriate science curriculum for preschool and primary age children.

Applications are presented in a developmental sequence designed to support young children's construction of the concepts and skills essential to a basic understanding of science. An emphasis is placed on activities and teaching strategies that relate constructivist principles to science teaching. A developmental approach to assessment provides an individualized program in which each child is presented at each level with tasks that can be accomplished successfully before moving on to the next level.

A further emphasis is placed on three types of learning: naturalistic, informal, and structured. Much learning can take place through the child's natural exploratory activities if the environment is designed to promote such activity. The adult can reinforce and enrich this naturalistic learning by careful introduction of information and structured experiences.

The back-to-basics and pressure-cooker instructional practices of the eighties produced a widespread use of inappropriate instructional practices with young children. Science has been largely ignored with the excuse that teaching the basics of math and reading preclude allowing time for science. This text is designed to counteract this trend and to bring to the attention of early childhood educators how interrelated science is with other subject areas and how necessary it is to provide young children with opportunities to concretely explore these domains of early concept learning.

Karen K. Lind is an Associate Professor in the Department of Early and Middle Childhood Education at the University of Louisville, Kentucky where she is the recipient of the 1993 Distinguished Teaching Professor award for lifetime achievement from the University. Dr. Lind's career in early childhood and science education has included teaching young children of differing socioeconomic backgrounds in a variety of settings. Dr. Lind was recently on leave from the University to the National Science Foundation and is a Program Director for the Teacher Enhancement and Instructional Materials Development Programs (prek-8) in the Division of Elementary, Secondary, and Informal Education.

Dr. Lind is past President of the Council for Elementary Science International (CESI). She is the Early Childhood Column Editor of *Science and Children,* a publication of the National Science Teachers Association (NSTA) and has been a member of the NSTA Preschool-Elementary Committee and the Publications Committee as well as serving on the NSTA Board of Directors.

Dr. Lind is past president of local chapters of Pi Lambda Theta and Delta Kappa Gamma Society International. She has received funding from the National Science Foundation, Kentucky Council for Higher Education, the Edna McConnell Clark Foundation, the Monsanto Foundation, and other agencies, and has served as a program evaluator for projects funded by the National Science Foundation. Her research, publications, and inservice programs focus on teaching and learning science in both formal and informal settings.

Dr. Lind has presented papers and workshops at conferences and annual meetings of the American Association for the Advancement of Science (AAAS), the American Educational Research Association (AERA), the National Association for Research in Science Teaching (NARST), the Association of Teacher Educators (ATE), National Association for the Education of Young Children, (NAEYC), the National Science Teachers Association (NSTA), and other national and state level organizations.

Acknowledgments

The author wishes to express appreciation to the following individuals and school settings:

- Rosalind Charlesworth, my co-author in the writing of our book, *Math and Science for Young Children,* which served as the basis for this book.
- Photographers Robert L. Knaster (University of Louisville), Mike Ogburn (Jefferson County Public Schools), and typist Linda Moore (University of Louisville) for their patience and expertise.
- Artist Bonita S. Carter, for the care and accuracy taken in her original art and photographs.
- My family, Eugene F. Lind and Paul and Marian Kalbfleisch, and Pamela J. Kalbfleisch for their encouragement during the writing process.
- The children and teachers who were photographed in the following early childhood centers and elementary schools:

    Walden School, Louisville, Kentucky.

    Anchorage Elementary School, Anchorage, Kentucky.

    Jefferson County Public Schools, Louisville, Kentucky.
- The following teachers, who provided a place for observation and/or cooperated with efforts to obtain photographs or provided firsthand examples of young children experiencing science:

    Maureen Awbrey and Jenny Fackler (Anchorage Schools), Susan Moore (Wilt), Elizabeth Beam (Zachary Taylor), Krista Robinson (Shryock Traditional) and Dr. Anna Smythe (Cochran, Jefferson County Public Schools).
- Anchorage Schools computer teacher Sharon Campbell, who provided recommendations for using computers with young children.
- University of Louisville graduate students Phyllis E. Ferrell, Stephanie Gray and Felicia Spaulding for their assistance with the details associated with compiling large amounts of information.
- Phyllis Marcuccio, Associate Executive Director and Director of Publications for the National Science Teachers Association, for generously facilitating the use of articles appearing in *Science and Children* and other NSTA publications.
- The staff of Delmar Publishers for their patience and understanding throughout this project.

DEDICATION

This book is dedicated to my mother

MARIAN ANGLUND KALBFLEISCH

and in loving memory of my father

PAUL ROGER KALBFLEISCH

K. Lind

SECTION I

Concept Development in Science

UNIT 1
How Concepts Develop

OBJECTIVES

After studying this unit, the student should be able to
- Define concept development
- Identify children developing concepts
- Describe the commonalities between math and science
- Label examples of Piaget's developmental stages of thought
- Compare Piaget's and Vygotsky's theories of mental development
- Identify conserving and nonconserving behavior, and state why conservation is an important developmental task
- Explain how young children acquire knowledge

Early childhood is a period when children actively engage in acquiring basic concepts. Concepts are the building blocks of knowledge; they allow people to organize and categorize information. As we watch children in their everyday activities we can observe concepts being constructed and used. For example:

- One-to-one correspondence: Passing apples, one to each child at the table; putting pegs in pegboard holes; putting a car in each garage built from blocks.
- Counting: Counting the pennies from the penny bank, the number of straws needed for the children at the table, the number of rocks in the rock collection.
- Classifying: Placing square shapes in one pile and round shapes in another; putting cars in one garage and trucks in another.
- Measuring: Pouring sand, water, rice, or other materials from one container to another.

As you proceed through this text, you will see that young children begin to construct many concepts during the preprimary period; they then apply them to the problem-solving tasks that are the beginnings of scientific inquiry.

During the preprimary period children learn and begin to apply concepts basic to both mathematics and science. As children enter the primary period (grades one through three), they apply these early basic concepts when exploring more abstract inquiries in science and to help them understand more complex concepts in mathematics such as addition, subtraction, multiplication, division, and the use of standard units of measurement.

As young children grow and develop physically, socially, and mentally, their concepts grow and develop as well. *Development* refers to changes that take place due to growth and experience. It follows an individual timetable for each child. Development is a series or sequence of steps that each child reaches one at a time. Different children of the same age may be weeks, months, or even a year or two apart in reaching certain stages and still be within the normal range of development. This text examines concept development in science from birth through the primary grades. For an overview of this development sequence, see Figure 1–5.

Concept growth and development begin in infancy. Babies explore the world with their senses (Figure 1–1). They look, touch, smell, hear, and taste. Children are born curious. They want to know all about their environment. Babies begin to learn ideas of size, weight, shape, time, and space. As they look about, they sense their relative small-

Figure 1–1 The infant learns about distance as she reaches and grasps.

ness. They grasp things and find that some fit their tiny hands and others do not. Infants learn about weight when items of the same size cannot always be lifted. They learn about shape. Some things stay where they put them, while others roll away. They learn time sequence. When they wake up, they feel wet and hungry. They cry. The caretaker comes. They are changed and then fed. Next they play, get tired, and go to bed to sleep. As infants begin to move, they develop an idea of space. They are placed in a crib, in a playpen, or on the floor in the center of the living room. As babies first look and then move, they discover space. Some spaces are big. Some spaces are small.

As children learn to crawl, to stand, and to walk, they are free to discover more on their own and learn to think for themselves. They hold and examine more things. They go over, under, and in large objects and discover their size relative to them. Toddlers sort things. They put them in piles—of the same color, the same size, the same shape, or with the same use. Young children pour sand and water into containers of different sizes. They pile blocks into tall structures and see them fall and become small parts again. They buy food at a play store and pay with play money. As children cook imaginary food, they measure imaginary flour, salt, and milk. They set the table in their play kitchen, putting one of everything at each place just as is done at home. The free exploring and experimentation of the first two years are the opportunity for the development of muscle coordination and the senses of taste, smell, sight, and hearing. Children need these skills as a basis for future learning.

As young children leave toddlerhood and enter the preschool and kindergarten levels of the preprimary period, exploration continues to be the first step in dealing with new situations; at this time, however, they also begin to apply basic concepts to collecting and organizing data to answer a question. Collecting data requires skills in observation, counting, recording, and organizing. For example, for a science investigation, kindergartners

might be interested in the process of plant growth. Supplied with lima bean seeds, wet paper towels, and glass jars, the children place the seeds in the jars where they are held against the sides with wet paper towels. Each day they add water as needed and observe what is happening to the seeds. They dictate their observations to their teacher, who records them on a chart. Each child also plants some beans in dirt in a small container such as a paper or plastic cup. The teacher supplies each child with a chart for his or her bean garden. The children check off each day on their charts until they see a sprout (Figure 1–2). Then they count how many days it took for a sprout to appear; they compare this number with those of the other class members, as well as with the time it takes for the seeds in the glass jars to sprout. The children have used the concepts of number and counting, one-to-one correspondence, time, and comparison of the number of items in two groups. Primary children might attack the same problem but can operate more independently and record more information, use standard measuring tools (i.e., rulers), and do background reading on their own (Figure 1–3).

COMMONALITIES IN MATH AND SCIENCE IN EARLY CHILDHOOD

The young child's understanding of math and science grows from the development of some of the same basic concepts during early childhood.

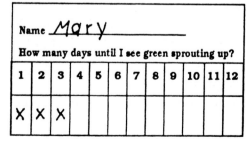

Figure 1–2 Mary records each day that passes until her bean seed sprouts.

Figure 1–3 This second grader learns through concrete activity in the first stages of the learning cycle.

Much of our understanding of how and when this development takes place comes from research based on Jean Piaget's theory of how concept development occurs. Piaget's theory is briefly described in the next part of the unit. First, the commonalities that tie math and science together are examined.

Math and science are interrelated in that the basic math concepts of comparing, classifying, and measuring are basic process skills of science (see Unit 5 for a more in-depth explanation). That is, basic math concepts are needed in order to solve problems

in science. The other science process skills (observing, communicating, inferring, hypothesizing, and defining and controlling variables) are equally important for solving problems in both science and mathematics. For example, consider the principle of the ramp, a basic concept in physics. Suppose a 2-foot-wide plywood board is leaned against a large block so that it becomes a ramp. The children are given a number of balls of different sizes and weights to roll down the ramp. Once they have the idea of the game through free exploration, the teacher might insert some questions such as, "What do you think would happen if two balls started to roll at exactly the same time from the top of the ramp?" or, "What would happen if you changed the height of the ramp or had two ramps of different heights? Of different lengths?" The students could guess, explore what happens, using ramps of varying steepness and length and balls of various types, observe what happens, communicate their observations, and describe commonalities and differences. They might observe differences in speed and distance traveled contingent on the size or weight of the ball, the height and length of the ramp, or other variables. In this example, children could use math concepts of speed, distance, height, length, and counting (how many blocks are propping each ramp?) while engaged in scientific observation. For another example, suppose the teacher brings several pieces of fruit to class: one red apple, one green apple, two oranges, two grapefruit, and two bananas. The children examine the fruit to discover as much about it as possible. They observe size, shape, color, texture, taste, and composition (juicy or dry, segmented or whole, seeds, and so on). Observations may be recorded using counting and classification skills (How many of each fruit type? Of each color? How many are spheres? How many are juicy? and so on). The fruit can be weighed and measured, prepared for eating, and divided equally among the students.

As with these two examples, it will be seen throughout the text that math and science concepts and skills can be acquired as children engage in traditional early childhood activities such as playing with blocks, water, sand, and manipulative materials, as well as during dramatic play, cooking, and outdoor activities. Additionally, commonalities in the problem-solving skills of science and the development of literacy will be explored in Units 5 and 6.

In 1987, the National Association for the Education of Young Children (NAEYC) published *Developmentally Appropriate Practice in Early Childhood Programs Serving Children From Birth Through Age Eight* as a guide for early childhood instruction. In 1989, the National Council of Teachers of Mathematics (NCTM) published standards for kindergarten through grade 12 mathematics curriculum, evaluation, and teaching.

The two NCTM publications, *Curriculum and Evaluation Standards for School Mathematics* (1989) and *Professional Standards for Teaching Mathematics* (1991), set forth developmentally appropriate practices in mathematics. The NCTM curriculum standards emphasize five goals for students:

1. Learning to value mathematics
2. Becoming confident of one's own ability
3. Becoming a mathematical problem solver
4. Learning to communicate mathematically
5. Learning to reason mathematically

There are two major national reform efforts for science education and a variety of state initiatives under development: The American Association for the Advancement of Science (AAAS) and the National Research Council (NRC). Although these groups do not disagree on the essentials of good science teaching, they do offer different perspectives.

Project 2061, the AAAS initiative, constitutes a plan to strengthen student literacy in science, mathematics, and technology. The first report, *Science for All Americans*, issued in 1989, describes the knowledge, skills, and attitudes that

students should possess as a result of their science experiences. Project 2061 recommends

1. Instructional methods based on classroom activities that engage students with science and teachers who help students actively construct meaning.
2. Science should be viewed as an activity and process, as well as a body of knowledge.
3. A focus on developing higher-order problem-solving skills, rather than rote memorization.
4. The development of students' scientific skills, scientific attitudes, and ability to make connections between science and other disciplines and between science and the real world.

Using a "less-is-more" approach to teaching, Project 2061 recommends that educators use six major themes that occur again and again in science to weave together the science curriculum: models, scale, evolution, patterns of change, stability, and systems and interaction. Although aspects of all or many of these themes can be found in most teaching units, *models and scale, patterns of change, and systems* are the themes considered most appropriate for younger children.

The second AAAS Project 2061 report, *Benchmarks for Science Literacy* (1994), categorizes the science knowledge all students need to know at all grade levels. The report is not in itself a science curriculum but is a useful resource for persons developing curriculum. Future AAAS Project 2061 reports plan to focus on exemplary instructional strategies and issues of teaching and assessment.

The second major national effort is the development of the *National Science Education Standards* (1995) coordinated by the National Research Council (NRC). The NRC initiated a process that proves qualitative criteria for judging science curricula, teaching, and assessment. The NRC coordinated the major professional organizations in science and individuals with expertise germaine to the process to produce the standards. The National Standards in Science Education echo the AAAS document and reaffirm that the AAAS document and reaffirm that elementary students should acquire information and construct knowledge through "examination, exploration, and manipulation of common objects and materials in their environment."

In addition to the two national efforts, there are state and local frameworks, such as the California Framework (1993), which guide curriculum development. Professional society position statements from the National Science Teachers Association (NSTA) (1994) and the Council for Elementary Science International (CESI) are also available.

The standards set by NCTM, NRC, and AAAS are congruent with and support the NAEYC guidelines and a constructivist approach to curriculum and instruction based on the theories of Jean Piaget and Lev Vygotsky as described next.

PIAGETIAN PERIODS OF CONCEPT DEVELOPMENT AND THOUGHT

Jean Piaget contributed enormously to understanding the development of children's thought. Piaget identified four periods of cognitive, or mental, growth and development. Early childhood educators are concerned with the first two periods and the first half of the third.

The first period identified by Piaget, called the *sensorimotor period* (from birth to about age 2), is described in the first part of the unit. It is the time when children begin to learn about the world. They use all their sensory abilities—touch, taste, sight, hearing, smell, and muscular. They also use growing motor abilities—to grasp, to crawl, to stand, and, eventually, to walk. Children in this first period are explorers and need opportunities to use their sensory and motor abilities to learn basic skills and concepts. Through these activities the young child *assimilates* (takes into the mind and comprehends) a great deal of information. By the end of this period, children have developed the concept of *object permanence*. That is, they realize that objects exist even when they are out of sight. They also

develop the ability of *object recognition*. They learn to identify objects using the information they have acquired about features such as color, shape, and size. As children near the end of the sensorimotor period, they reach a stage where they can engage in *representational thought*; that is, instead of acting impetuously, they can think through a solution before attacking a problem. They also enter into a time of rapid language development.

The second period, called the *preoperational period*, extends from about ages two to seven. During this period children begin to develop concepts that are more like those of adults, but these are still incomplete in relation to what they will be like at maturity. These concepts are often referred to as *preconcepts*. During the early part of the preoperational period, language continues to undergo rapid growth, and speech is used increasingly to express concept knowledge. Children begin to use concept terms such as big and small (size), light and heavy (weight), square and round (shape), late and early (time), long and short (length), and so on. This ability to use language is one of the *symbolic behaviors* that emerges during this period. Children also use symbolic behavior in their representational play, where they may use sand to represent food; a stick to represent a spoon; or another child to represent father, mother, or baby. Play is a major arena in which children develop an understanding of symbolic functions that underlie the later understanding of abstract symbols such as numerals, letters, and written words.

An important characteristic of preoperational children is *centration*. When materials are changed in form or arrangement in space, children may see them as changed in amount as well. This is because preoperational children tend to *center* on the most obvious aspects of what is seen. For instance, if the same amount of liquid is put in both a tall, thin glass and a short, fat glass, preoperational children say there is more in the tall glass "because it is taller." If clay is changed in shape from a ball to a snake, they say there is less clay "because it is thinner." If a pile of coins is placed close together, pre-operational children say there are fewer coins than they would if the coins were spread out. When the physical arrangement of material is changed, pre-operational children seem to be unable to hold the original picture of its shape in mind. They lack *reversibility*: that is, they cannot reverse the process of change mentally. The ability to hold or save the original picture in the mind and reverse physical change mentally is referred to as *conservation*. The inability to conserve is a critical characteristic of preoperational children. During the preoperational period children work with the precursors of conservation such as counting, one-to-one correspondence, shape, space, and comparing. They also work on *seriation* (putting items is a logical sequence, such as fat to thin or dark to light) and *classification* (putting things in logical groups according to some common criteria such as color, shape, size, use, and so on).

During the third period, called *concrete operations* (usually from ages 7 to 11), children are becoming *conservers*. That is, they are becoming more and more skilled at retaining the original picture in mind and making a mental reversal when appearances are changed. The time between ages five and seven is one of transition to concrete operations. Each child's thought processes are changing at their own rate. During this time of transition, therefore, a normal expectation is that some children are already conservers and others are not. This is a critical consideration for kindergarten and primary teachers because the ability to conserve number (the pennies problem) is a good indication that children are ready to deal with *abstract symbolic activities*. That is, they will be able to men-

Original	Physical Change	Question	Non-conserving Answer	Conserving Answer
Same amount of drink. 		Is there still the same amount of drink?	No, there is more in the tall glass.	Yes, you just put the drink in different size glasses.
Same amount of clay. 	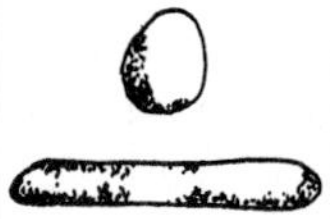	Is there still the same amount of clay?	No, there is more clay in the snake because it is longer.	Yes, you just rolled it out into a different shape.
Same amount of pennies. 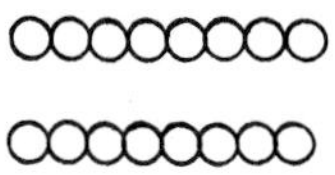	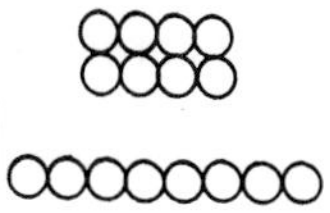	Are there still the same number of pennies?	No, there are more in the bottom row because it is longer.	Yes, you just moved the pennies closer together (points to top row).

Figure 1–4   Physical changes in conservation tasks

tally manipulate groups that are presented by number symbols with a real understanding of what mathematical operations mean. Section II of this text covers the basic concepts that children have to understand and integrate in order to conserve.

Piaget's final period is called *formal operations* (ages 11 through adulthood). During this period, children can learn to use the scientific method independently. That is, they learn to solve problems in a logical and systematic manner. They begin to understand abstract concepts and to attack abstract problems. They can imagine solutions before trying them out. For example, suppose a person who has reached the formal operations level is given samples of several colorless liquids and is told that some combination of these liquids will result in a yellow liquid. A person at the formal operations level would plan out how to systematically test to find the solution; a person still at the concrete operational level might start combining without considering all the parameters of the problem, such as labeling each liquid, keeping a record of which combinations have been tried, and so on. Note that this period may be reached as early as age 11; however, it may not be reached at all by many adults.

PIAGET'S VIEW OF HOW CHILDREN ACQUIRE KNOWLEDGE

According to Piaget's view, children acquire knowledge by constructing it through their interaction with the environment. Children do not wait to be instructed to do this; they are continually trying to make sense out of everything they encounter. Piaget divides knowledge into three areas:

- **Physical knowledge** is the type that includes learning about objects in the environment and their characteristics (color, weight, size, texture, and other features that can be determined through observation and are physically within the object).
- **Logico-mathematical knowledge** is the type that includes relationships each individual constructs (such as same and different, more and less, number, classification, and so on) in order to make sense out of the world and to organize information.
- **Social (or conventional) knowledge** is the type that is created by people (such as rules for behavior in various social situations).

Physical and logico-mathematical knowledge depend on each other and are learned simultaneously. That is, as the physical characteristics of objects are learned, logico-mathematical categories are constructed to organize information. For example, in the popular story *Goldilocks and the Three Bears*, papa bear is big, mama bear is middle sized, and baby bear is the smallest (seriation), but all three (number) are bears because they are covered with fur and have a certain body shape with a certain combination of features common only to bears (classification).

Constance Kamii, a student of Piaget's, has actively translated Piaget's theory into practical applications for the instruction of young children. Kamii emphasizes that according to Piaget, *autonomy* (independence) is the aim of education. Intellectual autonomy develops in an atmosphere where children feel secure in their relationships with adults; where they have an opportunity to share their ideas with other children; and where they are encouraged to be alert and curious, come up with interesting ideas, problems and questions, use initiative in finding out the answers to problems, have confidence in their abilities to figure out things for themselves, and speak their minds with confidence. Young children need to be presented with problems to be solved through games and other activities that challenge their minds. They must work with concrete materials and real problems such as the examples provided earlier in the unit.

VYGOTSKY'S VIEW OF HOW CHILDREN LEARN AND DEVELOP

Like Piaget, Lev Vygotsky was also a cognitive development theorist. He was a contemporary of Piaget's, but Vygotsky died at the age of 38 before his work was fully completed. Vygotsky contributed a view of cognitive development that recognized both developmental and environmental forces. Vygotsky believed that just as people developed tools such as knives, spears, shovels, tractors, and the like to aid them in the mastery of the environment, they also developed mental tools. People developed ways of cooperating and communicating and new capacities to plan and to think ahead. These mental tools helped people to master their own behavior. These mental tools Vygotsky referred to as *signs*. He believed that *speech* was the most important sign system because it freed us from distractions and allowed us to work on problems in our minds. Speech both enables the child to interact socially and facilitates thinking. In Vygotsky's view, *writing and numbering* were also important sign systems.

While Piaget looked at development as if it came mainly from the child alone, from the child's inner maturation, and spontaneous discoveries, Vygotsky believed this was only true until about the age of two. At that point, culture and the cultural signs were necessary to expand thought. He believed that the internal and external forces interacted to produce new thoughts and an expanded menu of signs. Thus, Vygotsky put more emphasis than Piaget on the role of the adult or more mature peer as an influence on children's mental development.

While Piaget placed an emphasis on children as intellectual explorers making their own discoveries and *constructing* knowledge independently, Vygotsky developed the concept of the *zone of proximal development* (ZPD). The ZPD is the area between where the child is now in mental development and where she might go with assistance from an adult or more mature child. Cultural knowledge is arrived at with the assistance or *scaffolding* provided by more mature learners. According to Vygotsky, good teaching involved presenting material that was a little ahead of development. Children might not fully understand it at first, but they would understand in time, with appropriate scaffolding. Instruction did not put pressure on development; instruction supported it as it moved ahead. Concepts constructed independently and spontaneously by children laid the foundation for the more scientific concepts that were part of the culture. Teachers must identify each student's ZPD and provide developmentally appropriate instruction. Teachers will know when they have hit upon the right zone because children will respond with enthusiasm, curiosity, and active involvement.

Piagetian constructivists tend to be concerned about pressuring children and not allowing them freedom to construct knowledge independently. Vygotskian constructivists are concerned with children being challenged to reach their full potential. Today many educators find that a combination of Piaget's and Vygotsky's views provides a foundation for instruction that follows the child's interests and enthusiasms while at the same time providing an intellectual challenge. The learning cycle view provides such a framework.

THE LEARNING CYCLE

The authors of the Science Curriculum Improvement Study (SCIS) materials designed a Piagetian-based learning cycle approach based on the assumption expressed by Albert Einstein and other scientists that "science is a quest for knowledge" (Renner & Marek, 1988). The scientists believed that if science was to be taught, students must interact with materials, collect data, and make some order out of that data. The order that students make out of that data is either a conceptual invention or it leads to a conceptual invention.

The learning cycle is viewed as a way to take students on a "quest for knowledge" that leads to the construction of knowledge. It is used as both a curriculum development procedure and a teaching strategy. Developers must organize student activities around phases, and teachers must modify their role and strategies during the progressive phases.

The phases of the learning cycle are sometimes assigned different labels and are sometimes split into segments. However, the essential thrust of each of the phases remain: exploration, concept development, concept application (Renner & Marek, 1988).

During the *exploration phase* the teacher remains in the background, observing and occasionally inserting a comment or question (see Unit 2 on naturalistic and informal learning). The students actively manipulate materials and interact with each other. The teacher's knowledge of child development guides the selection of materials and how they are placed in the environment so that they provide a developmentally appropriate setting in which young children can explore and construct concepts.

For example, in the exploration phase of a lesson about shapes, students examine a variety of wooden or cardboard objects (squares, rectangles, circles) and make observation about the objects. The teachers may ask them to describe how they are similar and how they are different.

During the *concept introduction* phase the teacher provides direct instruction; this begins with a discussion of the information the students have discovered. The teacher helps the children record their information. During this phase the teacher clarifies and adds to what the children have found out for themselves by using explanations, print materials, films, guest speakers, and other available resources (see Unit 2 on structured learning experiences). For example, in this phase of the lesson, the children exploring shapes may take the shapes and classify them in groups (squares, rectangles, and circles).

The third phase of the cycle, the *application phase*, provides children with the opportunity to integrate and organize new ideas with old ideas, relate them to yet other ideas, or apply them in a new way. The teacher or the children themselves suggest a new problem to which the information learned in the first two phases can be applied. In the lesson about shape, the teacher might introduce differently shaped household objects and wooden blocks. The children are asked to classify these items as squares, rectangles, and circles. Again, the children are actively involved in concrete activities and exploration.

The three major phases of the learning cycle can be applied to the ramp-and-ball example described earlier in this unit. During the first phase, the ramp and the balls are available to be examined. The teacher inserts some suggestions and questions as the children work with the materials. In the second phase, the teacher communicates with the children regarding what they have observed. The teacher might also provide explanations, label the items being used, and otherwise assist the children in organizing their information; at this point books and/or films about simple machines could be provided. For the third phase, the teacher poses a new problem and challenges the children to apply their concept of the ramp and how it works to the new problem. For example, some toy vehicles might be provided to use with the ramp(s).

Charles Barman (1989) describes three types of learning cycle lessons in his paper, *An Expanded View of the Learning Cycle: New Ideas About an Effective Teaching Strategy*. The lessons vary according to the way data is collected by students and the type of reasoning the students engage in. Most young children will be involved in *descriptive lessons*, in which they mainly observe, interact, and describe their observation. Although young children may begin to generate guesses regarding the reasons for what they observed, serious hypothesis generation requires concrete operational thinking (*empirical-inductive lesson*). In the third type of lesson, students observe, generate hypotheses, and design experiments to test their hypotheses (*hypothetical-deductive lesson*). This type of lesson requires formal operational thought. However, this does not mean that preoperational and concrete operational children should be discouraged from generating ideas on how to find out if their guesses will prove to be true; quite the contrary. They need to be encouraged to take the risk. Often they will come up with a variable solution, even though they may not yet have reached the level of mental maturation necessary to understand the underlying physical or logico-mathematical reasons.

ADAPTING THE LEARNING CYCLE TO EARLY CHILDHOOD

Bredekamp and Rosegrant (1992) have adapted the learning cycle to early childhood education (see Figure 1–5). The learning cycle for young children encompasses three repeating processes:

- Awareness: a broad recognition of objects, people, events, or concepts that develops from experience

CYCLE OF LEARNING AND TEACHING

	WHAT CHILDREN DO	WHAT TEACHERS DO
Awareness	Experience	Create the environment
	Acquire an interest	Provide opportunities by introducing new objects, events, people
	Recognize broad parameters	Invite interest by posing problem or question
	Attend	Respond to child's interest or shared experience
	Perceive	Show interest, enthusiasm
Exploration	Observe	Facilitate
	Explore materials	Support and enhance exploration
	Collect information	Provide opportunities for active exploration
	Discover	Extend play
	Create	Describe child's activity
	Figure out components	Ask open-ended questions—"What else could you do?"
	Construct own understanding	Respect child's thinking and rule systems
	Apply own rules	Allow for constructive error
	Create personal meaning	
	Represent own meaning	
Inquiry	Examine	Help children refine understanding
	Investigate	Guide children, focus attention
	Propose explanations	Ask more focused questions—"What else works like this?" "What happens if ___?"
	Focus	Provide information when requested—"How do you spell ___?"
	Compare own thinking with that of others	Help children make connections
	Generalize	
	Relate to prior learning	
	Adjust to conventional rule systems	
Utilization	Use the learning in many ways; learning becomes functional	Create vehicles for application in real world
	Represent learning in various ways	Help children apply learning to new situations
	Apply learning to new situations	Provide meaningful situations in which to use learning
	Formulate new hypotheses and repeat cycle	

Figure 1–5 Cycle of learning and teaching. *Note.* From *Reaching Potentials: Appropriate Curriculum and Assessment for Young Children* (Vol. 1, p. 33) by S. Bredekamp and T. Rosegrant (Eds.), Washington, DC: National Association for the Education of Young Children. Reprinted by permission.

- Exploration: the construction of personal meaning through sensory experiences with objects, people, events, or concepts
- Inquiry: learners compare their constructions with those of the culture, commonalities are recognized, generalizations are made that are more like those of adults
- Utilization: at this point in the cycle, learners can apply and use their understandings in new settings and situations.

Each time a new situation is encountered, learning begins with awareness and moves on through the other levels. The cycle also relates to development. For example, the infants and toddlers will be at the awareness level, gradually moving into exploration. Three-, 4-, and 5-year-olds may move up to inquire while 6-, 7-, and 8-year-olds can move through all four levels when meeting new situations or concepts. Bredekamp and Rosegrant (1992) provide an example in the area of measurement:

- Three- and 4-year-olds are aware of and explore comparative sizes
- Four-, 5-, and 6-year-olds explore with non-standard units, such as how many of their own feet wide is the rug
- Seven- and 8-year-olds begin to understand standard units of measurement and use rulers, thermometers, and other standard measuring tools.

Bredekamp and Rosegrant (1992) caution that the cycle is not hierarchical; that is, utilization is not necessarily more valued than awareness or exploration. Young children may be aware of concepts that they cannot fully utilize in the technical sense. For example, they may be aware that rain falls from the sky without yet understanding the technicalities of the water cycle. Using the learning cycle as a framework for curriculum and instruction has an important aspect: The cycle reminds us that children may not have had experiences that provide for awareness and exploration. To be truly individually appropriate in planning, we need to provide for these experiences in school.

The learning cycle fits nicely with the theories of Piaget and Vygotsky. For both, learning begins with awareness and exploration. Both value inquiry and application. The format for each concept provided in the text is from naturalistic to informal to structured learning experiences. These experiences are consistent with providing opportunities for children to move through the learning cycle as they meet new objects, people, events, or concepts.

THE ORGANIZATION OF THE TEXT

This text is divided into seven sections. The sequence is both integrative and developmental. Section I is an integrative section that sets the stage for instruction. Development, acquisition, and promotion of science concepts is described. A plan for assessing developmental levels is provided. Finally, the basic concepts of science and their application are described.

Section II encompasses the developmental science program for sensorimotor- and preoperational-level children (birth to age 7). Section II describes the fundamental concepts basic to science, provides suggestions for instruction and materials, and focuses on applying these fundamental concepts, attitudes, and skills at a more advanced level. Finally, Section II deals with higher level concepts and activities.

Section III encompass the acquisition of concepts and skills for children at the concrete operations level. Science continues to be integrated with other subject areas. Lessons, investigations, and concept applications are presented in all of the basic science content areas.

In Section IV, units provide suggestions of materials and resources and descriptions of science in action in the classroom, outdoors, and in the home. Finally, the appendices include concept assessment tasks, lists of children's books that contain math and science concepts as well as the NSTA Guidelines for animals in the classroom and food requirements for animals.

As Figure 1–6 illustrates, concepts are not acquired in a series of quick, short-term lessons; development begins in infancy and continues throughout early childhood and, of course, beyond. As you read each unit, keep referring back to Figure 1–6; it can help you relate each section to periods of development.

SUMMARY

Concept development begins in infancy and grows through four periods throughout a lifetime. The exploratory activities of the infant and toddler during the sensorimotor period are the basis of later success. As they use their senses and muscles, children learn about the world. During the preoperational period, concepts grow rapidly, and children develop the basic concepts and skills of science and mathematics, moving toward intellectual autonomy through independent activity, which serves as a vehicle for the construction of knowledge. Sometime between ages five and seven, children enter the concrete operations period and learn to apply abstract ideas and activities to concrete knowledge of the physical and mathematical world. The learning cycle lesson is described as an example of a developmentally inspired teaching strategy. This text presents the concepts, skills, and attitudes fundamental to math and science for young children.

Period	Concepts and Skills			
	Section II Fundamenal (Units 8, 9)	Section II Applied (Units 10,11)	Section II Higher Level (Unit 12)	Section III Primary (Units 13-17)
Sensorimotor (Birth to age Two)	Observation Problem-solving One-to-one correspondence Number Shape Space			
Preoperational (Two to seven years)	Sets and classifying Comparing Counting Parts and wholes Language	Ordering Informal measurement: Weight Length Temperature Volume Time Sequence	Sets and symbols Classifying Shape Space Informal measurement	
Transitional (Five to seven years)		Graphing	Graphing	
Concrete operations (Seven to eleven years)				Basic science concepts Whole number operations Geometry Measurement with standard units

Figure 1–6 The development of science concepts

FURTHER READING AND RESOURCES

Barman, C. R. (1989). *An expanded view of the learning cycle: New ideas about an effective teaching strategy* (Council of Elementary Science International Monograph No. 4). Indianapolis, IN: Indiana University.

Bredekamp, S. (Ed.). (1989). *Developmentally appropriate practice in early childhood programs serving children from birth through age eight.* Washington, DC: National Association for the Education of Young Children.

Bredekamp, S., & Rosegrant, T. (1992). *Reaching potentials: Appropriate curriculum and assessment for young children* (Vol. 1). Washington, DC: National Association for the Education of Young Children.

Charlesworth, R. (1992). *Understanding child development* (3rd ed.). Albany, NY: Delmar.

Crain, W. (1992). *Theories of development: Concepts and applications.* Englewood Cliffs, NJ: Prentice Hall.

Ginsburg, H. P., & Baron, J. (1993). Cognition: Young children's construction of mathematics. In R. J. Jensen (Ed.), *Research ideas for the classroom: Early childhood mathematics* (pp. 3–21). New York: Macmillan.

Inhelder, B., & Piaget, J. (1969). *The early growth of logic in the child.* NY: Norton.

Kamii, C. (1986). Cognitive learning and development. *Today's kindergarten.* NY: Teacher's College Press.

Karplus, R., & Thier, H. D. (1967). *A new look at elementary school science—Science curriculum improvement study.* Chicago: Rand McNally.

Labinowicz, E. (1985). *Learning from children: New beginnings for teaching numerical thinking.* Menlo Park, CA: Addison-Wesley.

Lawson, A. E., & Renner, J. W. (1975). Piagetian theory and biology teaching. *American Biology Teacher, 37*(6), 336–343.

National Council of Teachers of Mathematics. (1988). *Curriculum and evaluation standards for school mathematics.* Reston, VA: Author.

National Council of Teachers of Mathematics. (1991). *Professional standards for teaching mathematics.* Reston, VA: Author.

Piaget, J. (1965). *The child's conception of number.* NY: Norton.

Second standards document stresses inquiry and relevance. (1993). *NSTA Reports,* Feb./Mar., pp. 1, 6.

Social studies: Preparing responsible citizens. (1993). *AACTE Briefs, 14*(2), 4–5.

Sprung, B., Froschl, M., & Campbell, P. B. (1985). *What will happen if . . .* Mt. Ranier, MD: Gryphon House.

Sunal, C. S. (1982). Philosophical bases for science and mathematics in early childhood education. *School Science and Mathematics, 82*(1), 2–10.

SUGGESTED ACTIVITIES

1. Using the descriptions in the unit, prepare a list of behaviors that would indicate that a young child at each of Piaget's first three periods of development is engaged in behavior exemplifying the acquisition of math and science concepts. Using your list, observe four young children at home or at school. One child should be 6 to 18 months old, one 18 months to 2 1/2 years old, one age 3 to 5, and one age 6 to 7. Record everything each child does that is on your list. Note any similarities and differences observed among the four children.

2. Interview three mothers of children ages two to eight. Using your list from Activity #1 as a guide, ask them which of the activities each of their children do. Ask them if they realize that these activities are basic to the construction of math and science concepts, and note their responses. Did you find that these mothers appreciated the value of children's play activities in math and science concept development?

3. Observe science and/or math instruction in a prekindergarten, kindergarten, or primary classroom. Describe the teacher's approach to instruction, and compare the approach to Vygotsky's guidelines.

4. Interview two or three young children. Present the conservation of number problem illustrated in Figure 1–4 (see Appendix A for detailed instructions). Audiotape or videotape their responses. Listen to the tape, and describe what you learn. Describe the similarities and differences in the children's responses.

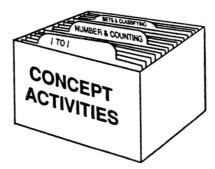

Figure 1–7 Start a math/science activity file now so you can keep it up to date.

5. You should begin to record on 5 1/2" × 8" file cards each math and science activity that you learn about. Buy a package of cards, some dividers, and a file box. Label your dividers with the titles of the units in this book. Figure 1–7 illustrates how your file should look.

R E V I E W

A. Define the term *concept development*.

B. Describe the commonalities between math and science.

C. Explain the importance of Piaget's and Vygotsky's theories of cognitive development.

D. Decide which of the following describes a child in the sensorimotor (SM), preoperational (P), or concrete operational (CO) Piagetian stages.
1. Mary watches as her teacher makes two balls of clay of the same size. The teacher then rolls one ball into a snake shape and asks, "Mary, do both balls still have the same amount, or does one ball have more clay?" Mary laughs, "They are still the same amount. You just rolled that one out into a snake."
2. Michael shakes his rattle and then puts it in his mouth and tries to suck on it.

3. John's mother shows him two groups of pennies. One group is spread out, and one group is stacked up. Each group contains 10 pennies. "Which bunch of pennies would you like to have, John?" John looks carefully and then says, "I'll take these because there are more," as he picks up the pennies that are spread out.

E. In review question D, which child, Mary or John, is a conserver? How do you know? Why is it important to know that a child is or is not a conserver?

F. Explain how young children acquire knowledge. Include the place of the learning cycle in knowledge acquisition. Provide examples from your observations.

REFERENCES

American Association for the Advancement of Science. (1989). *Science for all Americans: A Project 2061 report on literacy goals in science, mathematics and technology*. Washington, DC: Author.

American Association for the Advancement of Science. (1994). *Benchmarks in science literacy*. Washington, DC: Author.

Sachse, T. P. (1993). Curriculum assumptions: Underlying the current reforms in science education. In J. Walter (Ed.), *ASCD curriculum handbook* (pp. 5.83–5.90). Alexandria, VA: Association of Supervision and Curriculum Development.

National Research Council. (1995). *National science education standards*. Washington, DC: National Academy Press.

National Science Teachers Association. (1994). An NSTA position statement: Elementary school science. In *NSTA handbook*. Washington, DC: National Science Teachers Association.

Renner, R. W., & Marek, E. A. (1988). *The learning cycle and elementary school science teaching*. Portsmouth, NH: Heinemann Educational Books, Inc.

UNIT 2   How Concepts Are Acquired

OBJECTIVES

After studying this unit, the student should be able to
- List and define the three types of learning experiences described in the unit
- Recognize examples of each of the three types of learning experiences
- State possible responses to specific opportunities for the child to learn concepts
- Be aware of variations in individual and cultural learning styles

Concepts are acquired through children's active involvement with the environment. As they explore their surroundings, they actively construct their own knowledge. Specific learning experiences can be characterized as *naturalistic* (or *spontaneous*), *informal*, or *structured*. These experiences differ in terms of who controls the choice of activity: the adult or the child.

Naturalistic experiences are those in which the child controls choice and action; *informal* where the child chooses the activity and action, but at some point there is adult intervention; and *structured* where the adult chooses the experience for the child and gives some direction to the child's action (Figure 2–1).

In providing settings for learning and types of instruction, keep in mind that there are variations in learning styles among groups of children and among different cultural and ethnic groups. Some of these types of variations will be described later in the unit.

NATURALISTIC EXPERIENCES

Naturalistic experiences are those initiated spontaneously by children as they go about their daily activities. These experiences are the major mode of learning for children during the sensorimotor period. Naturalistic experiences can be a valuable mode of learning for older children.

The adult's role is to provide an interesting and rich environment. That is, there should be many things for the child to look at, touch, taste, smell, and hear. The adult should observe the child's activity and note how it is progressing and then respond with a glance, a nod, a smile, or a word of praise to encourage the child. The child needs to know when he is doing the appropriate thing.

Some examples of naturalistic experiences are listed:

- Kurt hands Dad two pennies saying, "Here's your two dollars!"
- Tamara takes a spoon from the drawer— "This is big." Mom says, "Yes."

TYPES OF ACTIVITY	INTERACTION EMPHASIZED
Naturalistic	Child/Environment
Informal	Child/Environment/Adult
Structured	Adult/Child/Environment

Figure 2–1 Concepts are learned through three types of activity.

- Roger is eating orange segments. "I got three." (Holds up three fingers.)
- Nancy says, "Big girls are up to here," as she stands straight and points to her chin.
- Cindy (age 4) sits on the rug sorting colored rings into plastic cups.
- Tanya and Tim (both age 4) are having a tea party. Tim says, "The tea is hot."
- Sam (age 5) is painting. He makes a dab of yellow. Then he dabs some blue on top. "Hey! I've got green now."
- Trang Fung (age 6) is cutting her clay into many small pieces. Then she squashes it together into one big piece.
- Sara (age 6) is restless during the after-lunch rest period. As she sits quietly with her head on her desk, her eyes rove around the room. Each day she notices the clock. One day she realizes that when Mrs. Red Fox says, "One-fifteen, time to get up," that the short hand is always on the one and the long hand is always on the three. After that she knows how to watch the clock for the end of rest time.
- Theresa (age 7) is drawing with markers. They are in a container that has a hole to hold each one. Theresa notices that there is one extra hole. "There must be a lost marker," she comments.
- Vanessa (age 8) is experimenting with cup measures and containers. She notices that each cup measure holds the same amount even though each is a different shape. She also notices that you cannot always predict how many cups of liquid a container holds just by looking at it. The shape can fool you.

INFORMAL LEARNING EXPERIENCES

Informal learning experiences are initiated by the adult as the child is engaged in a naturalistic experience. These experiences are not preplanned for a specific time. They occur when the adult's experience and/or intuition indicates it is time to act. This might happen for various reasons—for example, the child might need help or is on the right track in solving a problem but needs a cue or encouragement. It might also happen because the adult has in mind some concepts that should be reinforced and takes advantage of a *teachable moment*. Informal learning experiences occur when an opportunity for instruction presents itself by chance. Some examples are

- "I'm 6 years old," says 3-year-old Kate while holding up three fingers. Dad says, "Let's count those fingers. One, two, three fingers. You are 3 years old."
- Bob (age 4) is setting the table. He gets frustrated because he does not seem to have enough cups. "Let's check," says his teacher. "There is one placemat for each chair. Let's see if there is one cup on each mat." They move around the table checking. They come to a mat with two cups. "Two cups," says Bob. "Hurrah!" says his teacher.
- Juanita (age 4) has a bag of cookies. Mrs. Ramirez asks, "Do you have enough for everyone?" Juanita replies, "I don't know." Mrs. R. asks, "How can you find out?" Juanita says, "I don't know." Mrs. R. tells her, "I'll help you. We'll count them."
- Kindergartners George and Sam are playing with some small rubber figures called Stackrobats.® George links some together horizontally, while Sam joins his vertically. The boys are competing to see who can make the longest line. When George's line reaches across the diameter of the table, he encounters a problem. Miss Jones suggests that he might be able to figure out another way to link the figures together. He looks at Sam's line of figures and then at his. He realizes that if he links his figures vertically he can continue with the competition.
- Dean, a first grader, runs into Mrs. Red Fox's classroom on a spring day after a heavy rainstorm. He says, "Mrs. Red Fox! I have a whole bunch of worms." Mrs. Red Fox asks Dean where he found the worms and why there are so many out this morning. She suggests he put the worms on the sci-

ence table where everyone can see them. Dean follows through and places a sign next to the can: "Wrms fnd by Dean."

- Jason notices that each time he feeds Fuzzy the hamster, Fuzzy runs to the food pan before Jason opens the cage. He tells his teacher, who uses the opportunity to discuss *anticipatory responses*, why they develop, and their significance in training animals. He asks Jason to consider why this might happen so consistently and to think about other times he has noticed this type of response in other animals or humans. Several other children join the discussion. They decide to keep individual records of any anticipatory responses they observe for a week, compare observations, and note trends.

STRUCTURED LEARNING EXPERIENCES

Structured experiences are preplanned lessons or activities. They can be done with individuals or small or large groups at a special time or an opportune time. The following are examples of some of these structured activities (Figure 2–2):

- With an individual at a specific time. Cindy is 4 years old. Her teacher decides that she needs some practice counting. She says, "Cindy, I have some blocks here for you to count. How many are in this pile?"
- With a small group at a specific time. Mrs. Red Fox is sitting with a group of six in a semicircle in front of her. She says, "I have some balls in this basket. Look at them and tell me what you see." She places a basket of balls in front of the group. In the basket are about a dozen balls that range in size from a table tennis ball to a basketball. After the children examine the balls and discuss their characteristics, Mrs. Red Fox picks up the basketball and says, "Find a ball that is smaller." After the children respond, she puts the basketball and the table tennis ball aside. She picks up a tennis ball and says, "Find a ball in the basket that is larger."

- With an individual at an opportune time. Mrs. Flores knows that Tanya needs help with the concept of shape. Tanya is looking for a game to play. Mrs. Flores says, "Try this shape-matching game, Tanya. There are squares, circles, and triangles on the big card. You find the little cards with the shapes that match."
- With a large group at a specific time. Ms. Hebert realizes classification is an important concept that should be applied throughout the primary grades. It is extremely important in organizing science data. For example, to study skeletons, students brought bones from home. Ms. Hebert puts out three large sheets of construction paper and has the students explore the different ways bones can be classified (such as chicken, turkey, duck, cow, pig, deer) or placed in subcategories (such as grouping chicken bones into wings, backs, legs, and so on).

As a final example, consider how the same concepts might be constructed at all three levels with the same materials.

- Naturalistic experience. Mr. Flores places lids from various sized containers in a plas-

Figure 2–2 The child learns about measurement through a naturalistic activity.

tic tub on the rug where the children can examine them. At first, the children examined the lids one by one, then put them in the tub, and spilled them out. Recently, Mr. Flores noticed that some children separate the lids into groups by color, others sort them by size, and others line them up in order from large to small.

- Informal learning experience. One day Mr. Flores sits down on the rug with the children. He says, "Tell me about these lids and what you can do with them." The children tell him how some are the same color, some are the same size, and so on. As they talk, they show him examples. Then Mr. Flores asks some specific questions. "Bob, how many red lids do you have?" "Juanita, do you have more red lids or green lids?" He holds up a lid and says, "Everyone find a lid that is bigger than this one."
- Structured learning experience. Mr. Flores has the tub of lids, some large pieces of poster board, and an assortment of marking pens. The poster boards are marked off in squares like graph paper. He says, "Today we are going to make some graphs using information from this lid collection." He and the children then discuss what criteria they might use.

Note that throughout the examples in this unit the adults ask a variety of questions and provide different types of directions for using the materials. Questions and instructions can be *divergent* or *convergent. Divergent questions and instructions* do not have one right answer but provide an opportunity for creativity, guessing, and experimenting. Questions that begin "Tell me about ____," "What do you think ____?," "What have you found out ____?," "What can we do with ____?," and directions such as "You can examine these ____" or "You may play with these ____" are divergent.

Convergent questions or directions ask for a specific response or activity. There is a specific piece of information called for, such as "How many ____?," "Tell me the names of the parts of a plant," "Find a ball smaller than this one," and so on. Adults often ask only convergent questions and give convergent directions. Remember that children need time to construct their ideas. Divergent questions and directions encourage them to think and act for themselves. Convergent questions and directions can provide the adult with specific information regarding what the child knows, but too many of these questions tend to make the child think that there might be only one right answer to all problems. This can squelch creativity and the willingness to guess and experiment (See Unit 7 for more strategies and explanations).

LEARNING STYLES

In planning learning experiences for children, it is essential to consider individual and culturally determined styles of learning. The most broad-based theory of learning styles is Howard Gardner's theory of multiple intelligences. Gardner has identified seven intelligences: *linguistic, logical-mathematical, bodily kinesthetic, interpersonal, intrapersonal, musical,* and *spatial*. In planning learning experiences, it is important to include experiences in each area to provide for each child's area of strength and to strengthen his areas of weakness. Too often, conventional learning experiences focus on the linguistic (language) and logical-mathematical intelligences and ignore the other areas. Children who may have strength in learning through active movement and concrete activities (bodily kinesthetic learners) or those who learn best through interacting with peers (interpersonal learners) or one of the other modalities may lose out on being able to develop concepts and skills to the fullest.

Besides considering diversity in modality-related learning styles, also consider diversity in cultures and related differences in learning styles. Avoid stereotypes and misconceptions, while at the same time consider authentic culturally determined variations. Location and social class are also important sociocultural considerations. For example, Mexican-American and Native-American children may work well in cooperative groups because cooperation is an important factor in their cultures. Both African-American and Native-American cultures have strong oral traditions, which can be built on in instructional practices. Asian cultures tend to place an exceptionally strong value on respect for elders and especially for teachers.

Teachers need to become acquainted with the cultural learning styles of their students and build on their strengths. The customs and artifacts of a variety of cultures should be included in the curriculum. Multicultural education is not a topic to be presented one week and then forgotten; it should permeate the whole curriculum.

SUMMARY

Three types of learning experiences have been described and defined. The teacher and parent learn through practice how to make the best use of naturalistic, informal, and structured experiences so that the child has a balance of free exploration and specific planned activities.

FURTHER READING AND RESOURCES

Baratta-Lorton, M. (1976). *Math their way.* Menlo Park, CA: Addison-Wesley.

Benham, N. B., Hosticka, A., Payne, J. D., & Yeotis, C. (1982). Making concepts in science and mathematics visible and viable in the early childhood curriculum. *School Science and Mathematics, 82*(1), 29–37.

Charlesworth, R. (1992). *Understanding child development* (3rd ed.). Albany, NY: Delmar.

Forman, G. E., & Kuschner, D. S. (1983). *The child's construction of knowledge.* Washington, D.C.: National Association for the Education of Young Children.

Gardner, H. (1983). *Frames of mind: Theory of multiple intelligences.* New York: Basic Books.

Ginsburg, H. P., & Baron, J. (1993). Cognition: Young children's construction of mathematics. In R. J. Jensen (Ed.), *Research ideas for the classroom: Early childhood mathematics* (pp. 3–21). New York: Macmillan.

Kamii, C. (1985). *Children reinvent arithmetic.* New York: Teachers College Press.

Kamii, C., & DeVries, R. (1978). *Physical knowledge in preschool education.* Englewood Cliffs, NJ: Prentice-Hall.

Payne, J. N. (Ed.). (1990). *Mathematics for the young child.* Reston, VA: National Council of Teachers of Mathematics.

Smith, R. F. (1987). Theoretical framework for preschool science experiences. *Young Children, 42*(2), 34–40.

SUGGESTED ACTIVITIES

1. Observe a prekindergarten, kindergarten, and primary classroom. Keep a record of concept learning experiences that are naturalistic, informal, and structured. Compare the differences in the numbers of each type of experience observed in each of the classrooms.

2. During your observations, also note any times you think opportunities for naturalistic or informal learning experiences were missed.

REVIEW

A. Write a description of each of the three types of learning experiences described in this unit.

B. Decide if each of the following examples is naturalistic, informal, or structured:

1. "Mother, I'll cut this apple in two parts so you can have some." "Yes, then I can have half of the apple."

2. Nineteen-month-old John is lining up small blocks and placing a toy person on each one.

3. A teacher and six children are sitting at a table. Each child has a pile of Unifix Cubes®. "Make a train with the pattern A-B-A-B."

4. "I think I gave everyone two cookies", says Zang He. "Show me how you can check to be sure," says Mr. Brown.

5. Four children are pouring sand in the sandbox. They have a variety of containers of assorted sizes and shapes. "I need a bigger cup, please", says one child to another.

6. The children are learning about recycling. "Everyone sort your trash collection into a pile of things that can be used again and a pile of things that will have to be discarded."

7. Trang Fung brings her pet mouse to school. Each child observes the mouse and asks Trang Fung questions about his habits. Several children draw pictures and write stories about the mouse.

8. Children in Ms. Hebert's class are playing on the jungle gym. They are trying to find out who can hang upside down by the knees the longest. Several complain of being dizzy. After they rest for a few minutes, Ms. Hebert discusses with them why the human body might feel dizzy after hanging upside down too long.

9. Mrs. Red Fox introduces her class to LOGO through structured floor games. They take turns pretending to be a turtle and try to follow commands given by the teacher and the other students.

C. Read each of the following situations and explain how you would react:

1. George and Dina are setting the table in the home living center. They are placing one complete place setting in front of each chair.

2. Samantha says, "I have more crayons than you do, Hillary." "No, you don't." "Yes, I do!"

3. The children in Mr. Wang's class are discussing the show they must put on for the students in the spring. Some children want to do a show with singing and dancing; others do not. Brent suggests that they vote. The others agree. Derrick and Theresa count the votes. They agree that there are 17 in favor of a musical show and 10 against.

4. One of your students brings in a large crate of oranges, lemons, and grapefruit that his family purchased during a trip to Florida.

5. When you arrive at school you discover that Lollipop the mouse is giving birth.

D. Explain why it is important to consider individual and cultural learning styles when planning instruction for young children.

UNIT 3

Promoting Young Children's Concept Development

O B J E C T I V E S

After studying this unit, the student should be able to
- List in order and define the six steps in choosing concept objectives and activities
- Identify definitions of assessment and evaluation
- Discuss the advantages of using the six-step method
- Identify examples of each of the six steps
- Describe the choices the teacher must make after evaluation
- Evaluate whether a teacher uses the six steps

A teacher must know students well to help them learn to their fullest capacities. Objectives and activities must be chosen with care so that the children can move as fast and go as far as possible. The steps for planning concept experiences are the same as those used for any subject. Six questions must be answered (Figure 3–1):

- Where is the child now? **Assess**
- What should she learn next? **Choose objectives**
- What should the child do in order to accomplish these objectives? **Plan experiences**
- Which materials should be used to carry through the plan? **Select materials**
- Do the plan and the materials fit? **Teach** (do the planned experiences with the child)
- Has the child learned what was taught (reached objectives)? **Evaluate**

ASSESSING

Each child should be individually *assessed*. Two methods for this are used most frequently. Children can be interviewed individually using specific tasks, and they can be observed during their regular activities. The purpose of assessment is to find out what children know and what they can do before instruction is planned. The topic of assessment is covered in detail in Unit 4 (Figure 3–2).

Specific Task Assessment

The following are examples of some specific tasks that can be given to a child:

- Present the child with a pile of 10 counters (buttons, coins, poker chips, or other small things) and say, "Count these for me."
- Show the child two groups of chips: a group of three and a group of six. Ask, "Which group has more chips?"
- Show the child five cardboard dolls, each one a half inch taller than the next. Say: "Which is the tallest?" "Which is the smallest?" "Line them up from the smallest to the tallest."
- Give a 6-year-old a simple addition problem. Say, "You have three yellow cars," and place three yellow cars in front of the child. "Now you buy two blue cars," and place the blue cars next to the yellow cars. Say, "Write in numbers how many yellow cars you have,

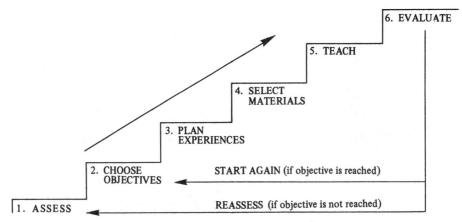

Figure 3–1 What should be taught and how?—FOLLOW THE STEPS.

how many blue cars you have, and how many cars you have altogether.''
- Put 30 counting chips in front of a 7-year-old. Say, "Here are 30 chips. Show me how many groups of 10 there are.''
- Place a pile of counting chips in front of an 8-year-old and ask, "Show me two times three using these chips.''

Assessment by Observation

The following are examples of observations that can be made as children play and/or work:
- Does the 1-year-old show an interest in experimenting by pouring things in and out of containers of different sizes?
- Does the 2-year-old spend time sorting objects and lining them up in rows?
- Does the 3-year-old show an interest in understanding size, age, and time by asking how big he is, how old he is, and "when will ____" questions?
- Does the 4-year-old set the table correctly? Does he ask for help to write numerals, and does he use them in his play activities?
- Can the 5-year-old divide a bag of candy so that each of his friends receives an equal share?

- If there are five children and three chairs, can a 6-year-old figure out how many more chairs are needed so everyone will have one?
- If a 7-year-old is supposed to feed the hamster two tablespoons of pellets each day, can she decide how much food should be left for the weekend?

Figure 3–2 A primary child is interviewed individually. "How many cubes did I hide? How many are left?"

- Four 8-year-olds are making booklets. Each booklet requires four pieces of paper. Can the children figure out how many pieces of paper will be needed to make the four booklets?

Through observation the teacher can find out if the child can apply concepts to real life problems and activities. By keeping a record of these observations, the teacher builds up a more complete picture of the child's strengths and weakness (Figure 3–3). The current trend is to collect samples of student work, photographs, audiotapes and videotapes and construct a portfolio that represents student accomplishments over time. Assessment will be discussed in more detail in Unit 4.

CHOOSING OBJECTIVES

Once the child's level of knowledge is identified, *objectives can be selected*. That is, a decision can be made as to what the child should be able to learn next. For instance, look at the first task example in the previous section. Suppose a 5-year-old child counts 50 objects correctly. The objective for this child would be different than the one for another 5-year-old who can count only 7 objects accurately. The first child does not need any special help with object counting. A child who counts objects at this level at age 5 can probably figure out how to go beyond 50 alone. The second child might need some help and specific activities with counting objects beyond groups of seven.

Suppose a teacher observes that a 2-year-old spends very little time sorting objects and lining them up in rows. The teacher knows that this is an important activity for a child of this age, one most 2-year-olds engage in naturally without any special instruction. The objective selected might be that the child would choose to spend five minutes each day sorting and organizing objects. Once the objective is selected the teacher then decides how to go about helping the child reach it.

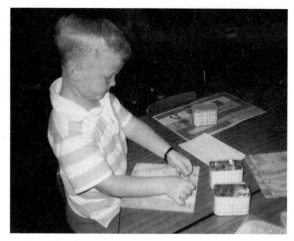

Figure 3–3   Assessment may also be done through observing children as they do their classroom activities.

PLANNING EXPERIENCES

Remember that young children construct concepts through naturalistic activities as they explore the environment. As they grow and develop, they feel the need to organize and understand the world around them. Children have a need to label their experiences and the things they observe. They notice how older children and adults count, use color words, label time, and so on. An instinctive knowledge of math and science concepts develops before an abstract understanding. When planning, it is important for adults to keep in mind the following:

- Naturalistic experiences should be emphasized until the child is into the preoperational period.
- Informal instruction is introduced during the sensorimotor period and increases in frequency during the preoperational period.
- Structured experiences are used sparingly during the sensorimotor and early preoperational periods and are brief and sharply focused.

Abstract experiences can be introduced gradually during the preoperational and transitional periods and increased in frequency as the child reaches concrete operations, but they should always be preceded by concrete experiences. Keep these factors in mind when planning for young children. These points are covered in detail in the section on selecting materials. In any case, the major focus for instructional planning is the promotion of individual and group problem solving.

Planning involves deciding the best way for each child to accomplish the selected objectives. Will naturalistic, informal, and/or structural experiences be best? Will the child acquire the concept best on her own? With a group of children? One to one with an adult? In a small group directed by an adult? Once these questions have been answered, the materials can be chosen and the lessons planned (See Unit 7 on lesson planning). Sections II, III, and IV tell how to plan these experiences for the concepts and skills that are acquired during the early years.

SELECTING MATERIALS

Three things must be considered when selecting science and math materials. First, there are some general characteristics of good materials. They should be sturdy, well made, and constructed so that they are safe for children to use independently. They should also be useful for more than one kind of activity and for teaching more than one concept.

Second, the materials must be designed for acquisition of the selected concepts. That is, they must fit the objective(s).

Third, the materials must fit the children's levels of development. As stated, acquiring a concept begins with concrete experiences with real things. For each concept included in the curriculum, materials should be sequenced from concrete to abstract and from three-dimensional (real objects), to two-dimensional (cutouts), to pictorial, to paper and pencil. Too often, however, the first steps are skipped and children are immersed in paper and pencil activities without the prerequisite concrete experiences and before they have developed the perceptual and motor skills necessary to handle a writing implement with ease. Five steps to be followed from concrete materials to paper and pencil are described as follows. Note that step one is the first and last step during the sensorimotor period; during the preoperational period, the children move from step one to step five; and during the transition and concrete operations periods, they move into step five.

- Step 1. Real objects are used for this first step. Children are given time to explore and manipulate many types of objects such as blocks, chips, stones, sticks, and materials such as sand, water, mud, clay, and playdough. Whether instruction is naturalistic, informal, or structured, concrete materials are used.
- Step 2. Real objects are used along with pictorial representations. For example, blocks can be matched with printed or drawn patterns. When cooking, each implement to be used (measuring spoons and cups, bowls, mixing spoons, and so on) can be depicted on a pictorial sequenched recipe chart. Children can draw pictures each day showing the height of their bean spouts.
- Step 3. Cutouts, which can be motorically manipulated, are introduced. For example, cardboard cutouts of different sizes, colors, and shapes can be sorted. Cutout dogs can be matched with cutout doghouses. Cutout human body parts can be put together to make a whole body. Although the materials have moved into two dimensions, they can still be manipulated.
- Step 4. Pictures are next. Commercially available pictorial materials, teacher-created or magazine pictures, and cut-up workbook pages can be used to make card games as well as sequencing, sorting, and matching activities. For example, pictures of people in various occupations might be matched with

pictures of their equipment. Pictures of a person at different ages can be sequenced from baby to old age. Groups of objects drawn on a card can be counted and matched with the appropriate numeral.

STOP HERE IF CHILDREN HAVE NOT YET REACHED THE TRANSITION STAGE.

- Step 5. At this level, paper and pencil activities are introduced. When the teacher observes that the children understand the concept with materials at the first five levels, this level is introduced. If the materials are available, children usually start experimenting when they feel ready.

An example of sequencing materials using the five steps follows. Suppose one of the objectives for children in kindergarten is to compare differences in dimensions. One of the dimensions to be compared is length. Materials can be sequenced as follows:

- Step 1. Real objects. Children explore the properties of Unifix Cubes® and Cuisinaire® Rods. They fit Unifix Cubes® together into groups of various lengths. They compare the lengths of the Cuisinaire Rods®. They do measurement activities such as comparing how many Unifix Cubes® fit across the short side of the table versus the long side of the table.
- Step 2. Real objects with pictures. The Unifix Cubes® are used to construct rows that match pictured patterns of various lengths. Sticks are used to measure pictured distances from one place to another.
- Step 3. Cutouts. Unifix® and Cuisinaire® cutouts are used to make rows of various lengths. Cutouts of snakes, fences, and so on are compared.
- Step 4. Pictures. Cards with pictures of pencils of different lengths are sorted and matched. A picture is searched for the long and the short

path, the dog with long ears, the dog with short ears, the long hose, the short hose, and so on.

STOP HERE IF THE CHILDREN HAVE NOT YET REACHED THE TRANSITION STAGE.

- Step 5. Paper and pencil activities are introduced. For example, students might draw long and short things.

At the early steps, children might be able to make comparisons of materials with real objects and even with cutouts and picture cards, but they might fail if given just paper and pencil activities. In this case it would be falsely assumed that they do not understand the concept when, in fact, it is the materials that are inappropriate.

The chart in Figure 3–4 depicts the relationship between the cognitive developmental periods—naturalistic, informal, and structured ways of acquiring concepts—and the five levels of materials. Each unit of this text has examples of various types of materials. Section IV contains descriptions of many that are excellent.

TEACHING

Once the decision has been made as to what the child should be able to learn next and in what context the concept acquisition will take place, the next step is teaching. *Teaching* occurs when the planned experiences using the selected materials are put into operation. If the first four steps have been performed with care, the experience should go smoothly. The children will be interested and will learn from the activities because they match their level of development and style of learning. They might even acquire a new concept or skill or extend and expand one already learned.

The time involved in the teaching step might be a few minutes or several weeks, months, or even years depending on the particular concept being acquired and the age and ability of the child. For instance, time sequence is initially learned through naturalistic activity. From infancy, children learn

PERIODS OF DEVELOPMENT	HOW CONCEPTS ARE ACQUIRED		
	Naturalistic	Informal	Structured
Sensorimotor	Real objects Objects and pictures Pictures	Real objects Objects and pictures Pictures	
Preoperational	Real objects Objects and pictures Cutouts Pictures	Real objects Objects and pictures Cutouts Pictures	Real objects Objects and pictures Cutouts Pictures
Transitional	Real objects Objects and pictures Cutouts Pictures	Real objects Objects and pictures Cutouts Pictures Paper and pencil	Real objects Objects and pictures Cutouts Pictures
Concrete Operations	Real objects Objects and pictures Cutouts Pictures	Real objects Objects and pictures Cutouts Pictures Paper and pencil	Real objects Objects and pictures Cutouts Pictures Paper and pencil

Figure 3–4 Two dimensions of early childhood concept instruction with levels of materials used

that there is a sequence in their daily routine: sleeping; waking up wet and hungry; crying; being picked up, cleaned, fed, and played with; and sleeping again. In preschool, they learn a daily routine such as coming in, greeting the teacher, hanging up coats, eating breakfast, playing indoors, having a group activity time, snacking, playing outdoors, having a quiet activity, lunch, playing outdoors, napping, having a small group activity time, and going home. Time words are acquired informally as children hear terms such as yesterday, today, tomorrow, o'clock, next, after, and so on. In kindergarten, special events and times are noted on a calendar. Children learn to name the days of the week and months of the year and to sequence the numerals for each of the days. In first grade, they might be given a blank calendar page to fill in the name of the month, the days of the week, and the number for each day. Acquiring the concept of time is a very complex experience and involves many prerequisite concepts that build over many years. Some children will learn

at a fast rate, others at a slow pace. One child might learn that there are seven days in a week the first time this idea is introduced; another child might take all year to acquire this information. Some children need a great deal of structured repetition; others learn from naturalistic and informal experiences. Teaching developmentally involves flexible and individualized instruction.

Even with careful planning and preparation, an activity might not work well the first time. When this happens, analyze the situation by asking the following questions:

- Was the child interested?
- Was the task too easy or too hard?
- Did the child understand what he was asked to do?
- Were the materials right for the task?
- Were they interesting?
- Is further assessment needed?
- Was the teacher enthusiastic?
- Was it just a "bad" day for the child?

You might try the activity again using the same method and the same materials or with a change in the method and/or materials. In some cases, the child might have to be reassessed to be sure the activity is appropriate for her developmental level.

EVALUATING

The sixth step is *evaluation*. What has the child learned? What does he know and what can he do after the concept experiences have been presented? The assessment questions are asked again. If the child has reached the objective, a new one can be chosen. The steps of planning, choosing materials, teaching, and evaluating are repeated. If the child has not reached the objective, the same activities can be continued or a new method may be tried. For example, a teacher wants a 5-year-old to count out the correct number of objects for each of the number symbols from 0 to 10. She tries many kinds of objects for the child to count and many kinds of containers in which to place the things he counts, but the child is just not interested. Finally she gives him small banks made from baby food jars and real pennies. The child finds these materials are exciting and goes on to learn the task quickly and with enthusiasm.

Evaluation may be done using formal, structured questions and tasks and specific observations as will be presented in Unit 4. Informal questions and observations of naturalistic experiences can be used for evaluation also. For example, when a child sets the table in the wrong way,

it can be seen without formal questioning that he has not learned from instruction. He needs some help. Maybe organizing and placing a whole table setting is more than he can do now. Can he place one item at each place? Does he need to go back to working with a smaller number (such as a table for two or three)? Does he need to work with simpler materials that have more structure (such as pegs in a pegboard)? To look at these more specific skills, the teacher would then return to the assessment step. At this point she would assess not only the child but also the types of experiences and materials she has been using. Sometimes assessment leads the teacher to the right objective but the experience and/or materials chosen are not (as in the example given) the ones that fit the child.

Frequent and careful evaluation helps both teacher and child avoid frustration. An adult must never take it for granted that any one plan or any one material is the best choice for a specific child. The adult must keep checking to be sure the child is learning what the experience was planned to teach him.

SUMMARY

This unit has described six steps that provide a guide for what to teach and how to teach it. Following these steps can minimize guesswork. The steps are (1) assess, (2) choose objectives, (3) plan experiences, (4) select materials, (5) teach, and (6) evaluate.

FURTHER READING AND RESOURCES

Assessing learning in preschool and primary programs. (1993). *Young Children 48*(5, Special Section), 20–47.

Baratta-Lorton, M. (1976). *Math their way*. Menlo Park, CA: Addison-Wesley.

Baroody, A. J. (1987). *Children's mathematical thinking*. New York: Teachers College Press.

Charlesworth, R. (1992). *Understanding child development* (3rd ed.). Albany, NY: Delmar.

Ginsburg, H. (1988). *Children's arithmetic: How they learn it and how you teach it*. Austin, TX: Pro Ed.

Hegland, S. M. (1991). Kindergarten mathematics: Teaching or controlling? *Arithmetic Teacher, 39*(2), 34–37.

Jacobs, H. H. (1993). Mathematics integration: A common-sense approach to curriculum development. *Arithmetic Teacher, 40*(6), 301–302.

Kamii, C. K. (1985). *Young children reinvent arithmetic*. New York: Teachers College Press.

Richardson, K. (1984). *Developing number concepts using Unifix Cubes*. Menlo Park, CA: Addison-Wesley.

Skinner, P. (1990). *What's your problem?* Portsmouth, NH: Heinemann.

Williams, C. V., & Kamii, C. (1986). How do children learn by handling objects? *Young Children, 42*(1), 23–26.

SUGGESTED ACTIVITIES

1. Interview two early childhood teachers. Ask them to tell you what kinds of science experiences they include in their programs. Find out how they decide what to teach, to whom, and which materials to use. Go through their responses later and try to evaluate whether they use any or all of the steps described in this unit.

2. Go to the library and look through recent issues of professional publications for teachers of young children. For your Activities File make a card for each article you find that gives ideas for using assessment and evaluation to help in choosing objectives, planning, and choosing materials. Summarize on each card the ideas that you feel will be helpful to you.

3. Spend a morning in an early childhood center. Note all the science experiences. Go through your notes and evaluate what you observed. What steps did you see? Did you see any incidents where you felt that the teacher needed to evaluate her own teaching or the child's learning? Why?

R E V I E W

A. List in order the six steps for instruction described in this unit.

B. Define each of the steps listed in A.

C. Read each of the following descriptions and label them with the correct step name:

1. From her Activities File, the teacher selects two cards from the Classification section.

2. Mrs. Brown has just interviewed Joey and discovered that he can count accurately through 12. He then continues, "15, 14, 19, 20." She thinks about what the next step in instruction should be for Joey.

3. The teacher is seated at the table with Fwang. "Fwang, you put three red teddy bears and two blue teddy bears together in one group. Then you wrote, 3 + 2 = 5. Explain to me how you figured out how to solve the problem."

4. During the first month of school, Mrs. Garcia interviews each of her students individually to find out which concepts and skills they know.

5. Mr. Black has set up the sand table, and the children are using standard-size measuring cups to pour and measure sand to learn the relationship between the different size cups.

6. Katherine needs to work on A-B-A-B type patterns. Her teacher pulls out three cards from the Pattern section of her Activity File.

7. Mr. Wang looks through the library of computer software for programs that require logical thinking strategies.

D. Describe the advantages of following the instructional steps suggested in this unit.

E. Read the description of Miss Conway's method of selecting objectives and activities. Analyze and evaluate her approach.

> Miss Conway believes that all her students are at about the same level in their mathematics and science capabilities and knowledge. She has a math and science program that she has used for 15 years and that she believes is satisfactory. She assumes that all students enter her class at the same level and leave knowing everything she has taught.

UNIT 4
Assessing the Child's Developmental Level

OBJECTIVES

After studying this unit, the student should be able to
- Explain how to find the child's level of concept development
- Explain the value of commercial assessment instruments for concept assessment
- Make a developmental assessment task file
- Be able to assess the concept development level of young children.
- Understand how to record, report, and evaluate using naturalistic/performance-based assessment
- Explain the advantages of portfolio assessment

Children's levels of concept development are found by seeing which concept tasks they are able to do. The first question in teaching is "Where is the child now?" To find the answer to this question, the teacher assesses. The teacher gives the child tasks to solve (such as those described in Unit 3). She observes what the child does as he solves the problems and records the answers he gives. This information is used to guide the next steps in teaching. The long-term objective for young children is to be sure that they have a strong foundation in basic concepts that will take them through the transition into the concrete operational stage when they begin to deal seriously with abstract symbols in math and independent investigations in science. Following the methods and sequence in this text helps reach this goal and at the same time achieves some further objectives:

- Builds a positive feeling in the child toward science
- Builds confidence in the child that he can do science activities
- Builds a questioning attitude in response to his curiosity regarding science problems

ASSESSMENT METHODS

Observation and interview are assessment methods the teacher uses to find out the child's level of development. Examples of both of these methods were included in Unit 3. More are provided in this unit. Assessment is appropriately done through observations and interviews using teacher-developed assessment tasks. Commercial instruments used for initial screening may also supply useful information but are limited in scope for the everyday assessment needed for planning. Initial screening instruments usually cover a broad range of areas and provide a profile that indicates overall strengths and weaknesses. These strengths and weaknesses can be looked at in more depth by the classroom teacher for information needed to make normal instructional decisions or by a diagnostic specialist (i.e., school psychologist or speech and language therapist) where an initial screening indicates some serious developmental problem. Individually administered screening instruments should be the only type used with young children. Child responses should require the use of concrete materials and/or pictures, verbal answers, or motoric responses such as pointing or rearranging some objects. Paper and pencil should be used only for assessment of perceptual motor development (i.e., tasks such as name writing, drawing a person, or copying shapes). Booklet-type paper and pencil tests administered to groups or individuals are inappropriate until children are well into concrete operations, can deal with abstract symbols, and have well-developed perceptual motor skills (Figure 4–1).

Observational Assessment

Observation is used to find out how children use concepts during their daily activities. The teacher has in mind the concepts the children should be using. Whenever she sees a concept reflected in a child's activity, she writes down the incident and places it in the child's record folder. This helps her plan future experiences.

Throughout this book, suggestions are made for behaviors that should be observed. The following are examples of behaviors as the teacher would write them down for the child's folder:

- Brad (18 months old) dumped all the shape blocks on the rug. He picked out all the circles and stacked them up. Shows he can sort and organize.
- Cindy (4 years old) carefully set the table for lunch all by herself. She remembered everything. Cindy understands one-to-one correspondence.
- Chris (3 years old) and George (5 years old) stood back to back and asked Cindy to check who was taller. Good cooperation—it is the first time Chris has shown an interest in comparing heights.
- Mary (5 years old), working on her own, put the right number of sticks in juice cans marked with the number symbols 0 through 20. She is ready for something more challenging.
- Trang Fung and Sara (6-year-olds), on their own decided to find out how many cups of water are needed to fill containers of various sizes and shapes. Each time they filled a container, they wrote down its name and how many cups of water it held. They learned how to set up an investigation.
- Derrick and Brent (7-year-olds) compare their baseball card collections and figure out how many more or fewer cards each has. They understand the concepts of more and less.
- Ann and Jason (8-year-olds) argue about which materials will float and sink. They asked their teacher if they could test their theories. They got the water, collected some objects, and set up a chart to record their predictions and then the names of the items that sink and those that float. This demonstrates understanding of how to develop an investigation to solve a problem.

Observational information may also be recorded on a checklist. For example, concepts can be listed, and each time the child is observed demonstrating one of the behaviors the date can be put next to that behavior. Soon there will be a profile of the concepts the child demonstrates spontaneously (Figure 4–2).

Interview Assessment

The individual interview is used to find out specific information in a direct way. The teacher

Figure 4–1 A parachute is an effective tool for helping children develop a sense of their bodies in space.

CONCEPT ACTIVITY OBSERVATION CHECKLIST

Child's Name _____ Birth Date _____

School Year _____ Grade/Group _____

Concept Activities (Concepts and activities are described in the text)	Dates Observed
Selects science center	
Selects cooking center	
Selects science concept book	
Selects science book	
Selects sand or water	
Sets the table correctly	
Counts spontaneously	
Sorts play materials into logical groups	
Uses comparison words (i.e., *bigger, fatter,* etc.)	
Builds with blocks	
Works with part/whole materials	
Demonstrates an understanding of order and sequence	
Points out number symbols in the environment	
Demonstrates curiosity by asking questions, exploring the environment, and making observations	

Figure 4–2   Concept observation checklist

can present a task to the child and observe and record the way the child works on the task and the solution she arrives at for the problem presented by the task (Figure 4–3). The rightness and wrongness of the answer are not as important as how the child arrives at the answer. Often a child starts out on the right track but gets off somewhere in the middle of the problem. For example, Kate (age 3) is asked to match four saucers with four cups. This is an example of one-to-one correspondence. She does this task easily. Next she is asked to match five cups with six saucers, "Here are some cups and saucers. Find out if there is a cup for every saucer." She puts a cup on each saucer. Left with an extra saucer, she places it under one of the pairs. She smiles happily. By observing the whole task, the teacher can see that Kate does not feel comfortable with the concept of "one more than." This is normal for a preoperational 3-year-old. She finds a way to do away with the problem by putting two saucers under one cup. She understands the idea of matching one to one but cannot have things out of balance. Only by observing the whole task can the teacher see the reason for what appears to be a "wrong" answer to the task.

For another example, Tim, who is just 4 1/2 years old, is given the following task. First he is shown cards with the number symbols zero to six. He is asked to name each number symbol and does so correctly. He is then asked to place the correct number of chips by each number symbol. Tim's responses tell the teacher that he recognizes and can name number symbols but that he cannot yet match the symbols with the right number of chips. He can recognize groups up to four but does not yet have the idea of groups of more than four. He tried to count out five chips and six chips but lost track after four. Tim's behavior is normal for a 4-year-old.

If Kate's and Tim's, answers were observed only at the endpoint and recorded as right or wrong, the crux of their problems would be missed. Only the individual interview offers the opportunity to observe a child solve a problem from start to finish without distractions or interruptions.

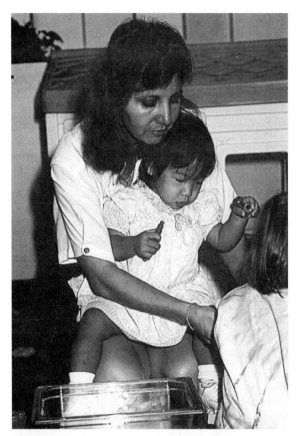

Figure 4–3   The child enjoys the individual interview.

An important factor in the one-to-one interview is that it must be done in an accepting manner by the adult. She must value and accept the child's answers whether they are right or wrong from the adult point of view. If possible, the interview should be done in a quiet place where there are no other things that might take the child's attention off the task. The adult should be warm, pleasant, and calm. Let the child know that he is doing well with smiles, words ("Good," "Fine," "You're a good worker," "Keep trying hard"), and gestures (nod of approval, pat on the shoulder).

If persons other than one of the teachers do the assessment interviews, the teacher should be sure that they spend time with the children before the interviews. Advise a person doing an interview to sit on a low chair or on the floor next to where the children are playing. Children are usually curious when they see a new person. One may ask, "Who are you? Why are you here?" The children can be told, "I am Ms. X. Someday I am going to give each of you a turn to do some special work with me. It will be a surprise. Today I want to see what you do in school and learn your names." If the interviewer pays attention to the children and shows an interest in them and their activities, they will feel comfortable and free to do their best when the day comes for their assessment interview.

If the teacher does the assessment herself, she also should stress the special nature of the activity for her and each child: "I'm going to spend some time today doing some special work with each of you. Everyone will get a turn."

ASSESSMENT TASK FILE

Each child and each group of children is different. The teacher needs to have on hand questions to fit each age and stage she might meet in individual young children. She also needs to add new tasks as she discovers more about children and their development. A card file or loose-leaf notebook of assessment tasks should be set up. Such a file or notebook has three advantages:

- The teacher has a personal involvement in creating her own assessment tasks and is more likely to use them, understand them, and value them.
- The file card or loose-leaf notebook format makes it easy to add new tasks and revise or remove old ones.
- There is room for the teacher to use her own creativity to add new questions and make materials.

Use the tasks in each unit and in Appendix A to begin the file. Other tasks can be developed as the student proceeds through the units in this book

and through her future career with young children. Directions for each task can be put on 5" × 8" inch plain white file cards. Most of the tasks will require the use of concrete materials and/or pictures. Concrete materials can be items found around the home and center. Pictures can be purchased or cut from magazines and readiness type workbooks and glued on cards.

The basic materials needed are: a 5" × 8" file card box, 5" × 8" unlined file cards, 5" × 8" file dividers or a loose-leaf notebook with dividers, a black pen, a set of colored markers, a ruler, scissors, glue, clear Contac® or laminating material, and preschool/kindergarten readiness workbooks with artwork.

In Appendix A each assessment task is set up as it would be on a five-by-eight-inch card. Note that on each card what the adult says to the child is always printed in CAPITAL LETTERS so the instructions can be found and read easily. The tasks are set up developmentally from the sensorimotor level (birth to age 2) to the preoperational level (ages 2 to 7) to early concrete operations (ages 6 to 8). The ages are flexible relative to the stages and are given only to serve as a guide for selecting the first tasks to present to each child.

Each child is at his own level. If the first tasks are too hard, the interviewer should start at a lower level. If the first tasks are quite easy for the child, the interviewer should start at a higher level. Figure 4–4 is a sample recording sheet format that could be used to keep track of each child's progress. Some teachers prefer an individual sheet for each child; others a master sheet for the whole class. The names and numbers of the tasks to be assessed are entered in the first column. Several columns are provided for entering the date and the level of progress (+, accomplished; √, needs some help; –, needs a lot of help) for children who need repeated periods of instruction. The column on the right is for comments on the process used by the child that might give some clues as to specific instructional needs.

DEVELOPMENTAL TASKS RECORDING SHEET

Child's Name _____ Birth Date _____

School Year _____ School _____ Teacher _____

Grade/Group _____ Person Doing Assessment _____

Levels: +, accomplishes; √, partial; −, cannot do task

Task	Levels			Comments
	Date	Date	Date	

Comments:

Figure 4–4   Recording sheet for developmental tasks

ASSESSMENT TASKS

The assessment tasks included in Appendix A represent the concepts that must be acquired by young children from birth through the primary grades. Most of the tasks require an individual interview with the child. Some tasks are observational and require recording of activities during playtime or worktime. The infant tasks and observations assess the development of the child's growing sensory and motor skills. As was discussed in the first unit, these sensory and motor skills are basic to all later learning.

The assessment tasks are divided into nine developmental levels. *Levels 1 and 2* are tasks for the child in the sensorimotor stage. *Levels 3 through 5* include tasks of increasing difficulty for the prekindergarten child. The *Level 6* tasks are those things that the child can usually do when he enters kindergarten between the ages of 5 and 6. This is the level he is growing toward during his prekindergarten years. Some children will be able to accomplish all these tasks by age 5; others not until 6 or over. *Level 7* is included as an assessment for advanced prekindergartners and for children in centers that have a kindergarten program. The child about to enter first grade should be able to accomplish the tasks at *Level 6* and *Level 8*. He should also be using most of the concept words correctly. *Level 9* includes tasks to be accomplished during the primary grades.

EXAMPLE OF AN INDIVIDUAL INTERVIEW

The following is a part of the *Level 5* assessment interview as given to Bob (4 1/2 years old). A corner of the storage room has been made into an assessment center. Mrs. Ramirez comes in with Bob. "You sit there, and I'll sit here, Bob. We have some important things to do." They both sit down at a low table, and Mrs. Ramirez begins.

An interview does not have to include any special number of tasks. For the preoperational child, the teacher can begin with matching and proceed through the ideas and skills one at a time so that each interview can be quite short if necessary.

If the person doing the interviewing has the time for longer sessions and the children are able to work for a longer period of time, the following can serve as suggested maximum amounts of time (Figure 4–5).

- Fifteen to twenty minutes for two-year-olds
- Thirty minutes for three-year-olds
- Forty-five minutes for four-year-olds
- Up to an hour with five-year-olds and older

Mrs. Ramirez:	Bob's Response:
HOW OLD ARE YOU?	"I'm four." (He holds up four fingers.)
COUNT TO 10 FOR ME, BOB. (Mrs. Ramirez nods her head up and down.)	"One, 2, 3, 4, 5, 6, 7, 8, 9, 10, . . . I can go some more. Eleven, 12, 13, 20!"
HERE ARE SOME BLOCKS. HOW MANY ARE THERE? (She puts out 10 blocks.)	(He points, saying) "One, 2, 3, 4, 5, 6, 7, 8, 9, 10, 11, 12." (He points to some more than once.)
GOOD, BOB. NOW COUNT THESE. (She puts out 5 blocks.)	(He counts, pushing each one he counts to the left.) "One, 2, 3, 4, 5."
(She puts the blocks out of sight and brings up five plastic horses and five plastic cowboys.) FIND OUT IF EACH COWBOY HAS A HORSE.	(Bob looks over the horses and cowboys. He lines up the horses in a row and then puts a cowboy on each.) "Yes, there are enough."
FINE, BOB. (She puts the cowboys and horses away. She takes out some inch cube blocks. She puts out two piles of blocks: five yellow and two orange.)	
DOES ONE GROUP HAVE MORE?	"Yes." (He points to the yellow.)
GOOD. (She puts out four blue and three green.)	
DOES ONE GROUP HAVE LESS?	(He points to the green blocks.)
WELL DONE.	
(She takes out five cutouts of bears of five different sizes.) FIND THE BIGGEST BEAR.	"Here it is." (He picks the right one.)
FIND THE SMALLEST BEAR.	(He points to the smallest.)
PUT ALL THE BEARS IN A ROW FROM BIGGEST TO SMALLEST.	(Bobby works slowly and carefully.) "All done." (Two of the middle bears are reversed.)
(Mrs. Ramirez smiles.)	
GOOD FOR YOU, BOB. YOU'RE A HARD WORKER.	

Figure 4–5   "Do this problem for me using these Unifix Cubes®." A primary child enjoys the one-to-one interview.

RECORD KEEPING AND REPORTING

The records of each child's progress and activities are kept in a *record folder* and a *portfolio*. The record folder contains anecdotal records and checklists, as already described. The portfolio is a purposeful collection of student work that tells the story of the student's efforts, progress, and achievements. It is a systematic collection of material designed to provide evidence of understanding and to monitor growth. Portfolios provide a vehicle for "authentic" assessment—that is, examples of student work done in many contexts. Students and teacher work together to gather work, reflect on it, and evaluate it.

The physical setup for portfolios is a critical place to begin. A box or file with hanging folders is a convenient place to begin. As work accumulates, it can be placed in the hanging folders. At regular intervals, teacher and child go through the hanging files and select work to place in the portfolio. An expanding legal-size file pocket makes a convenient portfolio container. It is important that each piece of work be dated so that growth can be tracked. Sticky notes or self-stick mailing labels can be used to write notations on each piece of work. Labels should include the date, the type of activity, and the reason for selecting each sample.

A critical attribute of a portfolio is that items are *selected* through regularly scheduled student/teacher conferences. Teachers have always kept folders of student work, but portfolios are more focused and contain specially selected work that can be used for assessment. A portfolio offers a fuller picture than traditional assessment does because it provides a vehicle for student reflection and self-evaluation.

Some examples of items that might be included in a portfolio are

- Written or dictated descriptions of the results of investigations.
- Pictures: drawings, paintings, photographs of the child engaged in a significant activity; teacher or student sketches of products made with manipulatives or construction materials such as unit blocks, Unifix Cubes®, buttons, etc.
- Dictated (from younger children) or written (from older children) reports of activities, investigations, experiences, ideas, plans, etc.
- Diagrams, graphs, or other recorded data.
- Excerpts from students' math, science, and/or social studies journals.
- Samples of problem solutions, explanations of solutions, problems created, etc.
- Videotapes and/or audiotapes.

This material is invaluable for evaluation and for reporting progress to parents. When beginning portfolio assessment, it is wise to start small. Pick one focus such as mathematics or science or even a focus on one area such as Problem Solving, Data from Thematic Investigations, Artwork,

Writing, etc. Beginning with a scope that is too broad can make the task overwhelming.

Evaluating a portfolio involves several steps. First, a *rubric* should be developed. A rubric is a list of general statements that define the attributes of the portfolio that should be evaluated; that is, a list of the qualities you believe are important. Rubrics should be developed based on what you are looking for in your class—not on isolated skills but on broad criteria that reflect understanding. The statements will vary with the content focus of the portfolio. Figure 4–6 provides a general format and sample statements. Next, a summary providing an overview should be written (see Figure 4–7). If grades must be assigned, then there is a final step: the *holistic evaluation* (see Figure 4–8). For a holistic evaluation, the portfolios are grouped into piles such as strong, average, and weak or very strong, strong, high average, low average, somewhat weak, and very weak based on the rubric and the summary. This comparative analysis can then guide grading. See the reference list for publications that offer additional ideas regarding the development of portfolio assessment

practices.

SUMMARY

The focus of assessment in science is on assessment integrated with instruction during naturalistic classroom activities and during activities that involve performance of concrete/ hands-on problem solving and child-directed investigations. There are two ways children can be assessed to find their developmental level. They can be observed and they can be interviewed. Observation is most useful when looking at how children use concepts in their everyday activities. The interview with one child at a time gives the teacher an opportunity to look at very specific ideas and skills.

Guidelines are given for doing an interview. There is a summary of the nine levels of developmental tasks, which are included in Appendix A. A sample of part of an interview shows how the exchange between interviewer and child might progress.

A system for record keeping, reporting, and evaluation using a record folder and a portfolio are described. A holistic approach to evaluation is recommended.

SAMPLE PORTFOLIO RUBRIC

	Strong, Well Established	Beginning to Appear	Not Yet Observed
1. Can organize and record data.			
2. Explores, analyzes, looks for patterns.			
3. Uses concrete materials or drawings to aid in solving problems.			
4. Investigations and activities help develope concepts.			
5. Persistent, flexible, self-directed.			
6. Works cooperatively.			
7. Enjoys math and science.			

Figure 4–6   A general format for a rubric

PORTFOLIO SUMMARY ANALYSIS

CHILD'S NAME _____ DATE _____

OVERALL EVALUATION

STRENGTHS AND WEAKNESSES

FURTHER RECOMMENDATIONS

Figure 4–7 Format for portfolio summary analysis

SAMPLE OF HOLISTIC SCORING FORMAT

4 Strong on all the characteristics listed in the rubric.

3 Consistent evidence of the presence of most of the characteristics.

2 Some presence of the characteristics but incomplete
communication or presence of ideas, concepts, and/or behaviors.

1 Little or no presence of desired characteristics.

Figure 4–8 Sample of a holistic scoring format

FURTHER READING AND RESOURCES

Assessing learning in preschool and primary programs [Special section]. (1993). *Young Children, 48*(5).

Bergman, A. B. (1993). Performance assessment for early childhood: What could be more natural? *Science and Children, 30*(5), 20–22.

Chambers, D. L. (1993). Integrating assessment and instruction. In N. L. Webb & A. F. Coxford (Eds.), *Assessment in the mathematics classroom, 1993 yearbook* (pp. 17–25). Reston, VA: National Council of Teachers of Mathematics.

Charlesworth, R., Fleege, P. O., & Weitman, C. (1993). *Research on the effects of standardized testing on instruction, pupils, and teachers: Implications for policy.* Manuscript submitted for publication.

Collison, J. (1992). Using performance assessment to determine mathematical dispositions. *Arithmetic Teacher, 39*(6), 40–47.

Garnett, C. M. (1992). One point of view: Testing—Do not disturb? A concerned parent's view of testing. *Arithmetic Teacher, 39*(6), 8–10.

Grace, C., & Shores, E. F. (1991). *The portfolio and its use.* Little Rock, AR: Southern Early Childhood Association.

Kamii, C. (Ed.). (1990). *Achievement testing in the early grades: The games grown-ups play.* Washington, DC: National Association for the Education of Young Children.

Kamii, C., & Lewis, B. A. (1991). Achievement tests in primary mathematics: Perpetuating lower order thinking. *Arithmetic Teacher, 38*(9), 4–9.

Meisels, S. J. (1987). Uses and abuses of developmental screening and school readiness tests. *Young children, 42*(2), 4–6, 68–74.

National Council of Teachers of Mathematics. (1989). *Curriculum and evaluation standards of school mathematics.* Reston, VA: Author.

Payne, J. N. (Ed.). (1990). *Mathematics for the young child.* Reston, VA: National Council of Teachers of Mathematics.

Portfolio news. Published quarterly by Teacher Education Program, University of California at San Diego, 9500 Gilman Drive, La Jolla, CA 92093-0070.

Richardson, K. 1984. *Developing number concepts using Unifix cubes®.* Menlo Park, CA: Addison-Wesley.

Robinson, G. E., & Bartlett, K. T. (1993). Assessment and evaluation of learning. In R. J. Jensen (Ed.), *Research ideas for the classroom: Early childhood mathematics.* New York: Macmillan.

Romberg, T. A., & Wilson, L. S. (1992). Alignment of tests with the standards. *Arithmetic Teacher, 40*(1), 18–22.

Sammons, K. B., Kobett, B., Heiss, J., & Fennell, F. (1992). Linking instruction and assessment in the mathematics classroom. *Arithmetic Teacher, 39*(6), 11–16.

St. Clair, J. (1993). Assessing mathematical understanding in a bilingual kindergarten. In N. L. Webb & A. F. Coxford (Eds.), *Assessment in the mathematics classroom, 1993 yearbook* (pp. 65–73). Reston, VA: National Council of Teachers of Mathematics.

Stenmark, J. K. (Ed.). (1991). *Mathematics assessment: Myths, models, good questions, and practical suggestions.* Reston, VA: National Council of Teachers of Mathematics.

Webb, N. L., & Coxford, A. F. (Eds.). (1993). *Assessment in the mathematics classroom.* Reston, VA: National Council of Teachers of Mathematics.

SUGGESTED ACTIVITIES

1. Find out what the expectations are for science concept development for students entering kindergarten and/or first grade in your local school system. Compare the school system list with the tasks suggested at levels 6 and 7 in the text and in Appendix A. What are the similarities and differences?
2. Get permission to assess the concept development level of two children at different age levels between 4 and 8. Make assessment cards, and obtain materials needed to administer two or three of the tasks to each child. Compare your results and reactions with those of the other students in the class. Make a class list of improvements and suggestions.
3. Find a prekindergarten, kindergarten, or first-grade teacher who has an established portfolio assessment system. Invite the teacher to be a guest speaker in your class.
4. Find three articles in professional journals that discuss assessment/evaluation of young children. What were the main ideas presented? Explain how you will apply these ideas in the future.

REVIEW

A. Explain why it is important to make assessment the first step in teaching.
B. Read incidents 1 and 2, which follow. What is being done wrong in each situation? What should be done?
   1. Ms. Collins is interviewing a child in the hallway. Other teachers and students are continuously passing by. The child frequently looks away from the materials to watch the passersby.
   2. Mr. Garcia is interviewing Johnny. Mr. Garcia places five rectangles on the table. Each is the same length, but they vary in width.

Mr. Garcia:
WATCH WHAT I DO. (Mr. Garcia lines up the objects from fattest to thinnest)

NOW I'LL MIX THEM UP. YOU PUT THEM IN A ROW FROM FATTEST TO THINNEST. (Mr. Garcia is looking ahead at the next set of instructions. He glances at Johnny with a rather serious expression.

Johnny's Response:
(Johnny picks out the fattest and the thinnest. He places them next to each other. Then he examines the other three rectangles and lines them up in sequence next to the first two. He looks up at Mr. Garcia.))
   ARE YOU FINISHED?

(Johnny nods that he is.)

TOO BAD, YOU MIXED THEM UP.
C. Describe the advantages of portfolio assessment.

UNIT 5

The Basics of Science

O B J E C T I V E S

After studying this unit, the student should be able to
- Define the relative importance of science content, processes, and attitudes in teaching young children
- Explain why science should be taught to young children
- Identify the major areas of science instruction
- List the science attitudes and process skills appropriate to preschool and primary grades
- Select appropriate science topics for teaching science to young children

SCIENCE AND WHY WE TEACH IT TO YOUNG CHILDREN

When people think of science they generally first think of the content of science. Science is often viewed as an encyclopedia of discoveries and technological achievements. Formal training in science classes often promotes this view by requiring memorization of seemingly endless science concepts. Science has been compiling literally millions of discoveries, facts, and data over thousands of years. We are now living in the age that is sometimes described as the "Knowledge Explosion." Consider the fact that the amount of scientific information created between the years 1900 and 1950 equals that which was learned from the beginning of recorded history until the year 1900. Since 1950 the rate of production of scientific information has increased even further. Some scientists estimate that the total amount of scientific information produced now doubles every two to five years.

If you tried to teach all that has been learned in science in preschool and continued daily straight through high school, you would make only a small

dent in the body of knowledge. It is simply impossible to learn everything. Despite this, however, far too many teachers approach the task of teaching children science as if it were a body of information that anyone can memorize. The fact is that it is nearly impossible to predict what specific information taught to primary age students today will be of use to them as they pursue a career through the next century (Figure 5–1).

It is entirely possible that today's body of science knowledge will change before a child graduates from high school. Scientists are constantly looking at data in different ways and coming to new conclusions. Thus, it cannot be predicted with any certainty which facts will be the most important for students to learn for life in the 21st century. What is known is that people in the next century will have to face new problems that they will attempt to solve. Life, in a sense, is a series of problems. The people who are most successful in future decades will be those who are best equipped to solve the problems they encounter.

This discussion is intended to put the nature of science in perspective. Science in pre-school

45

Figure 5–1 Exploring science

through college should be viewed more as a verb than a noun. It is not so much a body of knowledge as it is a way of thinking and acting. Science is a way of trying to discover the nature of things. The attitudes and thinking skills that have moved science forward through the centuries are the same attitudes and skills that enable individuals to solve the problems that they encounter in everyday life.

An approach to science teaching that emphasizes the development of thinking and the open-minded attitudes of science would seem to be most appropriate to the instruction of young children. This unit covers processes, attitudes, content, and the importance of science in language arts and reading.

TEACHING SCIENCE PROCESSES

Children discover the content of science by applying the processes of science. This can be done through science activities, class discussions, reading, and a variety of other teaching strategies. These are the thinking skills necessary to learn science.

Science Process Skills

Basic Process Skills

1. *Observing.* Using the senses to gather information about objects or events.
2. *Comparing.* Looking at similarities and differences in real objects. In the primary grades, students begin to compare and contrast ideas, concepts and objects..
3. *Classifying.* Grouping and sorting according to properties, such as size, shape, color, use, and so on.
4. *Measuring.* Quantitative descriptions made by an observer either directly through observation or indirectly with a unit of measure.
5. *Communicating.* Communicating ideas, directions, and descriptions orally or in written form such as pictures, maps, graphs, or journals so others can understand what you mean.

Intermediate Process Skills

6. *Inferring.* Based on observations but suggests more meaning about a situation than can be directly observed. When children infer, they recognize patterns and expect these patterns to recur under similar circumstances.
7. *Predicting.* Making reasonable guesses or estimations based on observations and prior knowledge.

Advanced Process Skills

8. *Hypothesizing.* Devising a statement, based on observations, that can be tested by experiment. A typical form for a hypothesis is, "*If* water is put in the freezer overnight, *then* it freezes."
9. *Defining and controlling variables.* Determining which variables in an investigation should be studied or should be controlled to conduct a controlled experiment. For example, when we find out if a plant grows in the dark, we must also grow a plant in the light.

Figure 5–2 Science process skills

Process skills are those that allow students to process new information through concrete experiences (Figure 5–2). They are also progressive, each building on and overlapping with one another. The skills most appropriate for preschool and primary students are the basic skills of *observing, comparing, classifying, measuring,* and *communicating* (Figure 5–3). Sharpening these skills is essential for coping with daily life as well as for future study in science and mathematics. As students move through the primary grades, mastery

Figure 5–3   Classifying keys

of these skills will enable them to perform intermediate process skills that include *gathering* and *organizing* information, *inferring*, and *predicting*. If students have a strong base of primary and intermediate process skills, they will be prepared by the time they reach the intermediate grades to apply those skills to the more sophisticated and abstract skills, such as *forming hypotheses* and *separating variables*, which are required in experimentation.

Grade level suggestions for introducing specific science process skills are given as a general guide for their appropriate use. Since students vary greatly in experience and intellectual development, you may find that your early childhood students are ready to explore higher-level process skills sooner. In such cases you should feel free to stretch their abilities by encouraging them to work with more advanced science process skills. For example, 4- and 5-year-olds can begin with simple ver-sions of intermediate process skills, such as making a guess about a physical change (What will happen when the butter is heated?) as a first step toward predicting. They can gather and organize simple data (such as counting the days until the chicks hatch) and make simple graphs like those described in Unit 10 of this text (Figure 5–4).

SCIENCE PROCESS SKILLS

Knowledge and concepts are developed through the use of process skills. It is with these skills that individuals think through and study problems.

Observing

The most fundamental of the scientific thinking processes is observation. It is only through this process that we are able to receive information about the world around us. The senses of sight, smell, sound, touch, and taste are the means by which our brains receive information and give us the ability to describe something. As young children use their senses in a firsthand exploratory

Figure 5–4   Graphing our family

way, they are using the same skills that scientists extend to construct meaning and knowledge in the world.

Sometimes we observe, but we do not always see very much. Teaching strategies that reinforce observation skills require children to observe carefully to note specific phenomena that they might ordinarily overlook. For example, when Mr. Wang's class observes an aquarium, he guides them by asking, "Which fish seems to spend the most time on the bottom of the tank? In what way do the fish seem to react to things like light or shadow or an object in their swimming path?"

Storybooks and informational books can also encourage the use of process skills. In the popular book *Bubbles*, Bernie Zubrowski asks children to note the colors they see and to describe the different patterns that bubbles make when viewed from several angles.

Observation is the first step in gathering information to solve a problem. Students will need opportunities to observe size, shape, color, texture, and other observable properties in objects. The following teacher statements and questions facilitate the use of this process: "Tell me what you see," "What do you hear?," "What does this feel like?," and "How would you describe the object?"

Comparing

As children develop skills in observation, they will naturally begin to compare and contrast and to identify similarities and differences. The comparing process, which sharpens their observation skills, is the first step toward classifying.

Teachers can encourage children to find likenesses and differences throughout the school day. A good example of this strategy can be seen when, after a walk through a field, Mrs. Red Fox asks her first graders, "Which seeds are sticking to your clothes?" and "How are these seeds alike?"

The comparing process builds upon the process of observing. In addition to observing the characteristics of an object such as a leaf, children learn more about the leaf by comparing it to other leaves. For example, a child finds a leaf and brings it to class to compare with other leaves in the leaf collection. Statements and questions that facilitate the comparing process include, "How are these alike?," "How are these different?," "Which of these is bigger, wetter, etc.?," and "Compare similarities and differences between these two animals.."

Classifying

Classifying begins when children group and sort real objects. To *group*, children need to compare objects and develop subsets. A *subset* is a group that shares a common characteristic unique to that group. For example, the jar may be full of buttons, but children are likely to begin grouping by sorting the buttons into subgroups of red buttons, yellow buttons, blue buttons and other colors.

Mrs. Jones has her kindergarten children collect many kinds of leaves. They place individual leaves between two squares of wax paper. Mrs. Jones covers the wax paper squares with a piece of smooth cloth and presses the cloth firmly with a warm steam iron. The leaf is now sealed in and will remain preserved for the rest of the year.

Once the leaves are prepared, the children choose a leaf to examine, draw, and describe. They carefully observe and compare leaves to discover each leaf's unique characteristics. Then, the children classify the leaves into subgroups of common characteristics.

Children initially group objects by one property, such as sorting a collection of leaves by color, size, shape, etc. As children grow older and advance in the classification process, objects or ideas are put together on the basis of two or more characteristics that are inherent in the items. Brown-colored animals with four legs, four example, can be grouped with all brown-colored animals, regardless of the number of legs, or they can be groups with different colored animals with four legs, or they can be classified with brown-colored animals with four legs.

Scientists from all disciplines use an organizational process to group and classify their work whether that work involves leaves, flowers, animals, rocks, liquids, or rockets. Statements and questions that facilitate this process include, "Put together all of the animals that belong together?," "Can you group them in another way?," "How are these animals organized?," and "Identify several ways that you used to classify these animals."

Measuring

Measuring is the skill of quantifying observations. This can involve numbers, distances, time, volumes, and temperature, which may or may not be quantified with standard units. Nonstandard units are involved when children say that they have used two "shakes" of salt while cooking or a "handful" of rice and a "couple" of beans when creating their collage.

Measuring involves placing objects in order, such as an ordered sequence (*seriation*), or it can be ordering according to length or shade. Children can also invent units of measure. For example, when given beans to measure objects, Vanessa may say, "The book is 12 beans long," but Ann finds that the same book is 11 beans long. Activities such as this help children see a need for a standard unit of measure—like an inch. Questions that facilitate the measuring process include, "How might you measure this object?," "Which object do think is heavier?," and "How could you find out?"

Communicating

All humans communicate in some way. Gestures, body postures and positions, facial expressions, vocal sounds, words, and pictures are some of the ways we communicate with each other and express feelings. It is through communication that scientists share their findings with the rest of the world.

In early childhood science explorations, communicating refers to the skill of describing a phenomenon. A child communicates ideas, directions, and descriptions orally or in written form, such as in pictures, dioramas, maps, graphs, journals, and reports. Communication requires that information be collected, arranged, and presented in a way that helps others understand your meaning.

Teachers encourage communication when they ask children to keep logs, draw diagrams or graphs, or otherwise record an experience they have observed. Children respond well to tasks such as recording daily weather by writing down the date, time of day, and drawing pictures of the weather that day. They will enjoy answering questions about their observations such as, "What was the temperature on Tuesday?" and "Was the sun out on Wednesday?," "What did you see?," and "Draw a picture of what you see."

Inferring

When children *infer*, they make a series of observations, categorize them, then try to give them some meaning. An inference is arrived at indirectly (not directly, like a simple observation). For example, you look out the window and see the leaves moving on the trees. You infer that the wind is blowing. You have not experienced the wind directly, but based on your observations and prior knowledge and experience, you know that the wind is blowing. In this case, your inference can be tested simply by walking outside.

The process skill of inferring requires that a reasonable assumption of prior knowledge be present. It requires that children infer something that they have not yet seen because it has not happened or because it cannot be observed directly. For this reason, the inferring process is most appropriate for middle level grades and the science content associated with those grades. However, science content associated with inferring what animal made a set of tracks, or the loss of water from plants, or the vapor in air can be appropriate for older primary children.

In another example, a teacher prepares four film canisters by filling them with different substances such as sand, chalk, stones, marbles, and paper clips. As the students observe the closed canisters, the teacher asks, "What do you think is inside of these canisters?," "What did you observe that makes you think that?," "Could there be anything else in the canister?," and "How could you find out?"

Predicting

The process of predicting is closely related to inferring. When you *predict*, you say what you expect to happen. You make a reasonable guess or estimation based on observations of data. Keep in mind that this process is more than a simple guess. Children should have the prior knowledge necessary to make a reasonable prediction. Children enjoy simple prediction questions.

After reading *Science in a Vacant Lot*, by Seymour Simon, children can count the number of seeds in a seed package and then predict how many of the seeds will grow into plants. As they prepare to keep a record of how two plants grow (one has been planted in topsoil; the other in subsoil), they are asked, "Which plant do you think will grow better?"

Hypothesizing and Controlling Variables = *Experiment*

To be called an *experiment*, an investigation must contain a hypothesis and control variables. A *hypothesis* is a more formal operation than the investigative questions that young children explore in the preschool and primary grades. A hypothesis is a statement of a relationship that might exist between two variables. A typical form of a hypothesis is: if ____, then ____. With young children, a hypothesis can take the form of a question such as, "What happens if the magnet drops?"

In a formal experiment, variables are defined and controlled. Although experiments can be attempted with primary age children, experimental investigations are most appropriate in the middle and upper grades.

DEVELOPING SCIENTIFIC ATTITUDES

In some ways, attitudes toward a subject or activity can be as important as the subject itself. Some examples are: individuals who know that cigarette smoking may kill but continue to smoke or people who know that wearing a seat belt greatly improves their chances of surviving an accident and preventing injury but choose not to wear it. The same is true with scientific attitudes.

The scientific attitudes of curiosity, skepticism, positive self-image, and positive approach to failure are highlighted, and other relevant attitudes are listed in Figure 5–5.

Curiosity

Preschool and primary students are obviously not mentally developed to a point where they can think consciously about forming attitudes for systematically pursuing problems, but they can practice behaviors that will create lifelong habits that reflect scientific attitudes.

Curiosity is thought to be one of the most valuable attitudes that can be possessed by anyone. It takes a curious individual to look at something from a new perspective, question something long believed to be true, or look more carefully at an exception to the rule. This approach that is basic to science is natural to young children. They use all their senses and energies to find out about the world around them. Often, years of formalized experiences in school, which allow little time for

Curiosity	Checking evidence
Withholding judgment	Positive approach to failure
Skepticism	Positive self-image
Objectivity	Willingness to change
Open-mindedness	Positive attitude toward change
Avoiding dogmatism	Avoiding superstitions
Avoiding gullibility	Integrity
Observing carefully	Humility
Making careful conclusions	

Figure 5–5 Scientific attitudes

exploration and questioning, squelch this valuable characteristic. Educational experiences that utilize firsthand inquiry experiences like the learning cycle make use of a child's natural curiosity rather than trying to suppress it.

Skepticism

Do you believe everything that you see? Are you skeptical about some things that you hear? Good! This attitude reflects the healthy skepticism required by both science and the child's environment. Children need to be encouraged to question, wonder, ask "why," and be cautious about accepting things at face value. Experiences designed around direct observation of phenomena and gathering data naturally encourage children to explore new situations in an objective and open-minded fashion. This type of experience can do much toward developing confidence and a healthy skepticism.

Positive Approach to Failure and Self-Image

A positive approach to failure and a positive self-image are closely related attitudes. Students need the opportunity to ask their own questions and seek their own solutions to problems. At times this may mean that they will pursue dead ends, but often much more is learned in the pursuit than in the correct answer. If children are conditioned to look to adult authority figures to identify and solve problems, they will have a difficult time approaching new problems both as students and as adults.

In the last 20 years, some educators believed that children should not be allowed to experience failure. Educational situations were structured so that every child could be successful nearly all the time. It was reasoned that the experience of failure would discourage students from future study. In the field of science, however, it is important to find out what does not work as it is to find out what does. In fact, real growth in science tends to happen when solutions do not fit what was predicted. Although students should not be constantly con-

fronted with frustrating learning situations, a positive attitude toward failure may better serve them in developing problem-solving skills. After all, in much of science inquiry, there are no "right" or "wrong" answers.

The remaining science attitudes, *willingness to change*, *positive attitude toward change*, *withholding judgment*, *avoiding superstitions*, *integrity*, and *humility*, are additional important attitudes both to science and functioning as a successful adult. These can be encouraged in science teaching both through the teacher's exhibiting these behaviors and acknowledging students when they demonstrate them. All of these attitudes that support the enterprise of science are also quite valuable tools for young students in approaching life's inevitable problems.

SCIENCE AND THE DEVELOPMENT OF LITERACY

An often-heard question is, "Why take time to teach science to young children?" Many teachers believe that they have too much to do in a day and they cannot afford to take the time to teach science. The answer to why science should be taught is, "You cannot afford *not* to teach science." Piaget's theory leaves no question as to the importance of learning through activity. The Council for Basic Education reports that there is impressive evidence that hands-on science programs aid in the development of language and reading skills. Some evidence indicates that achievement scores increase as a result of such programs. This statement is supported by many researchers. The following are possible explanations for this improvement:

In its early stages, literacy can be supported by giving children an opportunity to manipulate familiar and unfamiliar objects. During science experiences children use the thinking skills of science to match, discriminate, sequence, describe, and classify objects. These perceptual skills are among those needed for reading and writing (Figure 5–6). A child who is able to make fine dis-

EXAMPLES OF PROBLEM-SOLVING SKILLS IN SCIENCE	CORRESPONDING READING SKILLS
Observing	Discriminating shapes Discriminating sounds Discriminating syllables and accents
Identifying	Recognizing letters Recognizing words Recognizing common prefixes Recognizing common suffixes Recognizing common base words Naming objects, events, and people
Describing	Isolating important characteristics Enumerating characteristics Using appropriate terminology Using synonyms
Classifying	Comparing characteristics Contrasting characteristics Ordering, sequencing Arranging ideas Considering multiple factors
Designing investigations	Asking questions Looking for potential relationships Following organized procedures Reviewing prior studies Developing outlines
Collecting data	Taking notes Surveying reference materials Using several parts of a book Recording data in an orderly fashion Developing precision and accuracy
Interpreting data	Recognizing cause and effect relationships Organizing facts Summarizing new information Varying rate of reading Inductive and deductive thinking
Communicating results	Using graphic aids Logically arranging information Sequencing ideas Knowledge of technical vocabulary Illuminating significant factors Describing with clarity
Formulating conclusions	Generalizing Analyzing critically Evaluating information Recognizing main ideas and concepts Establishing relationships Applying information to other situations

Figure 5–6   Science and reading connection. *Note.* From "Science and Reading: A Basic Duo" by G. S. Carter and R. D. Simpson, 1989, *The Science Teacher*, *45*(3), p. 20. Reprinted by permission of the National Science Teachers Association.

criminations between objects will be prepared to discriminate between letters and words of the alphabet. As children develop conventional reading and writing skills they can apply their knowledge to facilitate their explorations in science by reading background material and recording hypotheses, observations, and interactions.

What better way to allow for children to develop communication skills than to participate in the "action plus talk" of science! Depending on the age level, children may want to communicate what they are doing to the teacher and other students. They may even start talking about themselves. Communication by talking, drawing, painting, modeling, constructing, drama, puppets, and writing should be encouraged. These are natural communication outcomes of hands-on science.

Reading and listening to stories about the world is difficult when you do not have a base of experience. If story time features a book about a hamster named Charlie, it might be difficult to understand what is happening if you have not seen a hamster. However, the communication gap is bridged if children have knowledge about small animals. Once a child has contact with the object represented by the written word, meaning can be developed. Words do not make a lot of sense when you do not have the background experience to understand what you read (Figure 5–7).

The relationship of language developed in the context of the direct experiences of science is explored in Unit 7 of this text. Ideas for working with experience charts, tactile sensations, listening, writing, and introducing words are included in curriculum integration.

Science also provides various opportunities to determine cause-and-effect-relationships. A sense of self-esteem and control over their lives develops when children discover cause-and-effect relationships and when they learn to influence the outcome of events. For example, a child can experience a causal relationship by deciding whether to add plant cover to an aquarium. Predicting the most probable outcome of actions gives children a sense of control,

Figure 5–7   Children prepare for animal visits

which is identified by Mary Budd Rowe as "fate control." She found that problem-solving behaviors seem to differ according to how people rate on fate control measures. Children scoring high on these measures performed better at solving problems.

Keep in mind that the child who is academically advanced in math and reading is not always the first to solve a problem or assemble the most interesting collection. If sufficient time to work with materials is provided, children with poor language development may exhibit good reasoning. It is a mistake to correlate language skills with mental ability.

APPROPRIATE SCIENCE CONTENT

The science content for preschool and primary education is not greatly different from that of any other elementary grade level, in that the depth and complexity of the science content and process skills are determined by the developmental level of the child. As already mentioned, the way that science is taught is probably far more important than the science content itself. The four main areas of science emphasis that are common in the primary grades are life science, health science, physical science, and earth and environmental science. Ideally, each of the four main areas should be given a balanced coverage. Appropriate science concepts for the early childhood years can be found throughout the text and specifically in the units dealing with science content.

Life Science

Science teaching at this level is traditionally dominated by life science experiences. This is not because it is most appropriate but rather because of tradition. Teaching at early elementary grades has its roots in the nature study and garden school movements of the first half of the 20th century. Many programs and materials for young children concentrate much time on life science to the exclusion of other science content. Although life science should not be the entire curriculum for young children, it can be an important part of the curriculum. Children are natural observers and enjoy finding out about the living world around them.

Life science investigations lend themselves quite readily to simple observations, explorations, and classifications. As with all science content at this level, hands-on experiences are essential to development of relevant concepts, skills, and attitudes. The areas of content typically covered with young children are plants, animals, and ecology. These experiences should build a foundation for students' understanding of environmental problems and solutions in higher grade levels and in adult life. Intelligent decision making regarding the interaction of science, technology, and the environment may well be a critical factor for survival in the next century. Examples of strategies for teaching appropriate life science content are found in Units 13, 14, 19, and 20.

Health Science

The study of health and the human body is receiving increased emphasis in elementary education. Recent concerns about problems of drug abuse, communicable diseases, and the relationship of nutrition and health have given rise to education in both factual information and "refusal skills like saying no." These learnings will help children take action to prevent the spread of disease, maintain a healthy body, and ask the types of questions that will ensure informed decisions.

Young children are curious about their bodies and are eager to learn more about themselves. They will enjoy exploring body parts and their relationships, body systems, foods, and nutrition. Misconceptions and worries that children have can be clarified by learning "all about me" in a variety of hands-on experiences (Figure 5–8).

Physical Science

Young children enjoy pushing on levers, making bulbs light, working with magnets, using a string-and-can telephone, and changing matter. This is the study of physical science—forces, motion,

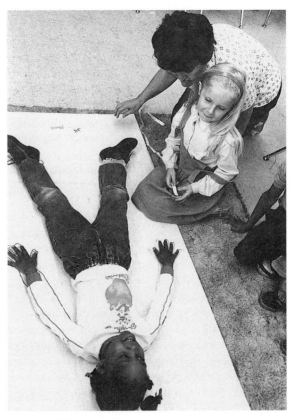

Figure 5–8 Measuring the body

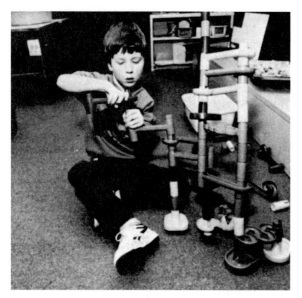

Figure 5–9 Controlling speed and action

energy, and machines. Teachers will enjoy watching a child assemble an assortment of blocks, wheels, and axles into a vehicle that really works. Physical science activities are guaranteed to make a child's face light up or ask, "How did you do that?"

Sometimes the content of this area is overlooked, which is unfortunate because physical science lends itself quite well to the needs of young children. One advantage of physical science activities is that they are more foolproof than many other activities. For example, if a young child is investigating the growth of plants, many things can go wrong that will destroy the investigation. Plants can die, get moldy, or take so long to give the desired effect that the children lose interest. Physical science usually "happens" more quickly. If something damages the investigation, it can always be repeated in a matter of minutes. Repeatability of activities is a significant advantage in developing a process orientation to science.

Keep in mind that children are growing up in a technological world. They interact daily with technology. It is likely that future lifestyles and job opportunities may depend on skills related to the realm of physical science.

Earth and Environmental Science

The study of earth science also allows many opportunities to help children develop process skills. Children are eager to learn about weather and how soil is formed. Air, land, water, rocks, and the sun, moon, and stars are all a part of earth science. Although these topics are attention grabbers, the teacher of young children must be certain to make the phenomena concrete for them to be effective. Hands-on experiences need not be difficult. Try making fossil cookies, weather and temperature charts, parachutes, and rock and cloud observation to teach a concept. Unit 16 gives a number of examples of how the earth sciences can be made appropriate for young children and how environmental awareness can be more more meaningful. Refer to Units 13, 14, 16, 19, and 20 for additional environmental education ideas.

SUMMARY

Our major goal in science education is to develop scientifically literate people who can think critically. In order to teach science to tomorrow's citizens, process skills and attitudes must be established as major components of any science content lesson. Facts alone will not be sufficient for children who are born into a technological world. Children interact daily with science. Their toasters pop; their can openers whir; and their televisions, VCRs, and computers are commonplace. Preparation to live in a changing world as productive individuals should begin early in a child's life.

The manipulation of science materials, whether initiated by the child and/or the teacher, creates opportunities for language and literacy development. Hands-on experiences, which emphasize the process skills of science, are essential if the child is to receive the maximum benefits from science instruction. The intent of this book is to tell how to plan and teach these kinds of experiences for young children.

FURTHER READING AND RESOURCES

Carter, G. S., & Simpson, R. D. (1978). Science and Reading: A basic duo. *Science Teacher*, *45*(3), 19–21.

Forman, G. E., & Hill, F. (1984). *Constructive play: Applying Piaget in the classroom*. Menlo Park, CA: Addison-Wesley.

Forman, G. E., & Kuschner, D. S. (1983). *The child's construction of knowledge*. Washington, D.C.: National Association for the Education of Young Children.

Harlan, J. (1991). *Science experiences for the early childhood years*. New York: Macmillan.

Howe, A. C., & Jones, L. (1993). *Engaging children in science*. New York: Macmillan.

Kamii, C., & Devries, R. (1993). *Physical knowledge in the classroom: Implications of Piaget's theory* (rev. ed.). Englewood Cliffs, NJ: Prentice-Hall.

Kamii, C., & Lee-Katz, L. (1979). Physics in preschool education: A Piagetian approach. *Young Children, 34*: 4–9.

Lind, K. K. (1991). Science process skills: Preparing for the future. In (Ed.), *Professional handbook: The best of everything*. Morristown, NJ: Silver Burdett & Ginn.

Lind, K. K., & Milburn, M. J. (1988). Mechanized childhood. *Science and Children. 25*(5), 32–33.

Mechling, K. R., & Oliver, D. L. (1983). *Science teaches basic skills*. Washington, D.C.: National Science Teachers Association.

Rowe, M. B. (1973). *Teaching science as continuous inquiry*. NY: McGraw-Hill.

Simon, S. (1970). *Science in a Vacant Lot*. New York: Viking Press.

Sunal, C. S. (1982). Philosophical bases for science and mathematics in early childhood education. *School, Science and Mathematics. 82*(1), 2–10.

Tipps, S. (1982). Making better guesses: A goal in early childhood science. *School Science and Mathematics. 82*(1), 29–37.

Zubrowski, B. (1979). *Bubbles*. Boston, MA: Little, Brown and Company.

SUGGESTED ACTIVITIES

1. The results of science are everywhere. Make a list of all of the science examples that you encountered on your way to class.

2. Recall a typical primary school day from your past. What type of science activities were introduced? How were the experiences introduced? Compare your experience with that of a child in a classroom you have observed. What are the similarities and differences? Do technological advancements make a difference?

3. Examine the teacher's edition of a recent elementary science textbook at the primary grade level. What science attitudes are claimed to be taught in the text? Decide if there is evidence of these attitudes being taught in either the student or teacher edition of the text.

4. Interview teachers of preschool and primary children to find out what types of science activities they introduce to students. Is the science content balanced? Which activities include the exploration of materials? Record your observations for class discussion.

5. If you were to teach science to urban children, what type of activities would you provide? Apply the question to rural and suburban environments. Would you teach science differently? Why or why not?

6. Pick one of your favorite science topics. Plan how you would include process, attitude, and content.

REVIEW

A. Discuss how the traditional view of science as a body of knowledge differs from a contemporary view of science as a process.

B. How does the knowledge explosion affect the science that is taught to young children?

C. List process skills that should be introduced to all preschool and primary age students.

D. What is meant by the term *healthy skepticism*?

E. What are the four major areas of science content appropriate for early childhood education?

F. Why has health education received increased attention in early childhood education?

UNIT 6

How Young Scientists Use Concepts

OBJECTIVES

After studying this unit, the student should be able to
- Develop lessons using a variety of science process skills such as observing, comparing, measuring, classifying, and predicting
- Apply problem-solving strategies to lessons designed for young students
- Use data collecting and analysis as a basis for designing and teaching science lessons
- Design experiences for young children that enrich their experience at the preoperational level and prepare them for the concrete operational level
- Describe the process of self-regulation
- Describe the proper use of a discrepant event in teaching science

CONCEPT FORMATION IN YOUNG CHILDREN

Young children try very hard to explain the world around them. Do any of the following statements sound familiar?

"Thunder is the sound of the angels bowling."
"Chickens lay eggs, and pigs lay bacon."
"Electricity comes from a switch on the wall."
"The sun follows me when I take a walk."

These are the magical statements of intuitive thinkers. These children use their senses or intuition to make judgments. Their logic is unpredictable, and they frequently prefer to use "magical explanations" to explain what is happening in their world. Clouds become the "smoke of angels," and rain falls because "it wants to help the farmers." These comments are typical of the self-centered view of intuitive children. They think that the sun rises in the morning just to shine on them. It never occurs to them that others might also benefit. They also have a difficult time remembering more than one thing at a time.

Statements and abilities such as these inspired Jean Piaget's curiosity about young children's beliefs. His search for answers about how children think and learn has contributed to our understanding that learning is an internal process. In other words, it is the child who brings meaning to the world and not vice versa. These misconceptions of a child are normal. This is what the child believes; thus, this is what is real to the child (Figure 6–1).

The temptation is to try and move children out of their magical stage of development. This is a mistake. Although some misconceptions can be corrected, others have to wait for more advanced thinking to develop. Students should not be pushed, pulled, or dragged through developmental stages. Instead, the goal is to enhance the development of young children at their present level of operation. In this way, they have the richness of experiences to take with them when the next level of development naturally occurs.

"The sun follows me!"

Figure 6–1 Children have misconceptions.

Enhancing Awareness

When teaching concepts that are too abstract for children to fully understand, try to focus on aspects of the concept that can be understood. This type of awareness can be enhanced by the use of *visual depictions*, *observing*, *drawing*, and *discussion*.

Although some aspects of weather might remain a mystery, understanding can be developed by recording the types of weather that occur in a month. Construct a large calendar, and put it on the wall. Every day, have a student draw a picture that represents the weather for the day. When the month is completed, cut the calendar into individual days. Then, glue the days that show similar weather in columns to create a bar graph. Ask the children to form conclusions about the month's weather from the graph. In this way, children can relate to weather patterns and visualize that these patterns change from day to day (Figure 6–2).

In a similar way, children will be better pre-

pared for later studies of nutrition if they have some understanding of their own food intake. Graphing snacks is a way for children to visually compare and organize what they eat. On poster board make five columns and mount pictures from the basic food groups at the bottom of each column. Discuss which food group each child's favorite snacks belong in. Have the children write their initials or attach a picture of themselves in the appropriate food column. Ask, "What do most of us like for snacks?" Discuss healthy snacks, and make a new chart at the end of the week. Is there a difference in choices? (Figure 6–3)

For observations to be effective, they should be done in 10 minutes or less, conducted with a purpose, and brought together by discussions. Unconnected observations do not aid in concept

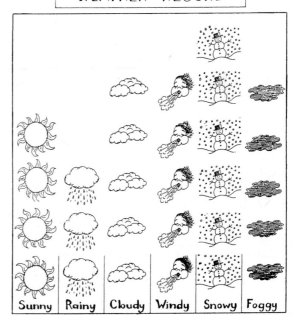

Figure 6–2 "How many cloudy days were there this month?"

SNACK GRAPH

Figure 6–3 Find your favorite snacks.

formation. For example, if a purpose is not given observing two flickering, different-sized candles, children will lose interest within minutes. Instead of telling children to "go look" at two burning candles, ask them to look and to find the difference between the candles. Children will become excited with the discovery that the candles are not the same size (Figure 6–4).

Discussions that follow observations heighten a child's awareness of that observation. A group of children observing a fish tank to see where the fish spends most of its time will be prepared to share what they saw happen in the tank. However, there may not be agreement.

Differences of opinion about observations stimulate interest and promote discussion. The children are likely to return to the tank to see for themselves what others say they saw. This would probably not happen without the focusing effect of discussion.

Drawing can provide excellent opportunities for observation and discussion. An effective use of drawing to enhance concept development would be to have children draw a tiger from memory before going to the zoo. Strategies like this usually reveal that more information is needed to construct an accurate picture. Children will be eager to observe details that they might not otherwise notice about the tigers in the zoo (Figure 6–5).

Teacher Magic and Misconceptions

Children need time to reflect and absorb ideas to fully understand a concept. Misconceptions can occur at any stage. Be sure to give them plenty of time to manipulate and explore. For example, when a teacher mixes yellow and blue paints to create green, children might think that the result is teacher magic. However, if given the paints and the opportunity to discover green, they might remember that yellow and blue mixed together make green. Because children cannot carry out most operations mentally, they need to manipulate materials to develop concepts (Figure 6–6).

Misconceptions can occur at any stage of development. Some children in the primary grades may be in a transitional stage or have moved into the concrete operation stage of development.

Figure 6–4 Children notice that the candles are not the same size.

Robin

Tiger

Figure 6–5   Robin's drawing of a tiger after a visit to the zoo.

Although these students will be able to do much logical thinking, the concepts they work with must still be tied to concrete objects that they can manipulate. Firsthand experiences with materials continue to be essential for learning.

The child in this developmental stage no longer looks at the world through "magical eyes." Explanations for natural events are influenced by other natural objects and events. For example, a child may now say, "The rain comes from the sky" rather than "It rains to help farmers." This linking of physical objects will first appear in the early concrete development stages. Do not be misled by an apparent new awareness. The major factor in concept development is still contingent upon children's need to manipulate, observe, discuss, and visually depict things to understand what is new and different about them. This is true in all of the Piagetian developmental stages discussed in this book.

SELF-REGULATION AND CONCEPT ATTAINMENT

Have you ever seen someone plunge a turkey skewer through a balloon? Did you expect the balloon to burst? What was your reaction when it stayed intact? Your curiosity was probably piqued—you wanted to know why the balloon did not burst. Actually, you had just witnessed a *discrepant event* and entered the process of self-regulation. This is when your brain responds to interactions between you and your environment. Gallagher and Reid (1981) describe *self-regulation* as the active mental process of forming concepts. Knowing a little bit about how the brain functions in concept development will help in an explanation of this process. Visualize the human mind with thousands of concepts stored in various sections of the brain, rather like a complex system of mental pigeonholes, much like a postal sorting system. As children move through the world and encounter new objects and phenomena, they assimilate and accommodate new information and store it in the correctly labeled mental category in their minds.

The brain, functioning like a postal worker, naturally classifies and stores information into the appropriate pigeonholes. (Figure 6–7). New information is always stored close to all of the related

Generate a list of topics, and construct questions to ask children.

For example:

Rain	What is rain?
	Where does rain come from?
Thunder	What do you think thunder is?
	Where does the loud sound come from?
Grass	What makes the grass green?
Night	Why does it get dark at night?
Seasons	Why are there seasons?
	Why do the leaves fall off the trees?
River	Why are there rivers in some places but not in others?
Sun	Why does the sun move?

Figure 6–6   Examples of questions to ask children

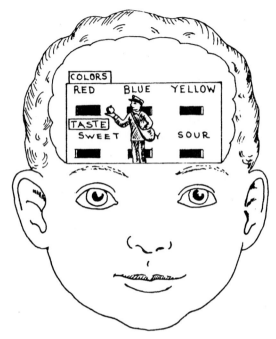

Figure 6–7 The brain functions like a postal worker.

information that has been previously stored. This grouping of closely related facts and phenomena related to a concept is called a *cognitive structure*. In other words, all that we know about the color red is stored in the same area of the brain. Our cognitive structure of red is developed further each time we have a color-related experience. The word *red* becomes a symbol for what we understand and perceive as the color red.

Our understanding of the world is imperfect because sooner or later, there is some point at which true understanding ends and misconceptions exist but go unquestioned. This is because incorrect interpretations of the world are stored alongside correct ones.

Continuing the postal worker analogy: If the information doesn't quite fit into an existing pigeonhole, it is stored somewhere else. The postal workers probably get frustrated trying to find a suitable pigeonhole.

A point can also be reached where new information conflicts with older information stored in a given cognitive structure. When children realize that they do not understand something they previously thought they understood, they are said to be in what Piaget calls a state of *disequilibrium*. This is where you were when the balloon did not behave as you expected. The balloon did not behave as you expected, and things no longer fit neatly together.

This is the *teachable moment*. When children are perplexed, their minds will not rest until they can find some way to make the new information fit. Since existing structures are inadequate to accommodate all of the existing information, they must continually modify or replace it with new cognitive structures. When in this state, children actively seek out additional information to create the new structure. They ask probing questions, observe closely, and inquire independently into the materials at hand. In this state, they are highly motivated and very receptive to learning. When children have had enough information to satisfy their curiosity and to create a new cognitive structure that explains most or all of the facts, they return to a state of *equilibrium*, where everything appears to fit together. As children move from disequilibrium to equilibrium, two mental activities take place. When confronted with something that they do not understand, children fit it into a scheme, something they already know. If this does not work for them, they modify the scheme or make a new one. This is called *accommodation*. Assimilation and accommodation work together to help students learn concepts. (Figure 6–8).

To make use of the process of self-regulation in your classroom, find out at what point your students misunderstand or are unfamiliar with the topic you are teaching. This will allow you to present information contrary to or beyond

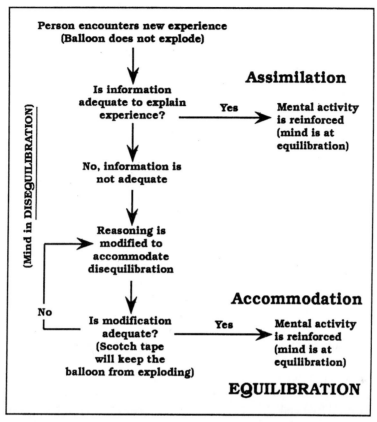

Figure 6–8   The self-regulation process (*Courtesy of the Council for Elementary Science International.*)

their existing cognitive structure and thus put them in a state of disequilibrium, where learning occurs.

Finding out what children know can be done in a number of ways. In addition to referring to the assessment units in this book, listen to children's responses to a lesson or question, or simply ask them to describe their understanding of a concept. For example, before teaching a lesson on animals, ask, "What does an animal look like?" You would be surprised at the number of young children who think that a life-form has to have legs to be considered an animal.

DISCREPANT EVENTS

A *discrepant event* puts students in disequilibrium and prepares them for learning. They are curious and want to find out what is happening. It is recommended that you take advantage of the natural learning process to teach children what you want them to understand. The following scenes might give you some ideas for discrepant events to improve lessons you plan to teach.

- Mr. Wang's second grade class is working on a unit on the senses. His students are aware of the function of the five senses, but they may not know that the sense of smell plays as large a role in appreciating food as the sense of taste. His students work in pairs with one child blindfolded. The blindfolded students are asked to pinch their noses shut and taste several foods such as bread, raw potatoes, or apples to see if they can identify them.

- Students switch roles and try the same investigation with various juices such as apple, orange, tomato, and so on. Most students cannot identify juices. Having experienced this discrepant event, the students will be more interested in finding out about the structures of the nose related to smell. They may be more motivated to conduct an investigation about how the appearance of food affects its taste.

- Mrs. Fox fills two jars with water while her first grade class watches. She fills one jar to the rim and leaves about an inch of space in the other jar. She puts a lid on each jar and places it on a tray in the school yard on a very cold winter day. Her students return later in the day and find that both have frozen, but the completely filled jar has burst. Students are eager to find out why.

- Kindergarten students Ann and Vanessa have been instructed to place two ice cubes in a glass and fill it to the brim with water. The ice cubes float on the water and extend about

Figure 6–9 Ann and Vanessa check their predictions.

half an inch above the edge of the glass. Ms. Hebert asks them what will happen when the ice cubes melt. Vanessa thinks the water will overflow because there will be more water. Ann thinks the water level will drop because the ice cubes will contract when they melt. They watch in puzzlement as they realize that the water level stays the same as the cubes melt (Figure 6–9).

USING THE LEARNING CYCLE TO BUILD CONCEPTS

You can assist your students in creating new cognitive structures by designing learning experiences in a manner congruent with how children learn naturally. One popular approach is the application of the learning cycle. The learning cycle, described in Unit 1, is based upon the cycle of equilibration originally described by Piaget. The learning cycle, which is used extensively in elementary science education, combines aspects of naturalistic, informal, and structured activity methods–suggested elsewhere in this book—into a method of presenting a lesson.

As you have learned, the discrepant event is an effective device for motivating students and placing them in disequilibrium. The learning cycle is a useful approach to learning for many of the same reasons. Learning begins with a period of free exploration. Exploration can be as simple as giving students the materials to be used in a day's activity at the beginning of a lesson so they can play with them for a few minutes. Minimal or no instructions should be given other than those related to safety, breaking the materials, or logistics in getting the materials. By letting students manipulate the materials, they will explore and very likely discover something they did not know before or something other than what they expected to happen. The following third grade example utilizes all three steps of the learning cycle (Figure 6–10).

MAKING THE BULB LIGHT

EXPLORATION PHASE

Mr. Wang placed a wire, a flashlight bulb, and a size D battery on a tray. Each group of three students was given a tray of materials and told to try to figure out a way to make the bulb light. As each group successfully lit the bulb, he asked them if they could find another arrangement of materials that would make the bulbs light. After about 10 minutes, most groups had found at least one way to light the bulb.

CONCEPT INTRODUCTION PHASE

After playing with the wires, batteries, and bulbs, Mr. Wang had the students bring their trays and form a circle on the floor. He asked the students if they had found out anything interesting about the materials. Jason showed the class one arrangement that worked to light the bulb. To introduce the class

Figure 6–10   Making the machine work

to the terms *open*, *closed*, and *short circuit*, Mr. Wang explained to the class that an arrangement that lights is called a closed circuit. Ann showed the class an arrangement that she thought would work but did not. Mr. Wang explained that this is an open circuit. Chad showed the class an arrangement that did not light the bulb but made the wire and battery very warm. Mr. Wang said this was a short circuit. Then he drew an example of each of the three types of circuit on the board and labeled them.

CONCEPT APPLICATION PHASE

Next, Mr. Wang showed the class a worksheet with drawings of various arrangements of batteries and bulbs. He asked the children to predict which arrangements would not light and form a closed circuit; which would form an open circuit by lighting; and which would heat up the battery and wire, forming a short circuit. After recording their predictions independently, the children returned to their small groups to test each of the arrangements. They recorded the actual answers beside their predictions (Figure 6–10).

After the students completed the task, Mr. Wang called them together. They discussed the results of their investigation, sharing which arrangements of batteries, wire, and bulbs they predicted correctly and incorrectly. Then Mr. Wang reviewed the terms learned during the lesson and asked the students to read a short section of their science text that talked about fire and electrical safety. The reading discussed the dangers of putting metal objects in wall sockets and fingers in light sockets and suggested precautions when flying kites near power lines.

After reading the section aloud, Mr. Wang asked the class if they could see any relationship between the reading and the day's activity. Chad responded that flying a kite into an electrical power line or sticking a dinner fork in a wall socket were

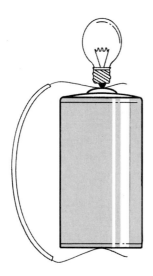

Figure 6–11 Battery prediction sheet.

In the preceding activity, you have seen a functioning model of the theory of cognitive development described by Piaget implemented in the classroom. The exploration phase invites assimilation and disequilibrium; the concept development phase provides for accommodation; and as the concept application phase expands the concept, reinforcement strategies for retaining the new concept are provided.

USING PART OF THE LEARNING CYCLE TO BUILD CONCEPTS

Although a formal investigation using the learning cycle is an excellent way to present lessons to children, teaching all lessons in this manner may not be possible or desirable. At times, exploration and observation might be the full lesson. Giving students an opportunity to practice their skills of observation is often sufficient for them to learn a great deal about unfamiliar objects or phenomena. In the following scenarios, teachers made use of exploration observations to create lessons:

- Mr. Brown constructed a small bird feeder and placed it outside the window of his prekindergarten room. One cold winter day his efforts were rewarded. Students noticed and called attention to the fact that there were several kinds of birds at the feeder. Brad said that they all looked the same to him. Leroy pointed out different characteristics of the birds to Brad. Diana and Cindy noticed that the blue jay constantly chased other birds away from the feeder and that a big cardinal moved away from the feeder as soon as any other bird approached. Students wondered why the blue jay seemed to scare all the other birds and the cardinal seemed to be afraid of even the small birds. They spent several minutes discussing the possibilities.

- On Richard's birthday, his preschool teacher, Miss Collins, decided that the class should make a microwave cake to celebrate the occasion. The students helped Miss Collins mix the ingredients and commented on the sequence of events as the cake cooked for seven minutes in the microwave. Richard was the first to observe how bubbles started to form in small patches. Then George commented that the whole cake was bubbling and getting bigger. After removing the cake from the microwave, many children noticed how the cake shrank, got glossy, then lost its gloss as it cooled (Figure 6–12).

Some lessons can be improved by having children do more than just observing and exploring. These exploration lessons include *data collection* as an instructional focus. Data collection and interpretation are important to real science and real problem solving. Although firsthand observation will always be important, most breakthroughs in science are made in the analysis of carefully collected data. Scientists usually spend much more time searching

Figure 6–12   The children help mix the ingredients.

through stacks of data than peering down the barrel of a microscope or through a telescope.

Data collection for young children is somewhat more abstract than firsthand observation. Therefore, it is important that students have sufficient practice in making predictions, speculations, and guesses with firsthand observations before they begin to collect and interpret data. Nevertheless, young students can benefit from early experience in data collection and interpretation. Initial data collections are usually pictorial in form. Long-term patterns and changes that children cannot easily observe in one setting are excellent beginnings for data collection.

- Weather records such as those discussed earlier in the unit can expose children to patterns during any time of the year. After charting the weather with drawings or attaching pictures that represent changing conditions, have children decide which clothing is most appropriate for a particular kind of weather.

Drawing clouds, sun, rain, lightning, snow, and so on that correspond to the daily weather and relating that information to what is worn can give students a sense of why data collection is useful.

- Growing plants provides excellent opportunities for early data collection. Mrs. Fox's first grade class charted the progress of bean plants growing in paper cups on the classroom windowsill. Each day students cut a strip of paper the same length as the height of their plant and glued the strips to a large sheet of newsprint. Over a period of weeks, students could see how their plants grew continuously even though they noticed few differences by just watching them. After pondering the plant data, Dean asked Mrs. Fox if the students could measure themselves with a strip of paper and chart their growth for the rest of the year. Thereafter, Mrs. Fox measured each student once a month. Her students were amazed to see how much they had grown during the year.

Another technique for designing science lessons is to allow students to have input into the process of problem solving and designing investigations. This might be called a *concept introduction lesson* because it utilizes the concept introduction phase of the learning cycle as the basis for a lesson. Although initial investigation and problem-solving experiences may be teacher designed, students eventually will be able to contribute to planning their own investigations. Most students probably will not be able to choose a topic and plan the entire investigation independently until they reach the intermediate grades, but their input into the process of planning gives them some ownership of the lesson and increases their confidence to explore ideas more fully. When solving real problems, identifying the problem is often more critical than the skills of attacking it. Students need practice in both aspects of problem solving.

The following examples depict students giving input into the problem to be solved and then helping to design how the problem should be approached.

- Mr. Wang's second grade class had had previous experience in charting the growth of plants. He told his class, "I'd like us to design an investigation about how fast plants grow. What things do you think could affect how fast a plant grows?" As Mr. Wang listed factors on the chalkboard, his students suggested a variety of factors including the amount of water, fertilizer, sunshine, temperature, type of seed, how much they are talked to, if they are stepped on, and so on. Students came up with possibilities that had never occurred to Mr. Wang. Next, he broke the class into small groups and told each group that they could have several paper cups, seeds, and some potting soil. They were asked to choose a factor from the list that they would like to investigate. Then, Mr. Wang helped each group plan their investigation.

- Derrick and Brent decided to study the effect of light on their plant. Mr. Wang asked them how they would control the amount of light their plants receive. Brent suggested that they bring a lightbulb to place near the plants so that they could leave the light on all day. Derrick said that he would put the plants in a cardboard box for the hours they were not supposed to receive light. Mr. Wang asked them to think about how many plants they should use. They decided to use three: one plant would receive light all day, one plant would receive no light, and one plant would receive only six hours of light.

PROBLEM SOLVING IN SCIENCE

The driving force behind problem-solving is curiosity, an interest in finding out. Problem solving is not as much a teaching strategy as it is a student behavior. The challenge for the teacher is to create an environment in which problem solving can occur. An example of the encouragement of problem-solving behavior in a primary classroom can be seen in the following examples.

- After studying the movement and structure of the human body Mr. Brown adds a final challenge to the unit. He has the children work with partners and poses the following situation and asks each pair to come up with a solution to the problem: "You like to play video games, but your family is worried because your wrists seem to be hurting from the motion you use to play the games. Plan a solution to the problem and role play the family discussion that might take place."

- Mr. Wang's class is studying the habitat of animals who live in water and the impact of humans on the environment. One of the problems that he poses to the class is to decide what they will do in the following situation. "You are looking forward to an afternoon of fishing at the lake near your home. When you get there you see a sign that was never there before. It says: NO Fishing. What do you do."

The asking and answering of questions is what problem solving is all about. When the situations and problems that the students wonder about are perceived as real, their curiosity is stimulated and they want to find an answer. This means a problem is some question or situation that is important to the student and thus gets her attention and enthusiasm focused on the search for a solution.

Problems should relate to and include the children's own experiences. From birth onward, children want to learn and naturally seek out problems to solve. Problem solving through the prekindergarten years focuses on naturalistic and informal learning, which promotes exploration and discovery. In kindergarten and primary, a more structured approach can be instituted. For an overall look at implementing a problem-solving approach for kindergarten and primary students, read Skinner's book, *What's Your Problem?*

Research indicates that working with concrete materials and drawing and/or writing explanations of solutions for problems are the best support for improving problem-solving skills. It is important to keep in mind that the process skills discussed in Unit 5 are essential to thinking and acting on a problem.

FOUR STEPS IN PROBLEM SOLVING

While people disagree about the exact number of steps it takes for a learner to solve a problem, there seem to be four basic steps that are essential to the problem-solving process:

1. *Identifying a problem and communicating it in a way that is understood.* This might involve assessing the situation and deciding exactly what is being asked or what is needed.

2. *Determining what the outcome of solving the problem might be.* This step involves the students in organizing a plan that will get them to their goals.

3. *Exploring possible solutions and apply them to the problem.* In this step, the plan is executed using appropriate strategies and materials. Children must learn that their first approach to solving a problem might be erroneous, but that if they keep trying, a solution will materialize. It is essential that children have the opportunity to explain solutions to others, this will help clarify the problem and help them be better able to explain the problem to themselves.

4. *Evaluating the possible solutions and revise solutions* if they do not seem to work as well as hoped. Since there is no one correct answer or way to arrive at an answer, there will be a variety of results. There may, in fact, be no answer to the problem.

Whether the lesson is part of the learning cycle, a culminating activity, or an unstructured experience, keep in mind first and foremost that for problem solving to occur, student curiosity must be stimulated with problems that engage, intrigue, and motivate. As students understand and learn how to apply the basic steps of the problem-solving process, they will be able to make connections with their past experiences, while keeping an open mind. The teachers role is that of a facilitator, using instructional strategies to create a classroom rich with opportunities, where students are enthusiastic about learning and developing the problem-solving skills that will last a lifetime.

SUMMARY

In all of the preschool and primary developmental stages described by Piaget, keep in mind that children's view of the world and concepts are not the same as yours. Their perception of phenomena is from their own perspective and experiences. Misconceptions arise. So, explore the world to expand thinking, and be ready for the next developmental stage. Teach children to observe with all of their senses and classify, predict, and communicate to discover other viewpoints.

There are many possible methods for designing science instruction for young children. The learning cycle is an application of the theory of cognitive development described by Piaget. The learning cycle can incorporate a number of techniques into a single lesson, or each of the components of learning cycle can be used independently to develop lessons. Other effective methods for designing lessons include discrepant events, data collection and analysis, and cooperative planning of investigations. All of these methods emphasize science process skills that are important to the development of concepts in young children.

FURTHER READING AND RESOURCES

Barman, C. (1990). *New ideas about an effective teaching strategy*. Council for Elementary Science International. Indianapolis: Indiana University.

Benham, N. B., Hosticka, A., Payne, J. D., & Yeotis, C. (1982). Making concepts in science and mathematics visible and viable in the early childhood curriculum. *School Science and Mathematics*, 82(1), 45–64.

Charlesworth, R. (1987). *Understanding child development*. Albany, NY: Delmar.

Confrey, J. (1990). A review of research on student conceptions in mathematics, science, and programming. In C. Cazden (Ed.), *Review of research in education*. Washington, DC: American Educational Research Association.

Gallagher, J. M., & Reid, D. K. (1981). The learning theory of Piaget and Inhelder. Monterey, CA: Brooks/Cole.

Gill, A. J. (1993). Multiple strategies: Product of reasoning and communication. *Arithmetic Teacher,* 40(7), 380–386.

Harlen, W., & Symington, D. (1988). Helping children to observe. In Spadek, B. (Ed.), *Primary science taking the plunge*. Portsmouth, NH: Heinemann.

Price, G. G. (1982). Cognitive learning in early childhood education: Mathematics, science, and social studies. In *Handbook of research in early childhood education* (pp. query author). New York: Free Press.

Renner, J. W., & Marek, E. A. (1988). *The learning cycle*. NH. Heinemann.

Shaw, J. M., & Owen, L. L. (1987). Weather–Beyond observation. *Science and Children*, 25(3): 27–29.

Skinner, P. (1990). *What's your problem?* Portsmouth, NH: Heinemann.

Sprung, B., Froschl, M., & Campbell, P. B. (1985). *What will happen if. . . . ?* New York: Educational Equity Concepts.

Tipps, S. (1982). Making better guesses: A goal in early childhood science. *School Science and Mathematics*, 82(1): 29–37.

Williams, C. V., & Kamii, C. (1986). How do children learn by handling objects? *Young Children,* 42(1), 23–26.

SUGGESTED ACTIVITIES

1. Interview children to determine their understanding of cause-and-effect relationships. Questions such as those in Figure 6–6 will be effective in gaining insight into the perceptions and misconceptions of young children. Compare remarks with classmates.
2. Brainstorm at least three strategies to prepare children to understand topics such as rain, lightning, clouds, mountains, and night. Pick a topic and prepare a learning experience that will prepare children for future concept development.
3. Pretend that you are presenting two lessons about seeds (seeds grow into plants) to a class of first graders. What types of learning experiences will you design for these students? How will you apply Piaget's theory of development to this topic? In what way would you adapt the experiences for a different developmental level?
4. Present a discrepant event to your classmates. After discovering how the event was achieved, analyze the process of equilibration that the class went through. Design a discrepant event that focuses on senses that would be effective for kindergarten age children.
5. The learning cycle has been presented as an effective way to build concepts in young children. What is your concept of the learning cycle, and how will you use it with children? Select a concept, and prepare a learning cycle to teach it.
6. Reflect on your own primary science experiences. What types of learning strategies did you encounter? Were they effective? Why or why not?

REVIEW

Briefly answer each of the following:

A. Describe what is meant by a discrepant event.
B. Why are discrepant events used in science education?
C. List the three major parts of the learning cycle.
D. Describe how cognitive structures change over time.
E. Why is data collection important with young children?
F. Create an example of a discrepant event that you might use with young children on a topic of your choice.

UNIT 7 Planning for Science

OBJECTIVES

After studying this unit, the student should be able to
- Develop science concepts with subject area integrations
- Explain and use the strategy of webbing in unit planning
- Identify and develop science concepts in a lesson; design lesson plans for teaching science to children
- Construct evaluation strategies

INTEGRATING SCIENCE INTO THE CURRICULUM

Concepts will be more likely to be retained by children if presented in a variety of ways and extended over a period of time. For example, after a trip to the zoo, extend the collective experience by having children dictate a story about their trip. Other activities could focus on following up previsit discussions, directing children to observe specifics at the zoo, such as differences in animal noses. Children might enjoy comparing zoo animal noses to those of their pets by matching pictures of similar noses on a bulletin board. In this way, concepts can continue to be applied and related to past experiences as the year progresses.

Additional integrations might include drawing favorite animal noses, creating plays about animals with specific types of noses, writing about an animal and its nose, and creating "smelling activities." You might even want to introduce reasons an animal has a particular type of nose. One popular idea is to purchase plastic animal noses, distribute them to children, and play a "Mother-May-I-Like" game. Say, "If you have four legs and roar, take two giant steps. If you have two legs and quack, take three steps forward" (Figure 7–1).

Think of how much more science can be learned if we make connections between it and other subjects. This requires preparing planned activities and taking advantage of every teachable moment that occurs in your class to introduce children to science.

Opportunities abound for teaching science in early childhood. Consider actively involving children with art, blocks, dramatic play, woodworking, language arts, math, and creative movement. Learning centers are one way to provide excellent integration. Centers are discussed in Unit 18 of this book. The following ideas may encourage your thinking.

- **Painting.** Finger painting helps children learn to perceive with their fingertips and demonstrates the concept of color diffusion as they

Figure 7–1 "If you have two legs and quack, take three steps forward."

clean their hands. Shapes can be recognized by painting with fruit and familiar objects.

- **Water center.** Concepts such as volume and conservation begin to be grasped when children measure with water and sand. Buoyancy can be explored with boats and sinking and floating objects.
- **Blocks.** Blocks are an excellent way to introduce children to friction, gravity, and simple machines. Leverage and efficiency can be reinforced with *woodworking*.
- **Books.** Many books introduce scientific concepts while *telling a story*. Books with pictures give views of unfamiliar things and an opportunity to explore detail and infer and discuss.
- **Music and rhythmic activities.** These let children experience the movement of air against their bodies. Air resistance can also be demonstrated by dancing with a scarf.
- **Playground.** The playground can provide an opportunity to predict weather, practice balancing, and experience friction. The concrete world of science integrates especially well with reading and writing. Basic words, object guessing, experience charts, writing stories, and working with tactile sensations all encourage early literacy development.

Children Learn in Different Ways

It is important to provide children with a variety of ways to learn science. Even very young children have developed definite patterns in the way they learn. Observe a group of children engaged in free play: some prefer to work alone quietly; others do well in groups. Personal learning style also extends to a preference for visual or auditory learning. The teacher in the following scenario keeps the wide range of learning styles in mind when planning science experiences:

Ms. Hebert knows that the children in her kindergarten class exhibit a wide range of learning styles and behaviors. For example, Ann wakes up slowly. She hesitates to jump in and explore and prefers to work alone. On the other hand, Vanessa is social, verbal, and ready to go first thing in the morning. As Ms. Hebert plans activities to reinforce the observations of flamingos that her class made at the zoo, she includes experiences that include both group discussion and individual work. Some of the visual, auditory, and small and large group activities include flamingo number puzzles; drawing and painting flamingos; and acting out how flamingos eat, rest, walk, and honk. In this way, Ms. Hebert meets the diverse needs of the class and integrates concepts about flamingos into the entire week (Figure 7–2). Organizing science lessons with subject matter correlations in mind insures integration. The following section outlines ways to plan science lessons and units.

ORGANIZING FOR TEACHING SCIENCE

In order to teach effectively, teachers must organize what they plan to teach. How they organize depends largely on their teaching situation.

Figure 7–2   A flamingo lacing card

Some school districts require that a textbook series or curriculum guide be used when teaching science. Some have a fully developed program to follow, and others have no established guidelines. Regardless of district directives, the strategies discussed in their chapter can be adapted to a variety of teaching situations.

Planning for Developing Science Concepts

After assessing, the first questions to ask when organizing for teaching are, "What do I want the children to know?" and "What is the best way to do this?" You might have a general topic in mind, such as air, but do not know where to go from there. One technique that might help organize your thoughts is *webbing*, a strategy borrowed from literature. A web depicts a variety of possible concepts and curricular experiences that you might use to develop concepts. By visually depicting your ideas, you will be able to tell at a glance the concepts covered in your unit. As the web emerges, projected activities can be balanced by subject area, e.g., social studies, movement, art, drama, and math, and by a variety of naturalistic, informal, or structured activities.

Start your planning by selecting what you want children to know about a topic. For example, the topic *air* contains many science concepts. Four concepts about air that are commonly taught to first graders begin the web depicted in Figure 7–3:

1. Air is all around us.
2. Air takes up space.
3. Air can make noise.
4. Air can be hot and cold.

After selecting the concepts that you plan to develop, begin adding appropriate activities to achieve your goal. Look back at Unit 6 and think of some of these strategies that will best help you teach about air. Remember, "messing around" time and direct experience are vital for learning.

The developed web in Figure 7–4 shows at a glance the main concepts and activities that will be included in this unit. You may not want to teach all

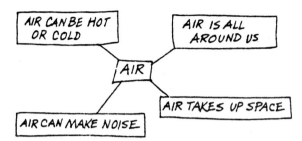

Figure 7–3 Begin by making each web of the science concepts you want to teach.

of these activities, but you will have the advantage of flexibility when you make decisions.

Next, turn your attention to how you will evaluate children's learning. Remember, preschool and primary age children will not be able to verbalize their true understanding of a concept. They simply have not advanced to the formal stages of thinking. Instead, have students show their knowledge in ways that can be observed. Have them explain, predict, show, tell, draw, describe, construct, and so on (Figure 7–5). These are the verbs that indicate an action of some kind. For example, as students explain to you why they have grouped buttons together in a certain way, be assured that the facts are there and so are the concepts, and one day they will come together in a fully developed concept statement. Concept development takes time and cannot be rushed.

The webbed unit you have developed is a long-term plan for organizing science experiences around a specific topic. Formal units usually contain overall goals and objectives, a series of lessons, and an evaluation plan. *Goals* are the broad statements that indicate where you are heading with the topic. *Objectives* state how you plan to achieve your goals. Practical teaching direction is provided by daily lesson plans. An evaluation plan is necessary to assess student learning and your own teaching. There is a variety of ways these components can be organized, but Figure 7–6 outlines the essential ingredients.

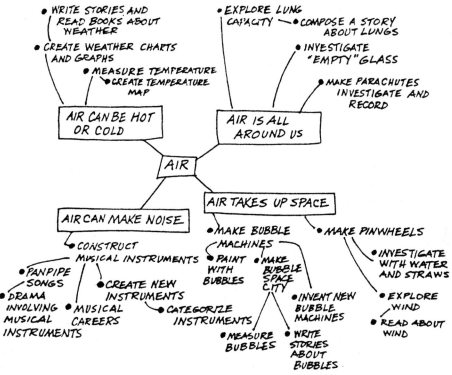

Figure 7–4   Example of a webbed unit

Lesson Planning

The *lesson plan* is a necessary component of the unit. It helps you plan the experiences that will aid in concept development. The following lesson plan is adaptable and focuses on developing a science concept, manipulating materials, and extending and reinforcing the concept with additional activities and subject area integrations. Refer to Figure 7–7, the Bubble Machine, for an example of this lesson plan format.

Basic Science Lesson Plan Components

Concept. Concepts are usually the most difficult part of a lesson plan. The temptation is to write an objective or topic title. However, in order to really focus your teaching on the major concept to be developed, you must find the science in what you

---

ACTION VERBS

Simple Action Words

arrange	design	match
attempt	distinguish	measure
chart	explain	name
circle	formulate	order
classify	gather	organize
collect	graph	place
compare	identify	point
compile	include	report
complete	indicate	select
contrast	label	sort
count	list	state
define	locate	tell
describe	map	

Figure 7–5   Verbs that indicate action

COMPONENTS IN A UNIT PLAN

TOPIC/CONCEPT	What is the topic or concept?
GOAL	Where are you heading?
OBJECTIVES	How do you plan to achieve your goals?
LESSONS	What will you teach?
EVALUATION	Did the students learn what you wanted them to learn?

Figure 7–6 Components in unit planning

---

intend to teach. For example, ask yourself, "What do I want the children to learn about air?"

Objective. Then ask, "What do I want the children *to do* to help them understand that air takes up space?" When you have decided on the basic experience, be sure and identify the process skills that children will use. In this way, you will be aware of content and process.

Define the teaching process in behavioral terms. State what behavior you want the children to exhibit. This will make evaluation easier because you have stated what you expect the children to accomplish. Although many educators state behavioral objectives with conditions, most teachers find that beginning a statement with "the child should be able to" followed by an action verb is an effective way to state objectives. Some examples might be

The child should be able to describe the parts of a flower.

The child should be able to construct a diorama of the habitat of a tiger.

The child should be able to draw a picture that shows different types of animal noses.

Materials. In order for children to manipulate materials, you must decide which materials should be organized in advance of the lesson. Ask, "What materials will I need to teach this lesson?"

Procedure. When planning the lesson ask, "How will this experience be conducted?" You must decide how you will initiate the lesson with children, present the learning experience, and relate the concept to the children's past experiences. Questions that encourage learning should be considered and included in the lesson plan.

It is recommended that an initiating experience begin the lesson. This experience could be the "messing around" with materials stage of the learning cycle, a demonstration or discrepant event, a question sequence that bridges what you intend to teach with a previous lesson or experience. The idea is that you want to stimulate and interest the children about what they are going to do in the lesson.

Extension. To ensure maximum learning of the concept, ways to keep the idea going must be planned. This can be done by extending the concept with additional learning activities, integrating the concept into other subject areas, preparing learning centers, and so on.

Assessment Strategies

You cannot teach a lesson or unit effectively if you do not plan for evaluation. To continue with another lesson before you know what students understand from the current lesson seems pointless. One reason for avoiding evaluation might be the tendency to associate the term *evaluation* with the term *grading*. This is a misconception. *Grading* takes place when a symbol that stands for a level of achievement is assigned to learning. *Evaluation*, on the other hand, is finding out what students understand. Evaluation takes place *before*, *during*, and *after* teaching.

Evaluation done before teaching is diagnostic in nature and takes place when you assess what children know about a topic and determine which stage of development they are in. For example, when you ask children where they think rain comes from, you are evaluating and discovering misconceptions.

As teachers evaluate student progress during teaching, changes in teaching strategies are

CONCEPT: "Air takes up space. Bubbles have air inside of them."
OBJECTIVE: The child will construct a bubble-making machine by manipulating materials and air to produce bubbles. The child will observe and describe the bubbles. The child will infer that air is inside of bubbles.
MATERIALS: Mix a basic bubble solution of 8 tablespoons liquid detergent and 1 quart water (expensive detergent makes stronger bubbles).

PROCEDURE:
Initiating Activity: Demonstrate an assembled bubble machine. Have children observe the machine and tell what they think is happening. (Refer to Figure 7–8).
How to do it: Help children assemble bubble machines. Insert straw into the side of the cup. Pour the bubble mixture to just below the hole in the side of the cup. Give children five minutes to explore blowing bubbles with the bubble machine. Then ask children to see how many bubbles they can blow. Ask: "What do your bubbles look like? Describe your bubbles." Add food coloring for more colorful bubbles.
    "What happens to your bubbles? Do they burst? How can you make them last longer?"
    "What do you think is in the bubbles? How can you tell? What did you blow into the bubble? Can you think of something else that you blow air into to make larger?" (balloon)

EXTENSIONS:
1. Have students tell a story about the bubble machine as you record it on chart paper.
2. Encourage children to make bubble books with drawings that depict their bubbles, bubble machines, and the exciting time they had blowing bubbles. Encourage the children to write or pretend to write about their pictures. Threes and 4s enjoy pretending to write; by 5 or 6 children begin to experiment with inventing their own spellings. Be sure to accept whatever they produce. Have children read their books to the class. Place them in the library center for browsing.
3. Make a bubbles bulletin board. Draw a cluster of bubbles and have students add descriptive words about bubbles.
4. Challenge students to invent other bubble machines. (Unit 35 of this book contains activities that teach additional concepts of air and bubbles.)

Figure 7–7   The bubble machine lesson

decided. If one strategy is not working, try something else.

As children work on projects, you will find yourself interacting with them on an informal basis. Listen carefully to children's comments, and watch them manipulate materials. You cannot help but assess how things are going. You might even want to keep a record of your observations or create a chart that reflects areas of concern to you, such as attitudes or interaction between students. When observations are written down in an organized way, they are called *anecdotal records* (Figure 7–9).

If you decide to use anecdotal records, be sure to write down dates and names and to tell students you are keeping track of things that happen. A review of your records will be valuable when you complete the unit. Recording observations can become a habit and provide an additional tool in assessing children's learning and your teaching strategies. Anecdotes are also invaluable resources for parent conferences.

Responses to oral questions can be helpful in evaluating while teaching. Facial expressions are especially telling. Everyone has observed a blank look that usually indicates a lack of understanding. This look may be because the question asked was

Figure 7–8   A bubble machine

EVALUATION

Things to record when observing, discussing, or keeping anecdotal records

Cognitive:

How well do the children handle the materials?

Do the children cite out-of-school examples of the science concept?

Is the basic concept being studied referred to as the children go about their day?

Attitude and skill:

Do the children express like or dislike of the topic?

Are there any comments that suggest prejudice?

Do children evidence self-evaluation?

Are ideas freely expressed in the group?

Are there any specific behaviors that need to be observed each time science is taught?

Figure 7–9   Keeping anecdotal records

too difficult. So, ask an easy question, or present your question in a different manner for improved results.

One way to evaluate during the after teaching component is to ask questions about the activity in a lesson review. Some teachers write main idea questions on the chalkboard. Then, they put a chart next to the questions and label it "What We Found Out." As the lesson progresses, the chart is filled in by the class as a way of showing progress and reviewing the lesson or unit.

Another strategy is to observe children applying the concept. For example, as "The Three Billy Goats" is being read, Joyce comments, "The little billy goat walks just like the goat that we saw at the zoo." You know from this statement that Joyce has some idea of how goats move. (Refer to units 3 and 4.)

Sometimes students have difficulty learning because an activity doesn't work. One basic rule

when teaching science is, "Always do the activity first." This includes noting questions or possible problems you may encounter. If you have trouble, students will too (Figure 7–10).

Evaluating the Unit

How well did you design your unit? Ask yourself some questions, such as the following, to help evaluate your work. These questions pull together the major points of this unit.

1. Have you related the unit to the children's past experiences?
2. Are a variety of process skills used in the activities?

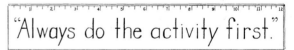

"Always do the activity first."

Figure 7–10   The golden rule

3. Have you integrated other subjects with the unit?
4. When you use reading and writing activities, do they follow hands-on experiences?
5. Do you allow for naturalistic, informal, and directed activities?
6. Is a variety of teaching strategies included?
7. Are both open-ended and narrow questions asked?
8. Will the evaluation strategy provide a way to determine if children can apply what they have learned?
9. What local resources are included in the unit?

Three Basic Types of Units

Some teachers like to develop *resource units*. The *resource unit* is an extensive collection of activities and suggestions focusing on a single science topic. The advantage of a resource unit is the wide range of appropriate strategies available to meet the needs, interests, and abilities of the children. As the unit is taught, additional strategies and integrations are usually added. For example, Mrs. Jones knows that she is going to teach a unit on seeds in her kindergarten class. She collects all of the activities and teaching strategies that she can find. When she is ready to teach the seed unit, she selects the activities that she believes are most appropriate.

Teachers who design a teaching unit plan to develop a science concept, objectives, materials, activities, and evaluation procedures for a specific group of children. This unit is less extensive than a resource unit and contains exactly what will be taught, a timeline, and the order of activities. Usually, general initiating experiences begin the unit, and culminating experiences end the unit. The specific teaching unit has value and may be used again with other classes after appropriate adaptations have been made. For example, Mr. Wang has planned a two-week unit on batteries and bulbs. He has decided on activities and planned each lesson period of the two weeks.

Extending the textbook in a textbook unit is another possibility. The most obvious limitation of this unit is a school district change in textbooks. A *textbook unit* is designed by outlining the science concepts for the unit and checking the textbook for those already covered in the book or teacher's manual. Additional learning activities are added for concepts not included in the text or sometimes instead of those in the text. Initiating activities to arouse interest in the topic might be needed. One advantage of this unit is using the textbook to better advantage. For example, after doing animal activities, use the text to confirm or extend knowledge.

Open-Ended and Narrow Questions

Asking questions can be likened to driving a car with a stick shift. When teaching the whole class, start in low gear with a narrow question that can be answered yes or no or with a question that has an obvious answer. This usually puts students at ease. They are happy; they know something. Then, try an open-ended question that has many answers. Open-ended questions stimulate discussion and

Figure 7–11 "Can you make a piece of clay float?"

offer opportunities for thinking. However, if the open-ended question is asked before the class has background information, the children might just stare at you, duck their heads, or exhibit undesirable behavior. Do not panic; quickly shift gears and ask a narrow question. Then, work your way back to what you want to find out.

Teachers who are adept at shifting between narrow and open-ended questions are probably excellent discussion leaders and have little trouble with classroom management during these periods.

Open-ended questions are excellent interest builders when used effectively. For example, consider Ms. Hebert's initiating activity for a lesson about buoyancy.

Ms. Hebert holds a rock over a pan of water and asks a narrow question, "Will this rock sink when dropped in water?" (yes, no) Then, she asks an open-ended question, "How can we keep the rock from sinking into the water?" The children answer, "Tie string around it," "Put a spoon under it," and "Grab it."

As the discussion progresses, the open-ended question leads the children into a discussion about boats. After talking about how boats are used, give each child a piece of clay and instruct her to design a boat that will float (Figure 7–11).

SUMMARY

Children are more likely to retain science concepts if they are integrated with other subject areas. Making connections between science and other aspects of a child's school day requires that opportunities for learning be well planned and readily available to children. Learning science in a variety of ways encourages personal learning styles and insures subject integrations.

The key to effective teaching is organization. Unit and lesson planning provide a way to plan what you want children to learn and how you want them to learn. A planning web is a useful technique for depicting ideas, outlining concepts, and integrating content.

The three basic types of planning units are resource units, teaching units, and textbook units. Teachers utilize whichever unit best suits their classroom needs. By asking open-ended and narrow questions, teachers develop science concepts and encourage higher-order thinking skills in their students.

FURTHER READING AND RESOURCES

Gega, P. (1993). *Science in elementary education.* New York: Macmillan.

Harlan, J. (1991). *Science experiences for the early childhood years.* New York: Macmillan.

Jacobson, W. J., & Bergman, A. B. (1990). *Science for children: A book for teachers.* Englewood Cliffs, NJ: Prentice-Hall.

Lind, K. K. (1993). Concept mapping: Making learning meaningful. In *Teacher's desk reference: A professional guide for science educators.* Englewood Cliffs, NJ: Prentice-Hall.

Rice, K. Soap films and bubbles. *Science and Children 23*(8), 4–9.

Schwartz, J. I. (1988). *Encouraging early literacy.* Portsmouth, NH: Heinemann.

Townsend, J., & Schiller, P. (1984). *More than a magnet, less than a dollar.* Houston: Evergreen Publishing Company.

Wassermann, S., & Ivany, J. W. G. (1990). *Teaching elementary science.* New York: Harper Collins.

SUGGESTED ACTIVITIES

1. Choose a topic, and construct a web of the major concepts that are important to know about the topic. Add the learning activities you plan to use to teach these concepts, and suggest appropriate evaluation techniques. Work in teams to brainstorm ideas.
2. Select a lesson from a primary level textbook. Compare how the book presents the concept with what you know about how children learn science.
3. Interview a teacher to determine his or her approach to planning; for example, whether a textbook series or curriculum guide is used, how flexibility is maintained, and what assessment techniques are found to be most effective. Ask teachers to describe how they plan units and lessons and to compare strategies used the first year of teaching with those used now. Discuss responses to your questions in a group.
4. Reflect on your past experiences in science classes. Which were the most exciting units? Which were the most boring? Do you remember what made a unit exciting or dull? Or do you primarily remember a specific activity?
5. Can you integrate a unit on seeds with language arts? Then, integrate drama/movement, art, math, and social studies with the seed unit. Try designing a puppet show that would help teach the concept.
6. Practice writing questions that will help you evaluate children's understanding of a lesson on taste.

REVIEW

1. What is webbing, and how can it be applied in designing a science unit?
2. Which process skills are involved in the bubble machine lesson, including extensions?
3. Identify learning cycle components in the bubble machine lesson.
4. What strategies could you use to integrate subject areas into science? Give an example.
5. List the major components of a science lesson plan.
6. Identify three ways of evaluating students other than paper and pencil tests.
7. What is a unit? List three basic types of units.
8. Explain the difference between narrow and open-ended questions and how each is used.

SECTION II

Fundamental Concepts, Skills and Activities

UNIT 8

Fundamental Concepts in Science

OBJECTIVES

After studying this unit, the student should be able to
- Define the concepts and skills that are fundamental to science for young children
- Explain how children apply and extend concepts and skills in science investigations
- Design lessons that integrate fundamental science concepts
  Develop naturalistic, informal, and structured activities that utilize science concepts

Children construct concepts during the preprimary period; they then apply them to the problem-solving tasks that are the beginnings of scientific inquiry. During this time, concepts grow rapidly and children develop the basic concepts and skills of science, moving toward intellectual autonomy through independent activity, which serves as a vehicle for the construction of knowledge.

This unit discusses the basic concepts and skills that are fundamental to science for young children. One-to-one correspondence, number and counting, sets and classifying, comparing, shape, space, and parts and wholes are concepts and skills that are fundamental to science as well as to mathematics and other subject areas. This unit shows how these concepts and skills can be explored and utilized in science with children in the sensorimotor and preoperational period. Recommendations for classroom assessment strategies can be found in Unit 4 and individual assessments are in Appendix A.

ONE-TO-ONE CORRESPONDENCE

One-to-one correspondence is the most fundamental component of the concept of number. It is the understanding that one group has the same number of things as another. For example, each child has a cookie, each foot has a shoe, each person wears a hat. It is preliminary to counting and basic to the understanding of equivalence and to the concept of conservation of number described in Unit I.

To obtain information of an informal nature, note the children's behavior during their work, play, and routine activities. Look for one-to-one correspondence that happens naturally. For example, when the child plays train, he may line up a row of chairs so there is one for each child passenger. When he puts his mittens on, he shows that he knows that there should be one for each hand; when painting, he checks to be sure he has each paint-brush in the matching color of paint. Tasks for formal assessment are given below and in Appendix A.

Exploring Science

Science topics such as animals and their homes lend themselves well to matching activities. Not only are children emphasizing one-to-one correspondence by matching one animal to a particular home, they are also increasing their awareness of animals and their habitats. The questions that teachers ask will further reinforce the process skills and science content contained in the activities. The following science-related activities work well with young children:

1. Create a bulletin board background of trees (one tree should have a cavity), a cave, a plant containing a spiderweb, and a hole in the ground. Hang a beehive from a branch, and place a nest on another branch. Ask the children to tell you where each of the following animals might live: owl, bird, bee, mouse, spider, and bear. Place the animal by the appropriate home. Then, make backgrounds and animals for each child, and let the children paste the animal where it might live (Figure 8–1). Ask, DO YOU THINK A PLANT IS A GOOD PLACE FOR A SPIDER TO SPIN A WEB? WHY DO YOU THINK SO? (Outdoor insects can land in the web.) Have the children describe the advantages of living in the different homes.

2. Another popular animal matching activity involves the preparation of six animals and six homes. The children must cut out a home and paste it in the box next to the animal that lives there. For example, a bee lives in a beehive, a horse in a barn, an ant in an anthill, a bird in a nest, a fish in an aquarium, and a child in a human home (Figure 8–2). Ask, WHY WOULD AN

Figure 8–1   "Find a home for the bear."

Figure 8–2   Cut out the pictures of animals and homes. Mount them on cardboard for the children to match.

ANT LIVE IN THE GROUND? Emphasize that animals try to live in places that offer them the best protection or source of food. Discuss how each is suited to its home.

3. Counters are effective in reinforcing the fundamental concept of one-to-one correspondence. For example, when the children study about bears, make and use bear counters that can be put into little bear caves. As the children match the bear to its cave, they understand that there are the same number of bears as there are caves. Lead the children in speculating why bears might take shelter in caves (convenient, will not be disturbed, hard to find, good place for baby bears to be born, and so on).

4. Children enjoy working with felt shapes. Cut out different sized felt ducks, bears, ponds, and caves for children to match on a flannel board. If children have the materials available, they will be likely to play animal matching games on their own, such as, "Match the baby and adult animals," or "Line up all of the ducks, and find a pond for each one." Have children compare the baby ducks to the adult ducks by asking, IN WHAT WAYS DO THE BABIES LOOK LIKE THEIR PARENTS? HOW ARE THEY ALIKE? CAN YOU FIND ANY DIFFERENCES? Emphasize camouflage as the primary reason that baby animals usually blend in with their surroundings. The number of animals and homes can be increased as the children progress in ability.

5. After telling the story "Goldilocks and the Three Bears," draw three bears of different sizes without noses. Cut out noses that will match the blank spaces, and have the children match the nose to the bear (Figure

8–3). You might want to do this first as a group, and then have the materials available for the children to work with individually. Point out that larger bears have bigger noses.

One-to-one correspondence and the other skills presented in this unit cannot be developed in isolation of content. Emphasize the science concepts and process skills as you utilize animals as a means of developing fundamental skills. Further animal matching and sorting activities can be created by putting pictures into categories of living and nonliving things, vertebrates and invertebrates, reptiles, amphibians, birds, and fish.

When comparing major groups of animals—reptiles, for example—try to include as many representatives of the group as possible. Children can study pictures of turtles (land turtles are called *tortoises*, and some freshwater turtles are called *terrapins*), snakes, lizards, alligators, and crocodiles, and match them to their respective homes. The characteristics of each reptile can be compared and contrasted. The possibilities for matching, counting, comparing, and classifying animals are limitless and are a natural math and science integration.

NUMBER SENSE AND COUNTING

The concept of number or understanding number is referred to as *number sense*. *Number sense* makes the connection between quantities and counting. Number sense underlies the understanding of more and less, of relative amounts, of the relationship between space and quanntity (i.e., number conservation), and parts and wholes of quantities, and number sense also helps children estimate quantities and measurements. Counting assists childrfen in the process of understanding quantity. Understanding that the last number named is the quantity in the group is a critical fundamental concept. It is the understanding of the "oneness" of one, "twoness" of two, and so on.

Quantities from one to four or five are the first to be recognized. Infants can perceive the difference between these small quantities, and children as young as $2\frac{1}{2}$ or 3 years may recognize these small amounts so easily that they seem to do so without counting. The concept of number is constructed bit by bit from infancy through the preschool years and gradually becomes a tool that can be used in problem solving.

Number's partner, counting, includes two operations—*rote counting* and *rational counting*. *Rote counting* involves reciting the names of the numerals in order from memory. That is, the child who says, "One, 2, 3, 4, 5, 6, 7, 8, 9, 10" has correctly counted in a rote manner from 1 to 10. *Rational counting* involves attaching each numeral name in order to a series of objects in a group. For example, the child has some pennies in her hand. She takes them out of her hand one at a time and places them on the table. Each time she places one on the table she says the next number name in sequence: "one," places first penny; "two," places another penny; "three," places another penny. She has successfully done rational counting of three objects. Rational counting is a

Figure 8–3 "Which nose belongs to Baby Bear?"

higher level of one-to-one correspondence (Figure 8-4). A basic understanding of rote counting and one-to-one correspondence is the foundation of rational counting tasks for formal assessment given in Appendix A.

Exploring Science

Emphasizing science content while learning number concepts enables children to relate these subjects to their everyday lives and familiar, concrete examples. The following example shows a kindergarten class using concrete experiences to reinforce counting and the science concept that apples grow on trees.

When Mrs. Jones teaches an apple unit in the fall, she sorts apples of different sizes and colors. Then she has the children count the apples before they cook them to make applesauce and apple pies.

For additional number concept extensions, she uses a felt board game that requires the children to pick apples from trees. For this activity, she creates two rows of apple trees with four felt trees in each row. The trees are filled with one to nine apples and the numerals are at the bottom of each row. As the children play with the game, Mrs. Jones asks, "How many apples can you pick from each tree?" As Sam picks apples off a tree, he counts aloud, "one, two, three, four, five—I picked five apples from the apple tree." He smiles and points to the numeral five (Figure 8–5).

When doing science activities, do not miss opportunities to count. The following activities emphasize counting:

1. If bugs have been captured for study, have your children count the number of bugs in the bug keeper. Keep in mind that insects can be observed for a couple of days but should be released to the area in which they were originally found.

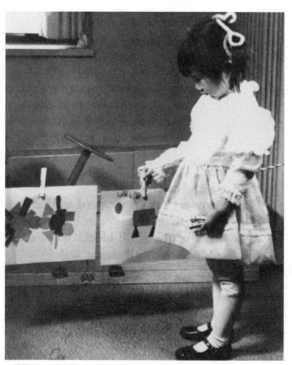

Figure 8–4 "One clothespin, two clothespins" is an example of rational counting.

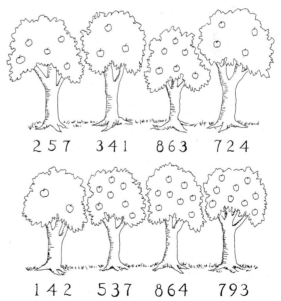

Figure 8–5 "How many apples can you pick?"

Figure 8–6 "Count the dots and stick the square on the correct tentacle."

a 12" × 20" rectangle made from light blue oak tag. Glue some of the fish, the treasure chest, rocks, and plants to the blue background. Then, using thumbtacks, attach a 13" × 21" clear plastic rectangle to the top of the light blue oak tag to create a fish tank bulletin board. Before the students arrive the next day, put more fish in the tank. Then ask, "How many fish are swimming in the tank?" Each day, add more fish, and ask the class, "How many fish are swimming in the tank today?" "How many were swimming in the tank yesterday?" "Are there more fish swimming in the tank today, or were there more yesterday?" Use as many fish as are appropriate for your students (Figure 8–7).

Children love to count. They count informally and with direction from the teacher. Counting cannot be removed from a context—you have to count something. As children count, emphasize the science in which they are counting. If children are counting the number of baby ducks following

2. Take advantage of the eight tentacles of an octopus to make an octopus counting board. Enlarge an octopus on a piece of poster board, and attach a curtain hook to each tentacle above a number. Make circles with dots (one to eight) to hang on hooks. Ask children to count the number of tentacles that the octopus has. Explain that all octopuses have eight tentacles. Discuss how an octopus uses its armlike tentacles. Then, have children count the dots on the circles and put the circles on the hook over the correct number (Figure 8–6).

3. A fish tank bulletin board display emphasizes counting and the science process skill of observation, and of the same time prepares children for future activities in addition. Prepare construction-paper fish, a treasure chest, rocks, and plants, and attach them to

Figure 8–7 "Create a fish tank bulletin board for counting fish."

an adult duck, lead the children in speculating where the ducks might be going and what they might be doing. Compare the behavior of ducks to the way chickens behave.

SETS AND CLASSIFYING

In both science and mathematics, an understanding of sets and classifying is essential. The term *sets* refers to things that are put together in a group based on some common criteria (such as color, shape, size, use). A set can contain from zero (an empty set) to an endless number of things (or members). However, most sets that children work with have some observable limit. A set of dishes is usually for a certain number of place settings such as service for 8 or service for 12. A set of tires for a car is usually 4 plus a spare, which equals 5. A set of tires for a large truck consists of more than 5 tires.

Before doing any formal addition and subtraction, the child needs to learn about sets and how they can be joined and separated. That is, children must practice *sorting* (separating) and *grouping* (joining). This type of activity is called *classification*. (Refer to the classification discussion in Unit 5).

The child learns that things may be grouped together using a number of kinds of common features:

- **Color:** Things can go together that are the same color.
- **Shape:** Things may all be round, square, triangular, and so on.
- **Size:** Some things are big, and some are small; some are fat, and some are thin; some are short, and some are tall.
- **Material:** Things are made out of different materials such as wood, plastic, glass, paper, cloth, and metal.
- **Pattern:** Things have different visual patterns such as stripes, dots, flowers, or they may be plain (no design).

- **Texture:** Things feel different from each other (smooth, rough, soft, hard, wet, dry).
- **Function:** Some items do the same thing or are used for the same thing (all are for eating, writing, playing music, for example).
- **Association:** Some things do a job together (candle and match, milk and glass, shoe and foot) or come from the same place (bought at the store or seen at the zoo) or belong to a special person (the hose, truck, and hat belong to the firefighter).
- **Class name:** There are names that may belong to several things (people, animals, food, vehicles, weapons, clothing, homes).
- **Common features:** All have handles or windows or doors or legs or wheels, for example.
- **Number:** All are groups of specific amounts such as pairs; groups of three, four, five; and so on.

Sorting and grouping are some of the most basic and natural activities for the young child. Much of his play is organizing and reorganizing the things in his world. The infant learns the set of people who take care of him most of the time (day care provider, mother, father, and/or relatives and friends), and others are put in the set of "strangers." He learns that some objects when pressed on his gums makes the pain of growing teeth less. These are his set of teething things.

As soon as the child is able to sit up, he finds great fun in putting things in containers and dumping them out. He can never have too many boxes, plastic dishes, and coffee cans along with safe items such as large plastic beads, table tennis balls, or teething toys (just be sure the items are too large to swallow). With this type of activity, children have their first experiences making sets.

By age 3 the child sorts and groups to help organize his play activities. He sorts out from his things those that he needs for what he wants to do. He may pick out wild animal toys for his zoo; people dolls for his family play; big blocks for his house; blue paper circles to paste on paper; girls for friends, and so on.

The adult provides the free time, the materials (junk is fine as long as it is safe), and the space. The child does the rest.

Adults can let children know that sorting and grouping activities are of value in informal ways by showing that they approve of what the children are doing. This can be done with a look, smile, nod, or comment.

Exploring Science

Sorting and grouping, which form the basis of classifying sets of things, lend themselves to one-to-one correspondence. Several things may be classified into any one set. The child must keep in mind the basis for his group as he sorts through all available things. Remembering that when given three pigs and three houses in separate piles he must find a pig for each house is easier than being given a mixed pile of pigs and houses that he must first sort into a pile of pigs and a pile of houses before he can find if there is a house for each pig. Classification is one of the most important fundamental skills in science. The following is an examples of how classification might be used during a science activity:

The following activities develop analytical

STRUCTURED ACTIVITIES

SETS AND CLASSIFICATION: COLOR

OBJECTIVE: To sort and group by color.

MATERIALS: Several different objects that are the same color and four objects each of a different color; for example, a red toy car, a red block, a red bead, a red ribbon, a red sock, and so on, and one yellow car, one green ribbon, one blue ball, and one orange piece of paper.

ACTIVITIES:
1. Hold up one red object, FIND THE THINGS THAT ARE THE SAME COLOR AS THIS. After all the red things have been found: THESE THINGS ARE ALL THE SAME COLOR. TELL ME THE NAME OF THE COLOR. If there is no correct answer: THE THINGS YOU PICKED OUT ARE ALL RED THINGS. Ask: WHAT COLOR ARE THE THINGS THAT YOU PICKED OUT?
2. Put all the things together again: FIND THE THINGS THAT ARE *NOT* RED.

FOLLOW-UP: Repeat this activity with different colors and different materials. During center time put out a container of brightly colored materials. Note if the children put them into groups by color. If they do, ask, "Why did you put those together?" Accept any answer they give but note whether they give a color answer.

---

many activities with many materials (Figure 8–8). As already mentioned, real objects are used first, then pictures and objects, then cutouts, and then pictures. One-to-one correspondence skills are needed to sort and group. Classification takes the child into higher levels of grouping that go beyond

thinking and encourage clear expression of thought in a variety of settings:

1. One way to encourage informal classifying is to keep a button box. Children will sort buttons into sets on their own. Ask, "How do these go together?" Let the children explain.

Figure 8–8 "Put the fruit in one bowl and the vegetables in the other."

2. Kindergarten age children can classify animals into mammals, reptiles, and amphibians by their body coverings. They can use pictures, plastic animals, or materials that simulate the body coverings of the animals.

3. Children can classify colors with color-coordinated snacks. As children bring in snacks, help them classify the foods by color. Some examples might include
   Green: lettuce, beans, peas
   Yellow: bananas, lemonade, corn, cake
   Orange: carrots, oranges, cheese
   White: milk, cottage cheese, bread
   Red: ketchup, cherry-flavored drinks, apples, jams, tomatoes
   Brown: peanut butter, whole wheat bread, chocolate

4. Display a collection of plant parts such as stems, leaves, flowers, fruit, and nuts. Have the children sort all of the stems into one pile, all of the leaves into another, and so on. Ask a child to explain what was done. Stress that things that are alike in some way are put together to form a group. Then, have the children re-sort the plant parts into groups by properties such as size (small, medium, and large).

5. Children might enjoy playing a sorting game with objects or pictures of objects. One child begins sorting a collection of objects. After he is halfway through, the next child must complete the activity by identifying the properties the first child used and continue sorting with the same system.

Using Charts and Lists in Classification

The following example shows a first grade teacher using classification activities to help make her class aware of the technological world around them.

First, Mrs. Red Fox has the children look around the classroom and name all the machines that they can see. She asks, "Is a chair a machine?" Dean answers, "No, it does not move." Mrs. Red Fox follows up with an open question, "Do you know what is alike about machines?" Mary and Judy have had experience in the Machine Center and say, "Machines have to have a moving part." This seems to jog Dean's memory, and he says, "And I think they have to do a job." (A machine has to have at least one moving part and do a task.) Mrs. Red Fox writes down all of the suggestions in a list called "Machines in Our Classroom." The children add the pencil sharpener, a door hinge, light switch, water faucet, record player, and aquarium to the list. Mrs. Red Fox then asks the children to describe what the machines do, and how they make work easier. After discussing the machines found in the classroom, the students talk about the machines that are in their homes (Figure 8–9).

The next day the children brainstorm, make a list called "Machines in Our Home," and hang it next to the classroom machine list. When the lists are completed, Mrs. Red Fox asks the children, "Do you see any similarities between the machines found at home and the machines found in our classroom?" Trang Fung answers, "There is a clock in our classroom, and we have one in the kitchen, too." Other children notice that both places have faucets and sinks. When the teacher

Figure 8–9 "Can a nail be a machine?"

asks, "What differences do you see between the machines found at home and at school?" Dean notices that there isn't a telephone or a bicycle at school, and Sara did not find a pencil sharpener in her home.

Mrs. Red Fox extends the activity by giving the children old magazines and directing them to cut out pictures of machines to make a machine book. The class also decides to make a large machine collage for the bulletin board.

COMPARING

When comparing, the child finds a relationship between two things or sets of things on the basis of some specific characteristic or attribute. One type of attribute is an informal measurement such as size, length, height, weight, or speed. A second type of attribute is *quantity comparison*. To compare quantities, the child looks at two sets of objects and decides if they have the same number of items or if one set has more. Comparing is the basis of ordering and measurement (Unit 10).

Some examples of measurement comparisons are listed:

- John is taller than Mary.
- This snake is long. That worm is short.
- Father bear is bigger than baby bear.

Examples of number comparisons are shown:

- Does everyone have two gloves?
- I have more cookies than you have.
- We each have two dolls—that's the same.

THE BASIC COMPARISONS

To make comparisons and understand them, the child learns the following basic comparisons:

- Informal Measurement

large	small
big	little
long	short
tall	short

fat	skinny
heavy	light
fast	slow
cold	hot
thick	thin
wide	narrow
near	far
later	sooner (earlier)
older	younger (newer)
higher	lower
loud	soft (sound)

• Number

more	less/fewer

The child also finds that sometimes there is no difference when the comparison is made. That is, the items are the same size, same length, same age, and so on. Relative to quantity they discover there is the same amount (or number) of things in two sets that are compared. The concept of one-to-one correspondence and the skills of counting and classifying assist the child in comparing quantities.

The young child has many contacts with comparisons in her daily life. At home mother says, "Get up, it's *late*. Mary was up *early*. Eat *fast*. If you eat slowly, we will have to leave before you are finished. Have a *big* bowl for your cereal; that one is too *small*." At school the teacher says, "I'll pick up this *heavy* box; you pick up the *light* one." "Sit on the *small* chair, that one is too *big*." "Let's finish this story." "Remember, the father bear's porridge was too *hot*, and the mother bear's porridge was too *cold*."

Small children are very concerned about size and number, especially in relation to themselves. They want to be bigger, taller, faster, and older (figure 8–10). They want to be sure they have the same, not less—and if possible more—of things that the other child has. These needs of the young child bring about many situations where the adult can help in an informal way to aid the child in learning the skills and ideas of comparing.

Exploring Science

When young children compare, they look at similarities and differences with each of their senses. Children are able to detect small points of difference and, because of this, enjoy spotting mistakes and finding differences between objects. Activities such as observing appearances, sizes, graphing, and dressing figures give experience in comparing.

1. Compare appearances by discussing likeness between relatives, dolls, or favorite animals. Then, make a chart to show the different hair colors in the room or any other characteristics that interest your students.
2. Size comparisons seem to fascinate young children. They want to know who is the biggest, oldest, tallest, shortest. Compare the lengths of hand spans, arm spans and lengths of paces and limbs. Have a few facts ready. Children will want to know which animals are the biggest, smallest, run the fastest, and so on. They might even decide to test which paper towel is the strongest or which potato chip is the saltiest.
3. Clothes can be compared and matched to paper dolls according to size, weather conditions, occupations, and activities such as swimming, playing outdoors, or going to a

Figure 8–10 "I can build a bigger machine."

birthday party. This comparison activity could be a regular part of a daily weather chart activity.

Comparing and Collecting

What did you collect as a child? Did you collect baseball cards, leaves, small cereal box prizes, shells, or pictures of famous people? Chances are you collected something. This is because young children are natural scientists; they are doing what comes naturally. They collect and organize their environment in a way that makes sense to them. Even as adults, we still retain the natural tendency to organize and collect.

Consider for a moment: Do you keep your coats, dresses, shoes, slacks, and jewelry in separate places? Do the spoons, knives, forks, plates, and cups have their own space in your house? In all likelihood, you have a preferred spot for each item. Where do you keep your soup? The cans are probably lined up together. Do you have a special place just for junk? Some people call such a place a junk drawer. Take a look at your house or room as evidence that you have a tendency to think like scientists and try to bring the observable world into some sort of structure.

In fact, when you collect, you may be at your most scientific. As you collect, you combine the processes of observation, comparison, classification, and measurement, and you think like a scientist thinks. For example, when you add a leaf to your collection, you observe it and compare it to the other leaves in your collection. Then, you ask yourself, "Does this leaf measure up to my standards?" "Is it too big, small, old, drab?" "Have insects eaten its primary characteristics?" You make a decision based on comparisons between the leaf and the criteria you have set (Figure 8–11).

Similarities and Differences

To find similarities, concepts, or characteristics that link things together may be even more

Figure 8–11   Gathering leaves

difficult than identifying differences in objects. For example, dogs, cats, bears, lizards, and mice are all animals. But to gain an understanding of a concept, children need to develop the idea that some similarities are more important than others. Even though the lizard has four legs and is an animal, the dog, cat, bear, and mouse are more alike because they are mammals. Unit 13 shows ways of teaching differences in animals.

In addition to quantitative questions such as "How long?" and "How many?," qualitative questions are necessary to bring about keener observations of similarities and differences. Observe the contrast in Chris's responses to his teacher in the following scenario:

Mrs. Raymond asks Chris, "How many seeds do you have on your desk?" Chris counts the seeds, says "Eight," and goes back to arranging the seeds. Mrs. Raymond then asks Chris, "Tell me how many ways your seeds are alike and how they are different." Chris tells his observations as he closely observes the seeds for additional differences and similarities. "Some seeds are small, some seeds are big, some have cracks, some feel rough." Chris's answers began to include descriptions that included shape, size, color, texture, structure, markings, and so on. He is beginning to find order in his observations.

Everyday Comparisons

Comparisons can help young children become more aware of their environment; for example:

1. Go for a walk, and have children observe different trees. Ask them to compare the general shape of the trees and the leaves. Let them feel the bark and describe the differences between rough or smooth, peeling, thin or thick bark. As the children compare the trees, discuss ways that they help people and animals (home, shelter, food, shade, and so on).

2. Activities that use sound to make comparisons utilize an important way that young children learn. Try comparing winter sounds with summer sounds. Go for a walk in the winter or summer and listen for sounds. For example, the students in Mrs. Hebert's class heard their boots crunching in snow, the wind whistling, a little rain splashing, and a few even noticed a lack of sound on their winter walk. Johnny commented that he did not hear any birds. This began a discussion of where the birds might be and what the class could do to help the birds that remained in the area all winter.

3. Insect investigations are natural opportunities for comparison questions and observation. Take advantage of the young childrens' curiosity, and let them collect four or five different insects for observation. Mr. Wang's class collected insects on a field trip. Theresa found four different kinds of insects. She put them carefully in a jar with leaves and twigs from the area in which she found them and punched holes in the jar lid. Mr. Wang helped her observe differences such as size, winged or wingless, and similarities such as six legs, three body parts, and two antennae. All insects have these characteristics. If your captive animal does not have these, it is not an insect. It is something else (Figure 8–12).

4. Snack time is a good time to compare the changes in the color and texture of vegetables before and after they are cooked. Ask, "How do they look different?" When you make butter ask, "What changes do you see in the cream?" Make your own lemonade with fresh lemons and ask, "What happens to the lemons?" Then let the children taste the lemonade before and after sugar is added. Ask, "How does sugar change the taste of the lemonade?"

SHAPE

Activities relating to shapes have their beginnings during the preprimary years.

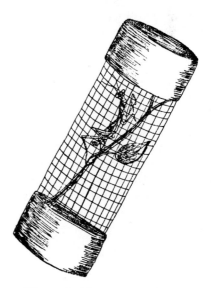

Figure 8–12   A bug collector

Each object in the environment has its own shape. Much of the play and activity of the infant during the sensorimotor stage centers on learning about shape. The infant learns through looking and through feeling with hands and mouth. Babies learn that some shapes are easier to hold than others. They learn that things of one type of shape will roll. They learn that some things have the same shape as others. Young children see and feel shape differences long before they can describe these differences in words (Figure 8–13). In the late sensorimotor and early preoperational stages, the child spends a lot of time matching and classifying things. Shape is often used as the basis for these activities.

As the child moves into the middle of the preoperational period, she can learn that there are some basic shapes (called geometric shapes) that have their own names. First the child learns to label circle, square, and triangle. Then she can learn rectangle, rhombus, and ellipse. Later on, these shape names will be used in science, geometry, art, and other areas of activity. There are two major purposes for learning about shape:

- It helps children to be more sensitive to similarities and differences in forms in the environment and aids in discriminating one form from another.
- Children learn some labels that they can use when describing things in the environment. ("I put the book on the square table.")

Exploring Science

Description of the physical environment is essential to the study of any aspect of science. Such descriptions are not possible without an understanding of spatial relationships, which include the study of shapes, symmetry, time, and motion.

Most things have a shape. Children identify and classify objects by their shapes. Basic two-dimensional geometric shapes include the circle,

Figure 8–13 The children experiment with the shape matching box.

triangle, square, and rectangle. Each of these shapes is constructed from a straight line. The following scenario is a fundamental kindergarten lesson that introduces shapes and applies them to how children learn:

Mrs. Jones arranges children in groups and gives each child a different sponge shape. After the children have had time to explore the outer edges of their sponge shape, she picks up one of the shapes and asks, "How many sides does this shape have?" Mary and Lai answer, "Three." Mrs. Jones says, "Hold your shape up if it is just like my shape." She makes sure that each child gets a chance to examine each shape. If the shape has sides, the children count the sides of the shape aloud. Then she asks all children who have circles to hold them up and pass them to other members of the group for examination. Yarn is passed out and the children begin to duplicate the shapes on the tabletop.

The next day, Mrs. Jones asks George to pick up a shape from the table. He selects a circle. Mrs. Jones asks George if he can find a shape in the room that matches the circle (clock, button, table, pan, record). Sam and Mary take turns finding triangle shapes (sailboat sails, diagonally cut sandwiches), and Lai finds square shapes (floor tiles, crackers, cheese slices, napkins, paper towels, bulletin boards, books, tables). Then, each child stands next to the shape and identifies its name. Mrs. Jones leads the group in shape-matching until everyone finds and reports objects of each shape.

To extend the activity, Mrs. Jones has the children use their sponge shapes to paint pictures. She prepares the paint by placing a wet paper towel in a pie tin and coating the towel with tempera paint. The towel and paint work like a stamp pad in which to dip damp sponge shapes. After the children complete their pictures, she asks, "Which shapes have you used in your picture?"

More Shape Activities

The following activities integrate shape with other subject areas:

1. Construction-paper shapes can be used to create fantasy animal shapes such as the shape from outer space, or the strangest insect shape ever seen. Have the children design an appropriate habitat and tell the background for their imaginary shape creature.

2. Take students on a shape walk to see how many shapes your children can find in the objects they see. Keep a record. When you return to your classroom, make a bar graph. Ask children to determine which shape was seen most often.

3. Shape books are an effective way of reinforcing the shape that an animal has. For example, after viewing the polar bears, make a book in the shape of a polar bear. Children can paste pictures in the book, create drawings of what they saw, and dictate or write stories about bears. Shape books can be covered with wallpaper or decorated in the way that the animal appears (Figure 8–14).

Figure 8–14   A polar bear book for writing

Shape and the Sense of Touch

Young children are ardent touchers; they love to finger and stroke different materials. The following activities are a few ways that touch can be used to classify and identify shapes:

1. A classic touch bag gives children a chance to recognize and match shapes with their sense of touch. Some children might not want to put their hands into a bag or box. Be sure and use bright colors and cheerful themes when decorating a touch bag or box. A touching apron with several pockets is an alternative. The teacher wears the apron, and students try to identify what is in the pockets.

2. Extend this activity by making pairs of tactile cards with a number of rough- and smooth-textured shapes. Have the children blindfold each other and match the cards with partners. Ask, "Can you find the cards that match?" and "How do you know they match?" Or, play "Mystery Shapes" by cutting different shapes out of sandpaper and mounting them on cards. Ask the children to close their eyes, feel the shape, and guess what it is.

3. Students will enjoy identifying shapes with their feet, so you can make a foot feely box.

Figure 8–15   Taking a tactile walk

SPACE

A sense of spatial relationships along with an understanding of shape are fundamental to interpreting, understanding, and appreciating our inherently geometric world. There are relationships in space, and there is the use of space. The relationship ideas are *position*, *direction*, and *distance*. Use of space includes organization and patterns and construction. Each space concept helps the child answer her own questions.

It is through everyday motor activities that the child first learns about space. As she moves her body in space, she learns position, direction, and distance relationships and about the use of the space. Children in the sensorimotor and preoperational stages need equipment that lets them place their own bodies on, off, under, over, in, out, through, above, below, and so on. They need places to go up and down, around and through, and sideways and across. They need things that they can put in, on, and under other things. They need things that they can place near and far from other things. They need containers of many sizes to fill; blocks with which to build; and paint, collage, wood, clay, and such, which can be made into patterns and

Students will probably infer that they can feel things better with their fingertips than with their toes. A barefoot trail of fluffy rugs, a beach towel, ceramic tiles, a pillow, and a window screen would be a good warm-up activity for identifying shapes with feet. Students should describe what they feel as they walk over each section of the trail (Figure 8–15).

Space Concept	Question	Answers
Position	Where (am I, are you, is he)?	on-off; on top of-over-under; in-out; into-out of; top-bottom; above-below; in front of-in back of-behind; beside-by-next to; between
Direction	Which way?	up-down; forward-backward; around-through; to-from; toward-away from; sideways; across
Distance	What is the relative distance?	near-far; close to-far from
Organization and Pattern	How can things be arranged so they fit in a space?	arrange things in the space until they fit, or until they please the eye
Construction	How is space made? How do things fit into the space?	arrange things in the space until they fit; change the size and shape of the space to fit what is needed for the things

organized in space. Thus, when the child is matching, classifying, and comparing, she is learning about space at the same time.

Exploring Science

Although young children are not yet ready for the abstract level of formal thinking, they can begin thinking about space and shape relationships. The following science board game being played in a primary classroom is a good example of this relationship:

"Put the starfish on top of the big rock."

"Which rock do you mean?"

"The big gray one next to the sunken treasure chest."

This is the conversation of two children playing a game with identical boards and pieces. One child gives directions and follows them, placing the piece in the correct position on a hidden game board. Another child, after making sure he understands the directions, chooses a piece and places it on the board. Then the first child continues with another set of directions: "Put the clam under that other rock."

The children are having fun, but there's more to their game than might first appear. A great deal about the child's concept of space can be learned through observation once the child responds to directions such as up-down, on-off, on top of, over-under, in front of, behind, etc. Is care taken to place the objects on the paper in a careful way?

Bird's-Eye View

Children sometimes have difficulty with concepts involved in reading and making maps. One reason for this is that maps demand that they look at things from an unusual perspective: a bird's-eye view of spatial relations. To help children gain experience with this perspective, try the following strategy:

Ask children to imagine what it's like to look down on something from high above. Say,

"When a bird looks down as it flies over a house, what do you think it sees?" You will need to ask some directed questions for young children to appreciate that objects will look different. "What would a picnic table look like to a bird?" "Does your house look the same to the bird in the air as it does to you when you're standing on the street?"

Then tell the children to stand and look down at their shoes. Ask them to describe what they can see from this perspective. Then ask them to draw their bird's-eye view. Some children will be able to draw a faithful representation of their shoes; others may only be able to scribble what they see. Give them time to experiment with perspective, and if they are having difficulty getting started, have them trace the outlines of their shoes on a piece of drawing paper. Ask, "Do you need to fill in shoelaces or fasteners?" "What else do you see?" Put the children's drawings on their desks for open house. Have parents locate their child's desk by identifying the correct shoes.

This lesson lends itself to a simple exercise that reinforces a new way of looking and gives parents a chance to share what is going on at school. Ask children to look at some familiar objects at home (television, kitchen table, or even the family pet) from their new bird's-eye perspective and draw one or two of their favorites (Figure 8–16). When they bring their drawings to school, other children can try to identify the objects depicted.

On the Playground

Playground distance can be a good place to start to get children thinking about space. Use a stopwatch to time them as they run from the corner of the building to the fence. Ask, "How long did it take?" Then, have the children walk the same route. Ask, "Did it take the same amount of time?" Discuss the differences in walking and running and moving faster or slower over the same space.

SPACE: RELATIONSHIPS, PHYSICAL SELF

OBJECTIVE: To help the child relate his position in space to the positions of other people and things.

MATERIALS: The child's own body, other people, and things in the environment.

ACTIVITIES:

1. Set up an obstacle course using boxes, boards, ladders, tables, chairs, and like items. Set it up so that by following the course, the children can physically experience position, direction, and distance. This can be done indoors or outdoors. As the child proceeds along the course, use space words to label his movement: "Leroy is going *up* the ladder, *through* the tunnel, *across* the bridge, *down* the slide, and *under* the table. Now he is *close to* the end."

2. Find Your Friend
   Place children in different places: sitting or standing on chairs or blocks or boxes, under tables, sitting three in a row on chairs facing different directions, and so on. Have each child take a turn to find a friend.
   FIND A FRIEND WHO IS ON A CHAIR (A BOX, A LADDER).
   FIND A FRIEND WHO IS UNDER A TABLE (ON A TABLE, NEXT TO A TABLE).
   FIND A FRIEND WHO IS BETWEEN TWO FRIENDS (BEHIND A FRIEND, NEXT TO A FRIEND).
   FIND A FRIEND WIIO IS SITTING BACKWARDS (FORWARDS, SIDEWAYS).
   FIND A FRIEND WHO IS ABOVE ANOTHER FRIEND (BELOW ANOTHER FRIEND).
   Have the children think of different places they can place themselves. When they know the game let the children take turns saying the FIND statements.

3. Put Yourself Where I Say
   One at a time give the children instructions for placing themselves in a position.
   CLIMB UP THE LADDER.
   WALK BETWEEN THE CHAIRS.
   STAND BEHIND TANYA.
   GET ON TOP OF THE BOX.
   GO CLOSE TO THE DOOR (GO FAR FROM THE DOOR).
   As the children learn the game, they can give the instructions.

4. Where Is Your Friend?
   As in Activity 2, "Find Your Friend," place the children in different places. This time ask WHERE questions. The child must answer in words. As WHERE IS (Child's Name)? Child answers, "Tim is under the table," or "Mary is on top of the playhouse."

FOLLOW-UP: Set up obstacle courses for the children to use during playtime both indoors and outdoors.

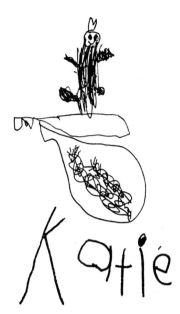

Figure 8–16   Katie's cat from a bird's-eye view

PARTS AND WHOLES

The young child learns that wholes have parts. Later the older child learns that parts are *fractions* of the whole. The child must learn the idea of parts and wholes before he can understand fractions. He learns that some things are made up of special (unique) parts, that sets of things can be divided into parts, and that whole things can be divided into smaller parts.

He learns about special parts:

- Bodies have parts (arms, legs, head).
- A car has parts (engine, doors, steering wheel, seats).
- A house has parts (kitchen, bathroom, bedroom, living room).
- A chair has parts (seat, legs, back).
   He learns that sets of things can be divided:
- He passes out cookies for snack.
- He deals cards for a game of picture rummy.
- He gives each friend one of his toys with which to play.

- He divides his blocks so each child may build a house.

He learns that whole things can be divided into parts:

- One cookie is broken in half.
- An orange is divided into several segments.
- A carrot or banana is sliced into parts.
- The contents of a bottle of soda pop are put into two or more cups.
- A large piece of paper is cut into small pieces.

The young child centers on the number of things he sees. Two-year-old Pete breaks up his graham cracker into small pieces. "I have more than you," he says to Tim, who has one whole graham cracker also. Pete does not see that although he has more pieces of cracker he does not have more crackers. Ms. Moore shows Chris a whole apple. "How many apples do I have?" "One," says Chris. "Now watch," says Ms. Moore as she cuts the apple into two pieces. "How many apples do I have now?" "Two!" answers Chris. As the child enters concrete operations, he will see that a single apple is always a single apple even though it may be cut into parts.

Gradually the child is able to see that a whole is made up of parts. He also begins to see that parts may be the same (equal) in size and amount or different (unequal) in size and amount. He compares number and size and develops the concepts of more, less, and the same. An understanding of more, less, and the same underlies learning that objects and sets can be divided into two or more equal parts and still maintain the same amount.

Exploring Science

After students are used to identifying shapes, introduce the concept of balanced proportions called *symmetry*. Bilateral symmetry is frequently found in nature. *Bilateral* means that a line can be drawn through the middle of the shape and divide it into two. Each of the shapes the students have worked with to this point can be divided into two matching halves. Point out these divisions on a square, circle, and equilateral triangle. Provide lots of pictures of animals, objects, and other living things. Have the children show where a line could be drawn through each picture. Ask, "How might your own body be divided like this?" Provide pictures for the children to practice folding and drawing lines (Figure 8–17).

Food activities commonly found in early childhood classrooms provide many opportunities for demonstrating parts and wholes. For example, when working with apples, divide them into halves or fourths. Ask, "How many apples will we need for everyone to receive a piece?" When you cut open the apples, let the children count the number of seeds inside. If you are making applesauce, be sure the children notice the difference between a whole cup of apples or sugar and a half cup. A pizza would be a natural food to order and talk about. Ask, "Can you eat the whole pizza?" or "Would you like a part of the pizza?"

During snack time, ask each student to notice how his or her sandwich has been cut. Ask, "What shape was your sandwich before it was cut?," "What shape are the two halves?," and "Can you think of a different way to cut your sandwich?" Discuss the whole sandwich and parts of a sandwich.

Many times during the day the teacher can help children develop their understanding of parts and wholes. The teacher can use the words *part*, *whole*, *divide*, and *half*.

Figure 8–17   A bear has symmetry

- "Today everyone gets *half* of an apple and *half* of a sandwich."
- "Too bad; *part* of this game is missing."
- "Take this basket of crackers, and *divide* them up so everyone gets some."
- "No, we won't cut the carrots up. Each child gets a *whole* carrot."
- "Give John *half* the blocks so he can build too."
- "We only have one apple left. Let's *divide* it up."
- "Point to the *part* of the body when I say the name."

PARTS AND WHOLES: PARTS OF THINGS

OBJECTIVE: To learn the meaning of the term *part* as it refers to parts of objects, people, and animals.

MATERIALS: Objects or pictures of objects with parts missing.

ACTIVITIES:
1. The Broken Toys
    Show the child some broken toys or pictures of broken toys. WHAT'S MISSING FROM
    THESE TOYS? After the child tells what is missing from each toy bring out the missing
    parts (or pictures of missing parts). FIND THE MISSING PART THAT COMES WITH
    EACH TOY.
2. Who (or What) Is Hiding?
    The basic game is to hide someone or something behind a screen so that only a part is
    showing. The child then guesses who or what is hidden. The following are some
    variations:
    a. Two or more children hide behind a divider screen, a door, or a chair. Only a foot or a
        hand of one is shown. The other children guess whose body part can be seen.
    b. The children are shown several objects. The objects are then placed behind a screen. A
        part of one is shown. The child must guess which thing the part belongs to. (To make
        the task harder, the parts can be shown without the children knowing first what the
        choices will be).
    c. Do the same type of activity using pictures:
        • Cut out magazine pictures (or draw your own), and mount on cardboard. Cut a piece
           of construction paper to use to screen most of the picture. Say, LOOK AT THE
           PART THAT IS SHOWING. WHAT IS HIDDEN BEHIND THE PAPER?
        • Mount magazine pictures on construction paper. Cut out a hole in another piece of
           construction paper of the same size. Staple the piece of paper onto the one with the
           picture on it so that a part of the picture can be seen. Say, LOOK THROUGH THE
           HOLE. GUESS WHAT IS IN THE PICTURE UNDER THE COVER.

FOLLOW-UP: Play *What's Missing Lotto* game. (Childcraft) or *What's Missing? Parts &*
Wholes, Young Learners' Puzzles (Teaching Resources)

The child can be given tasks that require
him to learn about parts and wholes. When the
child is asked to pass something, to cut up vegetables or fruit, or to share materials, he learns about
parts and wholes.

SUMMARY

One-to-one correspondence is the most basic
number skill. Children can increase their awareness of this skill and science concepts as they do
science-related matching activities such as putting
animals with their homes and imitating animal
movement.

Animal and plant life offer many opportunities for reinforcing concepts and number concepts

can be emphasized with familiar concrete examples of counting.

Sets are composed of items put together in a
group based on one or more common criteria.
When children put objects into groups by sorting
out items that share some feature, they are classifying. Comparing requires that children look for similarities and differences with each of their senses.
Activities requiring observation, measuring, graphing, and classifying encourage comparisons.

Adults help children learn shape when they
give them things to view, hold, and feel. Each
thing that the child meets in the environment
has a shape. The child also needs to use space in
a logical way. Things must fit into the space

available. As children make constructions in space, they begin to understand the spatial relationship between themselves and the things around them.

The idea of parts and wholes is basic to objects, people, and animals. Sets and wholes can be divided into smaller parts or pieces. The concept of bilateral symmetry is introduced when children draw a line through the middle of a shape and divide it into two halves.

Naturalistic, informal, and structured experiences support the learning of these basic science and math skills. A variety of evaluation techniques should be used. Informal evaluation can be done simply by observing the progress and choices of the child. Formal tasks are available in Appendix A.

SUGGESTED ACTIVITIES

1. How will you evaluate children's learning? How will you assess if children are developing science and math concepts and skills?

2. Select a science topic such as air, and identify possible ways the science and the math concepts in this unit can be integrated with the curriculum.

3. Teach a lesson that integrates science and math to a group of children. Assess the extent to which you think they understand both the science and the math concept you were emphasizing.

4. Describe your childhood collection to the class. Discuss the basis for your interest and where you kept your collection. Do you continue to add to this collection?

5. Begin a nature collection. Mount and label your collection, and discuss ways that children might collect objects in a formal way. Refer to Unit 13 of this book for nature collection suggestions.

6. Observe a group of students doing a science activity. Record the informal math and science discoveries that they make.

7. Design a questioning strategy that will encourage the development of classification and encourage student discussion. Try the strategy with children. Develop questioning strategies for two more of the concepts and skills presented in this unit.

REVIEW

Match each term to an activity that emphasizes the concept.

_____ Using the sense of touch to match similar objects   a. One-to-one correspondence

_____ Looking down on things from a bird's-eye view   b. Counting

_____ Matching animals to their homes   c. Sets and classifying

_____ Figuring out how many fish swimming in the tank   d. Comparing

_____ Classifying animals into groups of mammals and reptiles   e. Shape

_____ Duplicating yarn triangles and circles   f. Space

_____ Drawing an imaginary line through the middle of a sandwich   g. Parts and whole

UNIT 9

Language and Concept Formation

OBJECTIVES

After studying this unit, the student should be able to
- Explain the importance of language to communications, connections, and reasoning
- Explain two ways to describe a child's understanding of concept words
- Describe the whole language philosophy as it applies to science and mathematics
- Use literature, writing, drawing, and speaking to support the development of science and mathematics language

What the child does and what the child says tells the teacher what the child knows about math and science. The older the child gets, the more important concept words become. The child's language system is usually well developed by age 4; that is, by this age, children's sentences are much the same as an adult's. Children are at a point where their vocabulary is growing very rapidly (Figure 9–1).

The adult observes what the child does from infancy through age 2 and looks for the first understanding and the use of words. Between 2 and 4 the child starts to put more words together into longer sentences. She also learns more words and what they mean.

In assessing the young child's concept development, questions are used. Which is the big ball? Which is the circle? The child's understanding of words is checked by having her respond with the right action:

- "Point to the big ball."
- "Find two chips."
- "Show me the picture in which the boy is on the chair."

The above tasks do not require the child to say any words. She needs only point, touch, or pick up something. Once the child demonstrates her understanding of math words by using gestures or other nonverbal answers, she can move on to questions she must answer with one or more words. The child can be asked the same questions as above in a way that requires a verbal response:

- (The child is shown two balls, one big and one small.) "What is different about these balls?"
- (The child is shown a set of objects.) "How many are there in this set?"
- (The child is shown a picture of a boy sitting on a chair.) "Where is the boy?"

The child learns many concept words as she goes about her daily activities. It has been found that by the time a child starts kindergarten, she uses many concept words she has learned in a naturalistic way. Examples have been included in unit 8. The child uses both comments and questions. Comments would be like the following:

- "Mom, I want *two* pieces of cheese."
- "I have a *bunch* of birdseed."
- "Mr. Brown, this chair is *small*."
- "*Yesterday* we went to the zoo."
- "The string is *long*."

Figure 9–1 "Which circle is bigger?"

- "This is the *same* as this."
- "The foot fits *in* the shoe."
- "This cracker is a *square* shape."
- "Look, some of the worms are *long* and some are *short*, some are *fat* and some are *thin*."
- "The *first* bean seed I planted is *taller* than the *second* one."
- "Outer *space* is *far away*."

Questions would be like these:

- "How *old* is he?"
- "*When* is Christmas?"
- "*When* will I grow as *big* as you?"
- "*How many* are coming for dinner?"
- "Who has *more*?"
- "What *time* is my TV program?"
- "Is this a school *day*, or is it *Saturday*?"
- "What makes the bubbles when the water gets *hot*?"
- "Why does this roller always go *down* its ramp *faster* than that roller goes *down* its ramp?"
- "Why are the leaves turning *brown* and *red* and *gold* and falling *down on* the ground?"

The answers that the child gets to these questions can help increase the number of concept words she knows and can use.

The teacher needs to be aware of using concept words during center time, lunch, and other times when a structured concept lesson is not being done. She should also note which words the child uses during free times.

The teacher should encourage the child to use concept words even though she may not use them in an accurate, adult way, for example:

- "I can count—1, 2, 3, 5, 10."
- "Aunt Helen is coming after my last nap." (Indicates future time)
- "I will measure my paper." (Holds ruler against the edge of the paper.)
- "Last night Grandpa was here." (Actually several days ago)
- "I'm 6 years old." (Really 2 years old)
- "I have a million dollars." (Has a handful of play money)

Adults should accept the child's use of the words and use the words correctly themselves. Soon the child will develop a higher level use of words as she is able to grasp higher level ideas. For the 2- or 3-year-old, any group of things more than two or three may be called a *bunch*. Instead of using *big* and *little* the child may use family words: "This is the mommy block" and "This is the baby block." Time is one concept that takes a long time to grasp. A young child may use the same word to mean different time periods. The following examples were said by a 3-year-old:

- "*Last night* we went to the beach." (Meaning last summer)
- "*Last night* I played with Chris." (Meaning yesterday)
- "*Last night* I went to Kenny's house." (Meaning three weeks ago)

For this child, *last night* means any time in the past. One by one he will learn that there are words that refer to times past such as last summer, yesterday, and three weeks ago.

Computer activities can also add to vocabulary. The teacher uses concept words when explaining how to use the programs. Children enjoy working at the computer with friends and will use the concept words in communication with each other as they work cooperatively to solve the problems presented by the computer (Figure 9–2).

Books also afford a multitude of opportunities for building concept vocabulary. For example, a teacher was observed reading a story called *Julius*, by Syd Hoff. The following concept words were used:

- Show me the *front of* the book.
- Show me the *end of* the story.
- The giraffe has a very *long* neck.
- Carry *on top of* their heads.
- *Time* to rest.
- Who's *in* there?
- *On* the ship.
- I'm coming *in* for a landing.
- He landed *on* Julius's nose.
- If someone is *slim*, he is *thin* or *skinny*.
- She is *fat*—the *fattest* lady I've ever seen.
- Mr. and Mrs. *Tiny* are *small*.

- Mr. *Giant* is *in* the tree.
- We're *bigger* than you.
- Show me the *first* word; the *last* word.

Examples of other books with concepts are included in other units. Appendix B lists many books with concept ideas (Figure 9–3).

Many concept words have already been introduced, and more will appear in the units to come. The prekindergarten child continually learns words. The following presents those concept words that most children can use and understand by the time they complete kindergarten.

CONCEPT WORDS

The following words have appeared in Unit 8

- **One-to-One Correspondence:** one, pair, more, each, some, group, bunch, set, amount
- **Number and Counting:** 0, 1, 2, 3, 4, 5, 6, 7, 8, 9, 10, how many, count, group, one more than, next, number, computer

Figure 9–2 Working at the computer, children can communicate using concept language.

Figure 9-3 Books contain a rich variety of concept language.

- **Sets and Classifying:** sets; descriptive words for color, shape, size, materials, pattern, texture, function, association, class names, and common features; belong with; goes with; is used with; put with; the same
- **Comparing:** more, less, big, small, large, little, long, short, fat, skinny, heavy, light, fast, slow, cold, hot, thick, thin, wide, narrow, near, far, later, sooner, earlier, older, younger, newer, higher, lower, loud, soft (sound)
- **Shape:** circle, square, triangle, rectangle, ellipse, rhombus, shape, round
- **Space:** *where* (on, off, on top of, over, under, in, out, into, out of, top, bottom, above, below, in front of, in back of, behind, beside, by, next to, between); *which way* (up, down, forward, backward, around, through, to, from, toward, away from, sideways, across); *distance* (near, far, close to, far from); map, floor plan
- **Parts and wholes:** part, whole, divide, share, pieces, some, half

  Words that will be introduced later are
- **Ordering:** first, second, third; big, bigger, biggest; few, fewer, fewest; large, larger, largest; little, littler, littlest; many, more, most; thick, thicker, thickest; thin, thinner, thinnest; last, next, then
- **Measurement of volume, length, weight, and temperature:** little, big, medium, tiny, large, size, tall, short, long, far, farther, closer, near, high, higher, thin, wide, deep, cup, pint, quart, gallon, ounces, milliliter, kiloliter, liter, foot, inch, kilometer, mile, meter, centimeter, narrow, measure, hot, cold, warm, cool, thermometer, temperature, pounds, grams, kilograms, milligrams
- **Measurement of time and sequence:** morning, afternoon, evening, night, day, soon, week, tomorrow, yesterday, early, late, a long time ago, once upon a time, minute, second, hour, new, old, already, Easter, Christmas, Passover, Hanukkah, Juneteenth, Pioneer Days, Cinco de Mayo, birthday, now, year, weekend, clock, calendar, watch, when, time, date, sometimes, then, before, present, soon, while, never, once, sometime, next, always, fast, slow, speed, Monday and other days of the week, January and other months of the year, winter, spring, summer, fall
- **Practical:** money, cash register, penny, dollar, buy, pay, change, cost, check, free, store, map, recipe, measure, cup, tablespoon, teaspoon, boil, simmer, bake, degrees, time, hours, minutes, freeze, chill, refrigerate, pour, mix, separate, add, combine, ingredients

Words can be used before they are presented in a formal structured activity. The child who speaks can become familiar with words and even say them before he understands the concepts they stand for (Figure 9–4).

- **Primary Level Words:** addition, subtraction, number facts, plus, add, minus, take away, total, sum, equal, difference, amount, altogether, in all, are left, number line, place value, patterns, 1s, 10s, 100s, digit, multiplication, division, equation, times, divide, product, even, odd, fractions, halves, fourths, thirds, wholes, numerator, denominator, measure, inches, feet, yards, miles, centimeter, meter, kilometer

THE WHOLE LANGUAGE PHILOSOPHY AND SCIENCE AND MATHEMATICS

The emphasis on communication, reasoning, and making connections in science and mathematics relates naturally to the whole language philosophy in reading and language arts. Just as mathematics and science are turning toward a conceptual emphasis (vs. memorization, drill, and learning basic facts and formulas), so, too, have reading and language arts turned to an approach referred to as *whole language*, which integrates written

Figure 9–4   *"Today* it is sunny outside."

and spoken language into meaningful contexts. Reading and writing are learned through active involvement in the context of meaningful experiences with literature, drama, music, science, mathematics, and social studies. Immersion in language and print; opportunities and resources such as materials, time, space, and activities; meaningful communication; a teacher who is a communication role model; acceptance of children as readers and writers; and the expectation that children will become literate are the critical elements in the whole language approach (Raines & Canady, 1990). In the whole language classroom, children listen to good literature, experiment with writing, and learn to read naturally. They explain and discuss, record data, and write about their explorations in science and mathematics. Refer back to Unit 6 for applications to problem solving. Through these activities, children develop their spoken and written language vocabulary in a meaningful context.

SUMMARY

As children learn science and math concepts and skills, they also add many words to their vocabularies. Science and math have a language that is basic to their content and activities. Language is learned through naturalistic, informal, and structured activities. Computer activities are excellent for promoting communication between and among children. Books are a rich source of concept words. The current trend toward a whole language philosophy in the early childhood classroom fits well with the emphasis on communication, reasoning, and making connections in mathematics and science.

FURTHER   READING   AND   RESOURCES

Ballenger, M., Benham, N., & Hosticka, A. (1984). Children's counting books: Mathematical concept development. *Childhood Education,* September/October, 30–35.

Bayle, L. (1987). *Picture books for preschool nutrition education: A selected annotated bibliography.* Lexington, MA: Author.

Burke, D., Snider, A., & Symonds, P. (1988). *Box it or bag it mathematics: Kindergarten teachers' resource guide.* Portland, OR: The Math Learning Center.

Burke, D., Snider, A., & Symonds, P. (1992). *Math excursions K: Project-based mathematics for kindergartners.* Portsmouth, NH: Heinemann.

Capps, L. R., & Pickreign, J. (1993). Language connections in mathematics: A critical part of mathematics instruction. *Arithmetic Teacher,* 41(1), 8–12.

Carlile, C. (1992). Bag it for science. *Science and Children,* 29(6), 15–16.

Gee, T. C., & Olson, M. W. (1992). Let's talk trade books. *Science and Children, 29*(6), 13–14.

Harcourt, L. (1988). *Explorations for early childhood.* Menlo Park, CA: Addison-Wesley.

Kliman, M., & Richards, J. (1992). Writing, sharing, and discussing mathematics stories. *Arithmetic Teacher, 40*(3), 138–141.

Lewis, B. A., Long, R., & Mackay, M. (1993). Fostering communication in mathematics using children's literature. *Arithmetic Teacher, 40*(8), 470–473.

Maguire, B. E. (1992). Introducing Mr. I. M. Treeless. *Science and Children, 29*(7), 21–22.

McMath, J., & King, M. (1993). Open books, open minds. *Science and Children, 30*(5), 33–36.

Midkiff, R. B., & Cramer, M. M. (1993). Stepping stones to mathematical understanding. *Arithmetic Teacher, 40*(6), 303–305.

Nevin, M. L. (1992). A language arts approach to mathematics. *Arithmetic Teacher, 40*(3), 142–146.

Radencich, M. C., & Bohning, G. (1988). Pop up, pull down, push in, slide out: Natural science action books. *Childhood Education, 64*(3), 157–161.

Raines, S. C., & Canady, R. J. (1990). *The whole language kindergarten*. New York: Teachers College Press.

Scarnati, J. T., & Weller, C. J. (1992). The write stuff. *Science and Children, 29*(4), 28–29.

Schoenfeld, M. (1987). Rainy weather: Books for children. *Day Care and Early Education, 15*(2), 44–45.

Schon, I. (1992). Ciencia en español. *Science and Children, 29*(6), 18–19, 46.

Stiffler, L. A. (1992). A solution in the shelves. *Science and Children, 29*(6), 17, 46.

Wassermann, S. (1990). *Serious players in the primary classroom*. New York: Teachers College Press.

Whitin, D., & Wilde, S. (1992). *Read any good math lately? Children's books for mathematical learning, K-6*. Portsmouth, NH: Heinemann.

SUGGESTED ACTIVITIES

1. Visit a prekindergarten, a kindergarten, and a primary classroom. Observe for at least 30 minutes in each room. Write down every child and adult math and science word used. Compare the three age groups and teachers for number and variety of words used.

2. Make the concept language assessment materials described in Appendix A. Administer the tasks to 4-, 5-, and 6-year-old children. Make a list of the concept words recorded in each classroom. Count the number of times each word was used. Compare the number of different words and the total number of words heard in each classroom.

3. In the library, research the area of whole language and its relationship to mathematics and science instruction. Write a report summarizing what you learned.

4. Observe some young children doing concept development computer activities. Record their conversations, and note how many concept words they use.

5. Select one of the concept books suggested in Appendix B. Familiarize yourself with the content. Read the book with one or more young children. Question them to find out how many of the concept words they can use.

REVIEW

A. Explain how language learning relates to science and mathematics concept learning.

B. Describe how a whole language approach to instruction might increase the concept vocabulary of young children.

UNIT 10

Applications of Fundamental Concepts in Preprimary Science

OBJECTIVES

After studying this unit, the student should be able to
- Apply the concepts and skills related to ordering and patterning, measuring, and graphing to science lessons and units at the preprimary level
- Design science lessons that include naturalistic, informal, and structured activities

This unit presents activities, lessons, and scenarios that focus on the fundamental concepts, attitudes, and skills of ordering and patterning, measuring, and graphing. Units 8 and 9 of this book describe the fundamental concepts basic to both science and mathematics along with suggestions for instruction and materials. This unit focuses on applying these fundamental concepts, attitudes, and skills at a more advanced level.

ORDERING AND PATTERNING

Underlying the concept of patterning are the concepts of comparing and ordering. Ordering is a higher level of comparing (Unit 8). Ordering involves comparing more than two things or more than two sets. It also involves placing things in a sequence from first to last. In Piaget's terms, ordering is called *seriation*.

Patterning is related to ordering in that children need a basic understanding of ordering to do patterning. *Patterning* involves making or discovering auditory, visual, and motor regularities. Patterning includes (1) simple patterns such as placing Unifix Cubes® in a sequence by color and/or number, (2) number patterns on the 100s chart, (3) patterns in nature such as spiderwebs and designs on shells, (4) quilt patterns, and (5) graphs. Movement can also be used to develop pattern and sequence through clapping, marching, standing, sitting, jumping, and the like.

There are four basic types of ordering activities. The first is to put things in sequence by size. The second is to make a one-to-one match between two sets of different numbers of things in order from the last to the most. The last is ordinal numbers. Ordinal numbers are first, second, third, and so on.

Just as children's natural development guides them to sort things, it also guides them to put things in order and to place things in patterns. As children sort them often put the items in rows or arrange them in patterns. For example, Kate picks out blocks that are all of one size, shape, and color and lines them up in a row. She then adds to the row by lining up another group of blocks of the same size, shape, and color. She picks out blue blocks and yel-

Figure 10–1   A young child draws his family in order by size.

low blocks and line them up, alternating colors. Pete is observed examining his mother's measuring cups and spoons. He lines them up from largest to smallest. Then he makes a pattern: cup-spoon-cup-spoon-cup-spoon-cup-spoon.

As speech ability increases, the child uses order words. "I want to be *first*." This is the *last* one." "Daddy Bear has the *biggest* bowl." "I'll sit in the *middle*." As he starts to draw pictures, he often draws mothers, fathers, and children and places them in a row from smallest to largest (Figure 10–1).

Exploring Science

Ordering and patterning build on the skills of comparing. If children have not had prior experience in comparing, they will not be ready to order and find patterns. When we order we compare more than two things and place things in a sequence. Children must have some understanding of seriation to do the more advanced skill of *patterning*. The following activities involve using a science emphasis of shape, animals, color, and sound while making or discovering visual, auditory, and motor regularities:

1. **Sun, moon, and stars.** Use your flannel board to help children recognize pattern in flannel figures of the moon, sun, and star shapes. Start the activity by discussing the shapes in the night sky. Then, place the moon, sun, and star shapes in a pattern on the flannel board. Make a game of placing a figure in the pattern and having the children decide which figure comes next. As the children go through the process of making a pattern with the flannel figures, they are also reinforcing the concept of shapes existing in the night sky (Figure 10–2). The natural patterns found in the night sky are an ideal observational activity for young children; when the sun goes down and the child can see the moon and stars. Observing the changes in the sky from day to night reinforces the patterns that children learn very young. Children may also be aware of the changes in the shape of the moon and want to draw those shapes.

2. **Animal patterns.** Make patterns for shapes that go together in some way such as zebra, tiger, leopard (wild animals), or pig, duck, and cow (farm animals). After introducing children to the pattern game described above, have them manipulate tagboard animal shapes in the same way.

Figure 10–2   Cindy creates a pattern

3. **Changing colors.** Create original patterns in necklaces by dyeing macaroni with food color. Children will be fascinated by the necklace and by the change in the appearance of the macaroni. Have children help prepare the macaroni: mix 1 tablespoon of alcohol, 3 drops of food coloring, and a cup of macaroni in a glass jar. Screw the lid on tightly, and take turns shaking the jar. Then, lay the macaroni out on a piece of newspaper to dry overnight. Do this for each color you select. Have children compare the macaroni before and after dyeing and describe the similarities and differences.

4. **Stringing macaroni.** To help children string macaroni, tie one end through a piece of tagboard. Then, have students practice stringing the macaroni on the string. When they are comfortable, let each invent a pattern of colors. The pattern is then repeated over and over until the necklace is completed. Have the children say the patterns they are stringing aloud, for example, "Red, blue, yellow; red, blue, yellow," until they complete the necklace. In this way, the auditory pattern is reinforced as well as the visual pattern. To extend this activity, have children guess each other's patterns, tell patterns, and try to duplicate patterns. Children will enjoy wearing their creations when they dress up for a Thanksgiving feast (Figure 10–3).

5. **Animal movement.** Children can be encouraged to learn how different animals move as they learn one-to-one correspondence and practice the counting sequence. Arrange the children in a line. Have them stamp their feet as they count, raising their arms in the air to emphasize the last number in the sequence A bird might move this way, raising its wings in the air in a threatening manner or in a courtship dance. Have children change directions without losing the beat by counting "one" as they turn. For example, "One,

Figure 10–3   Macaroni necklaces make a pattern.

two, three, four (up go the arms, turn); one, two, three, four (up go the arms, turn); one, two, three, four," and so on. Now, have the children move to different parts of the room. Arm movements can be left out, and the children can tiptoe, lumber, or sway, imitating the ways various animals move. A bear has a side-to-side motion, a monkey might swing its arms, and an elephant its trunk. This activity is also a good preparation strategy for the circle game suggested in the next paragraph (Fig. 10–4).

A Circle Game

Practice in counting, sequence, one-to-one correspondence, looking for patterns, and the process skills of predicting are involved in the following circle game, which focuses attention on the prediction skills necessary in many science activities. Rather than be the source of the "right" answer, Mrs. Jones allows the results of the game to reveal this. For maximum success, refer to the move-like-an-animal activity in the previous section of this unit.

Mrs. Jones asks six children to stand in a circle with their chairs behind them. The child designated as the "starter," Mary, wears a hat and initiates the counting. Mary counts one and each child counts off in sequence, one, two, three, and so on.

Figure 10–4 "Move your arms like a bird."

The child who says the last number in the sequence (six) sits down. The next child begins with one and again the last sits down. The children go around and around the circle, skipping over those sitting down, until only one child is left standing.

Mrs. Jones repeats the activity exactly, starting with the same child and going in the same direction using the same sequence, neither adding nor removing any children. She asks the children to predict who they think will be the last one standing. Mrs. Jones accepts all guesses equally, asking, "Who has a different idea?" until everyone who wishes has guessed. She repeats the activity so children can check their predictions. Then the activity is repeated, but this time Mrs. Jones says, "Whisper in my ear who you think will be the last child standing." The kindergarten teacher plans to repeat this game until every child can predict correctly who will be the one left standing.

The game can be played with any number of players and with any length number sequence. Rather than evaluate the children's predictions, Mrs. Jones uses the predictions as a good indication of children's development. Try this game; you will be surprised by children's unexpected predictions.

Sound Patterns

In the following scenario, Mrs. Jones introduces sound patterns to her kindergarten children.

Mrs. Jones brings out plastic bells. She selects three widely varied tones, rings them for the children, and asks, "Can you tell me what you hear?" Jane responds, "Bells, I hear bells!" The teacher asks, "Do any of the bells sound different?" "Yes," the children say. "In what way do they sound different?" Mrs. Jones asks. "Some sound like Tinkerbell, and some do not," George responds. After giving the children a chance to ring the bells, Mrs. Jones puts out a red, a yellow, and a blue construction paper square on a table. She asks, "Will someone put the bell with the highest sound on the red card?" (Figure 10–5). After Lai completes the task, Mrs. Jones asks the children to find a bell that has a low sound, and finally, one with the lowest sound. Each bell has its own color square.

Patterns can be found in the sounds that rubber bands make. Construct a rubber band banjo by placing three different widths of rubber bands around a cigar box, the open end of a coffee can, milk carton, or margarine tub. Have children experiment with the rubber band "strings" of varying length, and see if they notice differences in sound. Playing around with strings and homemade instruments helps prepare children for future concept development in sound.

Rhythmic patterns can be found in classic poems and songs such as "There Was a Little Turtle." Have children add actions as they sing the song.

There was a little turtle
He lived in a box
He swam in a puddle
He climbed on the rocks
He snapped at a mosquito
He snapped at a flea
He snapped at a minnow

Figure 10-5   "Which bell has the highest sound?"

And he snapped at me.
He caught the mosquito
He caught the flea
He caught the minnow
But he didn't catch me.

MEASUREMENT: VOLUME, WEIGHT, LENGTH, TEMPERATURE

The initial introduction to measurement focuses on the attributes of length, capacity, weight, volume, time, and temperature as measured using informal tools such as nonstandard units and estimation.

Measurement is one of the most useful math skills and is essential to science explorations. *Measurement* involves assigning a number to things so they can compared on the same attributes. Numbers can be assigned to attributes such as volume, weight, length, and temperature. For example, the child drinks *1 cup* of milk. Numbers can also be given to time measurement. However, time is not an attribute of things and so is presented separately. Standard units such as pints, quarts, liters, yards, meters, pounds, grams, and degrees tell us exactly how much (*volume*); how heavy (*weight*); how long, wide, or deep (*length*); and how hot or cold (*temperature*). A number is put with a standard unit to let a comparison be made. Two quarts contain more than 1 quart, 2 pounds weigh less than 3 pounds, 1 meter is shorter than 4 meters, and 30° is colder than 80°.

Stages of Development

The concept of measurement develops through five stages as outlined in Figure 10-6. The first stage is a play stage. The child imitates older children and adults. She plays at measuring with rulers, measuring cups, measuring spoons, and scales as she sees others do. She pours sand, water, rice, beans, and peas from one container to another as she explores the properties of volume. She lifts and moves things as she learns about weight. She notes that those who are bigger than she can do many more activities and has her first concept of length (height). She finds that her short arms cannot always reach what she wants them to reach (length). She finds that she has a preference for cold or hot food and cold or hot bathwater. She begins to learn about temperature. This first stage begins at birth and continues through the sensorimotor period into the preoperational period.

The second stage in the development of the concept of measurement is the one of making comparisons (Unit 8). This is well under way by the preoperational stage. The child is always comparing: bigger-smaller, heavier-lighter, longer-shorter, and hotter-colder.

The third stage, which comes at the end of the preoperational period and at the beginning of concrete operations, is one in which the child learns to use what are called *arbitrary units;* that is, anything

Piagetian Stage	Age	Measurement Stage
Sensorimotor and Preoperational	0–7	1. Plays and imitates 2. Makes comparisons
Transitional: Preoperational to Concrete Operations	5–7	3. Uses arbitrary units
Concrete Operations	6+	4. Sees need for standard units 5. Uses standard units

Figure 10–6 Stages in the development of the concept of measurement

the child has can be used as a unit of measure. She will try to find out how many coffee cups of sand will fill a quart milk carton. The volume of the coffee cup is the arbitrary unit. She will find out how many toothpicks long her foot is. The length of the toothpick is the arbitrary unit. As she goes through the stage of using arbitrary units, she learns concepts she will need to understand standard units (Figure 10-7).

When the child enters the period of concrete operations, she can begin to see the need for standard units. She can see that to communicate with someone else in a way the other person will understand, she must use the same units the other person uses. For example, the child says that her paper is nine thumbs wide. Another person cannot find another piece of the same width unless the child and the thumb are there to measure it. But, if she says her paper is 8½ inches wide, another person will know exactly the width of the paper. In this case, the thumb is an arbitrary unit, and the inch is a *standard unit*. The same is true for other units. Standard measuring cups and spoons must be used when cooking in order for the recipe to turn out correctly. If any coffee cup or teacup and any spoon are used when following a recipe, the measurement will be arbitrary and inexact, and the chances of a successful outcome will be poor. The same can be said of building a house. If nonstandard measuring tools are used, the house will not come out as it appears in the plans, and one carpenter will not be communicating clearly with another.

The last stage in the development of the concept of measurement begins in the concrete opera-

tions period. In this last stage, the child begins to use and understand the standard units of measurement such as inches, meters, pints, liters, grams, and degrees.

Exploring Science

Measurement is basically a spatial activity that must include the manipulation of objects to be understood. If children are not actively involved with materials as they measure, they simply will not understand measurement. Water and sand are highly sensory science resources for young children. Both substances elicit a variety of responses to their physical properties, and they can be used in measurement activities. Keep in mind that for sand and water to be effective as learning tools, long periods of "messing around" with the substances should be provided. For further information on the

Figure 10–7 "My hand is 1 block long!"

Figure 10–8 "Can a tube be used to fill a container?"

logistics of handling water and sand and a discussion of basic equipment needs, see Unit 18 of this book. The following activities and lessons use sand and water as a means of introducing measurement.

1. **Fill it up.** Put out containers and funnels of different sizes and shapes, and invite children to pour liquid from one to the other. Aspects of pouring can be investigated. Ask, "Is it easier to pour from a wide- or narrow-mouthed container?," "Do you see anything that could help you pour liquid into a container?," and "Does the funnel take longer? Why?" Add plastic tubing to the water center. Ask, "Can a tube be used to fill up a container?" and "Which takes longer?" (Figure 10–8).

2. **Squeeze and blow.** Plastic squeeze bottles or turkey basters will encourage children to find another way to fill the containers. After the children have manipulated the baster and observed air bubbling out of it, set up the water table for a race. You will need table tennis balls, tape, and basters. The object is to move the ball across the water by squeezing the turkey baster. Children should practice squeezing the baster and moving the balls across the water. Place a piece of tape down the center of the table lengthwise, and begin. Use a piece of string to measure how far the ball is moved. Compare the distances with the length of string. Ask, "How many squeezes does it take to cover the distance?"

3. **A cup is a cup.** Volume refers to how much space a solid, liquid, or gas takes up or occupies. For example, when a 1-cup measure is full of water, the volume of water is 1 cup. Volume can be compared by having children fill small boxes or jars with sand or beans. Use sand in similar containers, and compare the way the sand feels. Compare the heft of a full container with an empty container. Use a balance scale to dramatize the difference. If you do not have a commercial balance, provide a homemade balance and hanging cups. Directions for constructing balances can be found in Unit 38. Children will begin to weigh different levels of sand in the cups. Statements such as, "I wonder if sand weighs more if I fill the container even higher?" can be overheard. Let children check predictions and discuss what they have found (Figure 10–9).

Figure 10–9 Children explore volume by weighing sand.

4. Sink or float. Comparisons between big-little and heavy-light are made when children discover that objects of different sizes sink and float. Make a chart to record observations. After discussing what the terms *sink* and *float* mean, give the children a variety of floating and nonfloating objects to manipulate. Ask, "What do you think will float? Big corks? Small marbles?" As children sort objects by size and shape and test whether they sink or float, they are discovering science concepts and learning about measurement (Figure 10–10).

Ms. Moore has her class predict, "Will it sink or float?" Her materials include a leaf, nail, balloon, cork, wooden spoon, and metal spoon. She makes a chart with columns labeled *sink* and *float* and has the children place the leaf and so on, where they think it will go.

Cindy excitedly floats the leaf. "It floats, it floats!" she says. Because Cindy correctly predicts that the leaf would float, the leaf stays in the *float* column on the chart. Diana predicts that the wooden spoon will sink. "Oh, it's not floating. The wooden spoon is sinking." Diana moves the wooden spoon from the *float* column to the *sink* column on

the chart. In this way, children can predict and compare objects as they measure weight and buoyancy (Figure 10–11).

5. Little snakes. Many children in preschool and kindergarten are not yet conserving length. For example, they still think that a stick may vary in length if it is changed in some way. Therefore, use care in assessing your students' developmental stages. The child must be able to conserve for measurement activities to make sense. In the following scenario, a teacher of young children assesses the conservation of length while relating length to animals:

Mrs. Raymond reinforces the shape/space concept by giving each child in her class two pipe cleaners. She instructs them to place the pipe cleaners side by side and

	Sink	Float
leaf		✓
nail		
balloon		
cork		
wooden spoon		
metal spoon		

Figure 10–11 "Do you think the leaf will sink or float?"

Figure 10–10 "Will it sink or float?"

asks, "Which pipe cleaner is longer?" Then she tells the children to bend one of the pipe cleaners and asks, "Which is longer now?" She repeats this several times, having the children create different shapes.

Then the children make the pipe cleaners into little snakes by gluing small construction paper heads on one end of each pipe cleaner. Mrs. Raymond shows the children pictures of a snake that is coiled and one that is moving on the ground (try to find pictures of the same kind of snake). She asks, "Is the coiled snake shorter?" "Yes," the children say. "Let's see if we can make our pipe cleaners into coiled snakes," instructs Mrs. Raymond. "Oh," says Jimmie, "This really looks like a coiled snake."

The teacher asks the students to lay out the other pipe cleaners to resemble a moving snake and asks, "Which is longer?" There are a variety of responses as the children manipulate the pipe cleaner snakes to help them understand that the coiled and moving snakes are the same lengths. Then, have the children glue a small black construction paper end on the end of the pipe cleaners. Let them practice coiling and coiling the "snakes" and discuss how snakes move. Ask, "Can you tell how long a snake is when it is coiled up?" and "Was your coiled-up snake longer than you thought?" (Figure 10–12).

6. **A big and little hunt.** Height, size, and length can be compared in many ways. For example, Mrs. Jones takes her children on a big and little hunt.

After taking the children outside, Mrs. Jones has them sit in a circle and discuss the biggest and smallest things that they can see. Then she asks them, "Of all the things we have talked about, which is the smallest?" George and Mary are certain that the leaves are the smallest, but Sam and Lai do not agree. "The blades of grass are smaller,"

Figure 10–12   *"Which snake is longer?"*

Sam observes. "Are they?" Mrs. Jones asks. "How can we tell which is smaller?" "Let's put them beside each other," Mary suggests. The children compare the length of each item and discuss which is longer and wider.

7. **Body part measures.** Children enjoy measuring with body parts, such as a hand or foot length. Ask, "How many feet is it to the door?," and let the children count the number of foot lengths they must take. Or ask, "How many hands high are you?"

Give children pieces of string and have them measure head sizes. Then take the string, and measure other parts of their bodies. Compare their findings.

8. **How long will it take to sink?** Let children play for 5 minutes with dishpans of water, a kitchen scale, a bucket of water, and an assortment of objects. Then, give the chil-

dren plastic tubes to explore and measure. As one child drops a marble into a plastic tube filled with water, count in measured beats the amount of time that the marble takes to sink (Figure 10–13). Ask, "Will it sink faster in cold water or hot water?"

9. **Hot or not.** The following activities and questions correlate with science and, in many cases, integrate into the curriculum of a preschool or kindergarten.

- Take an outdoor walk to see what influences the temperature. "Is it warmer or colder outside?"
- Visit a greenhouse. Predict what the temperature will be inside the greenhouse; discuss the reasons for these predictions.
- Notice differences in temperature in different areas of the supermarket. Ask, "Are some areas colder?" and "Which is the warmest area of the supermarket?"
- Melt crayons for dripping on bottles and painting pictures. Notice the effect of heat on the crayons. Ask, "Have you ever felt like a melted crayon?" and "Act out the changes in a melting crayon with your bodies."

Figure 10–13 "How long will it take for a marble to sink?"

- Put some finger paints in the refrigerator. Have children compare how the refrigerated paints and room-temperature paints feel on their hands.
- Ask, "What happens to whipped cream as we finger paint with it?" Have children observe the whipped cream as it cools off and melts.
- Ask, "What happens to an ice cream cone as you eat it?" and "Why do you think this happens?"

MEASUREMENT: TIME

There are two sides to the concept of time. There is sequence and there is duration. *Sequence* of time has to do with the order of events. It is related to the ideas about ordering presented in this unit. While the child learns to sequence things in patterns, he also learns to sequence events. He learns small, middle-sized, and large beads go in order for a pattern sequence. He gets up, washes his face, brushes his teeth, dresses, and eats breakfast for a time sequence. *Duration* of time has to do with how long an event takes (seconds, minutes, hours, days, a short time, a long time).

Kinds of Time

There are three kinds of time a child has to learn. Time is a hard measure to learn. The child cannot see it and feel it as she can weight, volume, length, and temperature. There are fewer clues to help the child. The young child relates time to three things: personal experience, social activity, and culture.

In her *personal experience*, the child has her own past, present, and future. The past is often referred to as "When I was a baby." "Last night" may mean any time before right now. The future may be "After my night nap" or "When I am big." The young child has difficulty with the idea that there was a time when mother and dad were little and she was not yet born.

Time in terms of *social activity* is a little easier to learn and makes more sense to the young child. The young child tends to be a slave to order and routine. A change of schedule can be very upsetting. This is because time for her is a sequence of predictable events. She can count on her morning activities being the same each day when she wakes up. Once she gets to school, she learns that there is order there too: first she takes off her coat and hangs it up, next she is greeted by her teacher, then she goes to the big playroom to play, and so on through the day.

A third kind of time is *cultural time*. It is the time that is fixed by clocks and calendars. Everyone learns this kind of time. It is a kind of time that the child probably does not really understand until she is in the concrete operations period. She can, however, learn the language (seconds, minutes, days, months, etc.) and the names of the timekeepers (clock, watch, calendar). She can also learn to recognize a timekeeper when she sees one.

Language of Time

To learn time is as dependent on language as any part of math and Science. Time and sequence words are listed in Unit 8.

The teacher should observe the child's use of time language. She should note if he makes an attempt to place himself and events in time. Does he remember the sequence of activities at school and at home? Is he able to wait for one thing to finish before going on to the next? Is he able to order things (Unit 8) in a sequence?

The following is an examples of the kind of interview task that is included in appendix A:

SAMPLE ASSESSMENT TASK

Preoperational Ages 4–5

Time, Labeling and Sequence: Unit 10

METHOD: Interview.

SKILL: Shown pictures of daily events, the child can use time words to describe the action in each picture and place the pictures in a logical time sequence.

MATERIALS: Pictures of daily activities such as meals, nap, bath, playtime, bedtime.

PROCEDURE: Show the child each picture. Say, TELL ME ABOUT THIS PICTURE. WHAT'S HAPPENING? After the child has described each picture, place all the pictures in front of him, and tell the child, PICK OUT (SHOW ME) THE PICTURE OF WHAT HAPPENS FIRST EACH DAY. After a picture is selected, ask WHAT HAPPENS NEXT? Continue until all the pictures are lined up.

EVALUATION: When describing the pictures, note whether the child uses time words such as breakfast time, lunchtime, playtime, morning, night, etc. Note whether a logical sequence is used in placing the pictures in order.

INSTRUCTIONAL RESOURCE(S):

Charlesworth, R., and Lind, K. 1995. *Math and Science for Young Children* (2nd ed.). Albany, N.Y.: Delmar.

Time: A Daily Schedule

The adult serves as a model for time related behavior. The teacher checks the clock and the calendar for times and dates. The teacher uses the time words in the "Language of Time" section. She makes statements and asks questions (Figure 10–14):

- "*Good morning*, Tom."
- "*Goodnight*, Mary. See you *tomorrow*."
- "What did you do over the *weekend*?"
- "Who will be our guest for lunch *tomorrow*?"
- "*Next week* on *Tuesday* we will go to the park for a picnic."
- "Let me check the *time*. No wonder you are hungry. It's almost *noon*."
- "You are the *first* one here *today*."

Children will observe and imitate what the teacher says and does before they really understand the ideas completely.

An excellent tool for informal classroom time instruction is a daily picture/word schedule placed in a prominent place. Figure 10–15 is an example of such a schedule. Children frequently ask, "When do we _____?," "What happens after this?," and so on. Teachers can take them to the pictorial schedule and help them find the answer for themselves. "What are

Figure 10–14 After breakfast it is time to leave for work and for school.

we doing now?" "Find (activity) on the schedule." "What comes next?" Eventually, children will just have to be reminded to "Look at the schedule," and they will answer their questions by themselves.

The young child can begin to learn that time has duration and that time is related to sequences of events. The child first relates time to his personal experience and to his daily sequence of activities. It is not until the child enters the concrete operations period that he can use units of time in the ways that adults use them.

The young child learns his concept of time through naturalistic and informal experiences for the most part. When he is around the age of 4 1/2 or 5, he can do structured activities also.

GRAPHS

This type of activity can begin before kindergarten as students collect sets of data from their real life experiences and depict the results of their data collection in simple graphs. Consider the following example as it takes place in Ms. Moore's classroom:

Ms. Moore hears George and Sam talking in loud voices. She goes near them and hears the following discussion.

George: "More kids like red than blue."

Sam: "No! No! More like blue!"

George: "You are all wrong."

Sam: "I am not. You are wrong."

Ms. Moore goes over to the boys and asks, "What's the trouble, boys?" George replies, "We have to get paint to paint the house Mr. Brown helped us build. I say it should be red. Sam says it should be blue."

Sam insists, "More kids like blue than red."

Ms. Moore suggests, "Maybe there is some way we can find out." She takes the boys to a table.

"On this table let's put a piece of blue paper and a piece of red paper and a bowl of red and blue cube blocks."

George's eyes light up, "I see, and then each child can vote, right?"

DAILY SCHEDULE

8:00 A.M.–8:30 A.M.
Breakfast

8:30 A.M.–9:00 A.M.
Playtime
Outdoors or in Gym

9:00 A.M.–9:15 A.M.
Group Meeting

9:15 A.M.–10:30 A.M.
Center Activities

10:30 A.M.–10:45 A.M.
Snack

10:45 A.M.–11:15 A.M.
Playtime
Outdoors or in Gym

Figure 10–15   A picture/word daily schedule supports the development of the concept of time sequence (continued on next page).

11:15–11:45 A.M.
Story and Language
Development Group Activities

11:45–12:00 A.M.
Wash Hands, Go to
Lunch

12:00–12:30
Lunch

12:30–1:00 P.M.
Playtime
Outdoors or in Gym

1:00–2:00 P.M.
Rest

2:00–3:00 P.M.
Art, Music, Writing,
Reading

3:00–3:30 P.M.
Clean-Up
Prepare to Leave or
Go to Extended Day

Sam and George go around the room. They explain the problem to each child. Each child comes over to the table. They each choose one block of the color they like better and stack it on the paper of the same color. When they finish, there are two stacks of blocks as shown in Figure 10–16.

Ms. Moore asks the boys what the vote shows. Sam says, "The red stack is higher. More children like the idea of painting the house red." "Good," answers Ms. Moore, "would you like me to write that down for you?" Sam and George chorus, "Yes!"

"I have an idea," says George, "Let's make a picture of this for the bulletin board so everyone will know. Will you help us, Ms. Moore?"

Ms. Moore shows them how to cut out squares of red and blue paper to match each of the blocks used. The boys write "red" and "blue" on a piece of white paper and then paste the red squares next to the word "red" and the blue squares next to the word "blue." Ms. Moore shows them how to write the title: "Choose the Color for the Playhouse." Then they glue the description of the results at the bottom. The results can be seen in Figure 10–17.

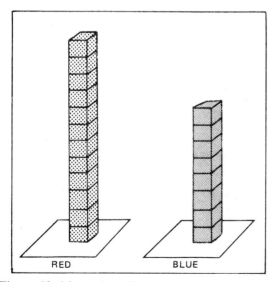

Figure 10–16   A three-dimensional graph that compares children's preferences for red or blue.

In the preceding example, the teacher helped the children solve their problem by making two kinds of graphs. *Graphs* are used to show visually two or more comparisons in a clear way. When a child makes a graph, he uses basic skills of classifying, comparing, counting, and measuring to make a picture of some information. A child who has learned the basics of science and math will find this to be an interesting and challenging activity.

Stages of Development for Making and Understanding Graphs

The types of graphs that young children can construct progress through five stages of development. The first three stages are described in this unit. The fourth and fifth are included in Unit 11. In Stage 1, the child uses real objects to make her graph. Sam and George used inchcube blocks. At this stage only two things are compared. The main basis for comparison is one-to-one correspondence (one block for each child) (Figure 10-16).

In the second stage, more than two items are compared. In addition, a more permanent record is made—such as when Sam and George in an earlier example glued squares of paper on a piece of paper for the bulletin board. An example of this type of graph is shown in Figure 10-18. The teacher has lined off 12 columns on poster board (or large construction paper). Each column stands for one month of the year. Each child is given a paper circle. Crayons, water markers, glue, and yarn scraps are available so each child can draw her own head and place it on the month for her birthday. When each child has put her "head" on the graph, the children can compare the months to see which month has the most birthdays.

In the third stage, the children progress through the use of more pictures to block charts. They no longer need to use real objects but can start right off with cut out squares of paper. Figure 10–19 shows this type of graph. In this stage, the children work more independently.

DISCUSSION OF A GRAPH

As the children talk about their graphs and dictate descriptions for them, they use concept words. They use words such as

less than	the same as
more than	none
fewer than	all
longer, longest	some
shorter, shortest	a lot of
the most	higher
the least	taller

When children make graphs, they use the basic process skills of observing, classifying, comparing, and measuring visually communicated information. In fact, the act of making a graph is in itself the process of communication. A graph is a way of displaying information so that predictions, inferences, and conclusions can be made.

When using graphs, it is essential that the meaning of the completed graph is clear to the children. With questions and discussion, it is possible for a graph to answer a question, solve a problem, or show data so that something can be understood. In the following scenario, Mrs. Jones uses common kitchen sponges to provide children with an opportunity to manipulate and construct two types of graphs:

Mrs. Jones distributes sponges of different colors to her kindergarten class. After allowing children time to examine the sponges, she suggests that they stack the sponges by color. As the sponges are stacked, a bar graph is naturally created. Mrs. Jones lines up each stack of sponges and asks, "Which color sponge do we have the most of?" Lai says, "The blue stack is the tallest. There are more blue sponges." "Good," answers Mrs. Jones. "Can anyone tell me which stack of sponges is the smallest?" "The yellow ones," says Mary. The

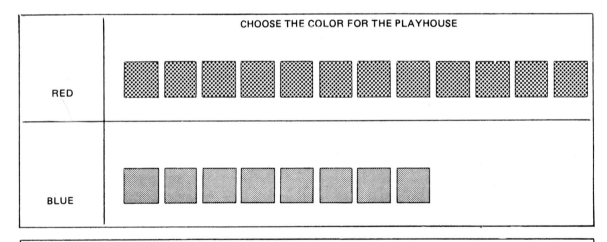

The red row is longer than the blue row. More children like red than like blue. We will buy red paint for our playhouse. 12 like red. 8 like blue.

by George and Sam

Figure 10–17 The color preference graph is copied using squares of red and blue paper, and the children dictate their interpretation.

Jan.	Feb.	March	April	May	June	July	August	Sept.	Oct.	Nov.	Dec.

April has the most birthdays. There are four.
March and October have no birthdays.
Three months have three.
One month has two.
Five months have one.

Figure 10–18   "When is your birthday?"

children count the number of sponges in each stack and duplicate the three-dimensional sponge graph by making a graph of colored oak tag sponges. The children place pink, blue, yellow, and green oak tag sponges that Mrs. Jones has prepared in columns of color on a tagboard background. In this way, children learn in a concrete way the one-to-one correspondence that a bar graph represents (Figure 10–20).

Mrs. Jones follows up the graphing activity with other sponge activities. Sam says, "Sponges in my house are usually wet." "Yes," chorus the children. George says, "Our sponges feel heavier, too." The children's comments provide an opportunity to submerge a sponge in water and weigh it. The class weighs the wet and dry sponges, and an experience chart of observations is recorded. The next day, Sam brings in a sponge with bird seed on it. He says, "I am going to keep it damp and see what happens."

Calendar Graph

Calendars are another way to reinforce graphing, the passage of time, and one-to-one correspondence. Mrs. Carter laminates small birthday cakes, and then writes each child's name and birth date on the paper cake with a permanent marker. At the beginning of the year, she shows the children the chart and points out which cake belongs to them. At the beginning of each month, the children with birthdays move their cakes to the calendar. Various animals, trees, and birds can be substituted for cakes (Figure 10–21).

Pets

Graphs can be used to compare sets and give early literacy experiences. Make a list of the pets that your children have. Divide a bristol board into columns to represent every pet named. Cover the board with clear laminate film. Make labels with pet categories such as dogs, cats, snakes, fish,

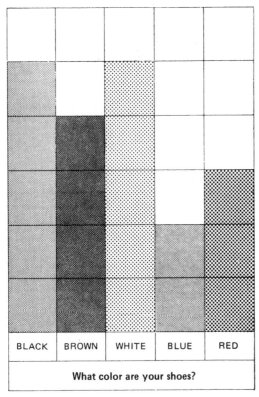

BLACK | BROWN | WHITE | BLUE | RED

What color are your shoes?

Figure 10–19 A block graph made with paper squares.

Figure 10–20 Making a sponge graph.

lizards, turtles, and so on. Glue the labels to clothespins. Then, place a labeled clothespin at the top of each column. Have the children write their names in the appropriate column (Figure 10–22).

Graphing Attractions

Simple magnets can be fun to explore. A real object graph can be made with ruled bristol board. Rule the board into columns to equal the number of magnets. Trace the shape of a magnet at the top of each column. Attach a drapery hook below each picture and proceed like Mrs. Carter.

After letting the children explore metal objects such as paper clips, Mrs. Carter places a pile of paper clips on the table along with different

types of magnets. She invites Cindy to choose a magnet and see how many paper clips it will attract. Cindy selects a horseshoe-shaped magnet and hangs paper clips from the end, one at a time, until the magnet no longer attracts any clips. "Good," says Mrs. Carter. "Now, make a chain of the paper clips that your magnet attracts." After Cindy makes the paper clip chain, Mrs. Carter

MARCH

SUNDAY	MONDAY	TUESDAY	WEDNESDAY	THURSDAY	FRIDAY	SATURDAY
			1	2	3 JAY	4
5	6	7 AMY	8	9	10	11
12	13	14	15	16	17	18
19	20	21	22 MIKE	23	24	25
26	27	28	29	30	31	

Figure 10–21 Calendars reinforce graphing, time, and one-to-one correspondence.

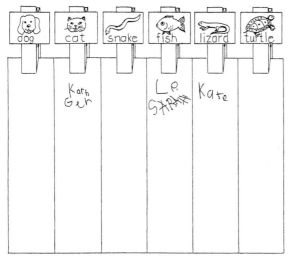

Figure 10–22   Graphing our pets.

directs her to hang it on the drapery hook under the drawing of the horseshoe-shaped magnet.

"I bet the magnet that looks like a bar will attract more paper clips," predicts Richard. He selects the rod magnet and begins to attract as many paper clips as he can. Then, he makes a chain and hangs it on the drapery hook under the rod magnet. The process is repeated until each child in the group has worked with a magnet. Mrs. Carter makes no attempt to teach the higher level concepts involved in magnetic force; rather, her purpose is to increase the children's awareness and give them some idea of what magnets do.

In this scenario, children observe that mag-nets can be different shapes and sizes (horseshoe, rod, disk, the letter U, ring, and so on) and attract a different amount of paper clips. They also have a visual graphic reminder of what they have accomplished. When snack time arrives, Mrs. Carter prepares a plate of metallic-paper-wrapped chocolate candy balls and a jar of peanut butter. She gives each child two large pretzel sticks. The children dip the pretzels into the peanut butter and then "attract" the metallic candy, imitating the way that the magnets attracted the paper clips.

SUMMARY

When more than two things are ordered and placed in sequence, the process is called seriation. If children understand seriation, they will be able to do the more advanced skills of patterning. Patterning involves repeating auditory, visual, or physical motor sequences.

Children begin to understand measurement by actively manipulating measurement materials. Water and sand are highly sensory and are effective resources for young children to develop concepts of volume, temperature, length, and weight. Time measurement is related to sequencing events. The use of measurement units will formalize and develop further when children enter the concrete operations period.

Graph making gives children an opportunity to classify, compare, count, measure, and visually communicate information. A graph is a way of displaying information so that predictions, inferences, and conclusions can be made.

FURTHER READING AND RESOURCES

Baratta-Lorton, M. (1976). *Mathematics their way.* Menlo Park, CA: Addison-Wesley.

Burk, D., Snider, A., & Symonds, P. (1988). *Box it or bag it mathematics.* Salem, OR: The Math Learning Center.

Council for Elementary Science International Sourcebook IV. (1986). *Science experiences for preschoolers.* Columbus, OH: SMEAC Information Reference Center.

Forman, G. E., & Kuschner, D. (1983). *Child's*

FURTHER READING AND RESOURCES

construction of knowledge. Washington, DC: National Association for the Education of Young Children.

Fowlkes, M. A. (1985). Funnels and tunnels. *Science and Children, 22*(6), 28–29.

Hill, D. M. (1977). *Mud, sand and water.* Washington, DC: National Association for the Education of Young Children.

James, J. C., & Granovetter, R. F. (1987). *Water works.* Lewisville, NC: Kaplan Press.

McIntyre, M. (1984). *Early childhood and science.*

Washington, DC: National Science Teachers Association.

Phillips, D. G. (1982). Measurement or mimicry? *Science and Children, 20*(3), 32–34.

Rockwell, R. E., Sherwood, E. A., & Williams, R. A. (1986). *Hug a tree.* Mt. Rainier, MD: Gryphon House, Inc.

Shaw, E. L. (1987). Students and sponges—Soaking up science. *Science and Children. 25*(1), 21.

Warren, J. 1984. *Science time.* Palo Alto, CA: Monday Morning Books.

SUGGESTED ACTIVITIES

1. What kind of problems do you anticipate in teaching ordering and patterning, measurement, and graphing to young children? Discuss problems you have encountered, and relate how they were overcome. How could the problem have been handled in a different way? What were the children like? Videotape or tape record yourself in a teaching situation; this can help to clearly illustrate a problem.

2. To measure is to match things. Observe and record every comparison that one child makes in a day. Record all forms of measuring that you observe this child performing. Teachers will probably tell you that children are not very interested in measuring for its own sake, so find the measuring in the child's everyday school life.

3. Reflect on measurement in your own life. What did you measure this morning? In groups, brainstorm all of the measuring that you did on your way to class. Predict the types of measuring that you will do tonight. Then reflect on ordering, patterning, and graphing in the same way.

4. Design a lesson that emphasizes one of the concepts and skills discussed in this chapter. Teach the lesson to a class, and note the reactions of the children to your teaching. Discuss these reactions in class. "Did you teach what you intended to teach?," "How do you know your lesson was effective?," and "If not, why not, and how could the lesson be improved?"

REVIEW

1. What is seriation? Why must children possess this skill before they are able to pattern objects?

2. Which activities might be used to evaluate a child's ability to compare and order?

3. How will you teach measurement to young children?

4. Explain how graphing assists in learning science concepts.

UNIT 11 Integrating the Curriculum Through Dramatic Play and Thematic Units

OBJECTIVES

After studying this unit, the student should be able to
- Describe how children apply and extend concepts through dramatic play
- Describe how children apply and extend concepts through thematic units
- Encourage dramatic role playing that promotes concept acquisition
- Recognize how dramatic role playing and thematic units promote interdisciplinary instruction and learning
- Use dramatic play and thematic units as settings for science investigations, mathematical problem solving, social learning, and language learning.

As discussed in Unit 1, the standards and guidelines of the major early childhood, mathematics, and science professional organizations all emphasize communications, connections, and reasoning. Curriculum that meets these standards can be implemented through the use of thematic units that integrate mathematics, science, social studies, language arts, art, music, and movement.

The purpose of this unit is to demonstrate how dramatic play and thematic units can enrich children's acquisition of concepts and knowledge, not only in science and mathematics, but also in the other content areas. Furthermore, these areas offer rich settings for social learning, science investigations, and mathematical problem solving. In Unit 1 the commonalities between math and science were described. and in Unit 5 the relationship of science to the development of lit-

eracy was described. Unit 7 provided a basic unit plan and examples of science units that incorporate math, social studies, language arts, fine arts, motor development, and dramatic play. Units 13 through 17 include integrated units and activities for the primary level. This unit emphasizes the natural play of young children as the basis for developing thematic units that highlight the potentials for an interdisciplinary curriculum for young children.

Concepts and skills are only valuable to children if they can be used in everyday life. Young children spend most of their waking hours involved in play. Play can be used as a vehicle for the application of concepts. Young children like to feel big and do "big person" things. They like to pretend they are grown up and want to do as many grown-up things as they can. Role playing can be used as

131

a means for children to apply what they know as they take on a multitude of grown-up roles.

Dramatic play is an essential part of thematic units. For example, using food as the theme for a unit could afford not only opportunities for applying fundamental concepts and carrying out science investigations and mathematics problem solving, but also could provide opportunities for children to try out adult roles and do adult activities. Children can grow food and shop for groceries; plan and prepare meals, snacks, and parties; serve food; and enjoy sharing and eating the results of their efforts. Opportunities can be offered that provide experiences for social education as children learn more about adult tasks, have experiences in the community, and learn about their own and other cultures. Teachers can use these experiences to assess and evaluate through observation.

DRAMATIC ROLE PLAYING

When children are engaged in dramatic role playing, they practice what it is like to be an adult. They begin with simple imitation of what they have observed. Their first roles reflect what they have seen at home. They bathe, feed, and rock babies. They cook meals, set the table, and eat. One of their first outside experiences is to go shopping. This experience is soon reflected in dramatic play. They begin by carrying things in bags, purses, and other large containers. At first, they carry around anything that they can stuff in their containers. Gradually, they move into using more realistic props such as play money and empty food containers. Next, they might build a store with big blocks and planks. Eventually, they learn to play cooperatively with other children. One child might be the mother, another the father, another the child, and another the store clerk. As the children move toward this stage, teachers can provide more props and background experiences that will expand the raw material children have for

Figure 11–1   Going shopping is a popular dramatic play activity.

developing their role playing. Problem-solving skills are refined as children figure out who will take which role, provide a location for the store and home, and develop the rules for the activity (Figure 11–1).

Children can learn about adult roles through field trips to businesses such as restaurants, banks, the post office, and stores both in the local neighborhood and in the extended community. Museums, construction sites, hospitals, fire stations, and other places offer experiences that can enrich children's knowledge of adult roles. Books, tapes, films, and classroom visitors can also provide valuable experiences for children. Following such experiences, props can be provided to support children's dramatic role playing. Each type of business or service center can be set up in the classroom with appropriate props.

Some examples of dramatic play centers and props are

- A toy store could be set up by having the children bring old toys from home that they could pretend to buy and sell.
- A grocery store can also be set up using items that might otherwise be discarded, such as empty food containers that the children could bring from home. The children could make food from playdough, clay, or papier-mâché. Plastic food replicas can be purchased.
- A clothing store can be organized into children's, ladies', and men's departments; children can bring discarded clothing and shoes from home.
- A jewelry store can be stocked with old and pretend jewelry (such as macaroni necklaces and cardboard watches).
- Services centers, such as the post office, fire station, police station, automobile repair shop, hospital, beauty shop, and the like can be stocked with appropriate props.
- Transportation vehicles such as space vehicles, automobiles, trucks, and buses can be built with large blocks, with lined-up chairs, and with commercially made or teacher-made steering wheels and other controls.
- Health and medical service centers can be organized. Provide props for medical play. Tie these in with discussions of good nutrition and other health practices. The children can "pay the bill" for the services.
- Space science vehicles can be created. Provide props for space travel (e.g., a big refrigerator carton that can be made into a spaceship, paper bag space helmets, and so on). Provide materials for making mission control and for designing other planetary settings.
- Water environments can be created. Provide toy boats, people, rocks for islands, and the like. Discuss floating and sinking. Outdoors, use water for firefighter play and for watering the garden. Have a container (bucket or large dishpan) that can be a fishing hole, and have waterproof fish with a safety pin or other metal object attached so they can be caught with a magnet fish bait. Investigate why the magnet/metal combination makes a good combination for pretend fishing. Count how many fish each child catches.
- Simple machines can be set up and materials for designing machines provided. Vehicles, a packing box elevator, a milk carton elevator on a pulley, a plank on rollers, and so on, make interesting dramatic play props, and their construction and functioning provide challenging problems for investigation.

Concepts are applied in a multitude of play activities such as those described above. The following are some examples:

- One-to-one correspondence can be practiced by exchanging play money for goods or services.
- Sets and classifying are involved in organizing each dramatic play center in an orderly manner; for example, placing all the items in the drugstore in the proper place.
- Counting can be applied to figuring out how many items have been purchased and how much money must be exchanged.
- Comparing and measuring can be used to decide if clothing fits, to determine the weight of fruits and vegetables purchased, to check a sick person's temperature, and to decide on which size box of cereal or carton of milk to purchase.
- Spatial relations and volume concepts are applied as items purchased are placed in bags, boxes, and/or baskets; and as children discover how many passengers will fit in the space shuttle or can ride on the bus.
- Number symbols can be found throughout dramatic play props; for example, on price tags, play money, telephones, cash registers,

scales, measuring cups and spoons, thermometers, rulers, and calculators.

Money is a basic part of most of these activities. For advanced preprimary and primary children who have a beginning understanding of earning and spending money, the computer program *Duck's Playground* can offer entertainment and practice in working and earning money. This program is available from Sierra On-Line, Inc., Coarsegold, California.

Pocket calculators are excellent props for dramatic play. Children can pretend to add up their expenses, costs, and earnings. As they explore calculators, they will learn how to use them for basic mathematical operations.

A THEMATIC UNIT EXAMPLE: FOOD

A thematic unit that focuses on food can involve many science, mathematics, social studies, language arts, art, music, and movement experiences. As scientists, children observe the growth of food, the physical changes that take place when food is prepared, and the effects of food on growth of humans and animals. They also compare the tastes of different foods and categorize them into those they like and those they dislike and into sweet and sour; liquid and solid; "junk" and healthful; and food such as meat/dairy products, cereals/ breads, and fruits/vegetables Refer to food experiences in Unit 17 (Figure 11–2).

As mathematicians, children pour, measure, count, cut wholes into parts, and divide full pans or full bowls into equal servings. They count the strokes when mixing a cake, make sure the oven is on the correct temperature setting, and set the clock for the required baking time. At the store, they exchange money for food and fruits and weigh vegetables. They count the days until their beans sprout or the fruit ripens.

Through food experiences, children learn much about society and culture. They can make foods from different cultures. They learn where food is grown, how it is marketed, and how it must

be purchased with money at the grocery store. They cooperate with each other and take turns when preparing food. Then they share what they make with others.

Children can sing about food and draw their food-related experiences. They can move like an eggbeater, like a stalk of wheat blowing in the wind, or like a farmer planting seeds. The following are some examples of dramatic play, mathematics, and science food experiences:

Food and Dramatic Play

In the home living center at school, children purchase, cook, serve, and eat food as part of their role playing. Children may want to set up a grocery store. The wide variety of items available in a grocery store allows students to observe many different forms in which matter exists. Forms of matter can be found in the shape of a cherry or in the changing shape of fruit juice as it is poured from a bottle into a cup. Exploring the form and function of matter helps children describe matter and compare it in its different states.

Food and Basic Concepts and Skills

Cooking activities are a rich source of science experiences. Following a recipe provides a sequenc-

Figure 11–2 Cooking affords an opportunity for measuring, mixing, and observing physical changes.

ing activity. Each ingredient must be measured exactly using a standard measuring tool. The correct number of cups, tablespoons, eggs, and so on must be counted out. Baked foods must be cooked at the correct temperature for the prescribed amount of time. Some foods are heated, while others are placed in the refrigerator or freezer. When the food is ready to eat, it must be divided into equal portions so that each person gets a fair share. A simple pictograph recipe can help children to be independent as they assemble ingredients (see Figure 11–3).

Children who live in the country or who have a garden have additional opportunities to apply basic concepts to real life experiences. They can count the number of days from planting until the food is ready to be picked. They can measure the growth of the plants at regular intervals. The number of cucumbers harvested and the weight of the

potatoes can be measured. If the child lives where livestock can be kept, the daily number of eggs gathered can be counted, the young calf can be weighed each week, and the amount of money collected for products sold can be counted.

Setting the table at the home living center or for a real meal is an opportunity for applying math skills. The number of people to be seated and served is calculated and matched with the amount of tableware and the number of chairs, napkins, and placemats needed. Putting utensils and dishes away is an experience in sorting things into sets. Pictographs can be used to provide clues about where each type of item should be placed.

Food and Science Concepts

Each of the activities described under "Food and Math" also involves science. Children can be

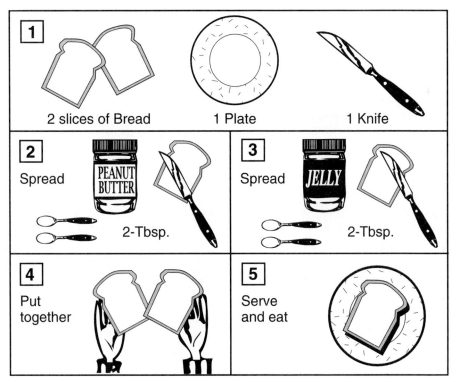

Figure 11–3   A pictograph for making a peanut butter and jelly sandwich

asked to predict what will happen when the wet ingredients (oil and milk) are mixed with the dry ingredients (flour, baking powder, and salt) when making the playdough biscuits. They can then make the mixture; observe and describe its texture, color, and density; and compare their results with their predictions. Next, they can predict what will happen when the dough is baked in the oven. When it is taken out, they can observe and describe the differences that take place during the baking process. They can be asked what would happen if the oven is too hot or if the biscuits are left in too long. Refer to the Exploring Cookies activity in Unit 16.

There are many opportunities to observe changes and make before and after comparisons. All of the scenes can be used to gather information about the food that we eat. For example. Applesauce exemplifies several physical changes: from whole to parts, from solid chunks to soft lumps, and to smooth and thick as cutting, heating, and grinding each have an effect. Children can also note the change in taste before and after the sugar is added. Stone soup offers an opportunity for discussion of the significance of the stone. What does the stone add to the soup? Does a stone have nutrients? What really makes the soup taste good and makes it nutritious? Refer to Stone Soup Recipe Cards in Unit 12.

Food and Social Studies

Each of the activities described also involves social studies. City children might take a trip to the farm. For example, a trip to an orchard to get apples for applesauce is an enriching and enjoyable experience. They might also take a trip to the grocery store to purchase the ingredients needed in their recipes. Then they can take turns measuring, cutting, adding ingredients, or whatever else is required as the cooking process proceeds. Stone soup is an excellent group activity because everyone in the class can add an ingredient. Invite people from different cultures to bring foods to class and/or help the children make their special foods. Children can note similarities and differences across cultures.

SUMMARY

Dramatic play and thematic units provide math, science, math and social studies experiences that afford children an opportunity to apply fundamental and applied concepts and skills. They can predict, observe, and investigate as they explore these areas. As children play home, store, and service roles, they match, count, classify, compare, measure, and use spatial relations concepts and number symbols. They also practice the exchange of money for goods and services. Through dramatic play they try out grown-up roles and activities.

Through thematic units, science and mathematics and science can be integrated with other content areas. The thematic experiences provide real life connections for abstract concepts. For teachers, these activities offer valuable opportunities for naturalistic and informal instruction as well as time to observe children and assess their ability to use concepts in everyday situations.

FURTHER READING AND RESOURCES

UNIT AND ACTIVITY RESOURCES

Baker, A., & Baker, J. (1991). *Counting on a small planet*. Portsmouth, NH: Heinemann.

Barrentine, S. J. (1991). Once around the paper route. *Science and Children*, 29(1), 27–30.

Brummett, D. C., Lind, K. K., Barman, C. R., DiSpezio, M. A. & Ostlund, K. L. (1995) *Destinations in Science*. Grade 1, Grocery Store, Menlo Park, CA: Addison-Wesley Publishing Company.

Charlesworth, R. (1988). Integrating math, science, and social studies: A unit example. *Day Care and Early Education*, 15(4), 28–31.

Charlesworth, R., & Lind, K. (In press). Whole language and the mathematics and science standards. In S. Raines (Ed.), *Whole language in grades 1, 2, and 3*. New York: Teachers College Press.

Corwin, R. B. (1993). Ideas: Using webs. *Arithmetic Teacher*, 40(6), 325–337.

Dalton, D. (1982). Resource list: Non-cooked food preparation. *Dimensions*, 10(1), 26–29.

Edwards, D. (1990). *Maths in context: A thematic approach*. Portsmouth, NH: Heinemann.

Hack, K., and Flynn, V. (1985). Green beans: Gardening with two's. *Day Care and Early Education*, 13(1), 14–17.

Harcourt, L. (1988). *Explorations for early childhood*. Menlo Park, CA: Addison-Wesley.

Hopkins, M. H., & Gard, D. M. (1992). Ideas: Exploring space. *Arithmetic Teacher*, 40(2), 93–95.

Irons, C., & Irons, R. (1991). Ideas: Toy shop numbers and other things in the environment. *Arithmetic Teacher*, 39(4), 18–25.

Katz, L. G., & Chard, S. C. (1989). *Engaging children's minds: The project approach*. Norwood, NY: Ablex.

Kerr, S. (1993). *Science centers A to Z*. Wheeling, IL: Look at me Productions, Inc.

Krogh, S. (1990). *The integrated early childhood curriculum*. New York: McGraw-Hill.

Martin, S. (1987). IDEAS! Nutrition: Avenue for discovery learning. *Dimensions*, 15(2), 15–18.

Mebane, R. C., & Rector, B. (1991). Ballooning interest. *Science and Children*, 29(3).

Raines, C. S., & Canady, R. J. (1990). *The whole language kindergarten*. New York: Teachers College Press.

Schafer, L. E., & Robinson, N. E. (1990). The Pepo Pumpkin mystery. *Science and Children*, 28(2), 12–15.

Skinner, P. (1990). *What's your problem?* Portsmouth, NH: Heinemann.

Smith, K. (1991). At the core of the curriculum. *Science and Children*, 29(1), 48–49.

Vandas, S. (1991). Water: The resource that gets used and used and used for everything! *Science and Children*, 28(8), 8–9.

Warner, L. (1981). Some basic concepts in the grocery store center. *Day Care and Early Education*, 8(4), 14–19.

Wasserman, S. (1990). *Serious players in the primary classroom*. New York: Teachers College Press.

COOKBOOKS

Albyn, C. L., & Webb, L. S. (1993). *The multicultural cookbook for students*. Phoenix, AZ: Oryx.

Christenberry, M. A., & Stevens, B. (1984). *Can Piaget cook?* Atlanta, GA: Humanics.

Faggella, K., & Dixler, D. (1985). *Concept cookery*. Bridgeport, CT: First Teacher Press.

McClenahan, P., & Jaqua, I. (1976). *Cool cooking for kids*. Belmont, CA: Fearon-Pitman.

Teddlie, A. T., & Turner, I. M. (1984). *Lots of action cooking with us*. Ruston, LA: Louisiana Association on Children Under Six.

Wanamaker, N., Hearn, K., & Richarz, S. (1979). *More than graham crackers*. Washington, DC: National Association for the Education of Young Children.

SUGGESTED ACTIVITIES

1. Observe young children at play in school. Note if any concept experiences take place during dramatic role playing or while doing thematic activities. Share what you observe with your class.
2. Add a section for dramatic play and thematic resources to your Activity File/Notebook.
3. Review several cookbooks (the ones suggested in this unit or some others) and examine recipes recommended for young children. Explain to the class which recipe books you think are most appropriate for use with young children.
4. Add to your Activities File five food experiences that enrich children's concepts and promote application of concepts.

REVIEW

A. Briefly answer each of the following:
   1. Why should dramatic role playing be included as a math, science, math, and social studies concept experience for young children?
   2. Why should food activities be included as math, science, math, and social studies concept experiences for young children?
   3. How can teachers encourage dramatic role playing that includes concept experiences?
   4. Describe four food activities that can be used in the early childhood math, science, and social studies program.
   5. Explain how thematic units promote an integrated curriculum.
B. Describe the props that might be included in three different dramatic play centers.

UNIT 12 Higher-Level Applications of Fundamental Concepts

OBJECTIVES

After studying this unit, the student should be able to
- Plan and do structured lessons in sets and symbols, classification, and measurement
- Plan activities for the child who develops at a fast rate and can do the higher-level assessment tasks with ease
- Design higher-level lessons that develop science concepts for children closer to the concrete level of development

Children in the transitional stage apply and develop fundamental concepts in sets and symbols, classification, shape, spatial relations, measurement, and graphs as they are exposed to higher level experiences. As they near the concrete operational level of development, they will continue to develop these concepts. The higher-level experiences described in this unit offer opportunities to build on many of the ideas presented in Unit 8 through 11 of this book.

SETS, SYMBOLS, AND CLASSIFICATION

Classifying Vegetables

Although children will be asked to bring vegetables from home for this lesson, you will need to prepare a variety of vegetables for maximum learning. Seed and garden catalogs and magazine pictures can provide illustrations of how the vegetables grow. Three major categories of vegetables that work well with children are *leaf* and *stem vegetables* (cabbage, lettuce, spinach, mustard, parsley), *root vegetables*

(sweet potatoes, carrots, beets, turnips, onions), and *seed vegetables* (cucumbers, peas, beans, corn, soybeans). Mrs. Red Fox conducts the following activity in the fall with her first grade class:

First, she invites the children to join her on a rug to examine the different vegetables. Then she asks her class to describe the vegetables in front of them. They answer, "Long, rough, smooth, peeling, hard, scratchy, lumpy, bumpy, crunchy, white, orange." Mrs. Red Fox holds up a potato and asks, "Can someone describe this potato?" "I can," Trang Fung says. "The potato is bumpy and brown." "Good," says Mrs. Red Fox. "Who can find another vegetable that is bumpy?" "A pea is a little bumpy," suggests Sara. Mrs. Red Fox writes the word *bumpy* on a 3 × 4 inch card and groups the potato and pea together. Then she holds up a carrot and asks, "Is there another vegetable that looks like this one?" Dean studies the assortment of vegetables and says, "How about the pumpkin?" "Yes, the pumpkin and the carrot are both orange." Mrs. Red Fox writes the word *orange* on a card and places the carrot and pumpkin together with the card. The children continue to classify by characteristics until each vegetable is in a group. Mrs. Red Fox refrigerates the vegetables overnight and readies them for a series of activities that emphasize a variety of concepts.

1. **Where do they grow?** The class discusses how the different vegetables looked while they were growing. After all, for all the children know, potatoes come from produce sections of supermarkets, and corn comes from a can. The children have fun matching the vegetable with pictures of the vegetable growing. Mrs. Red Fox makes a game of matching actual vegetables with how they look as they grow (Figure 12–1).

2. **Digging for potatoes.** After matching actual vegetables with pictures of growing vegetables, children practice digging for potatoes. Mrs. Red Fox fills the sandbox with rows of potatoes, and children take turns digging. Carrots, beets, and turnips are planted with their leafy tops above the soil, and children take turns gardening (Figure 12–2).

3. **What is inside?** Bowls of peas are set out to be opened and explored, and the idea of beginning a garden begins to occur to children.

4. **Under, on, and above.** Mrs. Red Fox makes

a bulletin board backdrop of a garden, and the children match cutout vegetables to where they grow. Onions are placed *under the ground*; peas, beans, and corn are shown *above the ground*; and lettuce, cabbage, and parsley are displayed *on the ground*.

5. **Patterns.** Children place the vegetables in patterns. Trang Fung made a pattern of potatoes, pumpkins, celery, and cucumbers. She said, "Bumpy, bumpy, bumpy, smooth. Look at my pattern. Dean, can you make a pattern?" Dean began his own pattern. "I am not going to tell you my pattern," said Dean. He laid out mustard, carrots, peas, cabbage, potato, and beans. Trang Fung smiled and continued the pattern. "On the ground, under the ground, and above the ground, spinach, onion, corn," she said (Figure 12–3).

6. **Vegetable prints.** As the week continued, some children wondered if the inside of the vegetables were alike and different, too. So, Mrs. Red Fox cut up several vegetables and let the children explore printing with vegetables. She poured tempera paint on sponges for a stamp pad. Then the children dipped the vegetable in paint and printed on construction paper. Mrs. Red Fox labeled some

Figure 12–1 George matches a carrot with the picture of a carrot that the teacher is holding.

Figure 12–2 Digging vegetables reinforces where they grow.

Figure 12–3 "Can you match my pattern?"

of the prints with vegetable words and hung them up for decoration. The prints were then classified by color and characteristics. Some children made patterns with their prints and asked others to guess the pattern and which vegetable made the pattern.

Stone Soup

Children can also learn about the vegetable members of the vegetable and fruit group through literature and cooking. After vegetables are identified as members of the vegetable and fruit food group, read the book *Stone Soup* (Paterson, 1981) and act out the story on the flannel board.

Print the recipe on poster board, add picture clues, and have the children wash vegetables for cooking. The children will quickly learn to use vegetable peelers and table knives as they cut the vegetables into small pieces. Then, act out the story once again. This time, really add the stone and vegetables to a crockpot to cook for the day. Bouillon cubes, salt, and pepper will spice up the soup. Do not be surprised if younger children think that the stone made all of the soup.

Prepare a set of cards with pictures of the ingredients, and have students put the cards in the correct sequence of the cooking activity. The children will want to make an experience chart of preparing the stone soup. They could even graph their favorite parts of the soup (Figure 12–4).

Animal Sets

Stuffed animals are familiar to the children and can be grouped in many ways. One way is to group stuffed animals on a table by sets: a group of one, two, three, and so on. Ask the children to draw the set of animals at their table on a piece of white paper. After the children have drawn the animals, include early literacy experiences by having them dictate or

Figure 12–4 "What did we add to the soup first? Then what did we add?"

write a story about the animals. Staple the drawings at each table into a book. The children at each table have made an animal book of ones, twos, and so on. Read each book with the children and make all books available for independent classroom reading.

More First Mapping Experiences

The everyday experience of reading maps is abstract and takes practice to develop. The following mapping activities include the use of symbols and build on the early "Bird's-Eye View" mapping experiences in Unit 8.

1. **Tangible mapping.** Children will not be able to deal with symbols on maps if they have not had experience with tangible mapping. Observe children as they create roads, valleys, and villages in clay or at the sand table. Keep in mind the perspective of *looking down* as children place objects on a huge base map. Such a map can be made from oil-cloth and rolled up when not in use.

2. **Pictorial mapping.** Take children to the top of a hill or building, and ask them to draw what they see. This activity can emphasize spatial relations and relative locations. After you have returned from a field trip, discuss what was seen on the bus ride. Use crayons or paint to construct a mural of the trip.

3. **Semipictorial mapping.** Children will use more conventional symbols when they construct a semipictorial map. As they discover that pictures take up a lot of room, they search for symbols to represent objects. Colors become symbolic and can be used to indicate water and vegetation.

4. **Base map.** The base map contains the barest minimum detail filled in by the teacher, i.e., outline, key streets, and buildings. This is a more abstract type of map; thus the area must be known to the child. Add tangible objects to the abstract base, i.e., toy objects and pictures (Figure 12–5). A flannel base map is a variation.

5. **Caution.** Never use one map to do many things. If your mapping experience tries to do too much, children cannot rethink the actual experience and relationships. Each mapmaking experience must fulfill some specific purpose. Each map must represent something in particular that children look for and understand.

Exploring Pumpkins: October Science

If you live where pumpkins grow, take a field trip to purchase some; if not, buy some at the grocery. You will need a pumpkin for each child. Plan to organize the children in groups with an adult helper. The following activities use the senses to apply and integrate the skills and fundamental concepts used in measuring, counting, classifying, and graphing in the exploration of pumpkins.

Time to Explore

Give children time to examine their pumpkins and their stems. Ask, "How does the pumpkin feel?," "How does it smell?," and "Do all pumpkins have stems?" Later, when the pumpkins are carved, encourage the children to describe the differences in texture between the inside and outside of their pumpkins.

Ask, "Which pumpkin is the heaviest?" and

Figure 12–5 Children add tangible objects to their maps.

"Who has the lightest pumpkin?" After the children decide, bring out a scale, and make an accurate measurement. The children probably cannot comprehend what the scale means or read the numbers, but they like to weigh things anyway. Tape the weight (mass) on the bottom of each pumpkin. Then, when jack-o'-lanterns are created, the children can compare the difference in mass.

Have children measure the circumference of a pumpkin with yarn. Ask, "Where shall we put the yarn on the pumpkin?" and "Why?" Instruct the children to wrap the yarn around the middle of the pumpkin. Then, help children cut the yarn and label it. Write the child's name on masking tape and attach it to the yarn length. After the children have measured their pumpkins and labeled their yarn, have them thumbtack the yarn length to a bulletin board. Ask, "Which pumpkin is the smallest around the middle?," "Which is the largest?," and "How can you tell?" Have the children refer to the yarn graph. Some kindergarten children might be ready to lay the yarn length along a measuring

stick and draw horizontal bar graphs instead of yarn ones (Figure 12–6).

Children will want to measure height as well as circumference. The major problem to solve will probably be where to measure from—the top of the stem or the indentation where the stem was. This time, cut a piece of yarn that fits around the height of the pumpkin. Label the yarn, and attach it to pieces of masking tape. Order the yarn lengths from shortest to tallest. Ask, "Which yarn is the longest?" and "Can you tell me who has the tallest pumpkin?"

Observing Pumpkins

Mrs. Jones has kindergarten children count the number of curved lines along the outside of the pumpkin. She asks, "How many lines are on your pumpkin?" She instructs the children to help each other. One child places a finger on the first line of the pumpkin and another child counts the lines. Then Mrs. Jones asks, "Do all the pumpkins have the same number of lines?" "No," answers

Figure 12–6   "How big is your pumpkin?"

Mary. "My pumpkin has more lines than Lai's pumpkin." Some children even begin to link the number of lines with the size of the pumpkin as they compare findings.

Mrs. Jones asks, "How does your pumpkin feel?" George says his pumpkin is rough, but Sam insists that his is smooth. "Yes," Mrs. Jones observes. "Some pumpkins are rough, and some are smooth." "Are they the same color?" This question brings a buzz of activity as the children compare pumpkin color. Mrs. Jones attaches the name of each child to his or her pumpkin and asks the children to bring their pumpkins to the front table. She asks the children to group the pumpkins by color variations of yellow, orange, and so on. Some of the children are beginning to notice other differences in the pumpkins such as brown spots and differences in stem shapes.

The children gather around Mrs. Jones as she carves a class pumpkin. She carefully puts the seeds and pulp on separate plates and asks the children to compare the inside color of the pumpkin with the outside color. She asks, "What colors do you see?" and "What colors do you see inside of the pumpkin?" "I see a lighter color," Mary says. "Do all pumpkins have light insides?" George is more interested in the stringy fibers. "This looks like string dipped in pumpkin stuff." "I am glad you noticed, George," Mrs. Jones comments. "The stringy stuff is called fiber. It is part of the pumpkin." Students learn the word *pulp* and also compare the seeds for future activities.

Children will also notice that *pumpkins smell*. Ask them to describe the smell of their pumpkins. Have them turn their pumpkins over and small all parts. Then ask them to compare the smell of the inside of their pumpkins with the outside rind and with the seeds, fiber, and pulp. "Does the pumpkin smell remind you of anything?" Record dictated descriptions and create an experience chart of pumpkin memories. Ask, "What do you think of when you smell pumpkins?"

As children make jack-o'-lantern faces, discuss the shapes that they are using. Then, using a felt-tip pen, ask them to draw faces on the surfaces of their pumpkins. Closely supervise children as they carve their pumpkins. Instruct them to cut away from their bodies. They will need help in holding the knife, and their participation might be limited to scooping out the pumpkin. Note: Apple corers work well for these experiences and are easier to use.

After the jack-o'-lanterns are cut and have been admired, Mrs. Jones begins a measurement activity. She asks, "How can we tell if the pumpkin is lighter than it was before it was carved?" "Lift it," say the children. "Yes," says Mrs. Jones, "that is one way to tell, but I want to know for sure." George suggests, "Let's use the scale again." But before the pumpkins are weighed, Mrs. Jones asks the children to whisper a prediction in her ear. She asks, "Do you think the pumpkin will weigh more or less after it has been carved and the seeds and pulp removed? Whisper 'More,' 'Less,' or 'The same.' " As the children respond, Mrs. Jones writes their responses on paper pumpkins and begins a more, less, and the same graph of predictions (Figure 12–7).

Last but not least in a series of pumpkin activities is tasting. Pumpkin pulp can be made into pumpkin bread or, for science and Halloween party time, make drop cookies with raisins for eyes, nose, and mouth. Or, for a tasty snack, cut some of the pumpkin pulp into chunks for cooking. Once cooked, dot the pieces with butter, and add a dash of nutmeg.

Try roasting some pumpkin seeds. Have the children wash the seeds to remove the pulp and fiber. The seeds can be dried between layers of paper towels, then roasted in a single layer on a cookie sheet. Bake in a 350° oven for 30° to 40 minutes. The children can tell when the seeds are ready by their pale brown color. To make a comparison lesson, show them seeds that you have previously roasted, and invite them to tell you when the color of the roasting seeds match yours. Cool the seeds, then have a snack.

MEASURING THE WORLD AROUND US

Playgrounds, yards, and sidewalks provide many opportunities for measuring in science. The following activities emphasize the science and measurement in outdoor adventures.

1. **How far will it blow?** After talking about air and how it moves, take the children outside to determine how far the wind will blow dandelion seeds. Draw bull's-eye-like circles on the playground with chalk. Label the circles. Have a child stand in the middle of the circle and hold a mature dandelion up to the

Figure 12–7   "Did your pumpkin weigh more, less, or the same after the seeds were removed?"

wind. Record which direction the wind blows the seeds and the circle in which most of them landed. This would be a good time to discuss wind as a way of dispersing seeds.

2. **Weed watch.** Place a stick next to a growing plant such as a dandelion or similar weed. Have the children mark the height of the weed on the stick. Check the weed each day for a week and see how tall it gets. (You might have to talk to the groundskeeper before trying this activity.) Children enjoy seeing the weeds grow. Discuss differences and possible factors in weed growth.

3. **How long does it take?** After students have had time to explore the water center, select some of the containers used in the center. Lead the children to an area that has pinecones, acorns, or other natural objects available. Recall the amount of time it took to fill the containers with water. Then, give a container to each group of children and instruct them to fill it with specific objects. Note the time that it takes to fill the containers. Vary the activity by assigning different groups of contrasting objects, i.e., small, big, rough, and so on, with which to fill the containers.

4. **Line them up.** Have children count the objects that they have collected in the containers. Ask each group to line up the objects. Compare the number of objects that it took to fill each container. If the objects collected were different, compare the number of each type of object that was needed to fill the container.

5. **How can we tell?** Children will probably find many ways to compare objects they have found. After they have examined and compared their objects visually, encourage them to weigh several of the objects. Ask, "Which container is the heaviest?" and "How can we tell?" A balance provides an objective measure. Balance the content of one container (acorns) against the content

of another (walnuts). Have children predict which will be heavier. Some might want to draw a picture of what they think will happen.

Popcorn Time

Children will sequence events as they act out a favorite snack. Have two or three children become popcorn by asking them to crouch down in the middle of a masking tape circle or hula hoop. As you pour imaginary oil on them, have the rest of the class make sizzling noises and wait for them to pop. When ready, each child should jump up, burst open like a popcorn kernel, and leap out of the popper circle. Children will want to take turns acting out the popcorn sequence.

Then, place a real popcorn popper on a sheet in the middle of the floor. Seat the children around the popper, remove the popcorn lid, and watch the popcorn fly. Before eating the popcorn, measure how far the popcorn popped with Unifix® cubes or string. (Be careful of the hot popper.) Ask, "Which popcorn flew the farthest?" and "Which flew the shortest?"

SPATIAL RELATIONS

Inside and Outside

Young children are curious about their bodies. They are familiar with outside body parts, which they can see and touch, but they are just beginning to notice that things happen inside their bodies. To increase this awareness and reinforce the concepts of inside and outside, Mrs. Jones has children look at, feel, and listen to what is going on inside of their bodies in the following scenario:

Mrs. Jones fills a garbage bag with an assortment of items—a wound-up alarm clock, rubber balls, book, a few sticks, and a bunch of grapes in a small sandwich bag. She places the bag on a chair in the front of the room, allowing it to drape down to show the outlines of some of the objects inside. She asks, "What is on the chair?" George says, "A garbage bag." "Is anything on the chair besides the bag?" asks the teacher. "No," the children respond. Mrs. Jones invites the children to gather around the bag and feel it. She asks, "Do you hear or feel anything?" "Yes," Mary says. "I feel something sharp." "And squishy," adds Sam. George is certain that he hears a clock ticking, and Lai feels a round and firm object that moves (Figure 12-8).

After the children guess what might be in the bag, Mrs. Jones opens it and shows the children what was inside. "Did you guess correctly?" "I did," says George. "I heard something ticking." "Good," answers Mrs. Jones. "How did you know that sticks were in the bag?" Mary says, "I could feel them poking through the plastic." "Yes," Sam adds, "the grapes must have been the squishy stuff."

After the children discuss the contents of the bag, Mrs. Jones takes the bag off the chair, asks the children to return to their places, and invites Mary to sit in the chair. She asks, "Now, what is on the chair?" The class choruses, "Mary."

Figure 12–8 Do you feel anything inside the bag?

"Yes, Mary is on the chair," says Mrs. Jones. "How is Mary like the bag?" After a few responses, George says, "Mary has something inside of her, too." The children come up to look at Mary, but do not touch her. Mrs. Jones asks, "Do you see what's inside showing through the way it did with the bag?" The children notice bones, knuckles, the funny bone, kneecap, and some veins. Mrs. Jones asks Mary to flex her arm muscles so the children can see muscles moving beneath her skin.

Mrs. Jones encourages the children to discover other muscles and feel them working. She has them stretch out on mats on the floor, curl up tightly, then slowly uncurl. "What have your muscles done?" Then she has them stretch out like a cat and curl up into a ball. Facial muscles are fun for the children. Mrs. Jones asks them to find and use all the muscles that they can on their faces. They wiggle noses, flutter eyelids, tighten jaws, and raise eyebrows. The teacher asks, "Does your tongue have muscles in it?" "How do you know?" Finally, the children move to music as they focus on what is happening inside their bodies. Mrs. Jones has them dancing like marionettes, stiffly with a few joints moving; then bending and curling the way rag dolls do; and finally, dancing like people, with muscles, joints, and bones controlling their movements.

The children are fascinated with the thought of something important inside of them. They make toy stethoscopes from funnels and rubber tubing and take turns finding and listening to their heartbeats. Some begin to count the beats; others enjoy tapping a finger in time with the sound of their hearts.

Mrs. Jones has the children simulate the way a heart works by folding their hands one over the other and squeezing and releasing them rhythmically. (This motion is somewhat like the way the heart muscles move to expand and contract the heart, pushing blood through.) She has them place their clasped hands close to their ears and asks,

"What do you hear?," "Is this squeezing sound like the soft thumping you heard through the stethoscope?," and "How is it different?"

Turtle Steps

Young computer users can talk to an electronic turtle and tell it where they want it to go in LOGO programs. They are actually talking to the "turtle," the leading edge of the drawing pen in turtle graphics, with a simplified form of Apple LOGO. By issuing commands in KINDER, the less difficult form of LOGO, Mrs. Campbell's students are able to draw pictures on their Apple II+ and Apple IIe monitors. Then, using a program called *Triple Dump*, described in the LOGO Tool Kit manual, they print their drawings.

Because Mrs. Campbell knows that children learn best by doing, she makes an analogy between the way children's bodies move and how the turtle draws on the screen. Before the children go to the computer terminals, she gets them ready by playing "turtle." Mrs. Campbell invites the children to

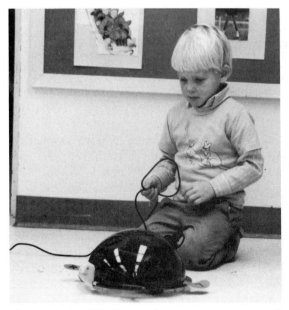

Figure 12–9   "Turtles, go forward two turtle steps."

put on their turtle caps, line up, and pretend that they are a band of marching turtles who can move only when commanded (a variation of "Mother, May I?"). She directs:

"Turtles, go forward two turtle steps."
"Turtles, go back one step."
"Turtles, turn right three steps."
"Turtles, left."

Oops! She has caught some turtles in an important mistake. For the turtles to move, they must be told how many steps to take. If children have trouble knowing left from right, she labels their hands with washable felt-tip pens and continues to direct them around the room (Figure 12–9).

Another preparatory game is "Turtle in the Pond." Mary is designated Mary Turtle and stands in a masking tape square "pond" on the floor (about 3 meters to a side). As other children give directions, Mary Turtle moves around the pond. "Turtle, forward three steps," commands George. The children take turns giving commands until the turtle has moved all around the pond.

"How do we know where Mary has already been?" asks George. "Good point," says Mrs. Campbell. "Mary Turtle has not left a trail to follow." The teacher gives Mary a ball of string to unwind as she takes her steps. In this way, a record of moves will be left (just like on the computer screen). The children direct Mary Turtle, who trails a string, around the pond.

"It is time for the turtle to hide," announces Mrs. Campbell. Mary jumps out of the pond and leaves the string design behind her. To start over again, the children clean the pond and leave a new trail.

A maze also helps children get ready for computer graphics. After making a masking tape maze on the floor, students take turns directing turtles through it with forward, right, and left directions. These are the basic commands for turtle graphics. A polluted pond can be simulated by having the turtle avoid books, chairs, and even chil-

dren. Mrs. Campbell asks, "Can you direct the turtle around the debris?"

When students are comfortable with activities such as the ones introduced, Mrs. Campbell takes them to the computer keyboard. Her activities have helped the children get ready to do graphics on the computer. Many versions of simplified turtle graphics are currently available for a variety of machines (Figure 12–10).

Lessons and activities such as "Turtle Steps" and "Inside and Outside" make children aware of the fact that there are different ways of looking at things. Taking a different view of things is a good way of reinforcing spatial relations and of beginning to see things like a scientist.

Assessment

If children can do the assessment tasks for Units 8 through 11, then they have the basic skills and knowledge necessary to connect sets and symbols and successfully complete higher-level learning activities in classification, shape, spatial relations, measurement, and graphs. The following example is a strategy many teachers use when children are at differing developmental levels.

As different concepts and activities are introduced to one child or a group of children,

Figure 12–10 Children are ready to do graphics on the computer.

any one activity could capture the interest of children who might be at a lower developmental level. Therefore it is not necessary to wait for all the children to be at the highest level to begin. Children at lower levels can participate in these activities as observers and as contributors. The higher-level child can serve as a model for the lower-level children. Or, the lower-level child might be able to do part of the task following the leadership of the higher-level child. Children can work in pairs to solve problems and can move into higher levels of symbol and measurement use as well as exploring calculators and computer software together. Most activities in science promote working in teams and sharing roles and responsibilities. This makes science an espe-

cially appropriate way to address differing development levels.

SUMMARY

Children in the transitional stage develop fundamental concepts in sets and symbols, classification, shape, spatial relations, measurement, and graphs as they are exposed to higher-level experiences. As children near the concrete operational level of development, they continue the need for hands-on exploration.

Science activities at this level allow children to pull together skills and ideas learned earlier. Most children incorporate these skills through naturalistic and informal experiences. Structured activities are also appropriate but should be brief.

FURTHER READING AND RESOURCES

Buckleitner, W. (1993). *Survey of early childhood software*. Ypsilanti, MI: High/Scope Press.

Burk, D., Snider, A., & Symonds, P. (1988). *Box it or bag it mathematics*. Salem, OR: The Math Learning Center.

Campbell, S. (1985). Preschoolers meet a high tech turtle. *Science and Children, 22*(7), 37–39.

Council for Elementary Science International Sourcebook IV. (1985). *Science experiences for preschoolers*. Columbus, OH: SMEAC Information Reference Center.

Davidson, J. I. (1989). *Children and computers together in the early childhood classroom*. Albany, NY: Delmar.

Council for Elementary Science International Sourcebook III. (1983). *Understanding the healthy body*. Columbus, OH: SMEAC Information Reference Center.

Kamii, C., & Devries, R. (1993). *Physical knowledge in the classroom: Implications of Piaget's theory* (rev. ed.). Englewood Cliffs, NJ: Prentice Hall.

Lind, K. K. (1984). A bird's-eye view: Mapping readiness. *Science and Children, 22*(3), 39–40.

Lind, K. K. (1985). The inside story. *Science and Children. 22*(4), 122–123.

McIntyre, M. (1984). Pumpkin science. *Early childhood and science*. Washington, DC: National Science Teachers Association.

Paterson, D. (1981). *Stone soup*. Mahwah, NJ: Troll Associates.

Rockwell, R. E., Sherwood, E. A., & Williams, R. A. (1986). *Hug a tree*. Mt. Rainier, MD: Gryphon House.

SUGGESTED COMPUTER PROGRAMS

Greeting Card option of *Print Shop*. [Computer program]. Broderbund Software.

Computergarten [Computer program]. Scholastic, Inc. (Pre-K–1)

Micros for micros: Estimation [Computer program]. Lawrence Hall of Science. (K–2)

SUGGESTED ACTIVITIES

1. Select a computer program for young children. What precomputer activities will you do with children before using the terminal? How will you use the computer program in your teaching? Will you conduct any follow-up activities?
2. Design a graphing experience for transitional children. Select an appropriate science topic, describe procedures, and develop a questioning strategy. Share the lessons in groups, and teach the lesson to a class.
3. Accompany a class on a field trip or walk around the block. Make a picture map of the field trip. Record the types of comments children make as they recall their trip. What types of objects made an impression on the children? Are the comments in keeping with what you know about children and the way they think?

REVIEW

1. List areas discussed in this unit that have higher-level concept activities.
2. Name three types of mapping activities that can be used with young children. Why use these strategies with children?
3. Why is it essential that children have time to explore materials when learning a science concept?
4. Should a computer be used in the classroom? Describe possible benefits. What should children do before they go to the keyboard?

SECTION III

Using Skills, Concepts, and Attitudes for Scientific Investigations in the Primary Grades

UNIT 13

Overview of Primary Science

OBJECTIVES

After studying this unit, the student should be able to
* Develop appropriate science learning experiences for the primary age child
* Design lessons that guide students in primary science investigations
* Incorporate process skills into science investigation lessons
* Guide students in collecting, observing, sorting, and classifying objects

This unit relates the skills needed for primary science investigations and the fundamental process skills to science lessons. Children in the primary grades continue to be avid explorers. Even though they are beginning to refine their inquiry skills, to identify changes in observed events, and to understand relationships among objects and events, they still require time to interact and manipulate concrete objects.

As children leave kindergarten and enter the primary level, they are also leaving the preoperational level and entering concrete operations. They begin to be able to use abstract symbols such as numbers and written words with understanding if they are tied to concrete experiences such as science investigations. They are also entering a period of industriousness in which they enjoy long-term projects, building things, making collections, and playing games that require taking turns, learning systems of rules, and making predictions. Peers are becoming increasingly important; thus working in small groups becomes a basic instructional strategy (Figure 13–1).

This unit begins with examples of how the love of collecting and the ability to play games can be applied in the science curriculum. Next, planning for investigations is described, followed by suggestions on how to manage the classroom. Finally, examples of how precomputer and computer activities can be used to enhance logical thinking are described.

COLLECTING

Primary children love to collect. They are increasingly aware of details, and their ability to compare and categorize objects is developing. They are apt to begin collecting pocketfuls of small and portable objects that they see around them. Use this natural inclination to encourage children to observe, compare, sort, and classify. Collections can consist of many things such as plants, animals, feathers, fur, rocks, sand, seashells, soils, and anything else that interests children.

Figure 13–1   Classifying and sorting shells

However, whatever the composition of the collection, it should be viewed as a means of encouraging inquiry, not as an end in itself. In this way, simple identification of objects does not become the focal point of collecting. Instead, children will learn the basic steps in scientific inquiry.

Getting Started by Using Magnifiers

Magnifiers are useful for both collecting and classifying. Handheld plastic magnifiers are perfect for all ages, are inexpensive, and have the advantage of being mobile for outdoor explorations. Magnifying boxes are hollow plastic boxes with a removable magnifier at the top. They are ideal for observing small treasures and animals such as live insects. When using magnifiers, carefully catch the insects, observe them, then return them to their environment without injury. In this way, you will encourage humaneness as well as observation.

Students can also use the jumbo-sized magnifier mounted on a three-legged stand. There is no need to hold objects with this type of magnifier, plus objects of different sizes can be examined at the same time. Although some dexterity is required for adjusting most magnifiers, the effort is important because the magnifiers are a bridge to using microscopes. In the following scenario, second graders are introduced to magnifiers before collecting (Figure 13–2).

> Mrs. Red Fox introduces magnifiers by letting the children explore for a period of time on their own. She does not tell them what to look at; rather, she gives them time to "mess around" with the magnifiers. "Wow!" observes Trang Fung. "Look how big the hair on my arm looks." As she continues to look around at objects close to her, Dean motions her over to his table. "Look, Trang. Look at the sleeve of my shirt." "It looks different. Something is in my shirt." "Mrs. Red Fox," asks Sara, "Do things always look bigger with magnifiers? Can we always see more?" "Let's look through them and see," suggests the teacher.
>
> Mrs. Red Fox plans several opportunities to view objects in different ways. She asks the children to describe the object before viewing with a magnifier, to describe what they see while they are viewing, to compare how objects look under different powers, and to compare and contrast appearances of objects after viewing is completed. She asks, "How does the object appear under the magnifier? Why do you think it looks different?"

The teacher groups the children and has them examine different areas of the room, their clothes, lunch, and a spiderweb. She explains that the magnifying glass itself is called a *lens* and confirms that things look different under a magnifier. She explains that this is because of the way the magnifier is constructed but does not suggest technical explanations. Primary children will enjoy noticing details not seen with the naked eye.

Focusing the Collecting

Practice collecting on the school grounds or in the neighborhood. Help children focus on their collections by giving them suggestions. After collecting, suggest classification systems, let children come up with their own, or try sorting objects in different ways. The primary purpose of collecting is not identification at this age. Rather, collecting should be viewed as an opportunity to encourage inquiry and become aware of the variety of similarities and differences in nature. As children collect, they observe, compare, classify, and begin to think as a scientist might think. The following collecting ideas will get the class started.

1. **Leaves.** Collect and sort leaves by color, shape, vein patterns, edges, and so on. Ask, HOW MANY RED LEAVES CAN YOU FIND? CAN YOU FIND LEAVES THAT ARE SMOOTH? DO SOME OF THE LEAVES FEEL DIFFERENT? TRY PUTTING ALL OF THE LEAVES THAT SMELL THE SAME IN A PILE. Children will want to associate the leaf with its name on a label. Suggestions for displaying collections are found in Unit 19 (see also Figure 13–3).

Figure 13–2   Introduce children to magnifiers.

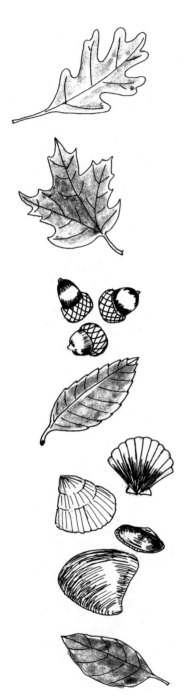

Figure 13–3 Leaves, shells, and seeds are fun to collect, sort, and label.

2. **Shells.** Collect different types of empty shells; for example, nutshells, eggshells, snail shells, seashells. Ask, WHAT KIND OF OBJECTS HAVE A SHELL? HOW DO YOU THINK THEY USE THEIR SHELL?

3. **Litter.** Collect litter around the school ground. Ask, WHAT TYPE OF LITTER DID YOU FIND MOST OFTEN? WHERE DID YOU FIND IT?

4. **Seeds.** Seeds can be found on the ground or flying in the air. Walk through a field, and examine the seeds clinging to your trouser legs and socks. Sort the seeds by size, color, and the way they were dispersed. Ask, WHAT TYPE OF SEED DID YOU FIND MOST OFTEN? Suggestions for setting up a center on seeds are found in Unit 18.

5. **Spiderwebs.** Spiderwebs are all around us, but children will need practice and patience to collect them. Spray powder on the web, then put a piece of dark paper on one side of it. Hold the web in place with hairspray. Ask, HOW ARE THE SPIDERWEBS THE SAME? HOW ARE THEY DIFFERENT? Children might enjoy pulling twine through white craft glue to duplicate the way a spider forms its web. Let dry and hang.

6. **Feathers.** Feathers can be found at home, at school, and on the way to school. Children will enjoy examining the feathers with magnifiers. Point out the zipperlike barbs that open and close the feathers. Ask, HOW ARE THE FEATHERS ALIKE? HOW DO THEY DIFFER? If children are studying birds, identify the function of the different types of feathers (Figure 13–4).

7. **Rubbings.** Another way to collect is to collect impressions of objects. Rubbings of bark and fossils are made by holding one side of a piece of paper against an object and rubbing the other side with a dark crayon. Mount the resulting patterns on colored construction paper, and display. Have the children compare and classify the patterns.

Figure 13-4 Zipperlike barbs can be seen with the help of a magnifier.

8. **Modeling clay.** Modeling clay can be used to create an impression of fossils, bark, leaves, and seeds. Simply press the clay against the object, remove, and compare impressions.

9. **Plaster molds.** Footprints can be preserved by forming a plaster mold. Mix plaster, build a small cardboard rim around the footprint, and pour plaster into the impression that you have found. Carefully remove the plaster when dry, and return the cast to the room for comparison (Figure 13-5).

Collecting Small Animals Without Backbones

Mr. Wang asks his students, "What is your favorite animal?" "That's easy," Derick says. "I like lions, seals, and cats." "Me, too," Theresa says. "But I really like horses the best." Brent chimes in that his favorite pet is a gerbil, and Liu Pei insists that dogs are the best animals because they guard your house.

A few students mention reptiles as a favorite animal, but most of the children name mammals. To introduce invertebrates as animals and clear up a common misconception, the teacher has the children to run their hands down their back. He asks, "What do you feel?" "Bones," says Theresa. "I feel my backbone." Mr. Wang asks the children if their favorite animals have backbones. "Yes, of course they do," Brent answers.

Mr. Wang explains that not all animals have backbones; these animals are called *invertebrates*. He mentions a few such as worms, sponges, mollusks, starfish, crayfish, spiders, and insects and is surprised at the children's interest.

The teacher decided to plan a collecting trip to a nearby pond and field. Each student was to wear old clothes, long-legged pants, and bring a washed peanut butter sized jar. Mr. Wang had prepared insect sweepers and a few catch jars (Figure 13-6).

Before leaving on the trip, Mr. Wang gave instructions. "We will need to be quiet and to look high and low." Derick cut in, "And under rocks,

Figure 13-5 Making a plaster mold of raccoon tracks. "What animal made these tracks?"

INSECT NET

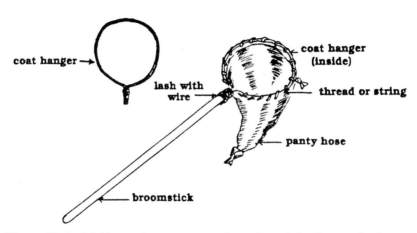

coat hanger →

coat hanger (inside)

lash with wire

thread or string

panty hose

broomstick

Figure 13–6 Making an insect sweeper from discarded nylons and a hanger.

bushes, and fallen branches." "Yes," the teacher said. "Look carefully where you walk."

The class worked in teams during the hunt, and each team tried to capture only one kind of animal. "Remember where you captured your animal," Mr. Wang reminded the children. "We will turn the insects loose in the same habitat that we found them."

After returning to the room, the teams used nature books to find out how to keep their captives alive. Each animal was displayed with an index card giving its name, habitat where it was found, and the collector's name. The animal was on display for 2 days and then released to its original habitat. Many questions were raised. "Does my worm like to eat raisins?" Derick wanted to know. Brent was interested in knowing if his worm was able to see, and Liu Pei wondered if her sow bugs would dig in the dirt of their container.

Mr. Wang encouraged close observation and investigation with such questions as, "Does the animal like rough or smooth surfaces? Does it spend most of its time in the light or in the dark?"

The next day, Liu Pei brought in animals she had found on her way to school. The display was growing. Children classified the animals by color,

number of legs, and where they were found. "Let's group the animals into those found on land and those found on water," Theresa said. "Don't forget the air," Brent suggested. "Mine were found in the air."

The invertebrate display was an excellent way to observe animals and their habitats. The students had an opportunity to classify, investigate characteristics, study life cycles, and expand their definition of animals. Some students developed a skit involving metamorphosis, others worked on a wall chart, and all gained an appreciation of the little creatures and their world.

GAMES

Primary age children enjoy games. "Put the Lobster Into the Chest" is a game that offers an opportunity for spatial awareness exploration and verbal communication, while reinforcing science content. Refer to Unit 8 for preliminary strategies for using this science board game.

Put the Lobster Into the Chest

To play this game, which is similar to "Battleship," you must first create two identical game boards and sets of playing pieces. Correlate the activity to a science topic of your choice. For instance, if you are doing a unit on farm animals, a pasture or a farmyard would be the obvious choice. For example, imagine that you are off the coast of Maine. For the game pieces, select animals commonly found in this setting. In this case, you might include lobsters, crabs, eels, clams, whales, dolphins, and seals. You will need two of each animal. Or, use three-dimensional game pieces.

It is best to play this game as a class before having the students break into pairs or small groups. When you give the instruction, "Put the lobster into the chest," students can consult with each other and ask you questions to make sure they know which is the lobster. Separate the players with a box or similar barrier so they cannot see each other's board (Figure 13–6a). A typical beginning interchange might go like this:

INITIATOR: Take the long thing with claws and put it beneath the floating green stuff.

FOLLOWER: Just on the sand?

INITIATOR: No. Put it on the sand under the plant.

FOLLOWER: Under the floating stuff near the brown fish?

INITIATOR: That's right.

The follow-up discussion is crucial to this game. After playing, always have the players compare their boards and talk about any differences between them.

DEFINING INVESTIGATIONS

You know that hands-on manipulative activities promote literacy skills and the learning of science concepts. Yet, many teachers shy away from including children in the active participation needed to develop these skills and concepts. Messy science investigations are avoided for several common reasons. One reason is that some teachers do not feel comfortable teaching science. Other teachers find managing children and materials an overwhelming task, and still others believe that investigations should be reserved for older children.

These fears should be put to rest. You do not need an extensive science background to guide children in science investigations. What you do need is instruction in how to do it. Explore strategies for teaching investigations to primary age children, and try the suggested strategies for managing children and materials. Early science experiences provide the necessary background for future, more sophisticated skill and concept development.

Teaching Science Investigations

Science investigations usually begin with a question. For example, ask, HOW LONG CAN YOU KEEP AN ICE CUBE FROM MELTING? Children can initiate investigations by asking their own questions, such as, HOW LONG WILL THIS ICE CUBE LAST IF I LEAVE IT ON MY PLATE?

After the initial question or questions, you usually predict what you think is going to happen. In the ice cube example, a child might predict, "I think the ice cube will last until lunch."

Determining variables simply means taking all the factors into account that might affect the outcome of the investigation. Although most third-grade students can handle the term *variable*, it is not advisable to introduce this term to kindergarten

Figure 13–6a   *"Put the lobster under the plant."*

through second-grade children. This component of investigation is usually too difficult for primary age children to understand. Instead, ask questions that help children consider variables in the investigation. For example, ask, WHAT ARE WE TRYING TO FIND OUT? WHAT SHALL WE CHANGE? The idea of keeping something constant can be understood by talking about the idea of fairness. It just would not be fair for everything not to be the same.

Keep records of observations, results, procedures, information obtained, and any measurements collected during the investigation. *Conclusions*, of course, are statements that tell if the original prediction, *hypothesis*, was rejected. Ask, WHAT HAPPENED? IS THIS WHAT YOU THOUGHT WOULD HAPPEN? DID ANYTHING SURPRISE YOU?

This procedure resembles the scientific method for a reason. This is because children are unconsciously using the scientific method as they observe, predict, and reach conclusions. Encouraging them to investigate capitalizes on their natural interest.

In fact, we could call investigations student research. Basically, children are trying to find the answers to questions for which they do not know the answers. As they investigate, they find answers to their questions in the same way as a scientist does. They are thinking like a scientist.

MANAGING THE CLASS

Distributing Materials and Working Together

A lack of classroom management can wreck your best plans. In addition to planning your lesson, give a few moments to consider how you will organize your children and the materials they will work with. The following suggestions will start you thinking:

Organize Children for Learning

Organize the class into teams of no more than four children. It is essential that each child

have responsibilities on the team. Designate a team leader, who is responsible for seeing that all materials are correctly obtained, used, and put away. The recorder is responsible for obtaining and putting away, recording, writing books, and reporting results to the class. Appoint a judge, who has the final word in any science activity related disputes, and an investigator, who is responsible for seeing that the team follows the directions when conducting the science activity. Make sure that the children understand their responsibilities.

Organize Materials for Learning

Materials can be organized several ways. One possibility is to distribute materials from four distribution centers in your room. Each center should be labeled 1, 2, 3, 4 and contain all of the equipment needed for an exploration. Then, number the children in the team 1, 2, 3, 4. The 1s are responsible for acquiring the materials at distribution center 1, the 2s at center number 2, and so on. Locate the distribution sites in separate areas of the room to reduce confusion, give a time limit for collection of materials, and provide a materials list so that the team leaders can check to see that everything needed is on their table.

If you are teaching a structured lesson, you may want to make a list that indicates what each individual will do during the exploration. For example, if you want the children to explore concepts of surface tension with soap and pepper, have the 1s pour the water into the cup, the 2s tap the pepper in the cup, the 3s coat the toothpick with liquid detergent, and the 4s plunge the toothpick into the pepper.

Science explorations are fun. To maintain discipline while conducting complex activities with the whole class, an organization system for children and materials is needed. Establish simple and clear rules for classroom operation. Once the children are comfortable with the rules and organization system, you will only need to periodically review what is expected to keep them on task.

Pocket Management Strategy

Primary teacher Maureen Awbrey prepares for managing children in learning areas by making a personalized library card pocket for each child in her class. Each pocket has the child's picture on it and a distinguishing symbol such as an orange triangle or a green square. Children learn their classroom jobs and become familiar with symbols as they review their job list each morning.

After the children are comfortable with their personal symbols and pockets, Mrs. Awbrey introduces them to the learning areas of the room. Each area is designated by a pocket and symbols that tell the children how many individuals may work in an area. For example, four circles mean that four children are permitted in the area. If Mrs. Awbrey does not want the children to use certain equipment, she places a "closed" sign in the area.

Colored strips of laminated paper containing the child's name and that of an available learning area are kept in the child's pocket. These strips are called *tickets*. When Scott wants to construct a zoo in the Block Center, he takes his block ticket to the block area and puts it in the pocket. When he is finished working in the block area, he removes his ticket and puts it in a basket. In this way, children rotate through the room and are exposed to a variety of learning experiences (Figure 13–7).

SAMPLE INVESTIGATIONS

The following investigations allow children to develop science processes as they conduct scientific investigations:

HOW LONG DOES IT TAKE FOR A PAPER TOWEL TO DRY?

CONCEPT: Water disappears into the air during evaporation.

OBJECTIVE: Children should be able to simulate clothes drying on a line by investigating the length of time it takes for paper towels to dry.

MATERIALS: Bowl of water, paper towels, cardboard, pie plates.

PROCEDURE: Ask children how their clothes get dry after they are washed. Are they put in a dryer? Are they hung on a line? Say, LET'S PRETEND THESE PAPER TOWELS ARE CLOTHES AND SEE HOW LONG THEY WILL TAKE TO DRY.

1. Soak a paper towel under water.
2. Squeeze out all the water that you can.
3. Open the towel and lay it on a pie plate.
4. Leave the plate on a table. Have children check and record the time.
5. Feel the towel at 30-minute intervals to see if it is dry. When it is dry, record the time.
6. How long did the towel take to dry? Have the groups share their findings on a class chart.

EXTENSIONS: Do you think it will make a difference if you put the towels in the sun or in the shade? Which wet towel do you think will dry first? Do you think wind will make a difference in how fast a paper towel dries? Set up a fan, and create wind. Measure the difference in drying time.

Figure 13–7 The boys cooperate as they explore worms.

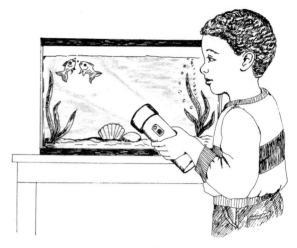

Figure 13–8 "Can a goldfish be trained to respond to light?"

CAN GOLDFISH BE TRAINED?

CONCEPT: Animals can be trained to respond to light and other signals.

OBJECTIVE: Children should be able to train a goldfish to respond to light.

MATERIALS: Goldfish (at least two), tank, flashlight, fish food.

PROCEDURE: Ask, HAVE YOU EVER TRAINED A PET TO DO SOMETHING? Children usually have a dog that sits or stays. DO YOU THINK THAT GOLDFISH KNOW WHEN IT IS TIME TO EAT? HOW COULD WE TRAIN THE GOLDFISH TO GO TO A CORNER OF THEIR TANK TO EAT? Discuss possibilities.

Shine the flashlight into a corner of the tank. Ask, DO THE GOLDFISH SWIM TOWARD THE LIGHT? (No.) Each day sprinkle a little food in the water as you shine the flashlight in the corner (Figure 13–8). Ask, WHAT ARE THE FISH DOING? (Swimming toward the light.)

Do this for several days in a row. Then, shine the light without adding food. Ask, WHAT HAPPENS WHEN YOU ONLY SHINE THE LIGHT? (Fish come to the light, but only for a couple of days if food is not offered.)

EXTENSIONS: Ask, WILL THE FISH RESPOND TO DIFFERENT SIGNALS? DO BOTH FISH RESPOND IN THE SAME WAY? WILL DIFFERENT TYPES OF FISH RESPOND IN THE SAME WAY? Have children record their attempts and successes. They may want to write stories about their fish, tell others, and invite other classes to see their trained fish.

Examples of Topics to Investigate

1. Can we design a container to keep an ice cube from melting?
2. Will mold grow on bread?
3. Can we get a mealworm to change direction?
4. What objects in our classroom will a magnet attract?
5. Can a seed grow without dirt?
6. Which part of a wet spot dries faster: the top, middle, or bottom? Or does it all dry at the same time (Figure 13–9)?

COMPUTER ACTIVITIES THAT ENHANCE LOGICAL THINKING

Children like to have fun when they learn. Why not make precomputer activities fun while developing early problem-solving skills? Have students look for patterns, guess the rules that might govern those patterns, and apply the rules to a situation.

The Floor Turtle

In the following scenario, Mrs. Red Fox is aware that young children learn best by becoming physically involved in activities. The teacher selects *Valiant Turtle*, by Harvard Associates, Inc., to spark interaction among her students. Commands typed into Terrapin LOGO move the cordless computerized floor turtle forward or backward and turn as far to the right or left as the child desires.

Sara types TFD 10 (turtle forward ten steps). "Oh, look, the turtle went forward," she says. Sara then types TBK (turtle backward), TRT, and TLT (turtle right or left turn, respectively), and a number of steps. The class is delighted with the floor turtle's response and everyone wants a turn.

Trang Fung gets ready to make a prediction. She asks, "What commands are you going to give the turtle, Sara? Okay, I think the floor turtle will stop right here." Trang Fung places a piece of masking tape with her name on it on the predicted spot. She waits as Sara gives commands. "Wow, I was really close. Let's try it again, Sara."

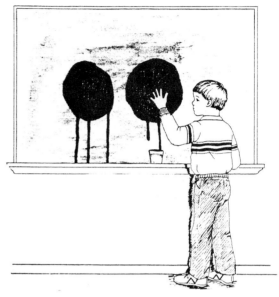

Figure 13–9   Use a chalkboard for investigating the drying time of wet spots.

As the children play with the floor turtle, they observe unit amounts and estimate distances. Steps and direction are predicted. The following are suggested floor turtle activities:

1. Put a sticker on the floor where the floor turtle will start and another where it stops. Measure the distance.
2. Have a child stand with feet apart in the path of the turtle. Ask, HOW MANY STEPS WILL THE TURTLE NEED TO TAKE TO PASS UNDER DEAN'S LEGS?
3. Have the turtle pass over two different types of floor surfaces. Have students investigate: WILL THE TURTLE TRAVEL THE SAME DISTANCE OVER CARPET AS IT WILL OVER TILE? This activity will also help children begin to understand friction.
4. Send the floor turtle over a certain path. Have students list the way it will have to move. Ask, WHICH WAY WILL INVOLVE THE FEWEST NUMBER OF STEPS? Chil-

dren can interact with each other, form and test hypotheses, list a sequence of steps that the floor turtle will follow, and become aware that they control the turtle.

Recognizing Rules for Patterns and Shapes

Elements of a pattern can be recognized and rules developed that apply to those patterns. *Gertrudes Secrets*, by the Learning Company, gives children a chance to keep patterns going by offering attribute games. Before learning the pattern games, introduce children to the space bar and the up, down, left, and right keys on the computer. Mrs. Red Fox designs an off-computer activity that prepares the students for the software.

Mrs. Red Fox makes squares, diamonds, and hexagons with three different colors of construction paper. She shows the children three pieces together that would fit a certain rule; for example, all shapes held up are red. She asks, "Can you tell me a rule for this group?" "Yes," says Dean. "Those shapes are all red." "Good," answers Mrs. Red Fox.

She continues to play games with a secret rule. For example, she holds up cutouts that are all diamonds or all yellow, and the children guess what the rule is. Then she asks, "If all of these pieces are yellows, what other pieces will also fit in this group?" When the children master this game they are ready to play the game "Loop" on *Gertrude's Secrets*.

The cutout shapes can also be used to make an attribute train. A piece is selected at random to make the train's "engine." "Cars" are made by attaching a shape that is different in only one way, either shape or color, to the previous one. The game continues until all the shapes have joined the train. Play a game called "Trains" on *Gertrude's Secrets* when children fully understand the off-computer train game.

SUMMARY

When children investigate, they develop science processes and science concepts. Science concepts are the "big ideas" in science; they explain the way the world is viewed.

Primary age children continue to be avid investigators. At this age, they refine their inquiry skills and begin to understand abstract symbols that are tied to concrete experiences. The unit suggests science learning experiences that enhance the primary child's special fondness for collecting and playing games. Ideas for classroom management and use of simple classroom investigations are also suggested.

FURTHER READING AND RESOURCES

Campbell, S. (1987). A playful introduction to computers. *Science and Children*, *24*(8), 38–40.

Green, B., & Schlichting, S. (1985). *Explorations and investigations*. Riverview, FL: The Idea Factory, Inc.

Kneidel, S. S. (1993). *Creepy crawlies and the scientific method*. Golden, CO: Fulcrum.

Lind, K. K. (1993). Collector's choice. *Science and Children*, *31*(3), 34–35.

McClurg, P. (1984). Don't squash it! Collect it! *Science and Children*, *21*(8), 8–10.

McIntyre, M. (1984). *Early childhood and science*. Washington, DC: National Science Teachers Association.

Smith, E., Blackmer, M., & Schlichting, S. (1987). *Super science sourcebook*. Riverview, FL: The Idea Factory, Inc.

VanDeman, B. (1984). The fall collection. *Science and Children*, *27*(1), 20–21.

Zeitler, W. R., & Barufaldi, J. P. (1988). *Elementary school science instruction—A perspective for teachers*. White Plains, NY: Longman.

SUGGESTED COMPUTER PROGRAMS

Balancing bears [Computer program]. Sunburst
    Publications.
Gertrude's secrets [Computer program]. The
    Learning Company.
LOGO revised [Computer program]. MECC.
Mystery objects [Computer program]. MECC.
Story starters: Science [Computer program]. Peli-
    can Software.
Windows on science—Primary science [Computer
    program]. Optical Data Corporation.

USING WORD PROCESSORS

Children can use word processors or speech syn-
thesizers to write about science topics. They
can then listen to output, or print out and illustrate what they have created. Some good
word processing programs for children are:
Magic Slate (20 Col.). Sunburst.
Milliken. Scholastic.
Bank Street Writer. Scholastic.

SUGGESTED ACTIVITIES

1. Observe differences in the ability to classify.
   Design lessons that take advantage of childrens' abilities to observe detail.
2. Begin a collection of twenty objects from nature. How could you use this collection in your
   teaching? Use the collection in this way and
   share children's response with others.
3. Select a collecting topic such as leaves. Describe naturalistic, directed, and structured collecting activities that might take place with

leaves. Observe children as they collect and
identify each of these three types of learning.
4. Identify the process skills and science concepts
   emphasized in the investigation activities in this
   unit. Design an investigation and introduce it to
   primary age children. Record children's responses. What type of questions did children
   ask? How did they go about conducting the
   investigation?

REVIEW

1. Give two differences in the way that primary
   age children learn and the way that kindergarten age children learn.
2. How are primary grade science experiences
   similar to kindergarten lessons?

3. Why encourage children to collect? When collecting, what preparations and procedures will
   you follow before, during, and after collecting?
4. What are invertebrates and why should they be
   mentioned in the early grades?

U^{NIT} 14 Life Science

O B J E C T I V E S

After studying this unit, the student should be able to
- Develop an understanding of life science topics that are appropriate for primary grade children
- Develop structured and unstructured life science learning activities with primary age children
- Describe appropriate conditions for the care of animals in the classroom
- Apply unit webbing strategies to life science content

Whether they live in large cities or small towns, children display an eagerness to learn about the living things around them. The countless opportunities that exist to acquire firsthand knowledge of plants and animals make learning fun for both children and teacher. This unit begins with life science concepts that are basic to primary grade learning; it then presents an example of a seed unit planned with the webbing strategy discussed in Unit 7. Next, guidelines for animal care and a variety of investigations and learning experiences with animals are described. Finally, sources for teaching about plants, animals, and the environment are suggested.

LIFE SCIENCE CONCEPTS

A knowledge of science concepts is basic to planning and teaching life science to primary age children. Remember, the concepts are the "big ideas" from science that we want students to understand. Thus, learning experiences are planned around them. For example, Figure 14–1 shows a unit planning web, as described in Unit 7, that focuses learning activities around three basic concepts from the topic of seeds. The following concepts are basic to understanding plants, animals, and all living things (Figure 14–1):

Living Things

1. Living things can be distinguished from non-living things.
2. Plants and animals are living things.
3. Animals and plants affect one another.
4. Living things have unique features that help them live in different kinds of places.
5. Most living things need water, food, and air.

Seeds and Plants

1. Seeds differ in size, shape, color, and texture.
2. Seeds germinate and grow into a specific type of plant.
3. Some seeds grow inside fruits.
4. Some seeds grow into flowers, shrubs, and trees.
5. Some seeds grow into food that we eat.
6. Seeds are dispersed in several ways.
7. Seeds need water, light, and warmth to grow.
8. Seeds and plants grow and change.
9. Leaves tend to grow toward light, and roots tend to grow into the soil.
10. Plants grow from seeds, roots, and stems.
11. Some plant forms do not have seeds, roots, or stems.

12. Some plants grow in the light, and some plants grow in the dark.
13. Some plants change in different seasons.

Animals

1. Animals need food, water, shelter, and a unique temperature.
2. Animals have individual characteristics.
3. Animals have unique adaptations. They move, eat, live, and behave in ways that help them survive.
4. Animals go through a life cycle.
5. Pets are animals that depend on us for special care. We love and take care of our pets.
6. There are many kinds of pets.
7. Different kinds of pets need different types of care to grow and be healthy.
8. Aquariums are places for fish and other living things to grow.

PLANNING AND TEACHING A SEED UNIT

The learning experiences suggested in this unit follow the format described in Unit 7 and are designed to meet the needs, interests, and developmental levels of primary age children described in Unit 13. Each lesson states a concept, a teaching objective based on what the child should be able to do, materials needed, and suggestions for teaching the concept. Extensions, integrations, and possible evaluation procedures are indicated in the body of the lesson when appropriate and at the end of the unit.

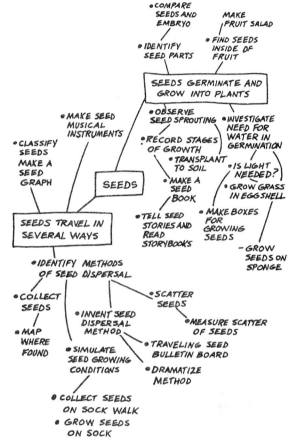

Figure 14–1   A planning web for a seed unit

SEEDS

CONCEPT: Seeds germinate and grow into plants; seeds contain a baby plant.

OBJECTIVE: Discover that a seed has three parts. Identify the embryo inside of the seed.

MATERIALS: Lima beans that have been soaked overnight (if you soak them longer, they may rot), paper towels, a variety of seeds.

PROCEDURE: Show children a lima bean seed. Ask, WHAT DO YOU THINK MIGHT BE INSIDE OF THIS SEED? CAN YOU DRAW A PICTURE OF HOW YOU THINK THE INSIDE OF THE SEED LOOKS?

Have children open the lima bean seed with their thumbnails. Ask, WHAT DO YOU NOTICE ABOUT YOUR SEED? HOW DOES THE SEED FEEL? IS THERE A SMELL? DOES THE INSIDE OF THE SEED LOOK LIKE THE PICTURE YOU HAVE DRAWN? Discuss similarities and differences. Have students draw a picture of the bean after it is opened.

Point out that there are three basic parts in all seeds: the seed cover (for protection), food for the baby plant (*cotyledon*), and the baby plant itself (*embryo*). Introduce the term *germinate*. (This is when the seed grows—it sprouts.) Have students paint a picture of the plant as they think it will look when it has grown.

EXTENSION: Soak different types of seeds, and have children compare the inside and outside of the seeds to the lima bean seeds. This could be done in an unstructured way as part of a Seed Center. In beans and peas, there are two seed halves. In seeds such as corn and rice, there is only one seed half or cotyledon (Figure 14–2).

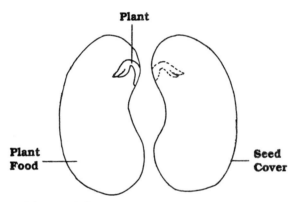

Figure 14–2   All seeds have three basic parts.

BABY PLANTS

CONCEPT: Seeds germinate and grow into plants.

OBJECTIVE: Observe and describe how seeds grow into plants. Describe how the embryo grows into a plant.

MATERIALS: Lima beans, paper towels, water, cotton, clear containers or glass tumblers.

PROCEDURE: Say, YESTERDAY WE SAW A BABY PLANT INSIDE OF A SEED. DO YOU THINK IT WILL GROW INTO A BIG PLANT? LET'S FIND OUT.

Soak lima beans overnight. Have children line the inside of a drinking glass with a wet, folded paper towel. Then, stuff cotton into the glass. This holds the paper towel in place.

Put soaked seeds between the paper towel and glass. Then, pour water to the edge of the bottom seed in the glass (the paper towel and cotton will absorb most of the liquid). The sprouting seeds will be easy for the children to see through the clear container. Have the children draw the sprouting lima bean and write a story about the investigation.

Ask, WHAT DO YOU SEE HAPPENING? WHAT COLORS DO YOU SEE? WHICH WAY ARE THE ROOTS GROWING? WHERE IS THE EMBRYO GETTING ITS FOOD? (From the cotyledon.) As the plant gets larger, the seed becomes smaller. In fact, the plant will begin to die when the cotyledon is used up.

When the food provided by the seed is used up, ask, WHAT OTHER TYPE OF FOOD CAN WE GIVE THE PLANT? Discuss the possibility of transplanting the young plants to soil as a continuation of the project.

EXTENSION: This concept can be extended throughout the year. It is a good science activity with the advantage of going from simple observation to experimentation. The concept lends itself to a short study of seeds or an extended study of how light, moisture, heat, color, soil, air, and sound affect the growth of plants.

GLASS GARDEN

CONCEPT: Moisture is needed for seeds to sprout.

OBJECTIVE: Observe the growth of seeds.

MATERIALS: Mung beans, cheesecloth, jar.

PROCEDURE: Soak a handful of mung beans in a jar, and cover the jar tightly with cheesecloth. Protect the jar from light by wrapping it in a towel. Then, have children simulate rain by rinsing and draining the seeds three times a day. Have children predict what will happen to the seeds. Ask, DID THE SEEDS SPROUT EVEN THOUGH THEY WERE IN THE DARK? (Yes.) DO YOU THINK THE SEEDS WILL SPROUT IF WE KEEP THEM IN THE DARK BUT DO NOT WATER THEM? (No.) Repeat the activity, and investigate what will happen if the seeds are kept in the dark and not watered.

EXTENSION: You may want to make a salad and top it off with the mung sprouts. Several variables can be tried, one at a time of course, so that children can investigate variables in sprouting seeds and growing plants.

TEACHING NOTE: Lima beans usually work well, but mung beans show the speedy growth that impatient young children may demand. Mung beans will not grow as tall as others, but they will show growth. Corn, on the other hand, takes longer than lima beans to germinate.

WHAT'S INSIDE?

CONCEPT: Seeds come from the fruit of plants.

OBJECTIVE: Discover that seeds develop inside of fruit.

MATERIALS: A variety of fruits, pinecones, flowers, plastic knives, paper towels.

PROCEDURE: Select several fruits, and place them on a table with plastic knives and paper towels. Have children examine the fruits and ask, WHAT DO YOU THINK IS INSIDE OF THE FRUIT?

Invite children to cut the fruits open. Ask, WHAT DID YOU FIND? HOW MANY SEEDS DID YOU FIND? ARE ALL OF THE SEEDS THE SAME COLOR? WHAT DO YOU THINK THE SEEDS ARE DOING INSIDE OF THE FRUIT?

Explain that a fruit is the part of a flowering plant that holds the seeds. Ask, CAN YOU NAME ANY FLOWERS IN YOUR BACKYARD THAT HAVE SEEDS? (Sunflowers, dandelions.) ARE THEY FRUITS? (Yes.) Point out that not all fruits are edible.

EXTENSION: Show a picture of a pine tree. Ask, DOES THIS TREE HAVE FLOWERS? (No.) DOES IT HAVE SEEDS? (Yes.) WHERE ARE THE SEEDS? (Cones.) Have children examine pinecones to find out how the seeds are attached. Compare the seeds enclosed in fruits to those attached to cones. Point out that seeds can grow inside of a flower, surrounded by fruit, or in a cone.

TRAVELING SEEDS

CONCEPT: Seeds need to travel to grow.

OBJECTIVE: Investigate why seeds travel by simulating growing conditions.

MATERIALS: Two containers, soil, seeds.

PROCEDURE: Have children bring in seeds from the school grounds or their neighborhood. Examine the seeds, and discuss where they were found. Hold up a seed and ask, DO WE HAVE THIS KIND OF PLANT ON OUR SCHOOL GROUNDS? (No.) HOW DID THE SEED GET HERE? (Wind.) I WONDER WHY IT BLEW AWAY?

After discussing ask, DO YOU THINK THAT SEEDS WILL GET A CHANCE TO GROW IF THEY ALL FALL AT THE BOTTOM OF THE PARENT PLANT? LET'S SEE WHAT HAPPENS WHEN SEEDS FALL IN ONE PLACE.

Fill two containers with seeds. Have children help plant seeds close together in one container and far apart in the other. Ask, WHICH CONTAINER DO YOU THINK WILL GROW THE MOST PLANTS? Discuss and list suggested reasons. Have children take turns giving all of the seeds water, light, warmth. Watch them for many days. Have children measure the growth of the plants and record what they see. Then ask, IN WHICH CONTAINER DO SEEDS GROW BETTER? (Spaced apart.) In this way, children will see a reason for a seed to travel.

SCATTERING SEEDS

CONCEPT: Seeds are adapted to disperse in several ways.

OBJECTIVE: Identify several ways of dispersing seeds.

MATERIALS: Seeds, magnifying glasses, mittens.

PROCEDURE: Arrange seeds from weeds, grasses, and trees in a Science Center. Have a magnifying glass and mitten available for students to examine seeds. Give basic directions, and let children "mess around" and explore the seeds. Ask, WHICH SEEDS SEEM TO CATCH IN THE MITTEN? (Hairy ones or ones with burrs.) Have children predict and draw what they think they will see when they observe a burr through a magnifying glass. Say, LET'S LOOK THROUGH THE MAGNIFYING GLASS AND DRAW WHAT WE SEE. Discuss the before and after pictures and describe the tiny hooks and how they are used. Introduce the term *disperse* and use it in sentences and stories about the burr with tiny hooks. Refer to Unit 13 for suggestions for the use of magnifiers.

EXTENSION: Take children outside to explore how different seeds are dispersed by shaking seeds from pods, beating grass seed spikes to release grains, brushing hairy seeds against clothes, and releasing winged seeds. Compare what happens to each seed.

INVENT A SEED

CONCEPT: Seeds are modified to travel in a specific way.

OBJECTIVE: Modify a seed for travel.

MATERIALS: Dried bean or pea seeds, a junk box (colored paper, glue, rubber bands, tape, cotton, ice cream bar sticks, balloons, pipe cleaners, paper clips, string), scissors.

PROCEDURE: Show children a coconut (the largest seed) and ask, HOW DO YOU THINK THIS COCONUT TRAVELS? (Water.) Display pods such as milkweed to demonstrate a pod that bursts and casts its seeds to the wind. HOW WILL THE BURR TRAVEL? (Catch on things.) Birds and other animals eat fruit such as berries. Then, they digest the fruit and leave the seeds somewhere else. WHY DID THE BIRD WANT TO EAT BERRIES? (They were good to eat.) Children will conclude that seeds have specific modifications to travel in specific ways. To reinforce the term *modify*, have students modify their clothes for different weather or activities.

Ask, IF YOU WERE A SEED, HOW WOULD YOU LIKE TO TRAVEL? Discuss preferences, and then assign one of the following means of travel to each small group of children: attract animal, catch on fur, pops or is shot out, floats on water, or carried by wind. Give each group seeds and junk box materials, and ask them to invent a way for their seed to travel. When the children have completed their creations, have them demonstrate how their seed travels (Figure 14–3).

EXTENSION: Make a bulletin board that displays the modified seeds traveling in the way the students intended. Have children examine seeds and think of other objects that work in the same way. (For example, the burr is the inspiration for the development of Velcro®.)

1. **Sock walk.** Drag a sock through a field. Then cover with soil and water, and wait for a variety of plants to grow from the seeds caught on the sock. Or put the sock in a plastic bag, shake the seeds out of the sock, and examine them. Ask, WHAT TYPES OF SEEDS DID THE SOCK ATTRACT?
2. **Egghead hair.** Draw a face on half of an eggshell. Place the egg in an egg carton, and fill the eggshell with moist soil. Sprinkle grass seed on top, then water. Grass will grow in 5 days. Attach construction paper feet with clay to display (plastic eggs also work well). To show the benefit of light on leaves, first grow the grass hair in the dark. Discuss the resulting pale, thin grass and ask, HOW CAN WE MAKE THE GRASS GREEN AND HEALTHY? Place the egg

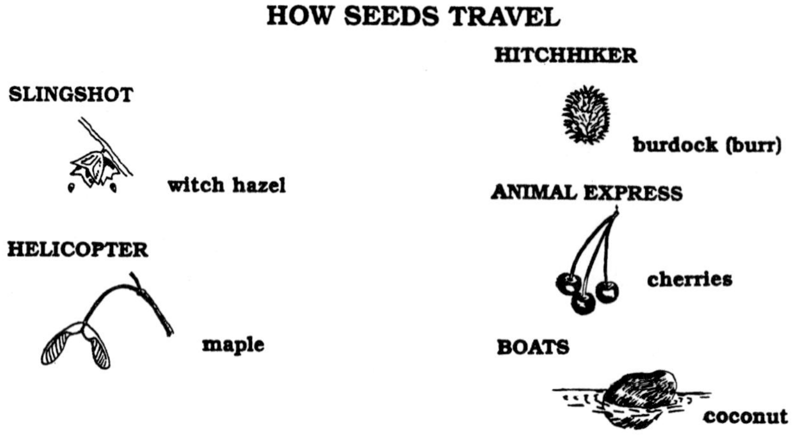

HOW SEEDS TRAVEL

SLINGSHOT

witch hazel

HELICOPTER

maple

HITCHHIKER

burdock (burr)

ANIMAL EXPRESS

cherries

BOATS

coconut

Figure 14–3 Seed dispersal methods

person in the light, and be prepared to trim the healthy green hair (Figure 14–4).
3. **Collections.** Seeds make an easy and fun collection. Collect from your kitchen, playground, or neighborhood.

Investigation Questions for Growing Seeds
1. How deep can you plant a seed and still have it grow?
2. If you crush a seed, will it still grow?
3. What direction will the sprouts in the glass garden grow if the glass is turned upside down?

SUBJECT INTEGRATIONS

Science and Math
1. **Seed walk.** Take a seed walk around the school. Ask, WHERE SHALL WE LOOK FOR SEEDS? WHAT DO YOU THINK WE MIGHT SEE? Gather seeds, and use as materials to sort, match, count, and weigh in the Science Center.
2. **How many ways.** Provide a box of seeds for students to classify. Compare size, shape, color, and texture of the seeds. Construct a seed graph.

3. **Greenhouse.** Simulate a greenhouse by placing a plastic bag over a container of germinating seeds. Place seeds in a jar on a moist paper towel. Put the jar inside of a plastic bag, and record the amount of time needed for sprouting. Compare sprouting time with seeds that are not placed in a plastic bag (Figure 14–5).

Figure 14–4 "Can you grow healthy grass hair for your eggshell people?"

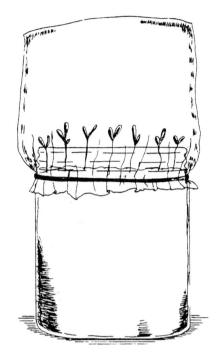

Figure 14–5   Make your own greenhouse.

4. **Cooking.** Create a fruit salad with the fruits gathered for seed activities. Or measure ingredients, and follow a recipe to make apple pie or other tasty dishes. Nut butter can be made by passing the seeds or nuts through a nut grinder. Store in the refrigerator, and use as spreads.

Science and Social Studies

1. **Seeds swell.** Years ago, seeds were used to stretch tight leather shoes. To simulate this, fill a small bottle with beans, cover beans with water, close the bottle with plastic wrap, and secure with rubber bands. Beans will swell and lift the plastic.
2. **Neighborhood map.** Have children bring in seeds that they have found. Make a map of where the seeds might be found.
3. **Seeds can be edible.** Try to bridge the gap between the processed food that the children eat and its raw form. Show pictures of wheat, fruit trees, and vegetables growing. Discuss edible seeds such as pumpkin, sunflower, peanuts, and those that are not eaten such as watermelon and apple seeds.
4. **Careers.** Discuss different jobs associated with growing plants. Make hats, and act out these jobs.
5. **Woodworking.** Create boxes and planters for growing seeds.

Science and Language Arts

1. Have students remove the *s* from *seed* and make new words (weed, feed, need, bleed).
2. Pretend you are a seed. Draw a picture, and write a story about how you will look and where you might travel.
3. Dramatize the growth of an embryo into a plant.
4. Make a seed book (in the shape of a lima bean), and fill it with bean stories and drawings.
5. Read, tell, and dramatize stories about seeds such as "Jack and the Beanstalk," "The Story of Johnny Appleseed," or "Popcorn" by Toni DePaola.

Science and Music

1. Sing songs about seeds and plants from your music book.
2. Use seeds to create musical instruments such as maracas and other types of "shaking" instruments in tubes with plastic lids.
3. Some children can make whistles from acorn caps. Hold thumbs in a V shape, with the top of the thumbs forming the V, under the hollow side of the cap. Blow gently at the base of the V to make a sound.

Science and Art

1. Create landscapes that would be favorable for seed growth.

2. Make faces on moist sponges with birdseed. Trim the green growth into different patterns.
3. Design seed mosaics. Glue seeds to paper or cardboard to make pictures.
4. Jewelry can be made by stringing seeds with thread and needle. You may need to boil seeds and wait for them to soften. Some children might want to paint the seeds and use them to decorate costumes.
5. Stick burrs together to make a basket. What else can you make from burrs? Pinecones and walnut shells can become birds and other creatures by adding glue and construction paper.

ADDITIONAL PLANT ACTIVITIES BASED ON SCIENCE CONCEPTS

When your unit on seeds is completed, you might want to develop additional concepts about plants. Here are a few suggestions:

Concept: Plants Grow from Roots and Stems

Growing plants from cuttings can be an exciting experience for primary age children. They will enjoy observing familiar products from a grocery bag doing unfamiliar things. Investigations with cuttings are long term and provide opportunities for record keeping, process skill development, and subject integration. You will need water, light, and common vegetables to reinforce that seeds are not the only way that plants reproduce.

1. **Dish garden.** To make a dish garden, cut off the top inch of carrots, beets, or white turnips. Keep the tops in dishes of water while the children observe the roots growing. Shoots will usually appear in a week to 10 days. Ask, CAN YOU TELL WHAT THIS PLANT IS BY THE LEAVES?
2. **Hanging around.** Suspend a yam or a fresh sweet potato, tapered end down, in a jar filled with water. Insert toothpicks so that only one-third of the sweet potato is in the water (Figure 14–6). Put the jar in a warm, dark place until buds and roots grow. Then put it in a sunny place, and prepare a string trellis for the upcoming foliage to climb. Children can chart the number of days for root and foliage growth and observe and record changes. Ask, WHAT HAPPENS TO THE SWEET POTATO AS THE VINE GROWS?
3. **Pineapple tops.** Cut a 2 1/2 inch section of pineapple fruit below the leaves. Put the pineapple top in a dish with water. When the roots develop, put the plant in potting soil and make a greenhouse by covering it with a plastic bag. Keep the pineapple greenhouse warm but not in direct sunlight. In about 3 weeks, take the new plant out of the green-

Figure 14–6 "Will a sweet potato grow in a glass of water?"

house, add water, and place it in the sun. Eventually, tiny pineapples may form (6 to 12 months).

Concept: Molds Grow in Dark, Moist Conditions

Children have probably seen mold in their own refrigerators or bread baskets but do not realize that mold is an organism called fungi. Observing a mold garden gives children an opportunity to focus on recording observations, keeping records, and writing predictions as they investigate the world of mold.

1. To begin the lesson, show the children a molding orange and ask, WHAT IS ON THE ORANGE? IS THE ORANGE GOOD TO EAT? WHERE HAVE YOU SEEN MOLD? Make a list of the conditions of the places where mold has been found. There should be replies of "moist," "dark," "types of materials such as fruit and bread."

2. To make the mold garden, fill a glass jar about one-third full of sand. Sprinkle water on the sand, and place items that the children bring in on top of the sand. Screw the lid on the jar and begin observations, discussion, and predictions. WHICH OBJECTS DO YOU THINK MOLD WILL GROW ON FIRST? WILL ANY OBJECTS NOT GROW MOLD? Place the mold garden in a dark place and prepare the children to observe. Changing colors, shapes, and sizes should prove interesting.

3. You might want to mention the important role that fungus plays in breaking down materials and in returning the components to the soil.

Teaching Notes

1. Most mold of this type is harmless, but do not take any chances. KEEP THE LID ON THE JAR. In addition, have children wash their hands if any moldy items are touched; do not sniff molds (check for mold allergies among students); and when the activity is completed, throw away all mold gardens without opening them and in a tightly sealed bag.

2. Growing mold in soil is speedy because it is rich in organic materials and for that reason is recommended by some science educators. However, a teacher does not know what else might be in the soil sample, ready to grow. Thus, play it safe and slow—stick to sand.

3. Mold is a type of fungus which lacks chlorophyll. Although warmth, darkness, and moisture are ideal conditions for mold growth, neither warmth nor darkness is necessary for growth. Further investigations of conditions for mold growth may be appropriate in your classroom.

ANIMALS IN THE CLASSROOM

Caring for and studying living things in the classroom and outdoors can be an excellent way to develop a respect for and knowledge of the daily requirements of all forms of life. As children care for a living thing, they seem to develop a sensitivity and sense of responsibility for the life around them. As they maintain the living organism, they become aware of the conditions under which that animal (or plant) survives as well as the conditions under which it will perish. You hope that these understandings and attitudes will carry over into the child's life and the human condition in general.

Before you think about caring for any living organisms, take the precautions listed in this unit. It is vital that living things do not suffer from too much care, such as overfeeding and handling and too little care, such as improper diet, water, temperature, and shelter. In other words, before allowing an animal in your classroom, be sure you know how to take care of it.

Care of the animal should begin before the animal arrives. It is recommended that the entire class has an opportunity to help prepare the cage or environment. As preparations are made, discuss why you are doing so to develop the children's understanding of the specific needs of a species.

When the animal arrives in class, give the new visitor time to become acclimated to its new surroundings. The expected enthusiasm and interest that an animal visitor is likely to generate may overwhelm the newcomer. Instruct children to quietly observe the animal in pairs for brief periods of time. Then, small groups can watch, always quietly, as everyone (animal and children) adjusts to the environment (Figure 14–7).

When planning for an animal guest, ask yourself and your students the following questions:

1. What type of cage or environment does this animal require?
2. What temperature must be maintained?
3. What type of food is needed, and how should that food be presented?
4. Will the animal be able to live in the room over weekends? What will happen to the animal during vacations?
5. Is this an endangered animal? Has this animal been illegally captured or imported? For example, for each parrot of many species that a child encounters, abut 10 parrots have perished in capture or transport. Or as in the case of a species such as the ball python, some animals will never eat in captivity. Limit animal use to those bred in captivity.
6. Does the animal need special lights? Many reptiles must have ultraviolet light, a warm and cool area of their cage, and live food.
7. Will this animal make a good classroom visitor? Should it be handled? Avoid impulse purchases that will lead to future problems.

Tips for Keeping Animals in the Classroom

When animals are in the classroom, care should be taken to insure that neither the children nor the animals are harmed. Mammals protect themselves and their young by biting, scratching, and kicking. Pets such as cats, dogs, rabbits, and guinea pigs should be handled properly and should not be disturbed when eating. For example, rats, rabbits, hamsters, and mice are best picked up by the scruff of the neck, with a hand placed under the body for support. In addition:

1. Check school district procedures to determine if there are any local regulations to be observed. Personnel at the local humane society or zoo are often very cooperative in assisting teachers to create a wholesome animal environment in the classroom. However, zoos receive numerous requests for adoption and usually do not want classroom animals for their collection or "feeder stock."
2. Caution students never to tease animals or to insert their fingers or objects through wire

Figure 14–7 John observes a gerbil as it acclimates to its new environment.

mesh cages. Report animal bites and scratches immediately to the school's medical authority. Provide basic first aid. Usually children follow the example set by the teacher. If you treat the animals with respect, the children will, too.

3. Purchase fish from tanks in which all fish appear healthy.

4. Discourage students from bringing personal pets to school. If they are brought into the room, they should be handled only by their owners, provided a place for fresh water, a place to rest, and then sent home.

5. Guidelines for collecting invertebrates and caring for them in the classroom are provided in Unit 13.

Teaching with Animals

Entire teaching units can be designed around observing animals in the classroom. Science concepts and subject integrations occur naturally as children observe, categorize, and communicate their experiences with animals. The benefits of observing animals far outweigh the cautions and are well worth your time and energy. Here are guiding questions and integrations that lead to investigations.

1. Describe how the animal moves. Do you move that way? See if you can figure out why the animal moves in the way that it does. Does anything make it move faster or slower? Add your observations to the observation list (Figure 14–8).

2. How does the animal eat its food? Does it use its feet or any other part of its body to help it eat? Does it prefer a specific type of food? Make a chart or graph showing preferences.

3. What do the animals do all day? Keep a record of the animal's activities, or pinpoint several specific behaviors such as recording the type of food eaten. Are there times when the animal is more or less active? Take

Michael Parker	Gerbils

They play.
The gerbils drink water.
They are hiding in their house.
He's lookin, playin.
He jumped back down in the house.

Figure 14–8 Michael observes and records some of the daily activities of gerbils.

black-and-white Polaroid® pictures of the animal at the same time of the day. Chart the results.

4. How do animals react to different objects in their environment? Offer gerbils paper towel tubes, and watch them play. Write a story that sequences the actions of the gerbils.

5. What type of sounds do the animals make? Identify different taped animal sounds, and decide if you can tell the size of an animal by its sound. Have children tape record different sounds made by the animal such as sleeping, eating, playing, drinking. Play the tape and have children make up stories about what they think is happening.

6. How can we keep earthworms in the classroom? Have children research what is required for keeping earthworms healthy. Earthworms make good pets because they can be handled with less stress to the animal than mammals, birds, reptiles, and amphibians.

7. Describe the animal's body covering. Why do you think it has this type of covering? Compare the body coverings of different animals. Design a center that allows children to feel objects that simulate animal coverings (refer to Unit 18). Observe these coverings on a trip to the zoo.

8. How does the animal drink? Can you think of other animals that drink in the same way? Categorize ways that animals drink (a cat laps water, a snake sucks water).

9. Seven- and 8-year-olds are not ready for formal outlining yet, but building a web is a good way to organize what they are learning about animals. This type of organization refreshes memory for what children have seen or studied and relates any information they are collecting. Figure 14–9 presents their ideas in a loosely structured way. The teacher selects the main divisions and writes them on the chalkboard. Then, the children give the main points. If the children are working in committees to research different aspects, this strategy illustrates the relatedness of the entire project.

A TRIP TO THE ZOO

A trip to the zoo is a terrific way to offer children opportunities to explore the world of animals. Observing animals in a zoo setting is a high interest activity that helps children learn about animals and

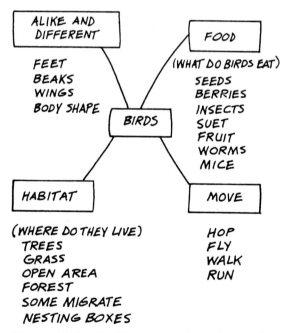

Figure 14–9 Webbing to review what we have learned

their needs. The following suggestions are designed to help maximize the unique setting of a zoo.

Before, During, and After

To make the most of your zoo visit, plan learning experiences that will be taught before going to the zoo, during the zoo visit, and after returning to the classroom. For example, you might want to focus your plans on the similarities and differences between reptiles and amphibians. In the following scenario, Mrs. Red Fox decides to relate class discussions and observations to turtles.

Before going to the zoo, Mrs. Red Fox prepares learning stations for her class. The stations will prepare the children for their zoo visit.

Station 1. Mrs. Red Fox prepares items that simulate body covering for the children to feel. To represent the dry, scaly skin of most reptiles, she rolls shelled sunflower seeds in clay. Oiled cellophane represents the moist, glandular skin of most amphibians. As children visit this station, they are invited to touch the simulated coverings and match picture cards of animals that might feel dry or slimy.

Station 2. To emphasize the role of camouflage in both reptiles and amphibians, the teacher prepares two pieces of black construction paper. A yellow pipe cleaner is taped to one piece of paper and a black pipe cleaner is taped to another. Ask, WHICH IS HARDER TO SEE? HOW DO YOU THINK THIS HELPS THE ANIMAL SURVIVE? DESIGN CAMOUFLAGE FOR A GREEN PIPE CLEANER THAT LIVES IN A DESERT.

Station 3. Some reptiles and amphibians rely on sensing vibrations to "hear" because they do not have outer ears. Mrs. Red Fox has the children tap a tuning fork on a surface and hold it near their ear. She says, DESCRIBE WHAT HAPPENS. TAP THE FORK AGAIN AND PRESS IT AGAINST YOUR CHEEK. WHAT HAPPENS THIS TIME? The class discusses how vibrations tell the animal what is happening. Some of the children begin comparing how birds and mammals hear and sense vibrations.

Station 4. Mrs. Red Fox has the children draw what they think a turtle will look like and what kind of home it will have.

At the Zoo

Mrs. Red Fox divides her class into small groups and assigns a chaperone to each small group. Each group has a turtle task card. When the groups come to the turtle exhibit, the chaperone helps the children complete the questions (Figure 14–10). The children are asked to observe and answer the following questions:

- How many turtles do you see?
- What are they doing?
- Are turtle toes like your toes?
- What are the turtles eating?
- Try walking around the areas as slowly as the turtle is moving. How does it feel?
- How are you and the turtle alike?
- How are you different?
- What other animals are living with the turtle?
- Is it easy to find the turtles in the exhibit?

As the children move to an amphibian exhibit such as frogs, toads, and salamanders, they make comparisons between the turtles and the amphibians. Mrs. Red Fox makes sure that the exhibit

Figure 14–10   "Can you see the animal?"

signs are read and questions are asked to gather additional information.

After the Zoo Visit

Mrs. Red Fox reinforces what the children have learned with a variety of learning experiences. The class makes turtle candy from caramels, nuts, and chocolate bits, and the children create a play about turtles and how they live.

Each child creates a shoebox diorama of the turtle habitat. The teacher asks, DID THE TURTLE LIVE IN THE SAME WAY THAT YOU THOUGHT IT WOULD? WHAT WAS DIFFERENT? WHAT WAS THE SAME? She has the children compare what they knew about turtles before the visit to the diorama that they have created. Mrs. Red Fox has storybooks and reference books available for children to find out more about reptiles and amphibians.

Additional Animal Activities

The following questions and activities can be used before, during, or after a trip to the zoo:

1. WHO MANY TOES DOES A GIRAFFE HAVE? WHAT COLOR IS A GIRAFFE'S TONGUE? CAN YOU TOUCH YOUR NOSE WITH YOUR TONGUE? Explain that giraffes use their tongues the way we use forks and spoons.
2. A snake is covered with scales. Ask, ARE THE SCALES ON A SNAKE'S STOMACH THE SAME SHAPE AND SIZE AS THOSE ON ITS BACK? DOES A SNAKE HAVE FEATHERS? DOES A SNAKE HAVE FUR?
3. People have several different types of teeth in their mouth. After looking in a few mouths, have the children look at a crocodile's teeth. ARE THE TEETH ALL THE SAME TYPE? WHY DO YOU THINK SO?
4. WHAT DO WE USE TO PROTECT OUR FEET? HOW ARE THE FEET OF THE SHEEP AND DEER ADAPTED TO WHERE THEY LIVE? When in front of the

hoofed animal display, have students stretch out their arms and then slowly move their arms together while looking directly ahead. WHEN CAN YOU SEE YOUR HANDS? Direct the children's attention to the hoofed animals. WHERE ARE THE DEER'S EYES LOCATED? Discuss the location of the eyes, and name some advantages of having eyes that can see behind you.

5. In front of the aquarium ask, HOW DO YOU THINK FISH BREATHE? DO FISH HAVE NOSES? FIND A FISH THAT FEEDS FROM THE TOP OF THE TANK. FIND ONE THAT FEEDS FROM THE BOTTOM OF THE TANK. DO ANY OF THE FISH FEED IN THE MIDDLE OF THE TANK?

6. DO ANY OF THE ANIMALS HAVE BABIES? Refer to these questions when observing animal babies. DO THE BABIES LOOK LIKE THE ADULT? HOW ARE THEY DIFFERENT? DOES THE BABY MOVE AROUND ON ITS OWN? IS ONE OF THE ADULTS TAKING CARE OF THE BABY? WHAT IS THE ADULT DOING FOR THE BABY?

Learning at the zoo can be an exciting experience. For a successful trip, plan activities for before, during, and after a zoo visit. If this is your first trip to the zoo, concentrate on familiar body parts and activities. For example, how does the animal move, eat, hear, see, or protect itself? Use these questions to encourage discussion of the special abilities and adaptations of animals (Figure 14–11).

SUMMARY

Teaching life science concepts on a firsthand basis is essential to planning and teaching science to primary age children. Children display an eagerness in learning about the living things around them. This unit provides activities about seeds, plants, and molds; contains suggestions for caring for and studying living things, both in the classroom and outdoors; and keeping animals in the classroom.

Figure 14–11 Touching a snake is fun in the zoo class.

Animal observations capitalize on the interest of children. The benefits of these observations far outweigh any cautions. A trip to the zoo can be a meaningful experience if specific plans are made for the visit. Prepare activities to do before, during, and after the trip.

RESOURCES FOR ANIMAL CARE

Science and Children, a journal of the National Science Teachers Association, has an informative monthly column on the care and maintenance of specific living organisms. Each month a different plant or animal receives in-depth treatment.

Dolensek, E. (1976). *A practical guide to impractical pets*. New York, NY: Viking Press.

Hampton, C., Hampton, C., Kammer, D. (1988). *Classroom creature culture*. Washington, DC: National Science Teachers Association.

Orlans, F. B. (1977). *Animal care from protozoa to small animals*. Menlo Park, CA: Addison-Wesley.

Nichol, J. (1989). *The animal smugglers*. New York: Facts on File Inc.

Smith, H. M. (1980). *Snakes as pets* (4th ed.) NJ: T.F.H. Publications, Inc. Ltd.

Smith, H. M. (1988). Snakes as pets. *Science and Children*, 25(6), 36.

FURTHER READING AND RESOURCES

Althouse, R. (1988). *Investigating science experiences for young children*. New York, NY: Teachers College Press.

Cobb, V. (1984). *Science experiments you can eat*. New York: J. P. Lippincott Company.

Council for Elementary Science International. (1984). *Outdoor learning experiences*. Columbus, OH: SMEAC Information Reference Center.

Dean, R. A., Dean, M. M., & Motz, L. (1987). *Safety in the elementary classroom*. Washington, DC: National Science Teachers Association.

DeVito, A., & Krockover, G. H. (1980). *Creative sciencing: Ideas and activities for teachers and children*. Boston: Little, Brown and Company.

Gega, P. (1993). *Science in elementary education*. New York, NY: Prentice-Hall.

Harlan, J. (1991). *Science experiences for the early childhood years*.

McIntyre, M. (1984). *Early childhood and science*. Washington, DC: National Science Teachers Association.

Tolman, M. N., & Morton, J. O. (1987). *Life science activities for grades 2–8*. West Nyack, NY: Parker Publishing.

SUGGESTED COMPUTER PROGRAMS

Animal homes and stories [Computer program]. Troll Associates.

Bumble games [Computer program]. The Learning Company.

"Cell"ebration [Computer program]. Science for Kids.

Elementary volume 4 math/science (#705) [Computer program]. MECC.

A field trip into the sea [Computer program]. Wings for Learning.

Fish scales [Computer program]. DLM.

Food chains [Computer program]. MCE, Inc.

Katie's farm [Computer program]. Lawrence Productions.

Life cycles [Computer program]. MCE, Inc.

Plant doctor [Computer program]. Scholastic.

The pond [Computer program]. Sunburst.

Wetlands [Computer program]. Optical Data.

Woolly's garden [Computer program]. MECC.

SUGGESTED ACTIVITIES

1. Use a web to plan a unit centered around two concepts important in teaching about animals to primary age children. Groups could brainstorm different concepts and put a web of the results on a large sheet of paper. Teach this unit to primary age children.

2. Would you web the example seed unit in the same way? There are countless ways to web a seed unit. Select different seed or plant concepts around which to focus your planning, and share them with the class. State your rationale.

3. Develop questions and evaluation strategies for the seed unit.

4. Design an activity for teaching with a classroom animal.

5. How many subject integrations will you use in your animal activity?

6. Identify the teaching strategies that were discussed in units 5, 6, and 7. Compare lists. Which strategies did you use in designing your activity?

REVIEW

1. List six life science concepts that are appropriate for primary age children.
2. What planning strategy can you use to develop a life science teaching unit?
3. Answer *True* or *False*:
   _____a. Animals can suffer from overfeeding and too much care.
   _____b. Wait until the animal arrives before preparing a home.
   _____c. Children should be encouraged to bring personal pets to the classroom.
   _____d. Most school systems do not have rules about animals in the classroom.
4. What are questions you should ask yourself as you prepare for an animal in your classroom?

UNIT 15 Physical Science

Physical science experiences are fun and exciting for primary age children. Even though these experiences can be dramatic and astounding for children, teaching the concepts is more foolproof than you might think. This is true for several reasons.

First, the physical sciences abound with opportunities for using discrepant events (discussed in Unit 6) that put students in disequilibrium and ready them for learning. Thus, they are eager and ready to explore. Second, most experiences are instantly repeatable. In this way, the child can continue exploring without elaborate preparation. And finally, the hands-on nature of physical science explorations make them ideal for use with primary age children.

This unit begins with the physical science concepts that are basic to primary grade learning and presents an example of ways that the topic of air can be integrated with science concepts of movement and changes in matter, gravity, light, and color. The subject integrations and lessons are part of the webbing scheme depicted in Figure 7–4 of Unit 7. Suggestions for the teaching of sound are also included (Figure 15–1).

Figure 15–1 "I can play a tune."

PHYSICAL SCIENCE CONCEPTS

The following concepts are basic to understanding the physical sciences. Use this list to identify concepts around which you can develop a planning web such as those described in units 7 and 14.

- Air takes up space.
- Air has weight.
- Air is all around us.
- Things that make sound vibrate.
- Moving air pushes things.
- Air slows moving objects.
- Things near the earth fall to the ground unless something holds them up.
- Everything is made from material called *matter*.
- All matter takes up space.
- Matter can change into a solid, liquid, or gas.
- Matter can be classified according to observable characteristics.
- Physical and chemical changes are two basic ways of changing things.
- In a physical change, appearances change, and the substance remains the same. (tearing paper, chopping wood)
- In a chemical change, the characteristics change so that a new substance is formed. (burning, rusting)
- A mixture consists of two or more substances that retain their separate identities when mixed together.
- Temperature tells how hot or cold an object is.
- There are many types of energy—light, heat, sound, electricity, motion, magnetic.
- Magnets can be used to make some things move without being touched.
- Static electricity is produced when two different materials are rubbed together.
- There are three parts to a simple electric circuit: a source of electricity, a path for electricity to travel, and something that uses the electricity (a light bulb or bell).
- Some materials allow electricity to pass through them.
- To see color, light is needed.
- The way to change how something is moving is to give it a push or a pull.
- Machines make it easier to move things.
- Things move in many ways, such as straight, zigzag, around and around, back and forth, and fast and slow.

PLANNING AND TEACHING A UNIT ABOUT AIR

The learning experiences suggested in this unit follow the format described in Unit 7 and used in the seed unit (refer to Unit 14). Each lesson states a concept, an objective, materials, and suggestions for teaching the concept. Extensions, integrations, and possible evaluation procedures are indicated in the body of the lesson, when appropriate, and at the end of the unit. The topic of air is explored with bubble and sound lessons (Figure 15–2).

Exploring Bubbles

Children love to play with bubbles. They love to create bubbles, chase bubbles, and pop bubbles. Why not take advantage of this interest to teach science concepts with a subject children already know something about?

Figure 15–2   "What is inside of the bubble?"

THE BUBBLE MACHINE

CONCEPT: Bubbles have air inside of them.

OBJECTIVE: The child will construct a bubble machine by manipulating materials to produce bubbles.

MATERIALS: Mix a bubble solution of 8 teaspoons (1/2 cup) liquid detergent and 1 quart water. Punch holes about halfway down the side of enough paper cups for each child. A box of drinking straws will also be needed. Write each child's name over the hole.

PROCEDURE: Assemble a bubble machine by inserting a straw through a hole in a paper cup and filling with detergent solution to just below the hole. Have the children observe the machine as you blow bubbles. Ask, WHAT DO YOU THINK IS HAPPENING? Have the children assemble bubble machines. Each child should insert a straw into the hole in the side of the paper cup and then pour some detergent solution into the cup just below the hole. Give children time to try bubble blowing and ask, WHAT DO YOUR BUBBLES LOOK LIKE? DESCRIBE YOUR BUBBLES. HOW MANY BUBBLES CAN YOU BLOW? WHAT IS INSIDE OF THE BUBBLE? (Figure 15–3).

EXTENSIONS: Make bubble books with drawings that depict the bubble machine experiences. Encourage children to write about their pictures. Read the books to the class; then put them in the Library Center for perusal.

INVENTING BUBBLE MACHINES

CONCEPT: Many different shapes will create bubbles.

OBJECTIVE: Make a shape that will create a bubble. Observe air entering bubbles and taking up space.

MATERIALS: Mixed bubble solution; soft, bendable wire; pans for bubble solution.

PROCEDURE: YOUR BUBBLE MACHINE WORKS WELL. CAN YOU BEND WIRE INTO SHAPES THAT WILL MAKE BUBBLES? Have children "mess around" with wire to create a variety of shapes for making bubbles. Have them test the shapes by blowing air into the bubble film or moving the wire shape through the air. Ask, DID YOU MAKE A BUBBLE? WAS YOUR BUBBLE THE SAME SHAPE AS THE WIRE? (Figure 15–3).

EXTENSION: Have other materials available for bubble machine making such as a pierced spatula, turkey baster, berry basket bottom, sieve, and other kitchen items. Ask, WHAT SHAPE DO YOU THINK THESE BUBBLES WILL BE? WHAT DO YOU NOTICE ABOUT THE SIZE OF THE BUBBLES? (Different sizes.) Have children record predictions and results for the different bubble blowers (Figure 15–4).

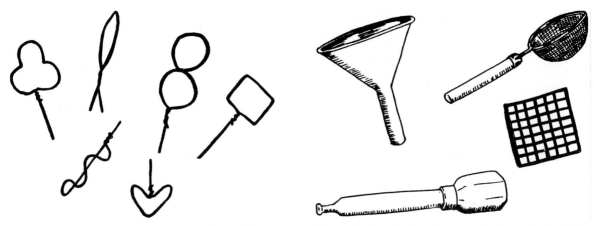

Figure 15–3 Wire shapes for blowing bubbles   **Figure 15–4** Kitchen shapes make interesting bubbles.

TABLETOP BUBBLES

CONCEPT: Air takes up space.

OBJECTIVE: Use air to create bubble sculpture. Predict how the bubbles will act on top of tables.

MATERIALS: Bubble solution, straws, cups, flat trays.

PROCEDURE: Have children dip out a small amount of bubble solution on a tray and spread it around. Ask, WHAT DO YOU THINK WILL HAPPEN IF YOU BLOW AIR INTO THE BUBBLE SOLUTION? (Bubbles will form.) Instruct children to dip a straw into the soap on the tray and blow gently. Give them time to "mess around" with tray top bubble blowing. Present challenges. CAN YOU BLOW A BUBBLE THE SIZE OF A BOWL? Have several children work together to make a community bubble. One child begins blowing the bubble and others join in by adding air to the inside of the bubble. (The straws must be wet to avoid breaking the bubble.) Bubble cities of the future can be made by adding more solution to the tray and blowing several bubble domes next to one another.

EXTENSION: Bubbles inside of bubbles. CAN YOU FIT A BUBBLE INSIDE OF A BUBBLE? Have children blow a bubble. Then insert a wet straw inside of the bubble and start a new bubble. WHAT HAPPENS IF THE SIDES TOUCH? (Figure 15–5). Make bubble chains. Have children blow a bubble with a straw. Then, wiggle the straw and blow another one. Soon, a chain of bubbles will form. Ask, HOW MANY BUBBLES CAN YOU MAKE?

Investigation Questions for Exploring Air and Bubbles

1. Will other liquids create bubbles?
2. Will adding a liquid called *glycerin* to the bubble solution make the bubbles stronger? (Yes.) Can you think of other things to add to the bubble solution to make the bubbles last longer? Test your formulas.

Figure 15–5   "Can you fit a bubble inside of a bubble?"

3. Are bubbles always round? (Yes, unless some of them stick together. Forces acting inside and outside of the soap film are the same all over it.)

SUBJECT INTEGRATIONS

Bubbles and Science

1. **Observe bubbles.** Describe color, movement, size, shape. How many different colors do you see in the soap bubble? How do the colors move and change? Look at the bubbles through different colors of cellophane or polarized sunglasses. Do the bubbles change?
2. **Classify bubbles.** Classify by color, size, shape (bubble machine bubbles will stick together and take different shapes), location, how the bubble was made.
3. **Changes in matter.** Ask children to describe some changes that they notice in bubbles. Ask, DID ANYTHING CHANGE? (Yes.) DID YOU SEE A PHYSICAL CHANGE IN THE BUBBLE SOLUTION? (Yes, matter only changes form in a physical change.)

Bubbles and Art

1. **Bubble painting.** Mix bubble solution with liquid poster paint. Put the mixture in a bowl. As the child blows into the paint with a straw, a paint bubble dome forms. Lay construction paper over the bubble. As the paint bubble bursts, it splatters paint on the paper. (Figure 15–6).
2. **Bulletin board.** Make a background of large construction paper bubbles. Display children's writing and art activities in this way.

Bubbles and Math

1. **How high?** Measure the height of the bubbles on a tray top. Measure how long a bubble lasts, predict and measure how many bubbles can be blown, and how far they can float.

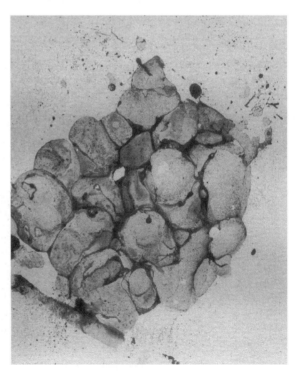

Figure 15–6   Cindy's bubbles break and make a pattern on the paper.

2. Lung capacity. Make a graph of who has the largest lung capacity. Have children discover a way of determining lung capacity by blowing bubbles.

Bubbles and Language Arts

1. Science experiences can provide inspiration for important first steps in writing.
2. **Bubble books.** Provide paper for children to record their bubble explorations. These can be bubble shaped and illustrated.
3. **Books about bubbles.** Read storybooks about bubbles (Appendix B).
4. **Chart story.** Have children write or dictate stories about what they observed when they examined air inside of bubbles (Figure 15–7).

Bubbles and Food Experiences

Children can observe the tiny air bubbles that go into various whipped mixtures. For example, whipped milk topping can be made for cookies. You will need 1/2 cup of instant dry skim milk and 1/2 cup cold water.

Beat with an electric mixer at high speed for 4 minutes. Have children watch the mixture change. Then, add 2 tablespoons of sugar and 1/2 teaspoon vanilla and beat at high speed until the mixture stands in peaks. You may want to add the ingredient "air bubbles" to your recipe. Remind children that air went into what they are eating.

Concept: Air Can Move Things and Slow Things Down

The following suggestions extend science concepts:

1. Moving bubbles. Have children move bubbles in the direction they want them to go by fanning them with paper (Figure 15–8).

2. Paper fans. Make paper fans to move air. These can be accordian-pleated sheets of paper or small paper plates stapled to ice cream bar sticks.

3. Glider designs. Make gliders, and find out how far they can fly.

4. Straw painting. Blow paint with plastic straws. Pick up the paint with air pressure (as with the bubble solution), drop it on paper, and blow the puddles of paint into a design.

5. Make pinwheels. Have children fold squares of paper and hold them in front of a fan or in the wind. Ask, WHAT HAPPENS TO THE PAPER? (It moves.) Help children make pinwheels from typing paper or wallpaper. A pushpin will hold the pinwheel to a pencil eraser and allow it to turn freely. Ask, HOW DID WE PRODUCE MOTION?

6. Air walk. Take children on a walk to find things that are moved by air. Discuss and write about what you have seen. Local windmills are ideal, but weather socks, flags, trees, seeds, clothes on a clothesline, and other moving things work well.

7. Exploring parachutes. Have children make parachutes out of squares of cloth. Tie each corner with string, then thread the four strings through a wooden bead or washer. Drop the parachute from various heights, and predict what will happen. Cut a hole in the top of the parachute, and observe any differences. Make parachutes out of different materials, such as plastic or cupcake liners, and compare their flight.

Matthew   October 12, 1988

To day we were sintest again it was a lot of fun. We were seeing if air took up space. Some people thoght that it did and some thoght it didn't. I blew a very very very very big bubble but it popped in my face. There were different colors and shapes. But they didn't taste good.

Figure 15–7 Matthew has made many observations about bubbles.

Figure 15–8 "Can you make bubbles move?"

8. Baby seeds. Open milkweed pods in the wind and watch the wind disperse the seeds. Refer to the seed lessons in Unit 14 for further investigations.

Exploring Sound

Children love to make music, but they probably do not know anything about the nature of sound. Help them understand that sound is caused when something vibrates by using the following lessons to teach children to see, hear, and feel the sound vibrations around them. Then, make musical instruments that reinforce the concepts.

GOOD VIBRATIONS

CONCEPT: Sound is caused when something vibrates.

OBJECTIVE: Observe objects vibrating and making sounds. Construct musical instruments based on concepts of sound.

MATERIALS: Paper plates, rubber bands, bottle tops, hole punch, paper cups, waxed paper, coffee cans, flexible tubing.

PROCEDURE:

1. Have children begin vibration observations by gently resting their fingers over their vocal cords and saying "Ahhhh" and "Eeee." Ask, WHAT DO YOU FEEL? (Something moving.) Explain that they are feeling vibrations occurring in their vocal cords, where all sounds they make with their voices come from.

2. Then have them place their fingertips against their lips while they simultaneously blow and hum. Reinforce the connection between vibration and sound by touring your classroom. Ask children to identify things that vibrate—the aquarium pump, kitchen timer, air vent, overhead lights. If possible, let them feel the vibrations in these objects and listen to the sounds each makes.

3. *Drum.* Make a simple drum out of a coffee can that has a plastic top. Place grains of rice on the can lid and tap lightly, while your students watch and listen. Ask, WHAT HAPPENS TO THE RICE WHEN YOU DO THIS? (It bounces up and down to the sound of the drum.)

4. *Drumsticks.* Make drumsticks from tennis balls and dowels. Punch a hole in the ball, apply glue to the end and edges of the dowel or stick, and push it into the center of the ball. Or use a butter brush, wadded up rubber bands, or a plastic lemon (Figure 15–9).

5. *Humming cup.* Make a humming cup by cutting the bottom out of a small paper cup. Then have the children cover the newly opened ends with waxed paper and secure with rubber bands. Say, PLACE YOUR LIPS LIGHTLY AGAINST THE WAXED PAPER END OF THE CUP AND HUM. They will get another feel for sound. Paper towel cups can be used in a similar way to make horns (Figure 15–10).

6. *More horns*. A yard of flexible tubing will provide a chance to whisper back and forth and feel sound traveling to their ears through a talking tube. Then, tape a funnel to one end and make a bugle-like horn.

7. *Tambourines*. You can construct this favorite instrument by decorating and shellacking paper plates in which you have already punched holes. Distribute bottle caps that also have holes punched in them, and have children tie two or three caps to each hole in their plates. This is a noisy but fun way to show the relationship between vibrations and sound.

EXTENSIONS: *Build a Band*. Making musical instruments will give children an opportunity to observe vibrations in other ways. Make a variety of instruments and decorate for a special occasion.

Figure 15–9 George makes drumsticks from tennis balls.

Figure 15–10 "Can you feel the vibrations of a humming cup?"

Wind Instruments

Wind instruments such as flutes, whistles, and panpipes depend on vibrating columns of air for their sound. The longer the column of air, the lower the pitch. (The highness or lowness of a sound is its *pitch*. The more vibrations per second, the higher the tone that is produced; the fewer vibrations, the lower the tone.) The following lesson demonstrates the relationship between the length of an air column and musical pitch:

BOTTLES, WATER, AND AIR

CONCEPT: Pitch is the highness or lowness of a sound.

OBJECTIVE: Recognize differences in sound. Construct wind instruments.

MATERIALS: Ten bottles of the same height, water.

PROCEDURE: Prepare by filling glass soda bottles to varying levels with water. (Plastic bottles are too easily knocked over.) Hold up an empty bottle and ask, WHAT DO YOU THINK IS IN THE BOTTLE? WHAT DO YOU THINK WILL HAPPEN IF THE AIR IN THE BOTTLE VIBRATES? Demonstrate by blowing across the top of the empty bottle. Teach children to direct air across the mouth of a bottle. This is worth taking the time to do. Instruct children to press the mouth of the bottle lightly against their lower lip and direct air straight across the mouth of the bottle. (Do not blow into the bottle. The secret is blowing straight across. Give them time to "mess around" with their new skill (Figure 15–11). Then ask, WHAT DO YOU THINK WILL HAPPEN IF YOU BLOW ACROSS A BOTTLE WITH WATER IN IT? Pour water into bottles, and have children find out what will happen. Children will discover that the bottles make sounds that vary in pitch. They might even play a tune (Figure 15–12).

EXTENSION: Emphasize the meaning of pitch by reading a familiar tale in which high- and low-pitched sounds figure. For example, ask children to imitate the three billy goats gruff. Dramatize differences in pitch with voice and body activities.

Figure 15–11   Marie has learned to make music with a bottle.

BOTTLES AND WATER

Collect eight bottles to make a scale—your job will be easier if they are all the same kind and size. To tune the bottles, you'll need to fill them to varying heights with water.

Start by dividing the volume of water that one of the bottles could accommodate by the number of notes you wish to produce. For example, if you want a one octave scale, divide the volume by eight. Then, leaving bottle one empty, put 1/8 of the volume into bottle two, 1/4 into bottle three, 3/8 into bottle four, and so on until bottle eight contains 7/8 of its volume of water. Adjust the amount of water up and down in the bottles until the scale intervals sound (more or less) true. Use masking tape to mark the correct level on each bottle.

Figure 15–12   Formula for bottle music.

FURTHER READING AND RESOURCES

Abruscoto, J. 1988. *Teaching science to children.* Englewood Cliffs, NJ: Prentice Hall.

Allison, L., and Katz, D. 1983. *Gee, wiz!* Boston, Mass.: Little, Brown and Company.

Althouse, R. (1988). *Investigating science experiences for young children.* New York: Teachers College Press.

Council for Elementary Science International Sourcebook V. (1988). *Physical science activities for elementary and middle school.*

Columbus, OH: SMEAC Information Reference Center.

Froschauer, L. (1993). *Teaching elementary science with toys: CESI sourcebook VII.* Columbus, OH: The ERIC Clearinghouse for Science, Mathematics, and Environmental Science.

Harlan, J. (1991). *Science experiences for early childhood years.* New York: Macmillan.

Hawkinson, J., & Faulhaber, M. (1969). *Music*

and instruments for children to make. Chicago: Whitman.

Lind, K. K. (1985). The beat of the band. *Science and Children, 23*(3): 32–33.

Lind, K. K. (1986). The beat goes on. *Science and Children, 23*(7), 39–41.

Perez, J. (1988). *Explore and experiment.* Bridgeport, CT: First Teacher Press.

Zubrowski, B. (1979). *Bubbles.* Boston: Little, Brown and Company.

SUGGESTED COMPUTER PROGRAMS

Balancing bears [Computer program]. Sunburst.

Kid-Leidoscope [Computer program]. Methods and Solutions/Mindplay.

Miner's cave [Computer program]. MECC.

Mystery matter [Computer program]. MECC.

An ocean of air [Computer program]. MCE, Inc.

Paper plane pilot [Computer program]. MECC.

Wood car rally [Computer program]. MECC.

SUGGESTED ACTIVITIES

1. Which process skills are used in the bubble unit? Identify each skill and how it is incorporated into the study of air inside of bubbles. Teach the unit to children. Which integrations and activities did you use?

2. Interview teachers of primary age children to find out what types of physical science activities they introduce to children. Do any of these activities include the exploration of materials? Record your observations for discussion.

3. Brainstorm strategies to prepare children to understand physical science topics such as magnets, light, and electricity. Pick a topic, and prepare a learning experience that will aid in future concept development.

4. Select a physical science concept, and prepare a learning cycle to teach that concept. Teach it to children. Record your observations for discussion.

5. Present a lesson about sound for primary age children. What types of learning experiences will you design for your students? Explain how you will apply Piaget's theory of development to this topic.

6. Go to a bookstore or library, and identify books to enhance the teaching of physical science. Present an evaluation of these materials and how you might use them to reinforce science concepts.

REVIEW

1. Explain why primary age children should explore physical science activities (give at least two reasons).

2. List six physical science concepts that are appropriate for primary grade science lessons.

3. What type of activities should be used to teach physical science concepts?

UNIT 16 Earth Science and Environmental Education

OBJECTIVES

After studying this unit, the students should be able to
- Design earth science and environmental education investigations for primary age children
- Develop an understanding of earth science concepts and environmental education topics that are appropriate for primary age children
- Develop structured and unstructured earth science learning experiences with primary age children
- Develop learning experiences in environmental education with primary age children
- Apply unit planning webbing strategies to earth science content
- Integrate earth science with other subject areas

Teaching children about rocks, fossils, weather, space, water, and the environment exposes them to new vocabulary and helps them gain experience with earth science concepts. It is not meant that children memorize words and ideas but rather "mess around" in preparation for future learning. In this way, when they are introduced to the same concepts at more advanced stages of development, they will have familiarity with the ideas and be open and receptive to learning.

This unit begins with appropriate earth science concepts that are basic to primary grade learning and suggests a way that the topic of rocks can be developed into a unit and integrated into the classroom. The rock lessons (Figure 16–1) are included to help you get started. You may find the other science and environmental education topics and lessons in this unit useful in introducing children to earth science and environmental concepts. The concepts listed below are appropraite for use with primary age children:

EARTH SCIENCE AND ENVIRONMENTAL EDUCATION CONCEPTS

- Rocks are formed in different ways.
- Rocks are nonliving things.
- Sand is made up of tiny pieces of rock.

Figure 16–1 Looking for a special rock.

- Water and wind change the surface of the earth.
- Mountains and land are made of rocks and soil.
- Dinosaurs are extinct, but fossil evidence tells us about them. Our only knowledge of some plants and animals that once lived on the earth is through the fossils we have found.
- *Evaporation* means a liquid changes into a gas (vapor) in the air.
- *Condensation* means a gas changes to a liquid. Water vapor is an example of condensation.
- The *atmosphere* is the air around us. It has conditions such as wind, moisture, and temperature. *Weather* is what we call the conditions of the atmosphere.
- There are four seasons, and each has unique weather.
- Temperature is how hot or cold something is.

- Clouds and fog are made of droplets of water.
- The earth has a layer of air and water around it.
- Water is a liquid and is called *ice* when it is solid.
- The sun gives off light and heats and warms the land, air, and water.
- A light source at a great distance looks small.
- The sun, moon, and stars all appear to move slowly across the sky. The moon appears to change in size and shape. Sometimes the moon can be seen at night, and sometimes it can be seen during the day.
- There are many stars in the sky. They do not look the same in brightness and color and are not scattered evenly.
- The patterns of stars stay the same and appear to move across the sky.

A CARTON OF ROCKS

CONCEPT: There are many kinds of rocks.

OBJECTIVES: Observe different types of rocks. Classify rocks in different ways.

MATERIALS: An egg carton for each child or group, small labels that can be glued on the box, pencils or pens, a handful of rocks.

PROCEDURE: Show the children the rocks in your hand. Ask the children, WHAT ARE THESE, AND WHERE ARE THEY FOUND? Give each small group of children a few rocks, and encourage them to develop classification schemes for them, such as flat, speckled, animal-shaped. Younger children will notice size and color first, then shape and the way the rock feels. Have the children develop labels for the categories.

Take the children to any place where there are rocks. Set a generous time limit, and have them search for different types of rocks to fill their egg cartons. Then, have the children share and classify what they have found. Use labels to identify rocks in the egg carton collections (speckled, round, and so on; Figure 16–2).

EXTENSION:
1. Older children are able to compare rock characteristics with pictures in rock identification handbooks.
2. Use various rocks to create a rock collage.
3. Read *Sylvester and the Magic Pebble*, by William Steig. A round red pebble makes a nice prop.

Figure 16–2   Kate and Sara sort the rocks they have collected.

Figure 16–3   Labeling rocks by hardness

THINKING LIKE A GEOLOGIST

CONCEPT: Some rocks are harder than other rocks.

OBJECTIVE: Examine rocks and minerals to determine how hard they are. Classify rocks by characteristics.

MATERIALS: An assortment of rocks (a rock and mineral set, if possible), roofing nails, pennies.

PROCEDURE: Give groups of children an assortment of rocks to observe. After they have had time to observe the rocks, ask, CAN YOU SCRATCH ANY OF THE ROCKS WITH YOUR FINGERNAIL? As they notice a difference in rocks, ask, CAN SOME ROCKS BE SCRATCHED IN THIS WAY? (Yes.) WHAT ELSE COULD YOU USE TO SCRATCH ROCKS?

After children try to scratch rocks with different objects such as the penny and fingernail, explain that finding out if a rock crumbles easily is one of the things a geologist does. (Even though children may not remember the term, the labeling is important.)

Tell the children that they are going to think like a geologist and determine how hard a rock is. Make a list of ways that the children will test the rocks. For example:

Can be rubbed off on fingers
Can be scratched with fingernail
Can be scratched with a penny
Hard to scratch

Have the children test the rocks and place them with the statement that best describes the rock. Ask, WHICH ROCKS DO YOU THINK ARE THE HARDEST? (Those that are hard to scratch; Figure 16–3).

Then, take the children outside to see which rocks can be used to draw streaks or lines on the sidewalk. Children might even see distinctive colors. Ask, WHAT COLORS ARE THE STREAKS? Have children compare the colors in the rocks with the colors of the streaks. Ask, CAN WE CLASSIFY ROCKS IN THIS WAY? (Yes.) You may want to review some of the ways that geologists classify rocks (appearance, texture, hardness, color).

EXTENSION: As children wash their hands, compare wet and dry rocks. What differences do they notice? Geologists use hardness and streak tests to identify minerals. Introduce the term "minerals" when children notice bits of color in the rocks. Explain that rocks are made up of many different ingredients (minerals).

EXPLORING COOKIES

CONCEPT: Rocks are formed in different ways.

OBJECTIVE: Identify similarities between rocks and cookies. Stimulate curiosity about earth processes.

MATERIALS: Oatmeal chocolate chip cookie recipe on chart and on index cards, ingredients for making cookies (two cookies for each child).

PROCEDURE: Pass out recipe cards to the small groups. Show the children what the various ingredients look like as you discuss those used in making oatmeal chocolate chip cookies. Give each small group of children samples of the cookie ingredients. Bake the cookies. Then, give each child two cookies (one to examine and one to eat).

Have the children explore the cookie and compare the ingredients and the information on the recipe card with the final product. Ask, CAN YOU SEE THE INGREDIENTS? (Some of them.) WHICH INGREDIENTS DO YOU SEE? CAN YOU TASTE ANY OF THE INGREDIENTS? (Figure 16–4) DO THE INGREDIENTS LOOK THE SAME? (No, some have changed.) Once the children recognize that some ingredients are still recognizable after baking and some are no longer in the same state, ask, IN WHAT WAY HAVE THEY CHANGED? (Melted, dissolved, and so on.) WHAT CHANGED THE INGREDIENTS? (Mixing, pressing, heat.) Discuss heat and chemical changes, if appropriate.

Give children an assortment of rocks, and tell them that rocks have ingredients, too. The earth acts like a baker and turns ingredients into rocks. (Rock ingredients, *minerals*, are turned into rock by pressure, heat, and moving around.) Let children handle mineral samples and try to find evidence of these samples in the rocks.

EXTENSION: Take a rock field trip. Have each child find an egg-sized rock. Wrap the rock in cloth and have an adult hit it with a hammer. Use hand lenses to examine the pieces of broken rock. Ask, HOW MANY PIECES OF ROCK ARE THERE NOW? Have the children explore the shape, size, and color of the fragments and describe the inside and outside appearance of the rock. The inside of a dull-looking rock is usually filled with pattern, texture, and color. Use a small light to help compare the shine and luster of various rocks. Have the children draw or color what they see through the hand lens.

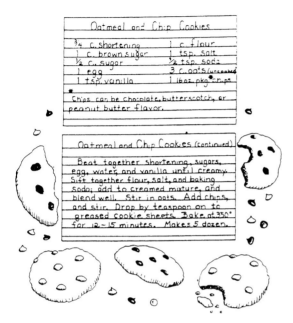

Oatmeal and Chip Cookies

¾ C. shortening	1 c. flour
1 c. brown sugar	1 tsp. salt
½ C. sugar	½ tsp. soda
1 egg	3 c. oats (uncooked)
1 tsp. vanilla	1 16 oz. pkg. chips

Chips can be chocolate, butterscotch, or peanut butter flavor.

Oatmeal and Chip Cookies (continued)

Beat together shortening, sugars, egg, water, and vanilla until creamy. Sift together flour, salt, and baking soda; add to creamed mixture, and blend well. Stir in oats. Add chips, and stir. Drop by teaspoon on to greased cookie sheets. Bake at 350° for 12-15 minutes. Makes 5 dozen.

Figure 16–4 "Compare the ingredients for making cookies with the cookies."

- *Environment* is the area around any given object or organism.
- The quality of air, water, and soil is affected by human activity.
- Keeping anything going uses up some resource.
- Water and wind change the surface of the earth.

PLANNING AND TEACHING A UNIT ON ROCKS

The learning experiences suggested in this unit follow the format described in Unit 7 and used in units 14 and 15. Each lesson states a concept, an objective, materials, and suggestions for teaching the concepts. Extensions, integrations, and possible evaluation procedures are indicated in the body of the lesson, when appropriate, and at the end of the unit.

The following basic geology lessons introduce fundamental concepts and stimulate children's curiosity about rocks, minerals, and earth

processes. The strategies will acquaint primary age children with the nature of rocks in a way that is immediate, exciting, and fun.

HOW ROCKS ARE FORMED

You can make the study of rocks more meaningful for your students if you know the basic way rocks are formed and a few common examples of each.

Igneous Rocks

Igneous rocks are formed through the cooling of magma or lava. Examples of igneous rocks formed by the rapid cooling of surface lava are pumice, obsidian, and basalt. Granite is the most common example of slow, below-surface cooling of molten rock. Refer to the "Igneous Rock Fudge" cooking experience integration.

Sedimentary Rocks

These rocks are formed from eroded rocks, sand, clay, silt, pebbles, and other stones. Compressed skeletons, shells, and dissolved chemicals also form sedimentary rocks. These rocks are usually deposited in layers and are compacted and cemented by the pressure of the overlying sediments. Examples of sedimentary rocks are conglomerate, sandstone, shale, and limestone. Fossils are frequently found in sedimentary rock. Refer to the "Pudding Stone" cooking experience integration.

Metamorphic Rocks

The term *metamorphic* means "changed in form." Metamorphic rock is formed when sedimentary and igneous rocks are completely changed in form through pressure and heat. For example, limestone becomes marble, shale becomes slate, and sandstone may become quartzite. These rocks are harder than most rocks.

Show the effect of pressure by pressing a bag of marshmallows or several spongy rubber balls under books on a flat surface. Have the children describe the change in the physical appearance of

ICICLE STALACTITES

CONCEPT: Stalactites are formed as mineral-rich water drips from the ceilings of caves.

OBJECTIVE: Observe the formation of stalactites in a simulated cave. Make a model of a cave.

MATERIALS: Cardboard box, pictures of caves, cotton string, small cardboard box, water, food coloring, eye dropper.

PROCEDURE: Prepare a model of a cave by cutting a large hole in one side of a cardboard box. Make a hole in the top of the box, tie heavy cotton string to a stick, and hang the string through the hole. The string should be about an inch above the bottom of the box. You may want to add a few rocks to the bottom of the box.

The box should be attached to the outside of a classroom window with the hole in the side of the box facing the inside of the classroom. The little cave should be placed in the shade so that the icicle stalactite will not melt. In this way, children can observe the formation of an icicle stalactite. On a cold day, begin forming the stalactite by dripping water down the string a few drops at a time. Each day add more drops of water. This model will take a long time to develop, much like the development of a cave stalactite. In this way, children learn about the formation of stalactites and that they take a long time to form (Figure 16–5).

Show children pictures of caves, and discuss features of caves. Explain that *stalactites* develop from the ceiling of a cave, and *stalagmites* develop from the floor of the cave.

As the icicle stalactite forms, begin adding food coloring to the drops of water to simulate the minerals found in the dripping cave water. Say, DESCRIBE THE CHANGES YOU SEE IN THE STALACTITE.

Have children predict if a stalagmite might form in their cave. Then, as the stalagmite begins to grow, ask, WHAT CAUSES THE STALAGMITE TO FORM? (Some water will drip on the bottom of the cave and begin building up to meet the stalactite.) Have children record and draw the changes inside of the classroom box cave. (Refer to the extension.)

A large calendar chart will emphasize the length of time required for a stalactite to develop. Have children take turns drawing the developing cave. Ask, WHAT CHANGES DO YOU SEE? DRAW WHAT YOU THINK WILL HAPPEN NEXT.

Children love caves and will enjoy making up stories about them. To encourage thinking, ask, WHAT KIND OF ANIMALS MIGHT LIVE IN OUR CAVE? COULD YOU LIVE IN A CAVE?

EXTENSION: Cover a table with blankets, and have children pretend they are cave explorers. (Or connect a series of large boxes to make a cave.) Papier-mâché hats and flashlights make good props for exploration. Help children decorate the cave with pillow rocks and paper stalactites and stalagmites. The children will enjoy discussing what they might see in a cave before they enter.

the objects, and relate the change to the metamorphic process.

To simulate the effect of heat on the rocks, melt several different colored marshmallows together into one interlocking marshmallow. Have children observe and describe the changes.

A CLASSROOM CAVE MODEL

Making a model is a way to simulate something that is difficult to observe firsthand. Keep in mind that the effectiveness of a model depends on the observations, comparisons, and predictions that children make. The following lesson is an example of model building that will help children gain understandings about caves and how some rocks are formed. Many additional questions, integrations, and strategies can be developed to design a cave unit.

Investigation Questions for Exploring Caves

1. Can plants break up rocks?
2. How does freezing water break up rocks?
3. How does weathering change a rock?

Figure 16–5   "What causes the stalactite to form?"

SUBJECT INTEGRATIONS

Rocks and Science

1. **Smooth rocks.** Additional ideas about rocks and their formation can be introduced by walking along a beach or stream and observing the smooth stones at the bottom of the stream or on the shore. Children can collect rocks and begin to draw comparisons about what makes the rocks smooth. Have them watch the action of the waves or stream. Ask, WHAT IS HAPPENING? Compare using sandpaper with the action of sand against the rocks.
2. **Sand from rocks.** Have children rub two rocks together to simulate wear on them. Discuss how this wear might take place in nature (water current, waterfalls, wind, and so on).

Rocks and Art

1. **Rock gardens.** Construct small rock gardens. Use pictures of Japanese gardens as inspiration.
2. **Rock necklaces.** Glue yarn to the back of flat, round rocks to make necklaces.
3. **Vegetable fossils.** Make mold fossils of vegetables. (See Additional Lesson Ideas for directions.)

Rocks and Language Arts and Reading

1. **Storybooks.** Read *Stone Soup*, and make vegetable soup. See Unit 11 for suggestions.
2. **Rock-shaped book.** Make rock-shaped covers for this bookmaking activity from brown construction paper. Inside pages should also be in the shape of the rock cover. Punch two holes in the top of the book, and fasten with metal rings or yarn. You may want to start the book with phrases like "A rock is a _____" (Figure 16–6).
3. **My rock.** Have each child select a rock and describe it. The children can record or dic-

Figure 16–6 "Record observations in your rock-shaped book."

tate descriptions. Encourage them by asking, WHAT DOES YOUR ROCK FEEL LIKE? DOES YOUR ROCK HAVE A SMELL? Stimulate thinking with, "My rock is as sparkly as a _____" Then have children write a biography of their rock.

Rock and Math

1. **Ordering rocks.** Put rocks in order of size, shape, and color, then from smoothest to roughest. Try doing this activity blindfolded.
2. **Weighing rocks.** Use a small balance to weigh rocks. Predict which rocks are the heaviest.
3. **Flannel board rocks.** Make flannel board rock shapes for math problem solving. Different sizes, colors, and shapes can be put in order, organized into patterns, sorted, and counted.
4. **Rock jar.** Fill a jar with rocks, and have the children estimate how many rocks are in the jar. Verify the number of rocks in the jar by counting by groups of 10.
5. **Dinosaur rocks.** Have children predict the number of rocks needed to build a dinosaur cave. Children can determine the needs of a dinosaur, such as enough rocks to shelter it and keep larger dinosaurs out of the cave.

Rocks and Cooking Experiences

1. **Igneous rock fudge.** After showing children pictures of volcanoes, find out what children know about them. Have pumice available for the children to examine. Some children might notice that the stone is light and has air bubble spaces. Explain that igneous means fire and that the pumice stone is an igneous rock that was once hot, liquid iron in a volcano that hardened as it cooled.

   To illustrate how lava cools, make fudge in a medium-sized pan. Mix 1/3 cup water, 1 cup sugar, a pinch of salt, 3 tablespoons of cocoa, and 1 teaspoon of vanilla. Boil the mixture for 3 minutes, and cool in one of two ways. To cool the fudge fast and produce a shiny, smooth surface, pour some of the mixture into a pie plate that is resting in a bowl of ice. For rough and lumpy granite-like fudge, cool at room temperature in another pie pan. Ask, WHICH WAY DO YOU THINK THE PUMICE WAS COOLED? (Fast, because it was blown out of the volcano. The black glassy obsidian is another example.)
2. **Pudding stones.** To illustrate conglomerate rock called pudding stone, have the children mix plaster and add various types of gravel and weathered stones to the mixture. Then, make pudding and add raisins and other food bits for a tasty pudding stone snack (Figure 16–7).

ADDITIONAL LESSON IDEAS

Fossils

Students will not be able to grasp the enormous time spans represented in the lessons about fossils and dinosaurs. It is most important that they understand that the dinosaurs existed long before humans; cartoon depictions of cave dwellers and dinosaurs are inaccurate.

Fossils can be shells and bones, prints of leaves, shells, or running feet, trees that have turned to stone, or insects that were trapped in tree sap. Discuss how the fossils might have been formed and whether they came from a plant or an animal. Ask, WHAT LIVING THINGS FROM THE PAST CAN BE IDENTIFIED BY FOSSILS?

On e way to illustrate this is to have students wear old shoes and go outside to make footprints in mud or damp sand. Have various students walk, jump, etc., and ask other students if they can figure out from the prints how each person was moving.

Fossils are most likely to be found in sedimentary rock. One way a chld can recognize this kind of rock is that it crumbles or scratches fairly easily and has a smell when it gets wet. To make a fossil, give the children pieces of plants, and have them coat the plant with petroleum jelly. Next, mix plaster of paris with water—according to the directions on the package—in the bottom of an aluminum foil pie plate. Instruct the children to gently press the plant into the surface of the mixture. After the plaster dries, remove the plant, and observe the imprint. Explain that this is one way a fossil is formed.

Children can press clay against the imprint, and the surface of the clay will take the shape of the original plant. Try making mold fossils of vegetables. Have children try to identify which vegetable made the print, children can form a fossils collage with the results (Figure 36–8).

WEATHER

Lessons in weather and seaons are especially appropriate for primary age children. In addition to discussing and studying the daily weather, take the children on a field trip to observe weather equipment in action. Local trip opportunities might include airports, television and radio stations, or high school or college weather stations. Visiting a weather station familiarizes children with the instruments and information they will study as they follow and record changes in weather and differences in seasons. Include constructing weather instruments, graphing, storybooks, subject integrations, and hands-on experiences as you teach children about weather.

Seasons

Temperature, rain, and snow tend to be high, medium, and low in the same months every year. Have children plot patterns of the freezing of water, melting of ice, and disappearance of water on cold surfaces. The following lessons in temperature and sunlight provide an opportunity for children to begin to correlate changes in daily temperature with seasons:

A Lesson on Temperature

Begin a discussion of temperature by asking children to explain how they know if it is hot or cold outside. After discussing observations, introduce the idea of using a thermometer as a way of measuring temperature. Distribute thermometers to

Figure 16–7   Making a conglomerate rock

Figure 16–8   Making a mold fossil

pairs or small groups to examine, and have the children record their observations. Ask, WHAT HAPPENS WHEN YOU HOLD THE THERMOMETER BETWEEN YOUR HANDS FOR A MINUTE? IS THE TEMPERATURE DIFFERENT WHEN YOU HOLD THE THERMOMETER AT THE BASE OF THE BULB? WHAT DO YOU THINK WILL HAPPEN IF YOU PUT THE THERMOMETER IN A GLASS OF COLD WATER? WHAT WILL HAPPEN IF YOU PUT THE THERMOMETER IN A GLASS OF HOT WATER?

Provide the groups with cups of hot and cold water, and let them investigate what will happen when the thermometers are placed in the cups of water. Have the children keep a record of their investigations and share results with other groups. Keeping records helps children to articulate their observations about how the thermometer works.

Pairs or groups of children will enjoy checking and recording temperature readings at different times of the day in a chosen location in the classroom or on the school grounds. Over a period of days, they can compare the pattern that emerges and make predictions. Since the goal of this lesson is for children to be aware that the temperature varies at different times of the day and thermometers can be difficult to read, temperature need not be measured precisely. Challenge children to find the hottest and coldest location in the room and on the playground.

Keep a class temperature chart so that the patterns seen over weeks and months can be related to the changing seasons. Identify clothing, activities, and food that are associated with each season. Include them on the temperature chart. A large paper body figure, such as those described in Unit 17, could be clothed to reflect seasonal changes.

Children may enjoy brainstorming words associated with each season and creating a "Hot and Cold" book following a pattern such as "as hot as ____" or "as cold as ____." Encourage the sensory aspect of the seasons by discussing seasonal smells, sounds, and tastes. One way to do this is to collect pictures from magazines that represent the sights, sounds, tastes, and activities of the season and display them as posters. A touch board made from objects found in the seasons provides an interesting class display.

Extending the Science Concept

To extend the concept ask, DO YOU THINK SHADOWS AFFECT TEMPERATURE? HOW COULD YOU TEST YOUR IDEA? RECORD WHAT HAPPENS. To continue the investigation of factors that can affect an object's temperature, such as color, ask, DO YOU THINK THERE WILL BE A DIFFERENCE BETWEEN A THERMOMETER PLACED IN A DARK-COLORED ENVELOPE AND ONE PLACED IN A LIGHT-COLORED ENVELOPE? WHY DO YOU THINK SO? Challenge children to find the hottest and coldest location in the classroom or on the playground, and ask them to give reasons for the varying temperatures. Encourage children to design ways to test different ideas.

In the same way, the length of sunlight at the same time of day each month can be recorded. Children can observe and record the daylight or dark when they come to school, eat supper, or go to bed. Discuss how the length of days affects our lives. As the year progresses, children will begin to correlate the changes in daily temperature and sunlight with the seasons.

A Thermometer Table.

Construct a thermometer table by having the children collect a variety of thermometers to compare and explore, such as oven thermometers, indoor-outdoor thermometers, and the many kinds of thermometers used to measure the body temperature.

A Party for All Seasons

At the beginning or the end of each season, children may want to have a season party. Planning groups will enjoy designing and creating the many aspects of the season party. The party could include single-portion recipes and samples of seasonal food, aromatic jars, touch boxes, and music and pantomime games of the indoor and outdoor activities typically done in each season. Children will enjoy painting murals and pictures of seasonal activities and constructing props for the activities.

WATER

Evaporation and *condensation* mean disappear and reappear. Years before children begin to understand that evaporating water, which appears to disappear, is still present in the form of small molecules (water vapor), they can observe the process and should be provided many opportunities to explore the phenomena. The following lesson is an example that allows children to see the effect of the science concept.

Puddle Pictures.

Ask, WHAT HAPPENS TO PUDDLES ON WARM SUNNY DAYS? Have children use a paintbrush to make a picture on the sidewalk. Carefully trace around the puddle with sidewalk chalk to create a picture. Ask, HOW DID THE WATER IN YOUR PUDDLE PICTURE CHANGE? WHERE DO YOU THINK THE WATER GOES WHEN IT DRIES? WHAT DOES IT CHANGE INTO? Have the children record the progress of the evaporating puddle on paper and with different colored chalk to mark the progress of the disappearing puddle. Ask, WHAT CAUSED THE WATER TO CHANGE INTO WATER VAPOR?

Relate this experience to observations of the drying process in the home. Have the children predict the fastest way to dry a shirt: lay it flat, hang it on a clothesline, or crumple it up in a bundle? Ask, HOW CAN YOU BE SURE THE WATER GOES INTO THE AIR? Help children design an investigation that does not expose the camp shirt (or paper towel) to the air. Develop the idea that when water dries, it *evaporates*, or changes into a gas called *water vapor*.

Ask children to look for examples of water changing from water vapor back into a liquid such as dew on the grass, frost on the window, and fog or steam on the mirror. Refer to the water activities and suggestions in this unit and other units in the text, such as Unit 13, for more suggestions for investigating water.

SPACE

Space travel, the moon, sun, and stars intrigue young children. They will not be able to comprehend the vastness of space or the enormity of the sun, moon, and earth, yet there are aspects of space science that they can readily observe.

The sun is the most observable object in the sky. (CAUTION: Children should never look directly into the sun.) Ask, ON WHAT SIDE OF THE BUILDING DOES THE SUN SHINE IN THE MORNING? Then, ON WHAT SIDE OF THE BUILDING DOES THE SUN SHINE WHEN WE LEAVE FOR THE DAY? Take the children for a walk around the building, and note where the sun's rays are shining at different times of the day. Draw these changes on a chart. Ask, WHY DO YOU THINK THAT THE SUN'S RAYS SHINE IN DIFFERENT PLACES?

Take the children outside of the building in the morning, and have them draw the school building and the location of the sun. Begin a bulletin board mural. Make the school building and surrounding features, and have the children place a construction paper sun where it belongs in the morning sky. Then make paper sun rays shining on the school building.

Shadow play is a natural for young children as they learn about the sun. Draw chalk outlines of the shadows cast, and then try casting shadows on a cloudy day. Ask, DO YOU HAVE A SHADOW TODAY? WHY NOT? Discuss the color of the sun and the moon. Ask, IS THE MOON THE SAME COLOR EVERY NIGHT? CAN YOU SEE THE MOON DURING THE DAY? (Yes.) Many children think that the moon goes to bed at night. Help them speculate on why the moon does not look as bright during the day.

If children think that the stars are held up with tape, do not discourage them. They are in good intellectual company. Aristotle, for example, thought that stars were embedded in concentric crystalline spheres. A primary age child cannot understand such concepts. Help the child notice that things in the sky look different at various times of the day and night.

Moon Patterns

The child's concept and grasp of the universe grows slowly over time. Ideas about light and sight are prerequisites to understanding the night sky. The priority in space-related lessons for young children is on describing what the sky looks like and identifying changes in shape and movement. The moon looks different every day and makes an ideal subject for observing and comparing.

Children can easily observe the pattern that the moon makes as it goes from one full moon to the next. Since moon phases appear at regular intervals, they can serve as a natural clock. It is not important that children remember the names of the phases of the moon, but that they see the pattern of change in the sky. As children record the differences that they see, they should describe and compare the various shapes the moon seems to have (Figure 16–9).

The Dos and Don'ts of Using Binoculars

This is an ideal time to introduce the children to binoculars and telescopes. By third grade, children should know that binoculars and telescopes magnify the appearance of objects in the sky. The craters, mountains, and other features on the moon's surface will provide a source of much discussion and imagination. Binoculars work especially well with young children.

The following are some binocular dos and don'ts: Do *not* try to find an object with the binoculars held up to your eyes. *Do* look at the object you want to look at, and *then* bring the binoculars

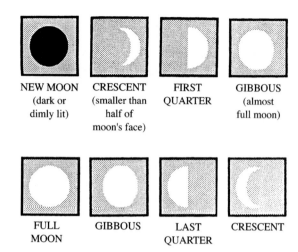

NEW MOON (dark or dimly lit) CRESCENT (smaller than half of moon's face) FIRST QUARTER GIBBOUS (almost full moon)

FULL MOON GIBBOUS LAST QUARTER CRESCENT

Figure 16–9 The phases of the moon

up to your eyes. This will work better if you focus the binoculars first. To do this, look at an object, bring the binoculars up to your eyes, and then focus until the object is clear. Caution children to *never* look at the sun with a pair of binoculars or a telescope. Possible blindness could be the result.

Craters of the Moon

As children look at the moon more closely and more often, they will begin to notice the many interesting features that can be seen by the naked eye or with binoculars. Take advantage of children's natural interest in the night sky, and let them record and draw their observations in greater detail.

Children will enjoy creating a lunar landscape. This can be done in the sand table by dropping different size balls into very wet sand. If a sand table is not available, a box of sand makes a good substitute. The children can compare the splatter marks extending from the impression made from the ball as it hits the sand to similar marks seen on the moon. Have the children compare the drawing that they have made of their moon observations with the sand craters they have made.

Features of the moon are ideal for simulation with clay and other sculpting materials. Murals, paintings, and other art forms provide reinforcement for the children's observations. If the child does not remember how a feature looks or her drawing is not as clear as she wants it to be, she can easily look at the moon the next night.

Observing the moon cycle will stimulate children's natural curiosity. They will want to know more about the night sky. There are a variety of things in the sky that can be seen at night. Planets, comets, meteors, stars, satellites, and airplanes fill the sky. The familiar patterns of stars called *constellations* will provide much excitement. Keep in mind that it is not important for children to know the names of the constellations. They need to be aware that the pattern of stars stays the same as it appears to move across the sky. This movement is another pattern of movement in the sky that is readily observed.

ENVIRONMENTAL AWARENESS

Environmental investigations are a natural way for children to enjoy and explore the world around them. When children explore the environment, they will engage in active participation and cooperation as they begin developing their own understanding. Experiences are often free or inexpensive and readily accessible to a variety of audiences and learning styles.

The suggestions and lessons in this section are based on one or more of the three common approaches to environmental education outlined by Dighe (1993).

1. **The Awareness Approach** focuses on children's feelings and appreciation of the world around them.
2. **The Environmental Concept Approach** introduces ideas that will lead to learning about environmental concerns.
3. **The Conservation Approach** provides opportunities for children to take action and see a result of that action.

The results of these lessons need to be observable and should not be too dramatic or controversial. To be effective, children need to see a direct result of their actions. For example, children can see a direct result of picking up trash or monitoring use of lights in the room.

To introduce the word *environment*, use a brainstorming approach: Write the word on the chalkboard and ask, WHAT DO YOU THINK THE WORD *ENVIRONMENT* MEANS? List the ideas named by the children, and keep that list posted. Children may want to modify the list as their awareness of the environment progresses. Periodically, have the children return to modify the list as meaning develops.

Water Changes the Earth

Water is everywhere. It flows in rivers and streams and makes up the oceans that cover the earth's surface. Draw children's attention to the bodies of water around them—rivers, lakes, oceans, and the like. Show pictures of different bodies of water, and discuss experiences.

Water is the single most important force that shapes the surface of the earth. Water from melting glaciers, rain, snow, forms streams and rivers and moves sand, which gradually wears away mountains and carves hills and valleys. To explore this concept, fill a tray with gravel and soil, and set the tray in a big pan. Raise one end of the pan with a block. Have children slowly pour water in the higher end of the tray and watch what happens.

Children can keep track of this investigation by drawing the sequence of changes in the tray as they happen. Encourage children to make a little channel for a stream to flow and to pour water into it. Ask, WHAT WILL HAPPEN WHEN ROCKS ARE ADDED TO THE SOIL AND GRAVEL? Take a class walk, and look for evidence of water changing the surface of the earth. Discuss how these changes can be beneficial or harmful (Figure 16–10).

Living Things Use Water

Living things—people, plants, and animals—consist mainly of water and must have it to live. In fact, water is more important for survival than

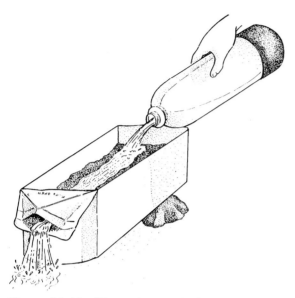

Figure 16–10 Water changes the face of the earth. From *Water, Stones, & Fossil Bones* (1991, p. 51), K. Lind (Ed.). Washington, DC: National Science Teachers Association.

food. Ask children to name some of the ways they use water. Encourage responses by asking, WHAT ARE SOME OTHER WAYS PEOPLE USE WATER? WHY IS WATER IMPORTANT TO BUSINESS? TO PEOPLE WHO FISH OR RAISE FARM ANIMALS? Begin a chart to record children's responses to the ways living things use water. Add to the chart throughout the lesson as other uses of water are discussed.

Ask, HOW DO YOU THINK WATER IS USED IN OUR SCHOOL? Assign groups of children locations or categories such as kitchen, bathrooms, art room, cleaning closets, water fountains. Invite the groups to think of questions about their location. What can they find out about where water comes from for the school and how water is used in their location? What could they count or measure? Have the children to work as a group to develop an investigation plan. Then each group may go to its research area and find out specifics about how water is used. Children may want to interview custodians and kitchen workers to find out how they use water in their work or devise a way to observe fountains for short periods of time.

When all groups have completed their research, meet as a whole class to share information. Help children summarize when they have learned about water use by asking, HOW MANY WATER SOURCES DID WE FIND IN THE SCHOOL? DO YOU THINK PEOPLE IN THE SCHOOL USE A LITTLE WATER, A MEDIUM AMOUNT, OR A LOT OF WATER? DO YOU THINK PEOPLE SOMETIMES WASTE WATER? WHAT CAN PEOPLE DO TO NOT WASTE WATER? WHAT WOULD WE DO IF WE DIDN'T HAVE WATER?

It will emerge that the school depends on water in many ways. Children may appreciate its availability and how difficult life would be without such access to water. Encourage children to draw or cut out pictures of water uses in their home or school.

Ask children to keep a personal "Water Use Log." They should record their use of water for one day. Begin by recording activities from the time they get up until the time they fall asleep.

Be a Water Saver

Discuss ways that people waste water, and begin a list of suggestions for how we can save water. To further the awareness of water that is sometimes wasted, suggest that children become water inspectors. Each child or team should list everything in the classroom and at home that requires water and investigate possible ways that water is wasted.

When children have completed their survey ask, WHERE DID YOU FIND LEAKY FAUCETS? DOES THE TOILET TANK LEAK? To find out if a toilet tank leaks, put food coloring in the tank, and wait 15 minutes. If the water in the bowl turns the color you put in the tank, you have a leak. Ask, HOW MANY LEAKY TOILETS CAN YOU FIND? HOW MANY LEAKY TOILETS ARE IN OUR SCHOOL? WHOM DO YOU NEED TO TELL ABOUT YOUR FINDINGS?

Water wasted from leaky faucets can be measured by placing a cup under the faucet and collecting the drips (Figure 16–11). Ask, HOW MUCH WATER DRIPS FROM THE FAUCET IN 1 HOUR? Collect the water, and have the children think of a way to use the water instead of pouring it down the drain.

After investigating and studying water waste, children may then want to explain how they personally plan to conserve water. Children can illustrate one way they use water wisely. Have students pantomime a scene to show a way to conserve water at home or at school.

Water for a Day

Provide each student with a paper cup and a 1-liter bottle of water. Tell them that this is their day's water supply for drinking, washing their hands, and so on. However, tell students they can flush the toilet. Tape faucets shut, and put a tub in the sink to collect water that would have gone down the drain. Have the children predict how much water they will use and record this information on a chart. At the end of the day, have the children use a large graduated cylinder to measure any water that remains in their bottles and the water in the tub. Record the data on charts, and water the plants with the remaining water. Ask, DID YOU USE AS MUCH WATER AS YOU THOUGHT YOU WOULD USE?

Is the Water Clean?

As more people use water, there has been an increase in water pollution. In some areas, raw sewage is pumped into rivers and streams, pesticides and fertilizers are washed from lawns and farmland into the water system, and pollutants such metals and petroleum products may enter a river or an ocean. It is important to point out that not all pollutants are visible. Some children think that because water looks clear, it is safe to drink. Emphasize to children they should never drink water unless they know that it is safe.

Figure 16–11   "How much water is wasted?"

Is It Safe to Drink?

Every day, wastes are being pumped into the world's water supply, but they are not always easy to detect. To develop the idea that you cannot always see pollution in water, cut off the bottom of a piece of celery, and divide the celery in half lengthwise. Fill two glasses halfway with apple juice, and add three drops of red food coloring to one and three drops of blue food coloring to the other. Place one-half of the celery in each glass, and let it stand for several hours. Take the celery out, and cut it into slices. Ask, WHAT COLOR IS THE CELERY AT THE TOP OF THE STALK? TASTE THE CELERY. CAN YOU TASTE THE APPLE JUICE? Try this investigation with food coloring and water.

How Much Garbage and Trash?

It is an understatement to say that humans throw away a lot of garbage and trash in a lifetime. To provide children with an opportunity to see how much garbage they use in one day, suggest that they place the garbage they normally toss out in a day or a week in a large biodegradable trash bag. They may be able to take this trash bag with them for a day. That night, sort the garbage from the trash bag into labeled categories of use such as organic, paper, plastics, metal, glass, clothes, and mysterious items that do not seem to fit the other categories. This is an especially appropriate classroom or family experience. The bags can be weighed. Most people create at least 4 pounds of garbage each day. Ways to recycle trash can be explored. Ask, WHICH BAG WEIGHS THE MOST? WHICH WEIGHS THE LEAST? WHICH BAG HAS THE MOST TRASH IN IT? WHO CREATED MOST OF THIS TRASH? CAN ANY OF THE ITEMS BE USED AGAIN?

RECYCLING

One of the best ways to recycle is to reuse materials instead of discarding them. Many of the items that are thrown away can be used again in the everyday classroom environment. Look around the classroom, and list the items being reused such as boxes, styrofoam chips, sheets of paper, larger pieces of cloth, rope, yarn, string, plastic jugs, wood scraps, old magazines, rug scraps, and many more.

The symbol in Figure 16–12 means *packaged in recycled materials*. How many items in your home come in recycled packaging? How many items can you find in the classroom or in the school?

Recycling Survey

Have children brainstorm a list of suggestions for a recycling survey. Ask them what they want to know about the recycling habits of their families. Items might include DO YOU RECYCLE? IF SO, DO YOU RECYCLE ALUMINUM

Figure 16–12   Packaged in recycled materials

CANS? Additional suggestions might be grocery bags, newspapers, magazines, plastic bottles, plastic containers, and glass bottles and jars. Ask, DO YOU THINK RECYCLING IS IMPORTANT? WHY OR WHY NOT? After developing the survey, have the children give their survey to their family and friends. Compile the results of the survey on a bulletin board made of a huge brown paper bag and discuss the results with the children. Ask, DOES ANYTHING ABOUT THE RESULTS ON OUR CHART SURPRISE YOU?.

Keeping the Earth Clean.

Make a class book of all of the things you can do to help keep the earth clean. Then take the class on a scavenger hunt. Put the children in pairs, and give each pair a short list of items to locate. Children can draw or plot on a map where they found each item (Figure 16–13). Have the

Figure 16–13   "Let's keep the earth clean." From *Water, Stones, & Fossil Bones* (1991, p. 121), K. Lind (Ed.). Washington, DC: National Science Teachers Association.

Figure 16–14   Saving a tree

children compare findings and discuss how the items might have ended up where they did. Items might include:

Take the class on a scavenger hunt. Put the children in pairs, and give each pair a short list of items to locate. Children can draw or plot on a map where they found each item.

- piece of garbage
- dripping faucet
- newspapers
- junk mail
- light turned on in an empty room
- aluminum can
- plastic bag
- bottle caps
- egg carton
- paper bag

Litter Collage.

Gather people's litter and nature's litter (fallen leaves, twigs, seed pods, and so on), and make a collage for each. Have the children write descriptions under the human litter and nature's litter. Bury some of the litter made by people and some of the litter made by nature. After a month, dig it up, and see what happened to the litter.

Save a Tree

Making paper is a fun and inexpensive way to emphasize the recycling process. Have the children save old newspapers instead of throwing them away. You will also need the following items: a large plastic pan or wading pool filled with warm water, an eggbeater, wire mesh screens, sponges, cotton cloth, and a rolling pin.

Shred paper into strips, and place them into water. Use the eggbeater, a whip, or an old blender to mash the paper into the consistency of oatmeal. For fancy paper, children can sprinkle bits of thread or flower petals into the pulp. To make the sheets of paper, spread and press the pulp onto a wire mesh screen, first dipping the screen under the pulp in the pan of water. Remove excess water from the sheet and underside of the screen (Figure 16–14).

Place the sheets of paper onto a cotton cloth, cover it with fabric, and squeeze out remaining moisture with a rolling pin. Let the sheets dry, trim them to a desirable size, and the children will be ready to write.

Paper logs can be made for holiday treats by putting 20 or 30 sheets of newspaper together and adding a cup of crushed pine cones or cedar shavings between every few pages. These sections are tightly rolled and tied loosely at the end. Fill the pool with water and enough cones and chips to cover half of the water's surface. Add 3 cups of salt to the mixture (for extra pretty flames), and put the logs in to soak for a week. Turn them once a day. Dry the logs, and give them as presents (Figure 16–15).

COMPUTER SUGGESTIONS

Dinosaur construction kit—Tyrannosaurus rex [Computer program]. D. C. Heath and Co.

Dinosaurs are forever [Computer program]. Polarware.

Eco-Saurus [Computer program]. First Byte/Davidson.

The energy education materials library [Computer program]. Energy Center, Sonoma State University.

Figure 16–15   Paper logs

A field trip into the sea [Computer program].
Wings for Learning.
How to start a rock collection [Computer program]. Danville, KY: Teacher Video Production Corporation.
An ocean of air [Computer program]. MCE, Inc.

Science explorers: Volume I [Computer program].
Scholastic.
Space subtraction (X–145) [Computer program].
MECC.
Stars and planets [Computer program]. Advanced Ideas.
Sun and seasons [Computer program]. MECC.
Wetlands [Computer program]. Optical Data.

SUMMARY

Rocks and minerals are not simply objects laying on the ground. They are part of the continually changing process of the earth. As children study earth science topics such as rocks, minerals, weather, water, and space, they study the conditions and forces that affect their planet and the environment. An early introduction to these difficult concepts exposes children to their world and helps ready them for future understanding.

FURTHER READING AND RESOURCES

Brummet, D. C., Lind, K. K., Barman, C. r., DiSpezio, M. A., & Ostlund, K. L. (1995) *Destinations in Science.* Menlo Park, CA: Addison-Wesley Publishing Company.

Dighe, J. (1993). Children and the earth. *Young Children, 48*(3), 58–63.

Gega, P. (1993). *Science in elementary education.* New York: Macmillan.

Herman, M. L., Passineau, J. F., Schimpf, A. L., & Treuer, P. (1991). *Teaching kids to love the earth.* Duluth, MN: Pfeifer-Hamilton.

Levine, S., & Grafton, A. (1992). *Projects for a healthy planet.* New York: John Wiley & Sons.

Lind, K. K. (1991). *Water, stones, and fossil bones.* Washington, DC: National Science Teachers Association.

McBiles, J. L. (1985). *Mining, minerals, and me.* Nashua, NH: Delta Education, Inc.

McCormack, A. (1979). *Outdoor areas as learning laboratories.* Council for Elementary Science International Sourcebook. Columbus, OH: SMEAC Information Reference Center.

Perez, J. (1988). *Explore and experiment.* Bridgeport, CT: First Teacher Press.

Renner, J. W., & Marek, E. A. (1988). *The learning cycle and elementary school science teaching.* Portsmouth, NH: Heinemann.

Spizman, R. F., & Garber, M. (1991). *What on earth you can do with kids?* Carthage, IL: Good Apple.

Williams, R. A., Rockwell, R. E., & Sherwood, E. A. (1987). *Mudpies to magnets.* Mt. Rainer, MD: Gryphon House, Inc.

SUGGESTED ACTIVITIES

1. Recall your rock collecting experiences in elementary school. Where did you find your rocks? Did you display your rocks? Did you know what your rocks were or how they were formed? What do you think the formation of rocks meant to your teachers?

2. Make your own teaching web. Select lessons from the rock unit, and design a unit that is appropriate for a group of children you are teaching. You should add ideas to the ones presented. Teach the lesson to children, and record your observations for class discussion.

3. Which process skills are used in the rock unit? Give an example of each skill and when it was used. Can you think of additional ways to integrate process skills into the unit on rocks?

4. Present a lesson on weather to primary age children. What types of learning experiences will you design for your students? How do you plan to apply what you know about Piaget's theory of development to the teaching of weather.

5. Examine a teacher's edition of an elementary school science textbook. Identify a lesson on rocks and one on weather. Do you agree with the way the lesson is presented? Explain why or why not. How would you teach the lesson?

6. Select an earth science or environmental topic and concept, and prepare a learning cycle lesson to teach that idea. Teach it to children.

7. Imagine that your class has just returned from collecting rocks. What types of questions will you ask to help students generate a list of characteristics that can be used to classify rocks into different groups? Your questions could take a variety of forms. Use your question list with children, and note the interactions for class discussion.

REVIEW

1. What is the purpose of introducing young children to earth science concepts?

2. List six earth science concepts appropriate for primary age children.

UNIT 17 Health and Nutrition

OBJECTIVES

After studying this unit, the student should be able to
- Design health and nutrition investigations for primary age children
- Develop an understanding of health and nutrition topics that are appropriate for primary age children
- Develop structured and unstructured learning experiences in health, nutrition, and the human body
- Integrate science in the primary grades with other subjects

Optimum growth and development depend on good nutrition, adequate experience, plenty of rest, and proper cleanliness. Concepts in health and nutrition need to be introduced to young children so they learn how to take care of their bodies and develop beneficial lifelong habits at an early age. This unit suggests experiences that help children learn about themselves through exploring the human diet, major food groups, and the human body. Lesson ideas for promoting good health habits are also presented.

The following health, nutrition, and human body concepts are basic to primary grade learning (Figure 17–1).

- Eating a variety of healthful foods and getting enough exercise and rest help people to stay healthy.
- Some things people take into their bodies from the environment can hurt them.
- A balanced diet consists of carbohydrates, fats, proteins, vitamins, minerals, and water.
- A diet that is a balance of foods plus water makes up a healthful regimen for normal people.
- You can help yourself stay healthy.
- The human body can be affected by a variety of diseases.
- Some diseases are caused by germs; some are not. Washing one's hands with soap and water reduces the number of germs that can get into the body or be passed on to other people.
- The human body carries on life processes.
- Food is the fuel and the building material of the body.
- The human body must take in and digest food.
- The human body consists of a number of groups of organs that work together to perform a particular function.
- Movement of the human body is made possible by the skeleton and muscles.

Figure 17–1 "How is a rock like our bones?"

- The human body takes in oxygen and gives off carbon dioxide.
- The circulatory system is the transportation system of the body.
- Humans reproduce and give off waste products.
- The brain enables human beings to think; it sends messages to other body parts to help them to work properly.
- Senses can warn individuals about danger; muscles help them fight, hide, or get out of danger.
- Humans observe and learn by seeing, hearing, feeling, tasting, and smelling.

EXPLORATIONS IN HEALTH AND NUTRITION

The learning experiences suggested in this unit introduce fundamental concepts that acquaint children with their bodies and how to stay healthy. Topics include good health habits; treatment of cuts and scrapes; how the body gains energy; the food pyramid and food activities; and bones, teeth, vitamins, and minerals.

Health Habits

Good health habits begin early in a child's life. Encourage children to begin an understanding of what healthy living really means by providing a variety of instructional techniques and subject integrations that relate to the child's life. Here are a few to get you started.

ARE YOUR HANDS DIRTY?

CONCEPT: Hands that look clean can still be dirty.

OBJECTIVE: Observe the growth of mold on potatoes. Compare the effect of mold growth resulting from handling potatoes with washed and unwashed hands.

MATERIALS: Two small potatoes, potato peeler, two clean jars with lids that seal, labels, marker.

PROCEDURE: Have children examine their hands. Ask, ARE YOUR HANDS CLEAN? DO YOU SEE ANY DIRT ON THEM? Discuss how hands look when they are dirty. WHAT IS THE DIRTIEST YOUR HANDS HAVE EVER BEEN? THE CLEANEST?

Peel two potatoes, ask a child to handle one of them, and put it in a jar. (Select a child who has not washed his or her hands for several hours.) Point out that the child's hands appear to be clean.

Label the jar with the name of the child and the words *unwashed hands*. Instruct a child to wash his or her hands, handle the second potato, and put it in the remaining jar. Label the jar with the child's name and the words *washed hands*. Discuss the relative cleanliness of the washed hands potato.

Place the two jars in a warm place where the children can observe and record what happens. Compare what is happening to the potatoes after a day or two. (Mold is likely to form on the unwashed potato.) Compare the potatoes, and discuss how the mold got on the potato (Figure 17–2). (Refer to Unit 14 for additional lessons about mold.)

EXTENSION: Have children describe and draw what the unwashed and washed hands looked like. Ask, DID THE UNWASHED HANDS LOOK DIRTY? (No.) This would be a good time to discuss germs and the importance of washing hands before handling food. Have children design posters to encourage hand washing before meals.

Good health habits chart. Keep a record of your health habits. Answer questions about yourself for a week. (For example: I brushed my teeth after every meal, I took a bath or shower. I washed my hands before meals today. I exercised today.) At the end of the week, look at all of your answers. What can you do to improve your health habits?

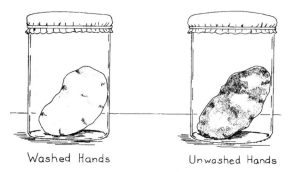

Washed Hands   Unwashed Hands

Figure 17–2 "What is happening in the unwashed hands jar?"

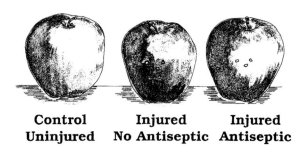

Control | **Injured** | **Injured**
Uninjured | **No Antiseptic** | **Antiseptic**

Figure 17–3 Apples with puncture wounds

APPLES AND ME

CONCEPT: Microorganisms (germs) can enter our body through cuts and scrapes in the skin.

OBJECTIVE: Compare the healing of injuries on an apple with injuries on our skin. Describe how antiseptic keeps germs out of our body.

MATERIALS: Three apples, soil or other type of dirt, antiseptic, two sewing needles.

PROCEDURE: Lead the children in a discussion of current injuries that they have received. Such incidents are a common happening in the primary grades. Encourage children to tell how the injury occurred and how it was treated.

Then hold an apple in your hand. Ask, HOW IS THE COVERING OF AN APPLE SIMILAR TO YOUR SKIN? HOW IS IT DIFFERENT? LET'S SEE WHAT HAPPENS WHEN THE SURFACE OF AN APPLE IS INJURED.

Label one apple the *control apple.* You will not injure this apple. Label the second apple *no antiseptic*, and the third apple *antiseptic*. Then, stir one of the needles in dirt, and puncture the second apple three times. Stir the other needle in dirt, sterilize the needle with antiseptic, and puncture the third apple. Place the three apples in a sunny place, and have the children keep a record of changes in the apples. Ask, WHAT DO YOU THINK THEY WILL LOOK LIKE IN ONE DAY? As children record the progress, discuss possible reasons for differences in the appearance of the apples. (The apple punctured by the unsterilized needle will rot fairly quickly.)

After several days, cut all of the apples in half, including the control apple. Ask, WHAT CHANGES DO YOU SEE IN THE APPLES? WHICH APPLE LOOKS THE WORST? DID STERILIZING THE NEEDLE MAKE ANY DIFFERENCE? WHAT DO YOU THINK WOULD HAPPEN IF THE SURFACE OF YOUR BODY WERE PUNCTURED? Discuss the best possible action to take in case of an injury (Figure 17–3). (Refer to the mold activities in Unit 14.)

EXTENSION: Sterilize the needles in different ways, such as using a candle flame to simulate heat sterilization or applying various commercial antiseptics to compare products.

Children will be interested in trying out this experiment with different types of foods and different types of injuries (scraping, cutting, slicing, and so on). Ask, IS THERE ANY SPECIAL WOUND THAT WILL LET THE MOST MICROORGANISMS FIND THEIR WAY THROUGH YOUR SKIN AND INTO YOUR BODY? (Puncture wounds.)

Test types of dirt. Fingernail dirt, shoe dirt, desk dirt. Find out if some dirt is "dirtier" than others.

Germ story. Write a story about the invading germs and what can be done to stop them. Children will enjoy acting out the invasions of germs into the body and their subsequent destruction by antiseptic.

FOODS WE EAT

PLANT POWER

CONCEPT: We get energy from plants.

OBJECTIVE: Identify the parts of plants that store food and the parts we eat.

MATERIALS: A variety of foods, toothpicks.

PROCEDURE: When teaching about foods, it is important to stress that they are necessary for growth and development. One way to do this is to compare children's bodies to the bean seeds in Unit 14. Ask, WHERE DID THE BEANS GET THE ENERGY TO SPROUT? (From the food stored in them.) Remind children that young plants use the food stored in the seed to grow. Ask, CAN YOU GET ENERGY FROM SEEDS? (Yes, when you eat them.)

Show the children different plants, and ask, WHERE DO YOU THINK GREEN PLANTS STORE THEIR FOOD? (Leaves.) Hold up carrots and turnip plants and ask, WHERE DO THESE PLANTS STORE THEIR FOOD? (Roots.) Show a picture of sugarcane plants (or a piece, if available) and ask, WHERE DO YOU THINK THE SUGARCANE STORES ITS FOOD? (Stem, which is between the root and the leaves.) Remember that the white potato is really a stem plant and the sweet potato is a root plant.

After you assess student progress, you may want to continue the lesson by introducing them to fruits, which store food, food for plants, and flowers which store food such as broccoli and cauliflower. Ask, WHERE DO YOU THINK THESE PLANTS STORE FOOD? (Flowers.)

EXTENSION: Reinforce the idea that energy comes from plants and their stored food with a plant-tasting party. You will need enough food samples for the entire class to taste. (You could ask each child to bring a sample.) Before the tasting party, have the children group plants by the parts that store food, wash the plants, cut them into bite-size parts, and put a toothpick in each piece. Ask, DO WE USE ALL OF THESE PLANT PARTS FOR FOOD? (Yes, taste, seeds, leaves, roots, stems, fruits, and flowers and discuss favorite plant parts.)

FOOD PYRAMID

CONCEPT: Foods from the basic groups provide the nutrients necessary for good health.

OBJECTIVE: Identify the food groups and the number of servings it includes (Figure 17–4).

MATERIALS: Magazine pictures of food.

PROCEDURE: Have children cut out magazine pictures from each food group. Mount the pictures on construction paper, add identifying food group labels, and pin to a bulletin board. Let the children decide if the pictures are labeled correctly. Move misplaced pictures to the correct categories and create a food Pyramid.

EXTENSION: *Bag it.* Label lunch bags for each food group. Then, cut out and laminate pictures of food. Have children sort the cutouts into the correct bags. You can use this idea in a center or as an interactive bulletin board.

Food group biography. Choose a group, and write your biography. If you were a food group, what one would you be? What would it be like to be this food group? Does your food group have a future?

Sell your food group. Make a television or radio commercial that will persuade the class that your food group is worthy of being eaten every day.

ADDITIONAL FOOD ACTIVITIES

1. *Fatty foods.* Ask, HOW CAN YOU FIND OUT IF FOOD HAS FAT IN IT? Place a drop of liquid fat on a piece of brown paper. Hold the paper up to the light and ask, DOES THE LIGHT COME THROUGH WHERE THE FAT IS? After a few hours ask, IS THE SPOT DRY OR DOES IT STAY THE SAME? (Stays the same.) Test the fat in foods such as peanut butter, nuts, olives, and milk by leaving the food on brown paper for a few hours. Then ask, IS THE SPOT DRY, OR DOES IT STAY THE SAME? After testing several foods ask, HOW DO YOU KNOW THERE IS FAT IN THESE FOODS? (Fatty oils stay on the paper.)

2. *Sugar time.* Show the children a variety of food containers (jars, boxes, and so on). Have them predict which foods contain sugar. After they write their predictions on a prediction sheet, have them read the ingredients on the food containers to check their predictions. Explain that the ingredients are listed in sequence from greatest amount to smallest. Also note information on vitamin, mineral, and calorie content. Compare results. Then, write the word *sugar* on the chalkboard. Ask, DOES THE LIST ON THE

LABEL SAY SUGAR? (Not always.) Introduce the children to some of the ways sugars are listed: corn syrup, maltose, sucrose, fructose, corn sweetener, syrup, dextrose, glucose, lactose, molasses. Discuss the amount of sugar in foods, and decide if eating a lot of sugar is a good idea.

3. *Classify foods.* Give children practice in identifying which foods belong in which food group by making charts and food group books. This can be done by using pictures; classifying individual children's diets; and analyzing school lunch menus, the contents of bag lunches, and the evening meal.

4. *Finding out.* Divide the class into small groups, and give each questions to explore about different food groups. Make a web of

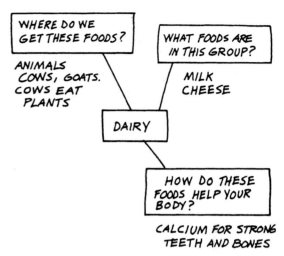

Figure 17–5   Web

their findings as they share with the class (Figure 17–5).

5. *Foods I like chart.* Have children write the names of the foods they would like to eat for breakfast, lunch, and dinner on a chart. Then, make a chart, and list the foods that they actually eat at these meals. Compare the charts and identify foods that are high in fats, carbohydrates, and sugar (potato chips, and so on). Discuss the nutritional value of the foods. Children might want to keep a log of foods that they eat for breakfast over a week's time (or food eaten for lunch or dinner). Compare class eating habits.

6. *Visitors.* Invite a cafeteria worker to talk about cleanliness and a nutritionist to explain how the lunch menus are created.

7. *Tasting party.* One effective method of eval-

Good Food for Growing Bodies

Your body needs food to give you energy for work and play.
What foods are good for your body?
This food pyramid can help you decide.

Figure 17–4   A Food Pyramid courtesy of *Destinations in Science.* Menlo Park, CA: Addison-Wesley Publishing Company.

KEEPING BONES AND TEETH STRONG

CONCEPT: Food supplies the body with important minerals. Calcium is a mineral that is used to make bones and teeth strong.

OBJECTIVE: Test rocks for the presence of calcium. Observe evidence of calcium.

MATERIALS: Pieces of limestone, chalk, marble, vinegar, hand lenses, medicine droppers.

CAUTION: Hydrochloric acid is usually used for this test. However, when working with young children, use vinegar.

PROCEDURE: Show children the rocks, and ask, WHAT ARE ROCKS MADE OF? (Many answers; one will probably be minerals.) Tell the children that they can test for the presence of a mineral called calcium by dropping acid or vinegar on a rock.

Give children samples of limestone. Ask, WHAT DO YOU THINK WILL HAPPEN IF WE DROP VINEGAR ON A ROCK? Instruct the children to fill the medicine dropper and carefully drop the vinegar on the rocks. Have the children observe and record what happens to the rocks. (Bubbles form.) Generate a list of words that describe children's observations. (Fizz, bubble, smell, and so on.) Explain that the bubbles indicate calcium is present (Figure 17–6).

EXTENSION: Children enjoy comparing the hard parts of their bodies to rocks. Ask, HOW ARE BONES AND TEETH LIKE ROCKS? (They both contain minerals.) Explain that two minerals, calcium and phosphorus, combine to make bones and teeth hard. Good sources include milk and other dairy foods, fruits, and vegetables. Other foods, such as eggs, leafy green vegetables, meats, grains, and nuts, have some calcium. Bring an end to the lesson by asking, WHERE DO WE GET THE CALCIUM TO MAKE OUR BONES AND TEETH STRONG? (From our foods, calcium.)

Chicken bones. Testing the brittleness of chicken bones can help children understand that bones are more likely to break if they do not have the necessary minerals. To conduct this test, scrub two large chicken bones thoroughly. Soak one in water and one in vinegar for several days. Have the children compare the bones with handheld lenses and note any differences. Then, predict which of the two bones will break more easily. (Vinegar dissolves calcium and phosphorus.) Compare the chicken bones to human bones.

Tear or crush? Have the children examine their teeth with mirrors and identify different sizes and shapes of teeth. How are the front teeth shaped? Ask, WHEN DO YOU USE YOUR FRONT TEETH? HOW DO YOUR FRONT TEETH HELP YOU EAT? WHAT TYPES OF FOOD DO YOU NEED TO CRUSH TO EAT? WHICH TEETH HELP YOU CRUSH FOOD?

This would be a good time to discuss carnivorous and herbivorous animals. Show pictures of the animals eating. Ask, WHAT TYPE OF TEETH DO THESE ANIMALS HAVE? After categorizing animals (and dinosaurs) by what they eat and discussing the shape and use of teeth, ask WHICH CATEGORY DO WE BELONG IN? (Both.) WHY? (We have several types of teeth. We eat both plants and animals.)

How do minerals get into food? To show how the roots of vegetables take in minerals from the soil, mix red food coloring and water. Have children observe the small rootlets that grow from the core of a carrot. Then, submerge the carrot in dyed water for 24 hours. Ask, WHAT HAPPENED TO THE RED COLOR? (Passes to the core of the carrot.) HOW DID IT GET THERE? (Through the rootlets.)

You may want to set up this observation with several different vegetables. Children will discover that dissolved minerals come into plants through plant roots. Let them decide that as we eat the plants, we take in the same minerals (Figure 17–7).

Then ask, IF PLANTS GET MINERALS FROM SOIL WATER, CAN WE GET MINERALS FROM WATER, TOO? (Yes.) Minerals in water are sulfur, chlorine, sodium, calcium, magnesium, potassium, fluorine. Discuss how we get minerals from water. (Drink, eat, plants, animals.)

Figure 17–6 "What will happen when vinegar is dropped on limestone?"

Figure 17–7 "Why is the celery turning red?"

uating food learning is to have a tasting party in which the children select their meal from a variety of foods. Simply observe which foods the children select to make up the meal.

8. *Recipes.* Integrate social studies by tasting foods from different countries or from different areas of town. Families also cook in different ways. Discuss similarities and differences, and make recipe books of favorite recipes. Have parents or other guests from a variety of ethnic backgrounds make one of their special dishes or share some special food with the class (refer to the many food activities in previous units).

We Are What We Eat

Study vitamins and minerals as far as the developmental level of your students permits. Here are a few ideas to get you started.

ADDITIONAL MINERAL ACTIVITIES

Iron. Iron is a mineral that you need in your blood. The iron combines with protein to form a compound that makes blood red. This compound also carries oxygen to all parts of your body. Meats, beans, peas, grains, and leafy vegetables are good sources of iron. Children will enjoy acting out the oxygen processing function of iron. Ask, HOW DO WE GET IRON INTO OUR BODIES?

Children can "become" blood platelets, oxygen, and food by wearing appropriate labels and drawings. Make a vein path with red yarn for the children to follow as they trace the journey of a blood platelet. Have children create a script about how iron enters the body and what it does to help them stay healthy.

Anemia. You can get sick if you do not get enough iron. Ask, DO YOU EAT FOODS THAT GIVE YOUR BODY IRON? Discuss foods that contain iron. Explain that when you have had a good night's sleep but still are tired all the time, you may be anemic. People with anemia get tired easily because their blood does not carry enough oxygen. Ask, WHAT CAN YOU DO TO AVOID GETTING ANEMIA? (Eat foods that contain iron.)

Plan a meal. Have children plan a meal for someone with anemia. If you are studying vitamins, children could plan a meal for someone with beriberi. (People with beriberi lack essential vitamins and minerals and are too weak to use their muscles to do work.)

Mineral people. Study the labels of common foods. Categorize cans and boxes of food by the minerals they contain. Then make mineral people such as an Iron Person or a Calcium Person. These figures can be made from the actual foods or boxes or pictures of these foods (Figure 17–8). Then, decide what foods are needed to create Vitamin People.

STRATEGIES FOR TEACHING THE HUMAN BODY

The internal anatomy of the human body is a difficult concept for young children to understand. Concrete experiences on which to base understandings can be difficult to provide. Refer to Unit 12 to review the garbage bag strategy for introducing children to the inside of the human body. In addition to the suggestions in Unit 12, the following suggestions will help you provide the children with concrete learning strategies:

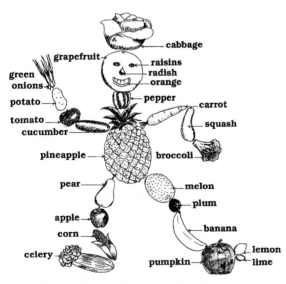

Figure 17–8 "Create a mineral person."

Inside of Me

Although it is difficult to observe the inside of the human body, children can infer that muscles, bones, and organs are inside of them. For example, bones give the body shape, help the body move, and protect the organs. Preliminary activities should include body awareness activities in which children explore, feel, and identify some of the major bones. Observation of X-ray films can further enhance the children's concept of bones. Then, trace a Halloween skeleton, cut out the bones, and assemble the skeleton using paper fasteners as joints. Try some of the following strategies for teaching about bones with children:

Our Skeleton has Joints

Have the children move their arms and legs in a way that explores the way joints work: marching, saluting, swinging arms and legs, and acting like a windmill. Ask, DO YOUR LEGS BEND WHEN YOU MARCH? CAN YOU MARCH WITHOUT BENDING YOUR LEGS? IS IT EASY TO DO? Point out and explore the joints that help your body move. Discover the difference between hinge joints, which bend one way, and ball and socket joints, which can bend, twist, and rotate (Figure 17–9).

Find the Joints

Have children work in pairs to make a paper body and locate joints. Have one child lie on a piece of butcher paper and the other child draw the outline of the body. Then, have the children locate joints on the paper body. Discuss why the type of joint used in the body is the most appropriate. Ask, WHAT WOULD HAPPEN IF WE HAD A BALL AND SOCKET JOINT IN OUR KNEES?

Writing about Bones

Explore the advantages and disadvantages of different types of joints by having children write stories about children with joints in different places. For example, if a child had a hinge joint where a shoulder joint is needed, how would the child move? What would a day in the life of that child be like?

Do Chickens have Joints?

Find out if the children think that a chicken has joints. Then, make chicken bones available to demonstrate how joints work. After children have had time to explore the chicken bones, ask, HOW IS YOUR SKELETON LIKE A CHICKEN SKELETON? (Both have joints and other similarities.)

Finger Bones

Have children place their fingers over the light of a flashlight. Ask, WHAT DO YOU SEE HOW CAN YOU TELL THAT YOU HAVE BONES INSIDE OF YOUR FINGERS? Have a

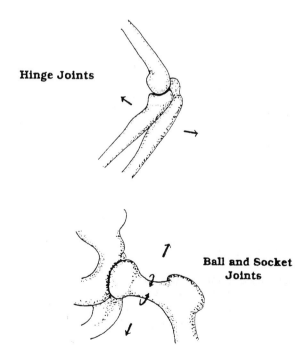

Hinge Joints

Ball and Socket Joints

Figure 17–9 A ball and socket joint and a hinge joint

doctor visit your class and discuss the use of X-rays. The children will enjoy seeing X-ray pictures of bones, especially broken bones. This would be a good time to discuss first aid for broken bones.

Bone Music and Art

Sing "Dry Bones." ("The toe bone's connected to the foot bone, the foot bone's connected to the ankle bone," and so on.) Children can compare skeleton poster bones as they sing, or a model of the backbone can be made with yarn and pieces of macaroni.

Make a Muscle

Young children enjoy flexing their arm muscles and feeling the muscles they can make, but they might think that arm muscles are the only ones they have. Encourage them to discover other muscles by raising their heels off the ground in a tiptoe position. Ask, CAN YOU FEEL YOUR MUSCLES MOVE AS THEY DO THIS? Have the children lie on mats, stretch out like a cat, then curl up into a ball. Ask, WHICH MUSCLES CAN YOU FEEL NOW?

Explore facial muscles by wiggling noses and raising eyebrows. Ask, DOES YOUR TONGUE HAVE MUSCLES? (Yes.) Give children time to find unexpected muscles in their bodies. Then, apply some of the bone and joint learning experiences to teaching about muscles.

All About Me

Children like to know that they are the same as others and that they are different, too. Discuss the similarities and differences in people that make them who they are. Give children opportunities to explore their bodies and what makes them an individual.

Exploring the Body: Using Hands and Feet to Help Us Move.

Ask children to find out how many things they can do with their hands such as wave, rub,

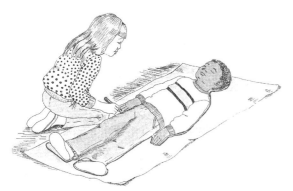

Figure 17–10   "Make a paper body."

scratch, or make a fist. Then, find out how many things can be done with their feet: skip, hop, walk, tiptoe. Have children write or dictate a list of their findings. Ask, CAN YOU THINK OF SOMETHING THAT YOU CANNOT DO WITH YOUR HANDS OR CANNOT DO WITH YOUR FEET? HOW IMPORTANT IS YOUR THUMB? Have the children do an activity without using their thumbs.

Paper Bodies

Full-sized paper outlines of a child's body can be used as a starting point for many learning experiences. Partners take turns tracing around each other on butcher paper with a crayon (Figure 17–10). Then, each child cuts out his or her body by following along the lines. Examples include:

- *My body.* After the paper body is made, have the children study their faces in a mirror and draw their features and clothes on one side of the paper body. The other side of the paper can be used to express yet a different look. Children will enjoy creating a fantasy body or storybook character on their own body shape.
- *Math body.* The cutout paper body can be an easy way for children to measure parts of their body. They can measure length of body, arms, and so on, and add weight and physical characteristics on a chart.

- *Action body.* After children are familiar with body tracing, let them trace each other in action poses and guess who is doing what and with what. Have magazines available for references of how a dancer uses muscles, how joints bend as an athlete runs, and how joints are used to sit in a chair.
- *I am curious.* Have children fill the paper body with magazine pictures depicting things that they like to do, are curious about, or want to learn about. Be careful not to limit paper body collages or subsequent "All About Me" books to simple biographies or listing of facts. This is not just a consumer activity or one about children's own acquisitiveness, but one that extends the exploration to include activities that enhance self-esteem. Children's interest in the world around them is worth learning more about. Ask, WHAT WOULD YOU LEARN MORE ABOUT? FIND THINGS THAT YOU ARE CURIOUS ABOUT. Make "I Am Curious" bodies and the like.

Figure 17–11   A body part bulletin board

- *Body mobile.* Separate this body at the joints and attach the body parts with yarn. These body mobiles can hang from the ceiling.
- *Body parts.* Cut up paper bodies can be added to a bulletin board or center. The body part bulletin board features an envelope of body parts that are assembled with thumbtacks. Labels may be added to name the parts, bones, joints, or organs that are being emphasized (Figure 17–11).

Senses

Studying the senses and how they can be used to gather information is a natural exploration for young children. Refer to units 8, 10, and 12 for exploration ideas and to the Senses Learning Center in Unit 18 for suggestions. The following sense walk experience is a useful beginning or extension for an ongoing study of the senses:

Sense Walk.

Ask the children to be absolutely silent as they take a walk around school. Plan to pass the lunchroom; office; custodian's area; gymnasium; other classrooms; and special area rooms, such as art and music. Instruct children to use their senses to notice as many things as they can. When you return to class, make a class chart or web of all the things noticed on the walk, such as different types of noises, smells, textures, sounds, and activity. Ask questions to encourage thinking, such as, DID THE FLOOR OF THE OFFICE FEEL LIKE THE FLOOR OF THE CLASSROOM? On a different day, take the class on an outside walk and brainstorm an experience web with the children to reinforce observations (Figure 17–12).

SUMMARY

Good health and nutrition habits begin early in a child's life. In order for children to begin to understand what it means to be healthy, they need to be exposed to a variety of learning experiences. These experiences need to be integrated into the

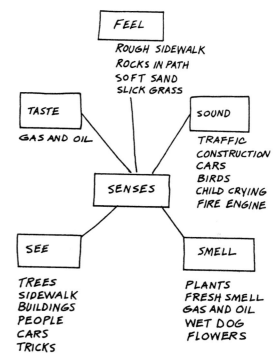

Figure 17–12   Brainstorm with an experience web.

child's life to have meaning and be as concrete as possible for better understanding.

Although children are curious about their bodies and how they work, their knowledge about internal anatomy is limited and especially difficult for children to understand. Concrete experiences on which to base learning about bones, muscles, and organs must be provided to ensure understanding.

MEDIA RESOURCES

Body movement, health and your Body. Chicago: Encyclopedia Britannica Educational Corporation. Each set contains six films with posters and teacher's guide.

Slim Goodbody: Your body, health, and feelings module. Chicago: Society for Visual Education.

FURTHER READING AND RESOURCES

Abruscato, J. (1991). *Teaching children science.* Englewood Cliffs, NJ: Prentice Hall, Inc.

Allison, L. (1976). *Blood and guts.* Boston: Little, Brown, and Company.

Bershad, C., & Bernick, D. (1979). *Bodyworks: The kids' guide to food and physical fitness.* New York: Random House.

Brummett, D. C., Lind, K. K., Barman, C. R., DiSpezio, M. A., & Ostlund, K. L. (1995) *Destinations in Science.* Grade 1, Grocery Store. Menlo Park, CA: Addison-Wesley Publishing Company.

Carter, C. D., & Phillips, F. K. (1979). *Activities that teach health.* New York: Instructor Publications, Inc.

Harlan, J. (1991). *Science experiences for the early childhood years.* Columbus, OH: Charles E. Merrill Publishing Co.

Hendry, L. (1987). *Foodworks.* Menlo Park, CA: Addison-Wesley.

Katz, L. G. (1988). *Early childhood education: What research tells us.* Bloomington, IN: Phi Delta Kappa Educational Foundation.

Lind, K. K. (1983). Apples, oranges, baseballs and me. In D. Stroak (Ed.), *Understanding the healthy body* (pp. 123–125). Columbus, OH: SMEAC Information Reference Center.

Lind, K. K. (1985). The inside story. *Science and Children, 22*(4), 122–123.

Science and Children. (1982). Skeleton Poster. Washington, DC: National Science Teachers Association.

Stronk, D. (1983). *Understanding the human body.* Columbus, OH: SMEAC Information Reference Center.

SUGGESTED COMPUTER PROGRAMS

Body-Awareness [Computer program]. Learning Well.

Bones and muscles: A team to depend on [Computer program]. Scholastic, Inc.

Incredible lab [Computer program]. Sunburst.

Science #5, House-a-Fire! Fire prevention [Computer program]. The Ellen Nelson Learning Library, Decision Development Corporation.

SUGGESTED ACTIVITIES

1. Assemble materials for one of the suggested learning activities. Try out the lesson with a small group of primary age children. Report to the class on what you did and how the children responded. How did you evaluate the children's responses? Would you change the activity if you were to teach it again?

2. Design a nutrition learning strategy for your Activity File. Which process skills will you emphasize? How many areas of the curriculum can you integrate into this lesson?

3. Develop your own teaching web. Select lessons from this unit, and design a teaching unit that is appropriate for a group of children you are teaching.

4. Prepare a learning cycle lesson to teach a health, nutrition, or human body concept. Teach it to a group of children, and report to the class. What was the advantage of using the learning cycle? Would another teaching strategy have worked better with this concept or group of children?

REVIEW

1. List two reasons health and nutrition education should be an essential part of the science curriculum in the primary grades.

2. Define health education as it applies to primary grade science.

SECTION VII

The Science Environment

UNIT 18 Materials and Resources for Science

OBJECTIVES

After studying this unit, the student should be able to
- Set up a science learning center
- Select appropriate materials for teaching science
- List examples of basic materials that can be used to support specific science concept development

Whether learning experiences are presented in an informal, unstructured, or structured approach or are used in learning centers or manipulated by an entire class at one time, manipulative science requires materials for children to explore. Hands-on science requires that materials be handled, stored, distributed, and replaced whenever they are used. Do not be discouraged. In the long

223

run, once the materials are accumulated and organized, less time is needed for teacher preparation because much of the classroom instruction will be carried out by the interaction of the child and the materials.

There are categories of math and science materials that can be used to guide selections. In Unit 3, six categories of materials were discussed: real objects, real objects used with pictorial representations, two-dimensional cutouts, pictures, wipe-off folders, and paper and pencil. These categories follow a developmental sequence from the concrete manipulative to the abstract representational. Preoperational children work with only the first four types of materials. During the transition to concrete operations, the last two categories may be available for those children who can deal with them. All through the concrete operations period, new concepts and skills should be introduced with concrete manipulative and pictorial materials before moving on to the abstract representational.

Many kinds of concrete manipulative materials have been introduced throughout the preceding units. Some are very versatile, and others serve specific functions. Pictorial manipulatives and other picture materials have also been suggested. Children's picture books are a potential source of pictorial and language information as was suggested in Unit 9. These materials help teach vocabulary, illustrate the use of math and science in a variety of settings, and expand children's ideas of how basic concepts can be used. However, it is important that these resources be carefully selected Be sure the illustrations accurately portray the concepts the book purports to help teach. Special care must be taken when selecting counting books because the illustrations are frequently inaccurate in their depiction of the set/symbol relationships. The teacher should ask, Which concept or concepts are illustrated in this book? How will reading this story or poem help Richard, Liu Pei, or Mary to better understand this concept?" Books should have good artwork and be colorful and well written.

There are several general categories of science materials. The most complete listing of available materials appears each January in *Science and Children*, a journal of the National Science Teachers Association, available through NSTA Publications. This useful supplement answers the question, "Where do I go for help?" The publication is organized into four main sections: equipment/supplies, media producers, computers/software, and publishers. This unit offers suggestions for the selection of basic science materials and resources and preparing science learning centers. The guidelines for selecting science materials for young children can also be applied to selecting other curricular materials.

BASIC SCIENCE MATERIALS

There are two basic types of science materials: those you purchase, and those you "scrounge." Purchased materials include textbook publishers' kits, general kits, and items purchased at supply houses or local retailers. Materials that are scrounged or contributed by parents and other benevolent individuals are known by many teachers as "good junk." Regardless of how the materials are acquired, they must be organized and managed in a way that promotes learning (Refer to Unit 13 for additional suggestions for classroom management.)

The Good Junk Box: Things to Scrounge

Many teachers rely on boxes of miscellaneous materials that have been gathered from many sources. Such a junk box comes in handy. Invite children, friends, businesspeople, and others to add to your junk box. Once people know you collect odds and ends, they will remember you when they are ready to throw something away; for example:

- Glass containers and 2-liter bottles make good aquariums, terrariums, and places to display animals (Figure 18–1).
- Aluminum foil, pie plates, and freezer food containers are useful for numerous activities.
- Film cans make smell and sound containers.

Figure 18–1   A pop bottle terrarium (*Reprinted from* Science and Children *1979). 16 (7), 47, with permission from the National Science Teachers Association, 1942 Connecticut Avenue, Washington, D. C. 20009. Gilmore, V. ""Helpful hints-Coca-Cola bottle terrarium.")*

- Hardware supplies are always welcome for the tool center; plastic tubing, garden hoses, and funnels are ideal for water play and making musical instruments.
- Candles, thumbtacks, paper clips, and sink and float items come in handy.
- Magnets from refrigerators are needed for magnet experiences; old, leaky aquariums make good housing for small mammals or reptiles.
- Oatmeal containers make drums; shoe boxes are great for dioramas and general organization and storage.
- Toys, clocks, and kitchen tools can be added to the Machine Center.
- Flashlights, batteries, and wire from telephone lines can be used for electricity experiments.
- Pipe cleaners are always useful for art; buttons and other small objects are needed for classifying and comparing.
- Straws, balloons, paper cups, pieces of fabric, and wallpaper are objects for the touch box.
- Some stores invite teachers to collect their old carpet and wallpaper sample books.

- Items that can be counted, sorted, graphed, and so on, such as plastic lids from bottles, jars, and other containers; thread spools; pinecones; seashells; buttons; and seeds are useful.
- Egg cartons and frozen food containers can be used for sorting.
- String, ribbon, sticks, and so on can be used for comparing lengths and for informal measuring
- Always keep an eye out for feathers, unusual rocks, shells, seed growing containers, plastic eggs—the list is endless.

Some teachers send home a list of "junk" items at the beginning of the year. Parents are asked to bring or send available items to school. Such a list will be easy to complete when you become familiar with "good junk" and have an idea of some of the items that you will use during the year. In addition, parents are usually responsive to special requests such as vegetables for the vegetable activities like those in Unit 12 and 17 or ingredients for the cooking activities in Unit 16.

Commercial Materials for Science

Your school district might decide to purchase a kit from a publisher when selecting a textbook for teaching science. Publisher kits are available from most major companies and contain materials specifically designed to implement the activities suggested in the textbook or teacher resource book. These kits can be helpful in providing the hands-on component of a textbook-based science program.

General kits are available from many sources and range in size from small boxes to large pieces of furniture with built-in equipment such as sinks and cabinets. General kits contain basic materials but may not be directed to your specific needs. An advantage of the boxes or rolling tables is that they are easy to circulate among teachers.

Specific topic kits such as "Mining, Minerals, and Me" from Delta Education (suggested in Unit 16) are boxed by topic and grade level. The idea is to provide the teacher with the materials necessary to teach a specific science topic. Teachers' manuals

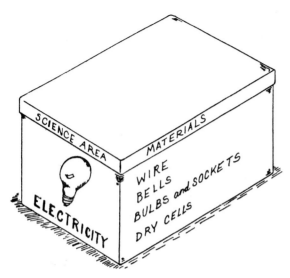

Figure 18–2 Store materials needed to teach concepts in a labeled shoebox.

and materials allow teachers to use the kit as a supplement to a textbook or as the major means of teaching a science concept.

Advantages and Disadvantages of Kits

Most kits contain a limited amount of consumable supplies, usually just enough for a class to do all of the activities covered in the teacher manual. Reordering must be continuous for the kit to be used again. However, the kits also contain permanent supplies such as magnifiers, clay, small plastic aquariums, petri dishes, balances, and the like.

The major drawbacks to commercial kits of any type are maintaining the consumables in the kits and finding the money to purchase the kits. Kits are self-contained, complete, and ready for use; consequently, they are also expensive.

Purchased Equipment

There are some items that you might have to purchase to be an effective science teacher. This list includes magnifiers, eyedroppers, plastic tub-

ing, mirrors, a rock and mineral set, magnets, batteries, and bulbs. If you select just one of these items, do not hesitate to choose magnifiers as the most useful piece of science equipment for the early childhood classroom. (Refer to Unit 14 for suggestions on using magnifiers.)

Although they are not interactive in the same way as rollers, ramps, and constructions, magnifiers provide children with their first look at fascinating magnified objects. Piaget was a biologist and probably would have wholeheartedly approved. It is hard to believe that he did not eagerly explore his environment up close at an early age.

Organizing and Storing Materials

As you collect and develop materials for teaching science and math, storage might become a problem. Most commercial kits have neat, ready-made labeled boxes, but the "junk box" system will need some organizing.

One way to manage a variety of materials is to place them in shoe boxes. The shoe boxes contain the equipment needed to teach a specific concept. If the boxes are clearly marked, they can be very convenient. The trick is to keep everything you need in the box such as homemade equipment materials, task cards, materials to duplicate, and bulletin board ideas. To be effective, the box, envelope, or grocery bag should display a materials list on the outside. In this way, you have a self-contained kit for teaching science (Figure 18–2).

Materials relating to a learning center can be stored in boxes under or near the Science Center. Materials will be handy, and older children will be able to get their own materials. Primary age children can be very effective organizers. They will enjoy and benefit from the job of inventorying science materials (Figure 18–3).

THE SCIENCE LEARNING CENTER

You know that the interests of children stem from the kinds of learning materials and experiences

Figure 18–3 Labeled boxes can be stored under a learning center.

available to them. One way to provide stimulating explorations is by setting up learning centers appropriate for an individual child or for a small group of children. As children work in centers, they learn to learn on their own in a planned environment. In this way, instruction is individualized, and children have time to explore science materials.

There are several different types of science learning centers, characterized by different purposes and modes of operation. The basic centers can be labeled Discovery Center, Open Learning Center, Inquiry Learning Center, and Science Interest Center.

Discovery Center

The word *discovery* implies that some action will be taken on materials and that questions and comments about what is happening take place. All is not quiet in a Discovery Center. Thus, it should be located away from listening and literacy centers. Discovery centers can be located on large tables, desks against a wall, or any spot that has room. Mobile discovery centers made of trays, shoe boxes, or baskets can simply be picked up and taken to a designated spot on the floor. An area

rug makes a good place to work without taking up too much space. (Figure 18–4).

In Figure18–5, activity trays are used to explore concepts about air. As with any learning center, the size of your center area and ages of the children must be taken into account. For the five activity trays described in Figure 18–5, it is recommended that the teacher use two trays with 5-year-olds and initially, one tray with younger children.

Open Learning Center

The Science Center in an open classroom is very creative and contains an abundance of manipulative materials, the majority of which are homemade. Using minimum directions, the child might be asked to "Invent something useful with these

Figure 18–4 Working with an activity tray

Activity Trays—Exploring Concepts About Air

TRAY	CONTENTS	CONCEPTS TO BE EXPLORED	INTRODUCTION	FURTHER EXPLORATION
1	2–4 each of several sizes and colors of paper bags Box of wire closures	Air can be felt even when it cannot be seen.	Open up bags and look inside. Do you see anything? Fold the bags up again. What do you feel as you do this? Try with several sizes and colors of bags.	How can you make the bag like a balloon? What is the closure used for?
2	12 plastic glasses, water pitcher, plastic drinking straws Red and blue food coloring, liquid soap	Bubbles are really air in water.	See how many different sizes of bubbles you can blow in a glass of water. What else can you do with the bubbles? What happens when you touch them?	Color the water with food coloring. What kinds of bubbles can you make now? What are the bubbles like when liquid soap is added?
3	Colored balloons, string, scissors, and felt-tip pens	Air can be felt even when it cannot be seen. Air makes a noise in some activities.	Blow up balloons. (A small air pump can be used for younger children.) Let the balloons go when they are large enough. What can you hear, feel, and see?	Draw faces and figures on your balloons. How do these change as the balloon is blown up? Tie balloons securely with a string and leave overnight. What changes are apparent the next day? What caused the changes?
4	Several sheets of heavy, colored paper; stapler; and crayons to decorate paper	Air can be moved with a fan.	Fold the colored paper accordion style to make a hand fan. Use a stapler to pull the bottom together. Use the fan to create air movement.	Try moving items from tray 5.
5	Feathers, cloth scraps, small plastic toy cars, plastic animals, packing forms, and cotton balls	Air moves many things.	Try to move these items using your fan. How many small items can you move across a table or floor space?	Try to guess which items will be more difficult to move. Why? Separate items that move easily from those that do not.

Figure 18–5 "Activity trays–Exploring concepts about air. Note. Early Childhood and Science by M. McIntyre, 1984. Reprinted by permission of the National Science Teachers Association.

materials." Guidance is provided in the way of helpful suggestions or questions as the children pursue and tinker with their invention.

Another example of an open center is a sink and float center. In this center, reinforcing the concept of sink and float is the central objective. The center contains a plastic tub half full of water and a box of familiar materials. On the backboard are the questions, "What will float?" and "What will sink?" With no further direction, the children explore the questions with the materials.

Teacher evaluation is not formal; rather, the teacher visits the center and satisfies any concerns about children's progress. The teacher might find

Figure 18–6   "Construct a beach."

children making piles of things that do and do not float or trying to sink something that they thought would float. Some teachers suggest that the children communicate what happened at the center by drawing or writing a few sentences (Figure 18–6).

Inquiry Learning Center

A more directed discovery approach focuses on a science concept or topic and contains materials to be manipulated by the children, directions for the investigation, and open-ended questions to be asked at the end of the inquiry. The objective is not to reinforce a concept but to engage the child in problem solving beyond what is known to gain new insights.

At an Inquiry Center, the child might find directions that say, "Using the materials in this box, find a way to light the bulb," or, "What kinds of materials are attracted to magnets?" Science concepts are turned into questions that are placed on activity cards. There might be a single task or a series of tasks that a primary age child can complete in 15 or 30 minutes.

It would be foolish to send children to an Inquiry Center without adequate preparation. Discuss directions, procedures, and task cards with the children before beginning center work. The children are expected to achieve a desired learning outcome. So, if things do not go smoothly, ask yourself the following questions: Were the directions clear? Did the children know where to begin and end? Did they know what to do when they were finished? Is the center appropriate for the age group? Did the first group using the center know how to restore the materials for the next group? (Figure 18–7).

Science Interest Center

Science interest corners, tables, and centers are popular in many schools. This Interest Center rein-

Figure 18–7   An Inquiry Center

forces, enriches, and supplements ongoing programs with materials that stimulate children's interest. The primary goal of the center is to motivate children to want to learn more about the subject at the center.

As general rules, children are not required to visit this center, and no formal evaluation of their activities is recorded. Many times the center repeats a lesson exploration. For example, if the class has done the "Thinking like a Geologist" lesson described in Unit 16, some children might want to try scratching minerals to test hardness or classifying the available rocks. Filmstrips, storybooks, and resource books on rocks and minerals should be available for the children to explore. Children could practice their measuring skills by using string to measure an assortment of objects or become acquainted with a balance scale by comparing the weight of different rocks.

Plan Your Center

State learning center objectives in such a way that you know what you want the child to learn. Know your children's developmental level. You can avoid inadvertently creating busywork for stu-dents by taking steps to carefully plan the concepts to be developed at the center. Start by writing a sentence that communicates what the child is expected to learn at the center. Children must be able participate in the activities and methods independently. Evaluate the center by asking yourself: Is the center effective in achieving my objectives? How can the center be improved? Figure 18–8 suggests a guide to planning a learning center.

SELECTING SCIENCE MATERIALS

Providing materials that encourage children to "mess around" and explore is the responsibility of the teacher. At the center, children use the process skills to observe, investigate, classify, and maybe hypothesize. Because this learning is not accidental, planning must go into setting up centers and selecting materials. After completing the planning guide suggested in Figure 18–8, consider the following criteria in selecting and arranging materials:

1. **Are the materials open-ended?** Can they be used in more than one way? For example, water play provides the opportunity to explore measuring or floating.

A Simple Outline for Planning a Learning Center

Purpose of Center	Characteristics of Students	Concepts and Skills	Activities and Materials	Expected Learning Outcomes	Evaluations	Suggestions for Change
					Students:	
					Center:	

Figure 18–8 A simple outline for planning a learning center. *Note.* From "Designing the Science Learning Center" by G. R. Sherfey and P. Huff, 1976, *Science and Children, 14*(3), p. 12. Reprinted by permission of the National Science Teachers Association.

2. **Are the materials designed for action?** In science, children do something to materials to make something else happen. If substances are to be dissolved, which will offer the best comparison: salt, sugar, or pudding mix?

3. **Are the materials arranged to encourage communication among children?** If appropriate, place materials to create cooperation and conversation. Arrange materials in categories such as pitchers of water in one section of the center, substances to be tested in another, and spoons and dishes for mixing in another. Children quickly learn to cooperate and communicate in order to complete the activity.

4. **Is there a variety of materials?** If the center is to be used over an extended period, some children will visit it many times. A variety of materials will prevent overexposure to the exploration.

5. **Do the materials encourage "What if _____ " statements?** The sink and float activity described in the open classroom learning center invites children to predict what will happen if they try to float a marble, toothpick, or sponge.

6. **Are the materials appropriate for the maturity of the children?** Consider the maturity level of the class. Select materials that the children can handle safely and effectively.

7. **Do the materials allow for individual differences such as ability, interest, working space, and style?** After considering floating and sinking, some children will begin to consider size and other characteristics of the available objects. Have objects with a variety of textures and features available.

8. **How much direction do the materials require?** In giving directions, consider the age of the children. Four- and 5-year-olds might receive directions from a cassette recording, but 3-year-olds and young 4s re-spond best to personal directions. Rebus-type directions are also appropriate.

9. **Do the materials stress process skills?** The process skills are the fundamental skills that are emphasized in science explorations with young children. These skills will come naturally from manipulating materials. However, a variety of appropriate materials is required for this to happen.

10. **Are the materials nonbiased?** Where appropriate, materials should illustrate authentic nonbiased dress and activities.

Sensory Learning Center

Children have a "sense-able" approach to the world around them. The approach that they use is as basic to science as it is natural to young children. Use the type of center you prefer to give children an opportunity to taste, smell, touch, observe, and hear their environment. Consider the following ideas as a starting point:

Thinking like a Criminologist

Skin prints are a way to take a closer look at the skin children live in. They enjoy examining their fingertips, taking their own fingerprints, and thinking like a criminologist at this center. Since a criminologist investigates crimes by analyzing clues in a systematic way, studying fingerprints is an important part of this job.

You will need one No. 2 pencil, white scratch paper, plain paper, a handheld lens, and a damp paper towel at this station. Show children how to rub soft pencil lead onto a sheet of paper and pick up a good smudge with one finger. Then, they carefully pick up the smudge with a piece of clear tape, pull it away, and press the fingerprint onto a clean paper.

Begin by having students make a set of their own fingerprints on a sheet of clean paper. If someone makes a mistake, simply peel off the tape and start over. Then create a classroom mystery for your students to solve. Ask, WHO WAS THE LAST PERSON TO USE THE PENCIL SHARPENER?

Figure 18–9 A rebus card gives the directions for mixing colors.

Each group that visits the center can be a group of "suspects." Prepare prints in advance, then show prints that were "found" on the pencil sharpener. Have the children use the handheld lens to compare their prints to the set belonging to the "criminal."

Integrate fingerprinting into art by letting the children use ink pads to make prints from their hands or fingers. Children can bring the prints to life by adding legs, arms, and other features. Fingerprint stories can be developed, and you may even want to include toe prints as a homework assignment. You could go further and classify fingerprints into three basic patterns: whorl, arch, and loop. Refer to the further readings list for resources.

Do You Hear What I Hear?

Walk in the hallway with a tape recorder and record five interesting sounds. Bring the tape back to the classroom, provide earphones, and have the children draw a picture of the sounds that they hear. Children enjoy using a tape recorder. Let them take turns tape recording sounds during recess, assemblies, or the lunch period. Challenge them to record unusual sounds and infer what is making the sounds. Add further interest to this center by sending the tape recorder home with a child to tape "home sounds." As children identify the home sounds at the center, have them compare and contrast the sounds in their own home and write a story about the sounds and how they are created.

The tape recorder also makes a good listening center for a variety of tapes and records. Many of the recordings should be stories. Children will enjoy illustrating the stories. Some will enjoy taping a story of their own for use in the center or as background for plays, puppet shows, and radio programs.

Red, Yellow, and Blue

The object of this center is to mix the primary colors and observe and record the results. Have the children record the color that results from dropping the correct amounts of color into the correct container (Figure 18–9).

Smells, Smells, Smells

Gather small amounts of familiar substances with distinctive odors, such as coffee, popcorn, orange extract, hot chocolate, onions, apples, and peanut butter. Put the items in jars, shoe boxes, plastic sandwich bags, or loosely tied brown paper bags—whichever seems appropriate—and leave small holes in the containers so that the odors can escape. As children take turns smelling the containers, ask them to describe the various odors and guess what might be producing these distinctive smells. Make a duplicate set of containers, and ask the children to match the ones that smell alike. Be sure to show children the safe way to smell an unknown substance: They should gently fan the air between their noses and the container with one hand and breathe normally. The scent will come to them.

Apple or Potato?

Figure 18–10   This center focuses on measurement activities and materials.

Spread vegetable pieces on a plate for children to taste. They will have to work in pairs. One puts on a blindfold, holds his nose, and tries to guess what he is tasting. The other child keeps a record by writing down what the vegetable piece really is and what his partner thinks it is. Then, the children trade places, redo the test, and compare their scores.

The children will be surprised that they made a lot of wrong guesses. This is because it is hard to tell one food from another of similar texture. The secret lies inside the nose. Tongues only tell if something is sweet, sour, salty, or bitter; the rest of the information comes from the odor of the food. Lead children to the conclusion that they would have a hard time tasting without their sense of smell.

Tasting liquids that children drink frequently is fun. Pour some milk, orange juice, water, soda, or other popular drinks into paper cups or clean milk cartons and provide clean straws for tasting. Have the children describe the taste and guess what it might be. Some children will enjoy drawing a picture of their favorite flavor. A sip of water or bite of bread in between items helps clear their palates.

A MEASUREMENT LEARNING CENTER

Materials in the center should be neatly organized and displayed. Place the materials in containers on low shelves where they are readily accessible to the students. Be sure the procedures for removing, using, and replacing materials are clearly understood by the children. Sometimes a specialized center (i.e., for measurement or classification; see Figure 18–10) can add to the excitement of learning.

Materials can be rotated according to the children's needs and interests and to keep their interest engaged. When new materials are introduced, the teacher should allow opportunities for exploration before the materials are used for structured activities.

A learning center can focus on specific concepts when these concepts are being introduced. For example, Figure 18–10 shows materials in a Measurement Center. Focused centers can be set up for any of the skills and concepts in the text. Notice the signs that call attention to the print associated with measurement language. A measurement center can be set up relative to available space and furnishings. A center might be a set of shelves with an adjacent table and chairs or carpeted area, a small table with a few different materials each day, or a space on the floor where math materials are placed. In one primary classroom in Guilderland, New York, a math bed was installed. A blackboard was at one end and shelves for books and materials at the other end: a comfortable and inviting Math Center.

Many teachers, especially in the primary grades, feel pressured to follow the directions in the textbooks and teach whole group measurement lessons without the use of manipulatives to introduce concepts as described throughout this text. It is possible to find a compromise that is beneficial for both students and teacher. For example, one first-grade teacher decided to try a new approach: She took the objectives for the text assigned to her class and found developmentally appropriate activities that correlated with each one. She selected the activities and assembled the necessary materials. She introduced each concept to the whole class and then divided the class into small groups to work with the concrete materials. The children felt more satisfied, performed their tasks with enthusiasm, and even commented on how much fun it was not to have to write! The teacher had time to circulate and help individual children. A positive side effect emerged from the opportunity to "talk" measurement: The children's language was extended, and unclear points were clarified. Peer tutoring developed naturally, to the advantage of both the tutors and those who needed help. The games and manipulatives were available for further use during the children's free choice time. The teacher's enthusiasm and the enthusiasm of the students were picked up by the other first-grade teachers and the principal. The teacher was asked to inservice the other first-grade teachers so that they could try the system.

SUMMARY

Stimulating science and math lessons do not happen by accident. The materials selected to teach science and math and the format that they are presented in are essential for successful explorations. Whether materials are purchased or scrounged, they must be flexible and appropriate to the developmental age of the child and the type of science and math learning that is required. Learning centers are designed and used to meet specific teaching objectives and must be evaluated for their effectiveness.

Lists of resource books for teachers and further reading lists are included in this unit. Lists of children's books and other resources are in Appendix B.

FURTHER READING AND RESOURCES

Carin, A. A., & Sund, R. B. (1992). *Teaching science through discovery*. New York: Macmillan.

Carroll, J. (1983). *Learning centers for little kids*. Carthage, IL: Good Apple, Inc.

Coombs, B., Harcourt, L., Travis, J., & Wannamaker, N. (1987). *Explorations 2*. Menlo Park, CA: Addison-Wesley.

Esler, W., & Esler, M. (1993). *Teaching elementary science*. Belmont, CA: Wadsworth Publishing Company.

Gilmore, V. (1979). Helpful hints—Coca-Cola bottle terrarium. *Science and Children, 16*(7).

Houle, G. B. (1987). *Learning centers for young children* (3rd edition). West Greenwich, RI: Tot-lot Child Care Products.

Kerr, S. (1993). *Science centers A to Z*. Wheeling, IL: Look At Me Productions, Inc.

McIntyre, M. (1984). *Early childhood and science*. Washington, DC: National Science Teachers Association.

Poppe, C. A., & Van Matre, N. (1985). *Science learning centers for the primary grades*. West Nyack, NY: Center for Applied Research in Education.

Sherfey, G. R., & Huff, P. (1976). Designing the science learning center. *Science and Children, 14*(3), 12.

Supplement of Science Education Suppliers. Published every January. Washington, DC: National Science Teachers Association.

Suydam, M. N. (1990). Planning for mathematics instruction. In J. N. Payne (Ed.), *Mathematics for the young child* (pp. 285–302). Reston, VA: National Council of Teachers of Mathematics.

Thornton, C. A., & Wilson, S. J. (1993). Classroom organization and models of instruction. In R. J. Jensen (Ed.), *Research ideas for the classroom: Early childhood mathematics*. New York: Macmillan.

Ziegler, N., Larson, B., & Byers, J. (1983). *Let the kids do it! Book 1: A manual for self-direction through indirect guidance.* Belmont, CA: Fearon.

Ziegler, N., Larson, B., & Byers, J. (1983). *Let the kids do it! Book 2: Symbols and rebus charts.* Belmont, CA: Fearon.

SUGGESTED ACTIVITIES

1. Obtain a copy of the current NSTA Supplement of Science Education Suppliers. Select a science concept and list materials that could be used in teaching that concept.

2. Reflect on the nature of science materials. Then, make a list of materials needed for teaching a science unit that you have developed. Where will you get these materials? How will you organize them for hands-on teaching?

3. Construct a learning center. Use the center with a group of children, and share the effectiveness of the materials with the class.

4. Compile a list of free and inexpensive science teaching materials. Send for some of these materials, and evaluate if they are appropriate for young children. Share this information with the class.

5. Visit a preschool, kindergarten, and primary class. Compare the science teaching materials used in these classes. What are the similarities and differences?

6. Visit a local educational materials store. Make a list of available science materials and their prices. Bring the list to class.

7. Participate in a small group in class, and compare math materials lists. Make cooperative decisions as to which materials should be purchased if a new prekindergarten, kindergarten, and/or primary classroom is to be furnished. Each group should consider cost as well as purpose.

8. Go to the library. Find and read at least 10 children's picture books that contain science concepts (see the Appendix B for suggestions). Write a description of each one. Tell how each book could be used with children.

9. Make two different "homemade" science resources that could be used with young children. Share the materials with the class. Be prepared to show the class how the resources can be made.

10. Visit two preschool, kindergarten, and/or primary classes. Ask to look at the science materials used. Diagram the Learning Centers that you see. Share the information with your class. Tell the purpose and strong and weak points of the center. List any changes that would make it better.

11. Add a science materials list to each of the activity units in your file/notebook.

12. Send for free commercial catalogs. Make a list of science materials that are new in each. Write down the descriptions presented in the catalogs. Share this information with your class.

REVIEW

A. Why are learning centers essential for science learning?

B. What are the two main types of science equipment?

C. List some useful items for a science junk box.

D. What are some of the advantages of science kits? What are some of the disadvantages?

E. Match the description with the center.

_____ Discovery Center
_____ Open Learning Center
_____ Inquiry Learning Center
_____ Science Interest Center

1. Children explore a concept with as little direction as possible. A leading question.

2. Little direction is given. Children "mess around" with materials at small tables or trays.

3. A directed discovery approach focuses on a concept. This center includes directions and is used to encourage children to go beyond what they know about a concept.

4. This center motivates children to want to learn about its materials.

F. Respond to each of the following situations:

1. Miss Collins says she doesn't believe it is appropriate to teach science or math to young children. When you observe in her kindergarten, you see children playing at a water table with various containers. Others are weighing toy cars on a balance scale and building with blocks. Is Miss Collins teaching science? If so, explain how.

2. Mr. Dominic teaches first grade. He is going to set up a Math Center. He has been given $300 to purchase basic materials. He asks for your help. What would you suggest?

3. Mrs. Edwards teaches second grade. She has just read this book. She is trying hard to provide a developmentally appropriate science environment. However, she cannot decide how to begin. What suggestions would you give her?

UNIT 19 Science in Action

OBJECTIVES

After studying this unit, the student should be able to
- Plan and use blocks for science experiences
- Describe the benefits of using blocks with primary age children
- Plan and use woodworking for math and science experiences
- Plan and use outdoor activities with young children

Math and science go on all the time in the developmentally appropriate classroom for young children. The block builder, like any engineer, builds her building so it will stand up and serve a planned function. The young carpenter measures wood and swings his hammer to get the most power when he hits the nail. Children do finger plays and action songs and explore the outdoors while they apply math and science concepts. As children move into concrete operations, math and science in action include more complex group games and activities and the introduction of team sports and preplanned building and science projects.

Children continue to be active learners in the primary grades. This is a fact from research based on Piagetian theory. Unfortunately, the active opportunities provided by blocks and outdoor explorations are not always considered in curriculum plans for primary age children. This is a mistake. Remember, primary age children are still concrete operation thinkers who learn to understand the world around them through actively engaging in explorations.

Block play and outdoor explorations give children many opportunities to investigate, test, and change objects. It is from these interactions that children build their own model of the world. (Refer to concept development in Units 1–6 to refresh your memory.)

This unit focuses on the relationship of blocks, woodworking, games, problem solving, and outdoor activities that meet the affective, cognitive, and psychomotor learning needs of the young child. The emphasis is on active learning both indoors and outdoors.

Children apply basic concepts as they explore the relationships among the various sizes and shapes in a set of unit blocks. They note that two of one size may equal one of another, some are longer and some shorter, some are square, some are rectangular, others are triangular, and still others are curved. They are working with fractions and parts and wholes.

BLOCKS, SCIENCE, AND CHILDREN

Block building and play are not isolated from science. The very nature of building a structure requires that children deal with the processes of science as discussed in Unit 5. As children build, they compare, classify, predict, and interpret problems. Scientific thinking is stimulated as children discover and invent new forms; expand experiences; explore major conceptual ideas in science;

237

Figure 19–1 The children create a block zoo.
measurement; and work with space, change, and
pattern.

Blocks Encourage Thinking

Blocks force children to distinguish, classify,
and sort. This can be seen as a group of second
graders learns the different properties of blocks by
recreating a field trip to the zoo. As they plan and
build, they deal with the fact that each block has
different qualities. Size, shape, weight, thickness,
width, and length are considered. As construction
progresses, the blocks become fulcrums and
levers. Guiding questions such as, CAN YOU
MAKE A RAMP FOR UNLOADING THE RHI-
NOCEROS? WHERE WILL YOU PUT THE
ACCESS ROAD FOR DELIVERING FOOD TO
THE ANIMALS? will help children focus on an
aspect of construction. Some children create zoo
animals, workers, and visitors to dramatize a day
at the zoo (Figure 19–1).

Allow time for children to verbalize why
they are arranging the zoo in a particular way. This
will encourage children to share their problem-
solving strategy and will help them to clarify

thinking. By observing the children at play, you
will also gain insight into their thinking.

Balance, Predictions, Interactions, and Movement

One emphasis in science is interactions
within systems. In block building, the blocks form
a system that is kept in equilibrium through balance. As children build, they work with a cause-
and-effect approach to predict stress and to keep
the forces of gravity from tumbling their structure.
The idea that each part added to the structure con-
tributes to the whole is constantly reinforced as
children maintain the stability of their structure.

Balancing blocks is an effective way to
explore cause and effect. By seeing the reaction of
what they do, children begin to learn cause and
effect. The following ideas emphasize action and
cause and effect:

1. **Dominoes.** Children develop spatial relationships as they predict what will happen to
   an arrangement of dominoes (Figure 19–2).
   Ask, CAN YOU ARRANGE THE DOMI-
   NOES IN SUCH A WAY THAT THEY
   WILL ALL BE KNOCKED DOWN?
2. **Construct and roll.** Arrange plastic bottles
   or blocks in a variety of ways, and have the
   children try to knock them over with a ball.
   This bowling-like game encourages children
   to keep score and establish a correspondence

Figure 19–2 "Arrange the dominoes so that they
will all be knocked down."

Figure 19–3   "Discuss how a swing is similar to a pendulum."

between the way blocks are arranged and how the ball is rolled. Ask, WHAT ACTION CAUSED THE BLOCKS TO FALL DOWN? WHAT ACTION STARTED THE BALL MOVING? DID THE BALL KNOCK DOWN EVERY BOTTLE THAT FELL? IF NOT, WHAT MADE THEM FALL?

3. **Pendulum release.** In a pendulum game, a ball moves without being pushed; it is released. Children structure space as they place blocks in a position to be knocked down by the pendulum bob. Have children predict, IF THE BALL PENDULUM IS PULLED BACK AND RELEASED, WILL IT KNOCK OVER THE BLOCK?

   Roomsize pendulums can be made life-sized by securing one end of a length of cotton string to the ceiling and attaching a weighted bob to the other end. Weighted bobs for the pendulum can be made by tying a plastic pill vial filled with sand to the cotton string. However, a smaller model may be more practical. Try this first and then tell the children how to expand to a life-sized model. One end of a length of cotton string or fish line must be attached to a stable support that allows for a swinging motion. A simple effec-tive pendulum can be constructed by placing an eye screw into a board, suspending the board between the backs of two chairs, and attaching the string with the pendulum bob. Children can sit on the floor and explore the action of the pendulum (Figure 19–3).

4. **Inclines.** In incline activities, the ball moves when released. Exactly where the ball goes is determined by manipulating the incline and the ball. Have children change the incline in different ways to control what happens to the ball. Children will enjoy cre-ating games such as catching the ball with a cup, racing different-sized balls down the incline, and measuring how far the ball trav-els (Figure 19–4).

5. **Buttons and bobby pins.** The object of this tilt game is to jiggle a button from start to finish without letting it fall off of the board or through a hole. The button or ball is guided by tilting and wiggling the board. To make the game, cut several holes in card-board, and rub the board with a piece of waxed paper. Position bobby pins with the raised side up on the board, mark a start and finish, and begin the game.

Figure 19–4   "Can you control the speed of the ball?"

Figure 19–5 Primary age children enjoy controlling the movement of blocks and marbles.

Pinball Wizards

Children can create pinball machines from scraps of plywood, strips of wood, glue, nails, plastic caps, and marbles. The challenge is for children to invent ways to make a marble fall down a series of ramps and make the trip as long as possible. Have the children glue wooden strips to a backboard at different angles. Then have them adjust their obstacles of nails and blocks as they try out the marble. Ask, CAN YOU THINK OF A WAY TO SLOW DOWN THE MARBLE? (You might want to introduce the concept of friction.)

Blocks and Marbles

Balance and action can be seen as children assemble plastic ramps and chutes with commercial toys such as Marbleworks® from Discovery Toys. Children gain a familiarity with concepts such as gravity, acceleration, and momentum when they design and create a maze of movement by fitting pieces together. To further introduce children to the principle of cause and effect, ask, WHAT ACTION STARTS THE MARBLE MOVING? Then have children predict the way in which the marble will move. Creating different pathways and exploring how the marble moves on them can be exciting.

Complex block and marble sets seem to fascinate primary age children. In these sets children arrange attractive wooden sections to allow marbles to travel through holes and grooved blocks of different lengths. Children enjoy controlling the movement of the marble down the construction and creating changes that determine direction and speed of the marble (Figure 19–5). Children can make their own marble runs from decorative molding that is available in paneling supply stores. The track can be nailed onto boards, taped down, or held for observing the movement of marbles (some will move at breakneck speeds). Have your students add a tunnel, try different types of balls, and find ways to use friction to slow down the marbles.

Another Type of Construction

Constructions introduce children to the conditions and limitations of space. They learn to bridge space with appropriate-sized blocks and objects and enclose space in different ways. The following ideas involve creating your own construction set with straws:

Use large straws for straw construction, and connect them with string, pipe cleaners, or paper clips. String is the most difficult to use but makes the most permanent construction. Simply stick the string in one end of the straw, and suck on the other end. The string will come through.

You will have to form a triangle with three straws. A triangle is the only shape made with straws that is rigid enough for building. If you are using string as a connector, tie the ends together to form a triangle, or thread three straws on one string to form the triangle.

Pipe cleaners as connectors are another method of building with straws. Push a pipe cleaner halfway into the end of one straw, then slip

Figure 19–6   "Can you make a bridge?"

another straw over the other end of the pipe cleaner. Double up the pipe cleaners for a tighter fit. Children can twist and turn this construction in many ways.

Many teachers recommend paper clips as ideal connectors in straw building. Open a paper clip, bend out the two ends, and slip each end into a straw. Paper clips are rigid and allow for complex building. You might have to add as many as three paper clips to give the structure strength. Paper clips may also be chained for a flexible joint between two straws. Challenge children to think and construct. Ask, HOW TALL A STRUCTURE CAN YOU MAKE? WHY DID YOUR STRUCTURE COLLAPSE? CAN YOU MAKE A BRIDGE?

When the straw frame stands by itself, test it. Ask, CAN YOU THINK OF A WAY TO TEST THE STRENGTH OF YOUR STRUCTURE? Place a paper clip through a paper cup and hang it somewhere on the straw structure. Ask, HOW MANY PAPER CUPS CAN YOUR STRUCTURE SUPPORT? HOW MANY PAPER CLIPS WILL MAKE THE FRAME WORK? (Figure 19–6).

Block City

Blocks in the classroom provide many opportunities to integrate basic reading and writing, science, math skills and concepts, and social studies into the construction process. Opportunities for integration abound as children explore the busy life of a block city.

Mr. Wang's second grade created a city of blocks. Buildings had to be accurate in the city, and each child builder represented herself in the daily acting out of city life. The block building sessions were preceded by class discussion as the children planned the daily block activities. Assessories (labeled boxes of food, clothing, computers, typewriters, and the like) were constructed from a variety of materials. Children played the roles of shopkeepers, bankers, and other workers. They made decisions such as where the people in the block city would get their money.

When the children had to put out an imaginary fire, they immediately saw a problem. How would they get water to the blaze? This discovery led to an investigation of how water gets into hydrants, utility covers, and water pipes. The children responded to the emergency by adding plastic tubing to the city as well as wire for electricity and telephones.

Not only was the city becoming more realistic, it was becoming less magical. Children no longer thought that water magically appeared when the water faucet was turned on. They knew that a system of pipes carried the water. In fact, the workings of a city in general became less magical. Many common misconceptions were dispelled, and understanding of how a city functions began to develop (Figure 19–7).

The Edible Village

Mrs. Moore's first grade class integrated the study of their neighborhood with block building. After finding out the different sections of the

Figure 19–7 A block city begins to take shape.

neighborhood and buildings they needed to create, each child was assigned a building. The class created their neighborhood with blocks made of graham crackers. They used flattened caramels for roadways and lollipops for streetlights. Coconut spread over white icing gave the illusion of snow.

The students mixed yellow and green food coloring into icing to create differently colored buildings. Recipes for icing provided opportunities to use measurements and follow directions in sequence. Writing about the creation of the village and what might be happening within graham cracker walls became a springboard for discussion.

Children made decisions about what should and should not be included in the village. They determined the authenticity of buildings and building size. This activity is especially appropriate for primary age children. Children in this age group are able to incorporate more detail and can be exposed to another's viewpoint. For example, the teacher asked, HOW WILL THE PEOPLE KNOW THAT SCHOOL IS OPEN? Children began asking each other, DO WE NEED A HOSPITAL? WHAT ABOUT A GAS STATION?

If your city or town is located near a river or lake, be sure to include it in construction. Paper straw bridges could be added and the geography of your area explored. You will find that as the children develop questions, they are motivated to find the answers because they need to know something for construction of the city. Thus, the block experience also becomes a first research experience.

The Block Area

The block area needs plenty of space. The blocks and the small vehicles, people dolls, and animals that enhance the accompanying dramatic play activities should be neatly organized on low shelves where they can be easily reached by the children. Shelves should be marked with outlines of each block shape so that the children can return the blocks to the proper place (and practice some one-to-one correspondence). Start the year with a small, easy-to-handle set. As time goes by, more blocks and more shapes can be introduced. The teacher can facilitate exploration

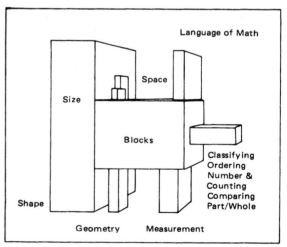

Figure 19–8 Children can construct many concepts as they work with blocks.

by asking questions and making comments. For example Mrs. Red Fox notes that Trang Fung has used all square blocks in her structure, whereas Sara has developed her structure with larger units. "It looks like each of you have your favorite sized blocks."

Blocks can be purchased in sets of various sizes. There are a variety of shapes and sizes in each set. The basic unit is a brick-shaped rectangle that is $1\,3/8" \times 2\,3/4" \times 5\,1/2"$. The variety of shapes and sizes is listed in Figure 19–9. Unit blocks should be made of good, strong, hard wood with beveled edges so that they will not wear down or splinter. They should be smoothly sanded. The sizes must be precise so that building can be done effectively.

Unit block sets are very expensive, but with good care, they last for many years. Keep them dry and free of dust. Occasionally they should be oiled or waxed.

At the beginning stage, the child may just handle the blocks and carry them from place to place. At the second stage, the children make rows and lines of blocks. At the third stage, children build bridges. At the fourth stage, children make simple enclosures. At the fifth stage, the children make patterns. These patterns may be balanced and symmetric. At the sixth stage, the children name the structures and use them for dramatic play. At the last stage, the children make structures that represent familiar buildings, such as their own home or even their whole city.

Children enjoy using other types of building materials besides unit blocks. Many preschools have large, hollow, wood blocks. At a lower cost, there are cardboard blocks. Cardboard boxes can enhance the imaginative activity of young children. Large boxes can be the focus of walking *around*, climbing *in*, and climbing *over*. Boxes can be moved about and combined in many different ways, providing experiences with weight, size, shape, and volume. Blocks and boxes provide rich learning opportunities.

Name	Nursery	Kgn. & Primary
Square	40	80
Unit	96	192
Double Unit	48	96
Quadruple Unit	16	32
Pillar	24	48
Half Pillar	24	48
Small Triangle	24	48
Large Triangle	24	48
Small Column	16	32
Large Column	8	16
Ramp	16	32
Ellipse		8
Curve	8	16
¼ Circle		8
Large Switch & Gothic Door		4
Small Switch		4
Large Buttress		4
½ Arch & Small Buttress		4
Arch & ½ Circle		4
Roofboard		24
Number of Shapes	12	23
Number of Pieces	344	760

Figure 19–9   Childcraft block sets

WOODWORKING

Most young children enjoy working with wood. Woodworking provides hands-on experience with measurement, balance, power, and spatial and size relationships. They use informal measurement as they check to see if they have a piece of wood that is the one they need and if they have a nail that is the correct length. As children move into the primary level, they can apply standard measurement: "I will need 12 pieces of 12" × 8" plywood for my birdhouse." The more advanced primary children can follow simple instructions and use patterns to make projects.

For effective woodworking, the classroom should have a sturdy workbench, good quality real tools, and assorted pieces of soft wood. The workbench should be large enough for at least two children to work at the same time. Woodworking must always be closely supervised. Workbenches designed for children can be purchased from the major school supply companies, or a large, old tree stump can be used.

The basic components of a high quality tool set for 4- and 5-year-olds are illustrated in Figure 19–10. Older children can use a greater variety of tools. The tools should be easily accessible when in use but kept in a locked closet or on a high shelf when not in use. Beginners do best with short nails with large heads.

Soft wood such as pine is easy to work with. When sawing is introduced, the wood should be put in a vise, so it will hold steady and so the child's hands will not be in the line of the saw.

Experienced woodworkers enjoy creating projects using odds and ends with their wood. Wheels can be made from bottle caps and windows from plastic lids. Scraps of cloth or ribbon can be glued on to the wood. Children can apply their math vocabulary as they explain their finished projects.

GAMES

Young children enjoy playing games. For the preschooler, games should be simple with a minimum of rules.

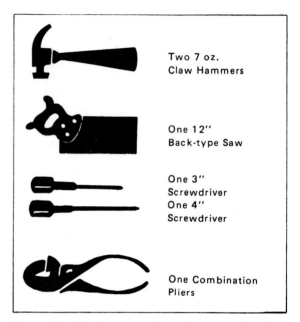

Two 7 oz. Claw Hammers

One 12" Back-type Saw

One 3" Screwdriver
One 4" Screwdriver

One Combination Pliers

Figure 19–10 Basic woodworking tools for four- and five-year olds: Start with these and add more as children become proficient

Board games provide an excellent way to teach basic concepts. *Candyland*®, *Chutes and Ladders*®, *Picture Dominoes*®, *Tri-ominos*®, and other bingo and lotto boxed games can be purchased. Some inexpensive board games are *Mailman*® (number recognition), *Down On the Farm*® (set recognition) in *Readiness Gameboards*® from Frank Schaffer Publications, and *Dog Bones*® and *Match the Shapes*® from the Dellosa and Carson publication *Fluttery Readiness*. For more advanced children, basic concepts can be practiced using board games such as *UNO*®, *UNO Dominoes*®, *Yahtzee*®, *Pay the Cashier*®, and *Count your Change*® are games that help children learn money concepts.

Card games enjoyed by primary children include those that are perennial favorites such as "Go Fish," "Concentration," "Crazy Eights," "Old Maid," "Flinch," "Solitaire," and "Fantan." Look through catalogs, and examine games at exhibitors' displays when you attend professional meetings. There is a vast selection available.

Young children enjoy bowling games and games that involve aiming. Dropping clothespins into a container or throwing beanbags through a hole or into a container are appropriate for young children. Once they learn the game they can keep track of their successes using Unifix Cubes® or making tick marks to keep score.

Outdoors or in the gym, children can have races. They can estimate how far they can throw a ball, a beanbag, or a paper plate. Primary children can measure with a yardstick and compare their estimates with their actual throwing distances.

Primary children enjoy jumping rope. A popular jingle that requires counting is:

Mabel
Mabel, Mabel,
Set the table,
Don't forget the red hot pepper
(turn the rope fast and count).

The children try to see who can jump the most red hot peppers. During the primary years, children are in the stage of industry versus inferiority. The struggle between these forces leads them into a natural interest in competitive activities, such as the games listed, and into team sports and races. Adults have to take care to find ways for each of the children to achieve so that they do not experience inferiority feelings. Primary children enjoy races that give them practice in time and distance relationships. Hurdle jumping can begin with high and low jumps then move into standard measures of height. Balls, beanbags, or frisbees can be thrown and the distances compared and measured. Team sports require scorekeeping and an understanding of *more*, *less*, and *ordinal relations* (that is, who is up first, second, third, and so on).

Primary children also enjoy math puzzlers and brainteasers that give them practice in problem solving. The following are examples:

Move one so each set has a sum of 15.

The Lady and the Tiger

How many different squares can you count?

How many different triangles can you count?

Answers: 11 squares   19 triangles

Finger Plays and Action Songs

Many finger plays and action songs include the application of basic concepts. Children may have to hear the song or finger play several times before they join in. If the teacher keeps repeating it, the students will gradually learn and participate. Favorite finger plays are "Five Little Monkeys Jumping On the Bed" and "Five Little Ducks Swimming in a Pond." A longtime favorite song is "Johnny Works With One Hammer." See the resources listed at the end of the unit. Finger plays and action songs help children learn math concepts through body actions.

SCIENCE IN ACTION: THE PLAYGROUND

Virtually all outdoors is science. This is where children can become a part of the natural world. Whether you use the outdoor environment around you to extend and enhance indoor science lessons or design lessons that focus on available outdoor resources, your students will benefit from the experience.

Children will be enthusiastic about exploring the "real" world. After all, "The real thing is worth a thousand pictures." Although this old saying and many of the suggestions for implementing outdoor learning overlap with field trip experiences, many of the learning strategies suggested can also be done in an urban setting. School yards, sidewalks, vacant lots, any strip of ground can be an area for outdoor learning. The important thing is to get your students outdoors and engage them in challenging learning.

Specific plans for outdoor learning will help ensure a successful experience. The following suggestions include teaching strategies that focus on specific science learnings. Refer to units 13, 14, 16, and 20 for more outdoor and environmental education ideas.

Animal Study Activities

Animal homes, habits, and behaviors fascinate children. To begin a successful outdoor experience, assess the previous experiences, skills, and attention spans of your students. Then, review the teacher preparation and control suggestions at the end of this unit, and begin.

Animal Homes

Involve children in the study of animal homes. First discuss, WHERE MIGHT AN ANIMAL LIVE? Then plan a field trip to look for animal homes. When planning a trip, keep in mind that most animals make their homes on southern slopes (sunny and warm). When you find a home, examine the area for tracks. Make a cast of the footprints and determine if the home is in use. Ask, HOW CAN WE TELL IF AN ANIMAL LIVES HERE? (One way is to look for signs such as food scraps and activity around the entrance.) Discuss possible reasons for the selection of this particular location for an animal home, and speculate on the possible enemies and living habits of the occupant (Figure 19–11).

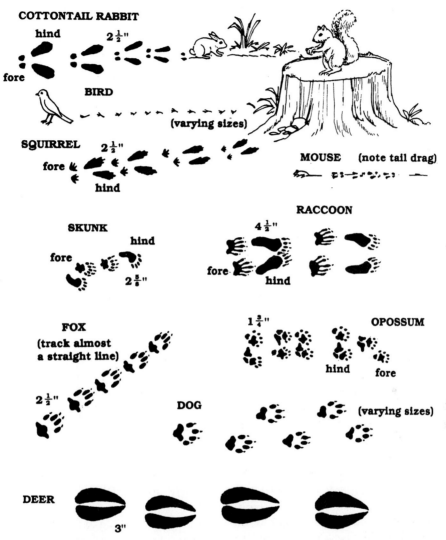

Figure 19–11   "You can identify an animal by the tracks that you see."

Finding Insects

Insects can be hard to find, but signs of their presence are common. The paper nest of a hornet or mud nest of a wasp can be found on buildings, rocks, or some tree branches. Be careful—if the nests are occupied, the owners may sting.

The presence of bark beetles can be seen by the "tunnel" left when they strip bark from logs. Most children are familiar with ant nests and know how to find them. Fallen logs are good locations for observing insects in the winter. The insects are usually sluggish, and the stinging types can be more easily observed.

Follow animal home observations with discussion. Ask questions such as, WHAT HAVE WE LEARNED ABOUT THE KINDS OF ANIMALS THAT LIVE AROUND OUR SCHOOL? WHAT ARE THEIR NEEDS? Pick one animal to focus on. Have children write about what one of the animals is thinking as it prepares a home.

A Different Type of Home

The next time you see a swollen, tumorlike bulge on the stem, flower head, stalk, or root of some plants, you might be looking at a unique insect home called a *gall*. The purpose of a gall is to provide an animal home. This happens when some species of insects causes specific kinds of plants to form galls around them. The gall has a hard outer wall and contains a food supply from the plant tissue. Have your students search for galls growing on flowers, bushes, or trees. Lead the children to discover that certain types of galls are found on specific plants. For example, a gall found on a Canada goldenrod (*Solidago canadensis*) is caused by a small, brown-winged fly. This fly (*Eurosta solidaginis*) only forms a gall on the Canada goldenrod (Figure 19–12).

Children will enjoy dramatizing the life of a gall insect. Say, PRETEND YOU ARE TINY AND HELPLESS. FIND A PLACE WHERE YOU CAN BE SAFE. Have the children pull jackets over their heads to simulate how protected the insect feels. Make a large papier-mâché gall for children to crawl into. Furnish it with a battery-powered light, and children will enjoy crawling in to read, write poems, or turn the light off and simply speculate about what it would be like to be a gall insect inside its home.

Interview a Spider

Children enjoy becoming reporters and interviewing various wildlife. After discussing what a reporter does and the techniques of interviewing, teams of children can decide on an animal they want to interview.

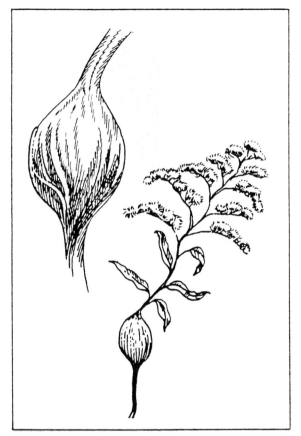

Figure 19–12 A gall is a different type of insect home.

Birds, Birds, Birds

A bird feeder is a good place to begin observing birds. If you do not have a suitable tree near your school, make your own with limbs or cornstalks tied together and propped up to provide perches and shelter. You will be providing birds with much-needed food, and as the birds come to eat, children will have a chance to observe them and their activities at close range.

Children will enjoy making seasonal ornaments and garlands for a holiday tree. Also, use ground feeders or seed dispensers as added attractions for the birds. To decorate a tree, have students string foods that appeal to a wide range of birds. Give them cubes of cheese, popcorn, raisins, and peanuts (in shells). To attract fruit-eating songbirds, add dried fruits to the strings.

Plain peanuts in their shells appeal to both insect- and seed-eating birds, so hang them on fishing line or skewer them on galvanized wire and attach the line to the tree. Then watch the antics of birds such as blue jays as they break open the shells.

Instruct children to keep a notebook of which foods various birds most like to eat. If you prefer, feed birds in aluminum TV dinner trays. Mount the trays on a board and puncture them so that excess moisture can drain out. Fill the different compartments in the trays with cracked corn, sunflower seeds, commercial birdseed, and fruit. Then watch as the birds come to feed, and ask questions that help students focus on the differences in the birds' feeding habits. WHICH BIRDS PREFER TO EAT ON THE GROUND? DO ALL OF THE BIRDS EAT SEEDS? WHICH LIKE FRUIT THE BEST?

Have children begin a class (and personal) list of the birds that visit your feeder. With a little practice, children might be beginning a lifelong hobby and interest. You need to be familiar with the birds in your area that will most likely appear at the feeder. Each bird has its own specific habits, food preferences, and actions. Take the children on a field trip and compare birds seen with the birds that visit the school yard feeder. (Refer to Unit 20 for additional bird activities.)

Outdoor Plants

My Wild Plant

Observing a wild plant and learning as much as possible through observation makes a good long-term activity for spring. Visit a vacant lot or school parking lot with the children, and try to find a spot not likely to be mowed, paved, or interfered with during spring months. Or contact your school maintenance personnel, and ask them to leave a small section of the school yard untouched for a month.

Have each child select one wild plant as her own for close study. A label with a child's name on it can be taped around the stems of the plant she selects. Encourage children to begin a plant notebook to make entries about their plant (Figure 19–13); for example:

1. Describe the plant as it appears today.
2. Measure everything you can with a tape measure.
3. Count all plant parts. Does the plant have an odor?
4. What textures did you find on the plant? (You might be able to record these with crayon rubbings.)
5. Does your plant make any sounds?
6. What other plants are the nearest neighbors of yours?
7. Do any animals live on or visit your plant?

During subsequent visits, determine how the plant has grown and changed. Decide what effect the plant has on other plants and animals living nearby, and determine what is good or bad about this plant.

Figure 19–13 "Describe your plant as it appears today."

Encourage children to make drawings and take photographs so that they will be able to share the story of their plant with others. Then, predict what the plant and growing site will be like in one year.

Hugging a Tree

A variation of selecting a special plant is to have children work in pairs to explore a tree. Blindfold one of the partners. Have the other partner lead the blindfolded one to a tree. Give the children time to touch, smell, and hug the tree. Then, bring the children back to a starting point, take the blindfold off, and ask, CAN YOU FIND THE TREE THAT YOU HUGGED? Children will enjoy finding a special tree to hug; some might even want to whisper a secret to the tree.

Adopt a Rock

Have children select a favorite rock for their collection and examine it closely. Then, put the rock in a bowl with other rocks. Ask, CAN YOU FIND YOUR ROCK? Blindfold students and pass the rocks around the group. Ask, WHICH ROCK FEELS LIKE YOUR ROCK? Then, help children trace the rock to the meal eaten last night. For example, rocks break down into soil, plants grow in soil, and animals live in plants.

What's for Dinner?

After adopting a rock, say to the children, GO HOME TONIGHT, AND LIST EVERYTHING YOU HAVE FOR DINNER. The next day, have children work in groups to discuss the dinner menu and analyze where their food comes from. Help children trace every food back to a plant; for example, milk to cow to grass. Have reference books available for children to consult. Encourage the children to reach the conclusion that all animals and people need food, and that we all depend upon plants for food. Ask, DO THE PLANTS NEED PEOPLE AND ANIMALS? After a lively discussion, point out the decay of animal life that nourishes plants. Then, create a food chain for

your bulletin board by using yarn to connect pictures of animals, plants, soil, and rocks. Add the sun, and have children create their own food chains to hang from a hanger (Figure 19–14).

Scavenger Hunts and Other 10-Minute Activities

Scavenger hunts are an excellent way to challenge children while focusing their attention on the task at hand. Make up a set of file cards to take with out. Each card should have a challenge on it; for example:

- Find a seed.
- Find three pieces of litter.
- Find something a bird uses for nesting material.
- Find something red.
- Find something a squirrel would eat.
- Find something that makes its own food.
- Find something that shows signs of erosion.
- Find something that shows change.
- Find a bird's feather.

Caution the children to collect only small quantities of the item on their card, or not to collect at all if they will damage something. In this case, write a description of the situation. Pass out the cards, and tell the individuals or teams that they have 10 minutes to meet the challenge. Discuss the findings back in the classroom.

Circle Game

If the ground is dry, sit in a circle, and pass an object such as a rock, leaf, or twig around the circle. As each child touches the object, he or she must say something that is observed about the object. Say, YOU WILL NEED TO LISTEN AND NOT REPEAT AN OBSERVATION MADE BY ANYONE ELSE. Remember, observations are made with the senses. Do not accept inferences or predictions.

While you are still in the circle, move the children apart so that they do not touch each other, and ask them to close their eyes and explore the

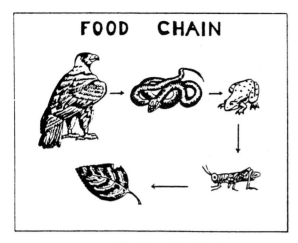

Figure 19–14   A food chain

area around them with just their hands (and bare feet, if the weather is nice). Then ask them to describe or write the textures that they felt.

Outdoor Learning and Writing Experiences

Writing, drawing, and dictating can be integrated with outdoor learning experiences. Here are a few suggestions:
- Write poems about something that was observed during an outdoor experience.
- Write a story about a living thing in the outdoors that has the power to speak to the humans that come to visit its outdoor area. What might the living thing say? What questions might it ask you?
- Write and draw posters that describe outdoor experiences.
- Keep a written log of outdoor activities.
- Write a short play about the outdoor trip.
- Write letters to someone about one aspect of the outdoor experience.
- Dictate stories about an incident or observation made during the outdoor experience.

- Write how you would feel if you were a plant and it didn't rain for a long time.

Planning for Outdoor Learning

Taking children outdoors can be a challenge if you are not prepared. To ensure the greatest value from the experience, teachers of all age groups should
1. Think about your purpose for including outdoor experiences. How will children benefit? What type of preparation do the children need before they go outdoors?
2. What are the logistics? Will you walk, drive, or ride in cars? What type of clothing is needed? Should you take snacks? Are there people to contact? What are the water and toilet facilities? How much help do you need?
3. Which science concepts will be developed? What do you hope to accomplish?
4. Have you planned what you will be teaching before the experience, during the activity, and after the experience?
5. How much talking do you really need to do?
6. How will you evaluate the experience?
7. What types of follow-up learning will be provided? What subjects can you integrate into the experience?

Attention Grabbers

Devices for grabbing the attention of a group can be physical, such as pulling out a huge beef thigh bone from your bag when you want to discuss animal bones. The bone will be heavy, but this action is guaranteed to grab the attention of your group.

More subtle attention grabbers include the following:
1. Look intently at an object to focus group attention on the same object.
2. Have children remind you of tasks, carry various items, assist with the activity, and

lead in other tasks. This participation helps keep their attention.

3. Lowering your voice when you want to make a point works well in the classroom and outdoors.
4. Change your position. Sit down with the children when they begin to wander, and regroup them.
5. Give the children specific items to look for or match, notes to take, or specific jobs. Children tend to lose interest if they do not have a task (Figure 19–15).

Additional Control Strategies

Although you might be proficient at controlling children indoors, the outdoors can be quite a different matter. Here are a few tips:

1. Before the outdoor experience, set up a firm set of rules (as you do indoors). As you know, it is far easier to relax rules than the other way around. However, hurting and frightening animals, crushing plants, and littering should not be tolerated.
2. When children become too active, try an attention grabber, or initiate an activity designed to give children a chance to run. For example, RUN TO THE BIG PINE TREE AND BACK TO ME. Relays with rocks as batons will also expend excess energy.
3. Have a prearranged attention signal for activities that require wandering. A whistle, bell, or hand signals work well.
4. When one child is talking and others desperately want your attention, place your hand on their hand to let them know that you recognize them.
5. Let different children enjoy leading the adventure. Occasionally, remove yourself from the line, take a different place in line, and go in a different direction. In this way, you lead the group in a new direction with different children directly behind you.
6. Play follow the leader with you as the leader as you guide the line where you want it to go. If there is snow on the ground, have the children walk like wolves: Wolves walk along a trail in single file, putting their feet in the footprints of the wolf ahead of them. If you are at the zoo, try walking to the next exhibit like the animal you have just been observing would walk.
7. Be flexible. If something is not working, just change the activity. Later you can analyze why something was not working the way you had planned.

Exciting outdoor activities do not happen by chance. Begin by planning carefully what you want the children to learn. Then teach the lesson, and evaluate the children's learning and your preparation. You will be off to a good start as an outdoor science educator.

Figure 19–15 "How many segments does a worm have?"

SUMMARY

Science in action mean children exploring the environment. This is done through woodworking, block constructing, game playing, and exploring the outdoor areas in their environment. Math and science in action mean children saying, singing, and acting out math and science language and basic concepts.

When children make block building decisions, they are thinking like scientists. They focus on a problem and use the thinking skills of math and science to arrive at a solution or conclusions. Block building and other indoor and outdoor explorations give children an opportunity to learn by manipulating and acting on their environment as they build their own model of the world.

The outdoor environment can be used to extend and enhance indoor lessons or as a specific place for engaging children in challenging learning. Suggestions have been given about how to work directly with outdoor learning as well as strategies for focusing children's attention on outdoor learning and encouraging higher-level science thinking. Once children learn how to learn outdoors, they will enjoy the fascinating world around them.

FURTHER READING AND RESOURCES

Woodworking

Skeen, P., Garner, A. P., & Cartwright, S. (1984). *Woodworking for young children.* Washington, DC: National Association for the Education of Young Children.

Blocks and Construction

Hirsch, E. (Ed.). (1984). *The block book.* Washington, DC: National Association for the Education of Young Children.

Kamii, S., & DeVries, R. (1993). *Physical knowledge in preschool education: Implications of Piaget's theory* (rev. ed.). Englewood Cliffs, NJ: Prentice-Hall.

Lind, K. K., & Milburn, M. J. (1988). The mechanized child. *Elementary School Notes*, *3*(5), 32–33.

Lind, K. K., & Milburn, M. J. (1988). More for the mechanized child. *Science and Children*, *25*(6), 39–40.

Zubrowski, B. (1981). *Messing around with drinking straw construction.* Boston: Little, Brown and Company.

Games

Arithmetic Teacher. See monthly articles and columns for problems and puzzles to solve.

Dellosa, J., & Carson, P. (1980). *Fluttery readiness.* Akron, OH: Carson-Dellosa.

Games for growing. (1984). *First Teacher, 5*(2).

Harte, S. W., & Glover, M. J. (1993). Estimation is mathematical thinking. *Arithmetic Teacher, 41*(2), 75–77.

Kamii, C. (1989). *Young children continue to reinvent arithmetic.* New York: Teachers College Press.

Kamii, C., & DeVries, R. (1980). *Group games in early education.* Washington, DC: National Association for the Education of Young Children.

Schutte, B. (1978). *Readiness game boards.* Palos Verdes Peninsula, CA: Frank Schaffer.

Warren, J. (1986). *1-2-3 games: No-Lose group games for young children.* Everett, WA: Totline Press, Warren Publishing House.

Finger Plays and Songs

Bayless, K. M., & Ramsey, M. E. (1987). *Music: A way of life for young children* (3rd ed.). Columbus, OH: Merrill.

Haines, B. J. E., & Gerber, L. L. (1988). *Leading young children to music* (3rd ed.). Columbus, OH: Merrill.

Moomaw, S. (1984). *Discovering music in early childhood.* Boston: Allyn & Bacon.

Music for march. (1985). *First Teacher*, 6(3).

Weimer, T. E. (1993). *Space songs for children.* Pittsburgh, PA: Pearce-Evetts Publishing.

Wiltcher, D. J. (1983). *Lots of wiggles.* Ruston, LA: Louisiana Association on Children Under Six.

Outdoors

Baker, A., & Baker, J. (1991). *Counting on a small planet: Activities for environmental mathematics.* Portsmouth, NH: Heinemann.

Cohen, S. (Ed.). (1992). Promoting ecological awareness in children [Special Issue]. *Childhood Education*, 68(5).

Lingelback, J. (1986). *Hands-on nature.* Woodstock, VT: Vermont Institute of Natural Science.

McCormack, A. J. (1979). *Outdoor areas as learning laboratories: Council for Elementary Science International sourcebook I.* Columbus, OH: SMEAC Information Reference Center.

Sisson, E. A. (1981). *Nature with children of all ages.* New York: Prentice-Hall.

SUGGESTED ACTIVITIES

1. Observe children interacting with blocks and other cause-and-effect materials. Record the children's behavior and comments. Do the children control the cause-and-effect reaciton? Do they predict what will happen?

2. Prepare a lesson that focuses on blocks, pendulums, inclines, or balls. Teach the lesson to primary age children and evaluate the activity. Share your findings with the class.

3. Observe some preschool, kindergarten, and/or primary students playing with blocks. See if you can categorize the developmental stages of their block building. Report on your observations in class.

4. Visit a local hardware store or a local discount store hardware department. Record the types of tools available and the prices. Compare your findings with the prices of similar toys in educational catalogs.

5. Design an outdoor activity, and teach it to a group of primary age children. Share your experience with the class.

6. Secure samples of outdoor education resources. Modify them for primary grades, and include them in your file.

7. Prepare a list of positive reinforcement statements that you will use when implementing outdoor education. How do the strategies compare with those used in an indoor setting? Discuss reasons for any differences.

REVIEW

A. Explain the benefits of block play for young children.

B. Name some activities that emphasize cause and effect. Why should they be used with young children.

C. Describe how to set up a woodworking area.

D. At which stage of block building is each of the following examples?

1. Putting blocks in rows.
2. Carrying blocks around.
3. Building structures for dramatic play.
4. Building simple enclosures.

E. Explain how finger plays and action songs can support math concept development.

F. What are the benefits of including outdoor activities with primary age children?

UNIT 20 Science in the Home

OBJECTIVES

After studying this unit, the students should be able to
- Explain the importance of parents as teachers
- Be knowledgeable about strategies for parent involvement in science
- Provide parents with strategies and activities for teaching children at home
- Describe a variety of science activities that relate science to a child's everyday life

Parents are their children's first teachers. Learning happens on a daily basis in the home: Children learn as they cook, set the table, sort laundry, observe ants, watch birds, or take a walk in the backyard, neighborhood, and/or the park (Figure 20–1). Teachers of young children are in a unique position to help parents make good use of these home learning opportunities. Unit 20 provides guidelines for parents as teachers. This unit focuses on specific suggestions for emphasizing science and math as vehicles for family learning.

Parents need to understand that children are eager to learn and can learn if the experiences are developmentally appropriate. As teachers of young children, you can assist parents in recognizing that they do not need to go overboard purchasing expensive materials when there are a multitude of learning opportunities that center on everyday activities using resources naturally present in the environment.

APPROACHES TO PARENT INVOLVEMENT IN MATH AND SCIENCE

Encourage parents to find the math and science in their homes. A large part of a child's time is spend in school, but the majority of time is still spent outside of the classroom. Every day at home is filled with opportunities to explore and ask questions that encourage thinking. It should be stressed that family entertainment does not have to be passive, such as watching TV. Activities that incorporate daily routines such as cooking, playing games, doing simple projects, finding materials to bring to school, and exploring the lives of living creatures and plants are suggested as opportunities for discovery, science and math, and family fun.

Figure 20–1 The parent is the child's first teacher.

Getting Parents Involved

Changes in our economy and lifestyles have resulted in a multitude of family configurations that were rare or nonexistent in the past. A large percentage of mothers of young children work either to boost the family income or because they are the major breadwinner, so they are not as available as their counterparts were in the past. Fathers work longer hours, sometimes holding down two jobs, and are also less able than in the past to participate in school-based activities. Parent involvement in education has changed from the view that parents can only be active participants by coming to school to the view that teachers must find ways to involve those parents who have difficulty finding time to schedule a visit to the school. The major focus today is setting up lines of communication and providing parents with learning tasks that can be performed as a part of everyday living. The following are suggestions for getting parents involved and engaging them in their roles as teachers:

A first step could be the publication of a newsletter that could be sent home each month telling about the past month's events and including information about upcoming activities. Future activities could be described and/or sent in the form of a monthly calendar. Children can contribute to the newsletter. They can draw pictures and dictate and/or write news stories describing their experiences at school. Two or three children might be asked to contribute to each newsletter. Suggested home activities may be included in the newsletter and/or sent home as a separate booklet.

Getting parents to school for a meeting can be difficult. However, it is important that they become acquainted with the activities, the environment, their child's teacher, and other parents. Parent meetings should provide important information and involve active experiences that will give parents an understanding of appropriate educational experiences that can be followed up in the home.

The students should be actively involved in

KINDERGARTEN NEWS

Published by Mr. Jones's Class *Carver School*
October 1, 1994

School Gets Off to a Good Start

The day after Labor Day, the children started kindergarten. Eight children came each day to get acquainted with the room and find out what we do in kindergarten. Several children have contributed descriptions of what they liked best about coming to kindergarten.

José: I like being bigger than the 4-year-old classes.

Mimi: I like painting and playing house.

Ronny: My favorite was drawing and writing with markers on big paper and playing with trucks and blocks.

Nina: I liked finding my new friend Marcus.

Buddy the Bunny Joins Us

Last week, we had a late arrival in our class. Mr. Ortiz, who manages a pet store at the mall, brought us a black-and-white rabbit with a cage and a supply of food. The class discussed a number of names. The majority voted for the name Buddy ("'cause he will be our best friend"). Buddy is very friendly and enjoys fresh vegetables. If your child asks to bring a carrot or a little piece of lettuce, please send it, if possible. The children are taking turns bringing treats for Buddy.

The Month Ahead

We are looking forward to fall. We are reading the outdoor temperature every morning and recording the data on a graph. We watch each day for the leaves to change. Our observations are written and drawn in our daily class journal. We are planning a walk around the block to collect samples of the leaves that fall from the trees. We will report next month on what we see and what we find.

the planning, so that their excitement and enthusiasm for the event will spill over to their parents. A program that has shown a great deal of success is *Family Math* (Stenmark, Thompson, & Cossey, 1986). Parents come to school and do math activities with their children. They are then provided with instructions for follow-up activities they can do at home. The same procedure could be followed with science (or better yet, math and science could be combined). Another procedure is to hold a Science and/or Math Fun Day (Carey, 1990). For a Fun Day, several activities are set up in a large area, such as a gym or cafeteria. Parents can be invited to take part as volunteer helpers and as active participants with their children. By having the Fun Day extend over several hours, busy parents can more likely find a time when they can join in.

Parents can also be asked to send waste materials to school as needed. The items listed in Figure 20–2 as aids to learning science at home are also useful at school. If the children each bring a pack of small brown paper lunch bags to school at the beginning of the year, when an item is needed the children can draw and/or write the name of the item on the bag, take it home, and ask their parents to put the item in the bag to take to school. Don't be concerned if the younger children write symbols that are not conventional pictures or words—they will know what it is and can read the symbol to adults.

Parents who have the time may volunteer to assist in the classroom. Parents who are not free during the day or prefer not to be involved in the classroom are often delighted to make games and other materials at home. There should always be an open invitation for parents to visit school.

Parents need to meet with their child's teacher in one-to-one conferences to exchange information about children's activities and progress. At these times, teacher and parent (and even the child) can review the student's portfolio of work and discuss goals for the future. At the same time, parents can describe what they have been doing at home with the child and relate any home events that may be affecting the child's behavior.

Homework often becomes an important type of activity in the primary grades. Children can work their way into the more formal homework activities by bringing things requested from home as a part of their prekindergarten and kindergarten experiences. These activities help them to develop responsibility and accustom parents to supporting classroom instruction. When it is required, homework should always be an extension of what has been taught at school. It may involve bringing some material to school; doing a simple project; or obtaining some information from a newspaper, magazine, or reference book. Be sure that parents have all the information needed to guide the child to completion of the assignment. Assignments for young children should be something that can be easily completed in 10 to 15 minutes.

An increasingly popular method for promoting developmentally appropriate home learning activities involves putting together small kits of materials that can be checked out and taken home for 2 or 3 days (Franklin & Krebill, 1993; Orman, 1993). Each kit includes materials and instruction for a home activity and some means for parents and children to return a report on the outcome along with the kit. Many of the activities suggested later in the unit could be made into take-home kits.

GUIDELINES FOR PARENTS AS TEACHERS AT HOME

Many parents may have questions about how they can provide learning experiences at home. They need to be reassured that naturalistic and informal experiences are at the heart of home learning. All during early childhood, play is the major vehicle for learning, both at school and at home. Exploration and discovery through play allow children to construct concepts. Parents need to be encouraged to be positive models for their children. If parents are enthusiastic learners, their children are more likely to be enthusiastic learners, too.

Parents and older siblings can provide a close relationship where exploration is encouraged and where one-to-one conversation can enrich the young child's math and science language development. Parents must be cautioned to be patient and allow children the opportunity to explore, reflect, and construct concepts. Parents need to understand that children learn through repetition. They do the same activities over and over before they assimilate what the experience has to offer and feel confident in their understandings. Parents also need to understand that children learn through concrete experiences. They need to learn how to use simple household items and waste materials (see Figure 20–2) as the focus for learning.

Provide examples of naturalistic, informal, and structured home learning experiences. *Naturalistic experiences* are those in which a concept is applied in an everyday activity, such as sorting laundry, counting out tableware, following an ant trail in the backyard, or watching the clock to get to an appointment on time. *Informal experiences* take place when the alert parent finds a way to involve the child in an activity such as asking the child to set the table, measure out cooking ingredients, learn his telephone number, and count the money in his piggy bank. The parent can also sing a song or chant a rhyme on the spur of the moment and providing materials the child can use on his own (such as blocks, sets of dishes, construction materials, and the like). *Structured activities* usually are not appropriate before age 3. Parents need to take care that, when they introduce structured activities, they do not pressure the child if he seems uninterested or not ready. Suggest that parents pull back and try again in 2 or 3 weeks. Emphasize that children need time to explore materials before parents present structured questions or problems to them.

SCIENCE IN THE HOME, YARD, NEIGHBORHOOD, AND PARK

There are many math and science activities that can be done in the home, backyard, neighborhood, park, or even on a vacation trip. Any of the following activities could be included in a parent newsletter and/or activity booklet or monthly calendar. Activities begin with daily home routines and then move into other areas.

Daily Routines

Parents should be encouraged to emphasize the skills of science as they go about their daily routines; for example:

1. As laundry is sorted and socks are matched, talk about the differences and similarities in the articles. Then fold the clothes, and put them in the correct places. Ask, WHERE DO THE PANTS GO? WHERE SHALL WE PUT THE T-SHIRTS? Even small children will begin the process of classification as they note the differences in characteristics.

2. Children can examine their bodies and compare themselves to animals in a concrete way. They have five toes on each foot, but a horse does not. When a family takes a trip to a farm or a duck pond, the differences and similarities in animal feet can be noted. Ask, HOW MANY TOES DO YOU HAVE? HOW ARE YOUR TOES DIFFERENT FROM A DUCK'S? WHY DO YOU THINK A DUCK HAS A WEB BETWEEN ITS TOES? Activities like this help children be aware of differences in animals and offer opportunities to discuss why an animal is structured in a certain way.

3. When kitchen utensils are returned to drawers after washing or food is put away after a shopping trip, discuss why they go where they do. Say, WHERE SHALL WE PUT THE SPOONS? SHOULD THE CRACKERS GO IN THE CUPBOARD OR THE REFRIGERATOR? Some parents might want to lay items such as spoons, spatulas, or cups on the table and see how many ways children can devise to group items; for example, things you eat with, things you cook with, things you stir with, and so on.

4. Begin a bottle cap collection for classifying, counting, and crafts. Have children sort caps

by size, color, and function. Trace around the caps to make designs. Then paste the caps on cardboard, and paint it.

5. Collect scraps of wood, and make things with the wood. Give children a hammer and some nails and say, LET'S MAKE SOMETHING WITH THIS WOOD. When the wood sculpture is completed, name it, and propose a function.

6. As children work with tools such as a hammer; screwdriver; tape measure; and various types of screws, bolts, and nails, ask WHAT DO WE DO WITH THIS? HOW IS THIS TOOL USED? If something needs to be fixed, let the children help fix the item. Children enjoy practicing tightening and loosening screws in a board. Simply begin the screws in a board, and let children practice the type of motion needed to operate a screwdriver (Figure 20–2).

Cooking With Children

Cooking provides many opportunities for parents to provide children with practical applications of science and math. When the parent is cooking, the child can measure the ingredients, observe them as they change form during cooking (or mixing), and taste the final product.

Children should be given as much responsibility for the food preparation as possible. This might include shopping for the food, washing, possibly cutting (carefully supervised, of course), reading and following the recipe, baking, cooking, or freezing, setting the food on the table, and cleaning up. The more the parent does, the less the child learns (Figure 20–3).

Try making an easy pizza. You will need muffins, tomato sauce, oregano, meat, and mozzarella cheese slices. Spread one-half of the muffin with a tablespoon of tomato sauce. Add a pinch of oregano. Sprinkle meat on the sauce, and add a layer of cheese. Place the little pizza on a cookie sheet, and bake for 10 minutes at 425°.

Figure 20–2   "What do we do with this tool?"

Children enjoy getting creative with food. Create Bugs on a Log by spreading peanut butter in pieces of celery. Top off the "log" with raisin "bugs" (Figure 20–4).

Make Summer Slush. Freeze a favorite fruit juice in ice cube trays. After the cubes are hard, place them in the blender, and blend. Add extra juice if needed for a slushy consistency.

The seeds from a jack-o'-lantern or a Thanksgiving pumpkin pie can be saved. They should be thoroughly cleaned and then dipped in a solution of salt water (1 tablespoon salt in 1 1/2 cups of water). Drain off the water, and spread the seeds on an ungreased cookie sheet. Bake at 350°. Stir every 5 minutes to be sure that they dry out and toast lightly on all sides. When lightly toasted, remove from oven, cool, crack, and eat.

Curious George's favorite is to spread a banana with peanut butter and roll it in ground

Figure 20–3 Give children responsibility in food preparation.

nuts or wheat germ. Also fun to make with peanut butter are Kid Feeders. Bird feeders made with peanut butter on pinecones can be made the same day children make Kid Feeders. Quarter an apple, and spread peanut butter on the cut sides. Roll the apple slices in one or more of the following: wheat germ, raisins, coconut, ground nuts, or sesame seeds.

Put ice or snow in a bowl, and place it in a warm place. Watch it melt. Then take the water in the bowl, and freeze it outside or in the refrigerator. Have the child describe what he observes.

Eye Spy

Encourage both observational and questioning skills. Take turns describing objects in the room and have the other person(s) guess what it is by asking up to 20 questions.

FAMILY SCIENCE IN NATURE

The outdoors affords many opportunities for family activities that center on nature. Whether in urban, suburban, small town, or urban settings, the outdoors affords rich opportunities for observation and interaction.

Who Invited the Ants?

Encourage families to use their backyard as a resource for teaching science. Many of the activities found in previous units are appropriate for use in the home. Select topics that are relevant to family life, and suggest them to parents. For example, the following suggestions turn uninvited picnic visitors into a family science exploration:

You will need a spoonful of tuna, a spoonful of honey, and a piece of fruit for this activity. Ask, WHAT WOULD ANTS EAT IF YOU INVITED THEM TO A FAMILY PICNIC? LET'S HAVE A PICNIC FOR THE ANTS IN OUR BACKYARD. Then let the fun begin. However, a few cautions should be noted. Ants belong to the same family as bees and wasps (some ants sting). They have strong jaws and their bites can hurt a lot, so be very careful when dealing with ants.

To begin explorations, go on an anthill hunt, usually a small pile of dirt with a hole in the middle of it. Or, if you spot any ants, follow them back to their home. If this doesn't work, any bare patch of ground will be fine for observing ants.

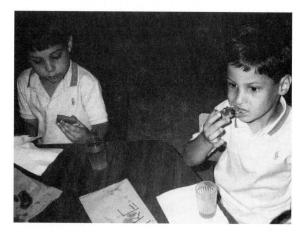

Figure 20–4 Children get creative and eat "Bugs on a Log."

Arrange the food on the ground (1 foot apart). Put the honey in a leaf and the meat and fruit directly on the ground. Observe closely. Ask, WHICH KIND OF FOOD DO THE ANTS GO TO FIRST? DO YOU THINK THE ANTS GO TO THEIR FAVORITE FOOD OR TO THE FOOD CLOSEST TO THEM? DO ALL OF THE ANTS CHOOSE THE SAME FOOD?

Observe ant behavior by asking, DO THE ANTS CARRY THE FOOD BACK TO THE ANTHILL, OR EAT IT ON THE SPOT? Sometimes ants act like messenger ants. When they find food, they go back to the nest and tell the others. Then everybody comes to your picnic.

This activity extends to the sense of smell. Ask, HOW DO YOU THINK THAT THE ANTS KNOW WHERE TO FIND THE FOOD? CAN THEY SEE THE FOOD? CAN THEY HEAR THE FOOD? Explain that as the ant runs to tell about the picnic, it leaves a scent trail for the other ants to follow. (Figure 20–5).

Scent Trails

Which member of the ant family can smell the best? Make a scent trail on your lawn by placing drops of extract on pieces of cut-up sponge. Use several distinctive scents such as peppermint, cinnamon, or lemon, and create trails. See if family members can find and follow the trail. Mixing extract with water and spraying it with a spray bottle in a trail pattern on the ground also works well.

Families will enjoy learning more about their picnic visitors. Most of the ants that we see are worker ants. Their job is to build and maintain the nest and find food for the colony. Soldier ants live up to their name by defending the anthill against invaders. There is only one queen ant. She rules the nest and lays the eggs that populate the colony. Some queen ants can live 15 years.

There is a variety of ants with interesting habits and lifestyles to discover. For example,

some ants even keep tiny insects called aphids to produce a sweet juice for them. The ants "milk" them for the sweet juice in much the same way that cows are milked. Another kind of ant farmer chews up leaves and spreads them out so that an edible fungus will grow. Some worker honey pot ants use their second stomach to store honeydew. They get so fat with honeydew that they hang in their nest like honey pots. Other ants take the honeydew from them when they are hungry.

Feed the Birds in the Backyard or Park

To help the children recognize different kinds of birds and to find differences in birds' sizes, shapes, feeding styles, and food preferences, create your own bird feeding program. In addition to the suggestions for learning about birds found in Unit 19, make beef suet—hard fat from about the kidneys and loins—to help keep up the birds' energy. The suet helps birds maintain their high body temperature. Ask a butcher for suet that is short and not stringy (stringy suet is hard for the birds to eat and does not melt down smoothly).

You can offer the suet to the birds in many ways. Try putting it in a soap dish attached to a tree limb with chicken wire, or hang it in an onion bag or lobster bait bag. Or make suet ornaments with grapefruit rinds or coconut shells. To do so, chop the suet, or put it through a meat grinder, and

Figure 20–5   Watching ants find the food.

then melt it in a double boiler. Pour the liquid suet into the rinds or shells to which you have already attached wire or string hangers, and set the containers aside in a cool place until the suet hardens. Then hang them on your tree.

How about a bottle cap suet log? Simply nail bottle caps to one side of a dead bough. Pour melted suet into the caps and set the bough aside until the suet hardens. Woodpeckers and other medium-sized birds will gather around to eat from the suet log.

Or make attractive suet pinecones. Melt the suet, and spoon it over the pinecones (to which you have already attached string or wire). Sprinkle the cones with millet, push sunflower seeds down into the cone's scales, and spoon more warm suet over the cones to secure the seeds. Place the cones on waxed paper and refrigerate until firm. Later, hang the cones from the tree as a snack for small birds like chickadees.

Peanut butter mixture makes great food for birds, too, since peanuts have high nutritional content and mixtures made with them can be spread on tree bark, placed in the holes of a log or a bottle cap feeder or hung from pinecones. But before giving the peanut butter to birds, be sure to mix corn-

meal into it (one cup of peanut butter to five cups cornmeal). This will make the peanut butter mixture easier for the birds to swallow. It is possible for birds to choke on peanut butter when it is not mixed with anything.

Try mounting a whole ear of dried corn in a conspicuous place, perhaps by nailing it to a post. Then have the children predict which birds will be able to eat the corn (Figure 20–6). (Only birds with large beaks will be able to crack the whole kernels of corn.)

A Family Bird Walk

A bird walk will heighten the observational skills of everyone involved. Here are some things to look for. Families can look for birds that

- Hop when they move on the ground
- Peck at the ground
- Hold their heads to one side and appear to be listening to something in the ground
- Flap their wings a lot when they fly
- Glide and hardly move their wings
- Climb on the side of trees
- Fly alone
- Fly with many other birds
- Make a lot of noise
- Eat alone
- Blend in well with the grass, trees, or sky

Select a favorite bird, and find out as much as you can about it. This can be a family project. Use birdcall audiotapes or videotapes to identify the birds that have been seen and heard on the bird walk. Children will enjoy creating bird stories, art projects, puzzles, and reading more about the birds they have observed (Figure 20–7).

The following books are helpful in identifying birds and creating a backyard habitat:

Albyn, C. L., & Webb, L. S. (1993). *The multicultural cookbook for students.* Phoenix, AZ: Oryx.

Burke, K. (1983). *How to attract birds.* San Fran-

Figure 20–6 "What kind of food do you think birds feed their young?"

Figure 20–7 Children enjoy putting together bird puzzles.

cisco: Ortho Books. A well-illustrated book with an informative text about providing food, water, and nest sites for both eastern and western birds.

Cook, B. C. (1978). *Invite a bird to dinner*. New York: Lathrop. A children's book about feeding birds with good ideas for making feeders out of everyday materials.

Cosgrove, I. (1976). *My recipes are for the birds*. New York: Doubleday. A book full of recipes, featuring treats such as Cardinal Casserole, Finch Fries, and Dove Delight.

Kress, S. W. (1985). *The Audubon Society guide to attracting birds*. New York: Scribner's.

SUMMARY

Science can provide many opportunities for informal family sharing. Parents can encourage children to explore, ask questions, and think about the world around them. A single guiding question from a parent can turn a daily routine into a learning experience. As children cook, observe, sort, investigate, and construct, they are using the skills needed to learn science mathematics, and other subject areas.

FURTHER READING AND RESOURCES

Baratta-Lorton, M. (1975). *Workjobs for parents*. Menlo Park, CA: Addison-Wesley.

Bennett, S., & Bennett, R. (1993). *The official playroom activity book*. New York: Random House.

Carey, J. H. (1990). Science fund: Have a field day in the gym. *Science and Children*, 28(2), 16–19.

Franklin, J., & Krebill, J. (1993). Take-home kits. *Arithmetic Teacher*, 40(8), 442–448.

Gardner, H. (1991). *The unschooled mind*. New York: Basic Books.

Gesell Institute Series. *Your one year old* up to *Your seven year old*. New York: Delta.

Lind, K. K. (1986). The bird's Christmas. *Science and Children*, 24(3), 34–35.

MCCPTA-EPI Hands-on-Science (1987). *Putting together a family science festival*. Washington, DC: National Science Teachers Association.

Orman, S. A. (1993). Mathematics backpacks: Making the home-school connection. *Arithmetic Teacher*, 40(6), 306–308.

Pearlman, S., & Pericak-Spector, K. (1992). Helping hands from home. *Science and Children*, 29(7), 12–14.

Smithsonian Family Learning Project (1987). *Science activity book*. New York: Galison Books.

Stenmark, J. K., Thompson, V., & Cossey, R. (1986). *Family math*. Berkeley, CA: University of California.

Trelease, J. (1989). *The new read-aloud handbook*. Middlesex, England: Penguin.

Wannamaker, N., Hearn, K., & Richard, S. (1979). *More than graham crackers*. Washington, DC: National Association for the Education of Young Children.

SUGGESTED ACTIVITIES

1. Observe a parent-teacher conference. Note how the teacher reports on the child's science and math concepts development and how the parents respond.
2. Write a parent newsletter that focuses on science in the home. Share the newsletter with the class.
3. Reflect on your own science in the home experiences, either as a child or as a parent. What kinds of opportunities were available to you? Which do you provide?
4. Make a list of guidelines for parents to follow when teaching science to their young children at home.
5. Add 15 home science activities to your Activities File/Notebook: 5 prekindergarten, 5 kindergarten, and 5 primary.
6. Plan a science in the home workshop for parents. Present the workshop to the class.
7. Interview at least three parents. Ask them what types of science activities they do with their children. Find out what problems, concerns, or needs they might have in doing science with their children.

REVIEW

A. Why is the home a good place to emphasize science?
B. List three opportunities for learning science in the home.
C. How does cooking relate to science?
D. Describe two family nature activities involving science.

APPENDIX A

Developmental
Assessment
Tasks

CONTENTS

Sensorimotor Levels

Preoperational Levels

Concrete Operations

SENSORIMOTOR: LEVEL 1

1A   **Sensorimotor**
                                                                 Age 2 months

General Development

METHOD: Interview.

SKILLS: Perceptual/motor.

MATERIALS: Familiar object/toy such as a rattle.

PROCEDURES/EVALUATION:
1. Talk to the infant. Notice if he seems to attend and respond (by looking at you, making sounds, and/or changing facial expression).
2. Hold a familiar object within the infant's reach. Note if he reaches out for it.
3. Move the object through the air across the infant's line of vision. He should follow it with his eyes.
4. Hand the small toy to the infant. He should hold it for 2 to 3 seconds.

1B

Sensorimotor
Age 4 months

General Development

METHOD: Observation.

SKILLS: Perceptual/motor.

MATERIALS: Assortment of appropriate infant toys.

PROCEDURES/EVALUATION:

1. Note each time you offer the infant a toy. Does she usually grab hold of it?
2. Place the infant where it is possible for her to observe the surroundings (such as in an infant seat) in a situation where there is a lot of activity. Note if her eyes follow the activity and if

---

1C

Sensorimotor
Age 6 months

General Development

METHOD: Interview and observation.

SKILLS: Perceptual/motor.

MATERIALS: Several nontoxic objects/toys including infant's favorite toy.

PROCEDURES/EVALUATION:

1. One by one, hand the infant a series of nontoxic objects. Note how many of his senses he uses for exploring the objects. He should be using eyes, mouth, and hands.
2. Place yourself out of the infant's line of vision. Call out to him. Note if he turns his head toward your voice.
3. When the infant drops an object, note whether or not he picks it up again.
4. When the infant is eating, notice if he can hold his bottle in both hands by himself.
5. Show the infant his favorite toy. Slowly move the toy to a hiding place. Note if the infant follows with his eyes as the toy is hidden.

1D

Sensorimotor
Age 12 months

General Development

METHOD: Interview and observation.

SKILLS: Perceptual/motor and receptive language.

MATERIALS: Two bells or rattles; two blocks or other small objects; two clear plastic cups; pillow or empty box; a cookie, if desired.

PROCEDURES/EVALUATIONS:

1. Note if the infant will imitate you when you do the following activities (for each task provide the infant with a duplicate set of materials):

a. Shake a bell (or a rattle).
b. Play peek-a-boo by placing your open palms in front of your eyes.
c. Put a block (or other small object) into a cup; take it out of the cup, and place it next to the cup.
2. Partially hide a familiar toy or a cookie under a pillow or a box as the child watches. Note whether the infant searches for it.
3. Note whether the infant is creeping, crawling, pulling up her feet, trying to walk, or is actually walking.
4. Note whether the infant responds to the following verbal commands:
a. NO, NO.
b. GIVE ME THE (name of object).

SENSORIMOTOR: LEVEL 2

2A   **Sensorimotor**
                                                                          Ages 12–18 months

General Development

METHOD: Interview and observation.

SKILLS: Perceptual/motor and receptive language.

MATERIALS: Several safe containers (i.e., plastic is good) and a supply of safe, nontoxic objects.

PROCEDURES/EVALUATION:
1. Give the child several containers and the supply of small objects. Note if he fills the containers with objects and dumps them out repeatedly.
2. Tell the child, POINT TO YOUR NOSE, HEAD, EYES, FOOT, STOMACH.
3. Hide a familiar object completely. Note whether the child searches for it.

2B   **Sensorimotor**
                                                                          Ages 18–24 months

General Development

METHOD: Interview and observation.

SKILLS: Perceptual/motor and receptive and expressive language.

MATERIALS: Child's own toys (or other assortment provided by you, such as a ball, toy dog, toy car, blocks, baby bottle, doll, and the like).

PROCEDURES/EVALUATIONS:
1. During playtime observations, note if the child is beginning to organize objects in rows and put similar objects together in groups.
2. Ask the child to point to familiar objects. POINT TO THE BALL (CHAIR, DOLL, CAR).
3. Note whether the child begins to name the parts of her body (usually two parts at 18 months).

PREOPERATIONAL: LEVEL 3

3A **Preoperational**
Ages 2–3

One-to-One Correspondence: Unit 8

METHOD: Observation, individuals or groups.

SKILL: Child demonstrates one-to-one correspondence during play activities

MATERIALS: Play materials that lend themselves to one-to-one activities, such as small blocks and animals, dishes and eating utensils, paint containers and paintbrushes, pegs and pegboards, sticks and stones, and the like

PROCEDURE: Provide the materials and encourage the children to use them.

EVALUATION: Note if the children match items to one such as putting small peg dolls in each of several margarine containers or on top of each of several blocks that have been lined up in a row

---

3B **Preoperational**
Ages 2–3

Number and Counting: Unit 8

METHOD: Interview.

SKILL: Child understands the concept of "twoness" and can rational count at least two objects.

MATERIALS: Ten counters (cube blocks, Unifix Cubes®, or other objects.

PROCEDURES:
1. Ask, HOW OLD ARE YOU?
2. Give the child two objects. HOW MANY (name of objects) ARE THERE? If the child succeeds, try three objects. Go on as far as the child can go.

EVALUATION:
1. May hold up appropriate number of fingers or answer "two" or "three."
2. Should be able to rational count two objects (or possibly recognize two without counting).

3C **Preoperational**
Ages 2–3

Sets and Classifying, Informal Sorting: Unit 8

METHOD: Observation and informal interviewing.

SKILL: While playing, the child groups toys by various criteria such as color, shape, size, class name, and so on.

MATERIALS: Assortment of normal toys for 2- to 3-year-olds.

PROCEDURE: As the child plays, note whether toys are grouped by classification criteria (see Unit 8). Ask, SHOW ME THE RED BLOCKS. WHICH CAR IS THE BIGGEST? FIND SOME SQUARE BLOCKS.

EVALUATION: The child should naturally group by similarities, should be able to group objects by at least one or two colors, and should be able to find objects from the same class.

3D   Preoperational
                                                                   Ages 2–3

Comparing, Informal Measurement: Unit 8

METHOD: Interview.

SKILL: Child can respond to comparison terms applied to familiar objects.

MATERIALS: Pairs of objects that vary on comparative criteria, such as

large-small	heavy-light
long-short	cold-hot
fat-skinny	higher-lower

PROCEDURE: Show the child the pairs of objects one pair at a time. Ask, POINT TO THE BIG (BALL). POINT TO THE SMALL or LITTLE (BALL). Continue with other pairs of objects and object concept words.

EVALUATION: Note how many of the objects the child can identify correctly.

3E   Preoperational
                                                                   Ages 2–3

Comparing, Number: Unit 8

METHOD: Interview.

SKILL: Shown a set of one and six or more, the child can identify which set has more.

MATERIALS: Twenty counters (i.e., pennies, Unifix Cubes®, cube blocks).

PROCEDURE: Place two groups of objects in front of the child: one group with a set of one object and one group with a set of six or more. Ask, WHICH HAS MORE (object name)? POINT TO THE ONE WITH MORE.

EVALUATION: Note if the child identifies the group that contains more.

3F   Preoperational
                                                                   Ages 2–3

Shape, Matching: Unit 8

METHOD: Interview.

SKILL: Child can match an object or cutout shape to another of the same size and shape.

MATERIALS: Attribute blocks or shape cutouts; one red circle, square, and triangle; one green circle, square, and triangle. All should be the same relative size.

PROCEDURE: Place the three green shapes in front of the child. One at a time, show the child each of the red shapes and tell the child, FIND A GREEN SHAPE THAT IS THE SAME AS THIS RED ONE.

EVALUATION: The child should be able to make all three matches.

3G Preoperational
  Ages 2–3

Space. Position: Unit 8

METHOD: Interview.

SKILL: Given a spatial relationships word, the child can place objects relative to other objects on the basis of that world.

MATERIALS: A small container such as a box, cup, or bowl and an object such as a coin, checker or chip

PROCEDURE: PUT THE *(object name)* IN THE BOX (or CUP or BOWL). Repeat using other space words: ON, OFF, OUT OF, IN FRONT OF, NEXT TO, UNDER, OVER.

EVALUATION: Note if the child is able to follow the instructions and place the object correctly relative to the space word used.

3H Preoperational
  Ages 2–3

Parts & Wholes, Missing Parts: Unit 8

METHOD: Interview.

SKILL: Child can tell which part(s) of objects and/or pictures of objects are missing.

MATERIALS: Several objects and/or pictures of objects and/or people with parts missing. Some examples are:

Things:	Doll with a leg or arm missing
	Car with a wheel missing
	Cup with a handle broken off
	Chair with a leg gone
	Face with only one eye
	House with no door
Pictures:	Mount pictures of common things on poster board.
	Parts can be cut off before mounting

PROCEDURE: Show the child each object or picture. LOOK CAREFULLY. WHICH PART IS MISSING FROM THIS *(name of object)?*

EVALUATION: Note if the child is able to tell which parts are missing in both objects and pictures. Does she have the language label for each part? Can she perceive what she is

---

3I   **Preoperational**
                                                                     Ages 2–3

Ordering, Size: Unit 8

METHOD: Interview.

SKILL: Child can order three objects that vary in one size dimension.

MATERIALS: Three objects of the same shape that vary in one size dimension, such as diameter:

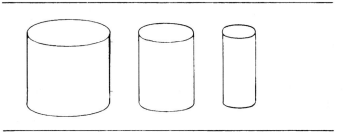

     Paper towel rolls can be cut into proportional lengths (heights) for this task. More objects can be available in reserve to be used for more difficult seriation tasks.

PROCEDURE: WATCH WHAT I DO. Line up the objects in order from fattest to thinnest (longest to shortest, tallest to shortest). NOW I'LL MIX THEM UP. (Do so.) PUT THEM IN A ROW LIKE I DID. If the child does the task with three objects, try it with five.

EVALUATION: Note whether the objects are placed in a correct sequence.

3J   **Preoperational**
                                                                     Ages 2–3

Measuring, Volume: Unit 8

METHOD: Observation.

SKILL: Child evidences an understanding that different containers hold different amounts.

MATERIALS: A large container filled with small objects such as small blocks, paper clips, table tennis balls, or teddy bear counters or with a substance such as water, rice, or legumes; several different sized small containers for pouring.

PROCEDURE: Let the children experiment with filling and pouring. Note any behavior that indicates they recognize that different containers hold different amounts.

EVALUATION: Children should experiment, filling containers and pouring back into the large container, pouring into larger small containers, and into smaller containers. Note behaviors such as if they line up smaller containers and fill each from a larger container or fill a larger container using a smaller one.

PREOPERATIONAL: LEVEL 4

4A   **Preoperational**
                                                                          Ages 3–4

One-to-One Correspondence, Same Things/Related Things:
Unit 8

METHOD: Interview.

SKILLS:

1. Child can match, in one-to-one correspondence, pairs of objects that are alike.
2. Child can match, in one-to-one correspondence, pairs of objects that are related but not alike.

MATERIALS:

1. Four different pairs of matching objects (such as two toy cars, two small plastic animals, two coins, two blocks).
2. Two groups of four related objects such as four cups and four saucers, four cowboys and four horses, four flowers and four flowerpots, four hats and four heads.

PROCEDURES:

1. Matching like pairs. Place the objects in front of the child in a random array. FIND THE THINGS THAT BELONG TOGETHER. If there is no response, pick up one. FIND ONE LIKE THIS. When the match is made, FIND SOME OTHER THINGS THAT BELONG TOGETHER. If there is no spontaneous response, continue to select objects, and ask the child to find the one like each.
2. Matching related pairs. Place two related groups of four in front of the child in a random array. FIND A CUP FOR EACH SAUCER (or COWBOY FOR EACH HORSE).

EVALUATION:

1. Note if the child matches spontaneously, and if he makes an organized pattern (such as placing the pairs side by side or in a row).
2. Note if the child is organized and uses a pattern for placing the objects (such as placing the objects in two matching rows).

4B   **Preoperational**
                                                                          Ages 3–4

Number and Counting, Rote and Rational: Unit 8

METHOD: Interview.

SKILL: Child can rote and rational count.

MATERIALS: Twenty counters (i.e., cube blocks, pennies, Unifix® Cubes).

PROCEDURE: First have the child rote count. COUNT FOR ME. START WITH ONE AND COUNT. If the child hesitates, ONE, TWO, _____. WHAT COMES NEXT? Next ask, HOW OLD ARE YOU? Finally, place four counters in front of the child. COUNT THE (objects). HOW MANY (_____) ARE THERE? If the child cannot count four items, try two or three. If she counts four easily, put out more counters, and ask her to count as many as she can.

EVALUATION: Note if she can rote count more than five and rational count at least five items. When she rational counts more than four, she should keep track of each item by touching each methodically or moving those counted to the side.

4C

Preoperational
Ages 3–4

Sets and Classifying, Object Sorting: Unit 8

METHOD: Interview.

SKILL: Child can sort objects into groups using logical criteria.

MATERIALS: Twelve objects: 2 red, 2 blue, 2 green, 2 yellow, 2 orange, 2 purple. There should be at least 5 kinds of objects; for example:

Color	Object 1	Object 2
red	block	car
blue	ball	cup
green	comb	car
yellow	block	bead
orange	comb	cup
purple	bead	ribbon

In addition, you will need 6 to 10 small containers (bowls or boxes).

PROCEDURE: Place the 12 objects in random array in front of the child. Provide him with the containers. PUT THE TOYS THAT BELONG TOGETHER IN A BOWL (BOX). USE AS MANY BOWLS (BOXES) AS YOU NEED.

EVALUATION: Note whether the child uses any specific criteria as he makes his groups.

4D

Preoperational
Ages 3–4

Shape, Identification: Units 8 and 10

METHOD: Interview.

SKILL: When given the name of a shape, the child can point to a drawing of that shape.

MATERIALS: On pieces of white poster board or on 5 1/2 × 8 file cards, draw the following shapes with a black marker (one shape on each card): circle, square, and triangle.

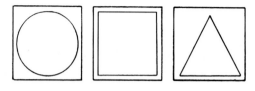

PROCEDURES: Place the cards in front of the child POINT TO THE SQUARE. POINT TO THE CIRCLE. POINT TO THE TRIANGLE.

EVALUATION: Note which, if any, of the shapes the child can identify.

4E

Preoperational
Ages 3–4

Space, Position: Units 8 and 10

METHOD: Interview.

SKILL: Child can use appropriate spatial relationship words to describe positions in space.

MATERIALS: Several small containers and several small objects; for example, four small plastic glasses and four small toy figures such as a fish, dog, cat, and mouse.

PROCEDURE: Ask the child to name each of the objects so you can use his name for it if it is different from yours. Line up the glasses in a row. Place the animals so that one is *in*, one *on*, one *under*, and one *between* the glasses. Say,

TELL ME WHERE THE FISH IS. Then, TELL ME WHERE THE DOG IS. Then, TELL ME WHERE THE CAT IS. Finally, TELL ME WHERE THE MOUSE IS. Frequently, children will insist on pointing. Then say, DO IT WITHOUT POINTING. TELL ME WITH WORDS.

EVALUATION: Note whether the child responds with position words and whether or not the words used are correct.

4F

Preoperational
Ages 3–6

Rote Counting: Units 8 and 10

METHOD: Interview.

SKILL: Child can rote count.

MATERIALS: None.

PROCEDURE: COUNT FOR ME. COUNT AS FAR AS YOU CAN. If the child hesitates or looks puzzled, ask again. If the child still doesn't respond, say ONE, TWO, WHAT'S NEXT?

EVALUATION: Note how far the child counts and the accuracy of the counting. Young children often lose track (i.e., "One, two, three, four, five, six, ten, seven,...") or miss a number name. Two's and three's may just count their ages, whereas fours usually can count accurately to ten and may try the teens and even beyond. By five or six children will usually begin to understand the commonalities in the twenties and beyond and move on toward counting to 100. Young children vary a great deal at each age level, so it is important to find where each individual is and move along from there.

4G   Preoperational
Ages 3–6

Rational Counting: Units 8 and 10

METHOD: Interview, individual or small group.

SKILL: Child can rational count.

MATERIALS: Thirty or more objects such as cube blocks, chips, or Unifix® Cubes.

PROCEDURE: Place a pile of objects in front of the child (about ten for a three-year-old, twenty for a four-year-old, and thirty for a five-year-old, and as many as 100 for older children). COUNT THESE FOR ME. HOW MANY CAN YOU COUNT?

EVALUATION: Note how accurately the child counts and how many objects are attempted.

In observing the process, note:

1. Does the child just use her eyes or does she actually touch each object as she counts?

2. Is some organizational system used such as lining the objects up in rows or moving the ones counted to the side, and so on?

3. Compare accuracy of rational counting with rote counting.

4H   Preoperational
Ages 3–6

Time, Identify Clock or Watch: Units 8 and 10

METHOD: Interview.

SKILL: Child can identify a clock and/or watch and describe its function.

MATERIALS: One or more of the following timepieces: conventional clock and watch, digital clock and watch. Preferably at least one conventional and one digital should be included. If real timepieces are not available, use pictures.

PROCEDURE: Show the child the timepieces or pictures of timepieces. WHAT IS THIS? WHAT DOES IT TELL US? WHAT IS IT FOR? WHAT ARE THE PARTS AND WHAT ARE THEY FOR?

EVALUATION: Note whether the child can label watch(es) and clock(s), and how much he is able to describe about the functions of the parts (long and short hands, second hands, alarms set, time changer, numerals). Note also if the child tries to tell time. Compare knowledge of conventional and digital timepieces.

4I

Preoperational
Ages 3–6

Symbols, Recognition: Units 8 and 10

METHOD: Interview.

SKILL: Child can recognize numerals zero to ten presented in sequence.

MATERIALS: 5 × 8 cards with one numeral from zero to ten written on each such as:

1	2	3	4

PROCEDURE: Starting with zero, show the child each card in numerical order from zero to ten. WHAT IS THIS? TELL ME THE NAME OF THIS.

EVALUATION: Note if the child uses numeral names (correct or not), indicating she knows the kinds of words associated with the symbols. Note which numerals she can label correctly.

PREOPERATIONAL: LEVEL 5

5A

Preoperational
Ages 4–5

One-to-One Correspondence, Same Things/Related Things: Unit 8

Do tasks in 4A (1 and 2) using more pairs of objects.

5B

Preoperational
Ages 4–5

Number and Counting, Rote and Rational Counting: Unit 8

See 4B, 4F, and 4G.

5C

Comparing, Number: Unit 8

METHOD: Interview.

SKILL: The child can compare the amounts in groups up to five and label the ones that are more, less, and fewer.

MATERIALS: Ten counters (i.e., chips, inch cubes, Unifix Cubes®).

PROCEDURE: Present the following groups for comparison in sequence:

> 1 versus 5
> 4 versus 1
> 2 versus 5
> 3 versus 2
> 5 versus 4

Each time a pair of groups is presented, ask, DOES ONE GROUP HAVE MORE? If the answer is yes, POINT TO THE GROUP THAT HAS MORE. Ask, HOW DO YOU KNOW THAT GROUP HAS MORE? If the child responds correctly to *more*, present the pairs again using LESS and FEWER.

EVALUATION: Note for which comparisons the child responds correctly. Can she give a logical reason for her choices (such as "Four is more than one" or "I counted them"), or does she place them in one-to-one correspondence?

5D

Comparing, Informal Measurement: Units 8 and 10

SKILL: Child can point to big (large) and small objects.

MATERIALS: A big block and a small block (a big truck and a small truck, a big shell and a small shell), and so on.

PROCEDURE: Present two related objects at a time. Say, FIND (POINT TO) THE BIG BLOCK. FIND (POINT TO) THE SMALL BLOCK. Continue with the rest of the object pairs.

EVALUATION: Note if the child is able to identify big and small for each pair.

5E

Part/Whole, Parts of a Whole: Units 8 and 10

METHOD: Interview.

SKILL: Child can recognize that a whole divided into parts is still the same amount.

MATERIALS: Apple and knife.

PROCEDURE: Show the child the apple. HOW MANY APPLES DO I HAVE? After you are certain the child understands there is one apple, cut the apple into two equal halves. HOW MANY APPLES DO I HAVE NOW? HOW DO YOU KNOW? If the child says "Two," press the halves together and ask, HOW MANY APPLES DO I HAVE NOW? Cut the apple into fourths, then eighths, following the same procedure.

EVALUATION: If the child can tell you that there is still one apple when it is cut into parts, he is able to mentally reverse the cutting process and may be leaving the preoperational period.

5F   **Preoperational**
                                                                        Ages 4–5

Ordering, Sequence/Ordinal Number: Units 8 and 10

METHOD: Interview.

SKILL: Child can order up to five objects relative to physical dimensions and identify the ordinal position of each.

MATERIALS: Five objects or cutouts that vary in equal increments of height, width, length, or overall size dimensions.

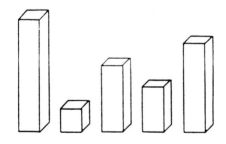

PROCEDURE: Start with five objects (cutouts). If this proves to be difficult, remove the objects (cutouts), then put out three and ask the same questions. FIND THE (TALLEST, BIGGEST, FATTEST) or (SHORTEST, SMALLEST, THINNEST). PUT THEM ALL IN A ROW FROM TALLEST TO SHORTEST (BIGGEST TO LITTLEST, FATTEST TO THINNEST). If the child accomplishes this task, ask, WHICH IS FIRST? WHICH IS LAST? WHICH IS SECOND? WHICH IS THIRD? WHICH IS FOURTH?.

EVALUATION: Note whether the children find the extremes, but mix up the three objects (cutouts) that belong in the middle. This is a common approach for preoperational children. Note if children take an organized approach to solving the problem or if they seem to approach it in a disorganized, unplanned way.

5G

Time, Labeling, and Sequence: Units 10 and 12

METHOD: Interview.

SKILL: Shown pictures of daily events, the child can use time words to describe the action in each picture and place the pictures in a logical time sequence.

MATERIALS: Pictures of daily activities such as meals, nap, bath, playtime, bedtime.

PROCEDURE: Show the child each picture. TELL ME ABOUT THIS PICTURE. WHAT'S HAPPENING? After the child has described each picture, place all the pictures in front of her. PICK OUT (SHOW ME) THE PICTURE OF WHAT HAPPENS FIRST EACH DAY. After a picture is selected, WHAT HAPPENS NEXT? Continue until all the pictures are lined up.

EVALUATION: When describing the pictures, note whether the child uses time words such as breakfast time, lunch time, playtime, morning, night, and so on. Note whether a logical sequence is used when placing the pictures in order.

5H

Practical Activities, Money: Unit 11

METHOD: Observation and interview.

SKILL: Child understands that money is exchanged for goods and services and can identify nickel, dime, penny, and dollar bill.

MATERIALS:
1. Play money and store props for dramatic play.
2. Nickel, dime, penny, and dollar bill.

PROCEDURE:
1. Set up play money and props for dramatic play as described in Unit 22. Observe the child, and note if he demonstrates some concept of exchanging money for goods and services and of giving and receiving change.
2. Show the child a nickel, dime, penny, and dollar bill. TELL ME THE NAME OF EACH OF THESE.

EVALUATION: Note the child's knowledge of money during dramatic play and note which, if any, of the pieces of money he recognizes.

The following tasks can be presented first between ages 4 and 5 and then repeated as the child's concepts and skills grow and expand.

5I

Sets and Classifying, Free Sort: Unit 10

METHOD: Interview.

SKILL: Child can classify and form sets in a free sort.

MATERIALS: Twenty to twenty-five objects (or pictures of objects or cutouts) that can be groped into several possible sets by criteria such as color, shape, size, or category (i.e., animals, plants, furniture, clothing, or toys).

PROCEDURE: Set all the objects out in front of the child in a random arrangement. PUT THE THINGS TOGETHER THAT BELONG TOGETHER. If the child looks puzzled, backtrack to the previous task and hold up one item. FIND SOME THINGS THAT BELONG WITH THIS. When a set is completed, NOW FIND SOME OTHER THINGS THAT BELONG TOGETHER. Keep on until all the items are grouped. Then point to each group. Ask, WHY DO THESE BELONG TOGETHER?

EVALUATION: Note if the child can make logical-looking groups and provide a logical reason for each one. That is, "Because they are cars" ("They are all green," "You can eat with them").

5J

Sets and Classifying, Clue Sort: Unit 10

METHOD: Interview.

SKILL: Child is able to classify and form sets using verbal and/or object clues.

MATERIALS: Twenty to twenty-five objects (or pictures of objects or cutouts) that can be grouped into several possible sets by criteria such as color, shape, size, or category (i.e., animals, plants, furniture, clothing, or toys).

PROCEDURE: Set all the objects in front of the child in a random arrangement. Try the following types of clues:

1. FIND SOME THINGS THAT ARE _____. (Name a specific color, shape, size, material, pattern, function, or class).

2. Hold up one object, picture, or cutout. FIND SOME THINGS THAT BELONG WITH THIS. After the choices are made, ask, WHY DO THESE THINGS BELONG TOGETHER?

EVALUATION: Note if the child can make a logical-looking group and provide a logical reason for her choices. That is, "Because they are cars" ("They are green," "You can eat with them").

5K

Symbols, Sequencing: Units 10 and 12

METHOD: Interview.

SKILL: Child is able to sequence numerals from zero to ten.

MATERIALS: 5 × 8 cards with one numeral from zero to ten written on each.

3	7	4	0	9	5
1	6		10	8	2

PROCEDURE: Place all the cards in front of the child in random order. PUT THESE IN ORDER. WHICH COMES FIRST? NEXT? NEXT?

EVALUATION: Note whether the child seems to understand that numerals belong in a fixed sequence. Note how many are placed in the correct order and which, if any, are labeled.

5L

Naturalistic and Informal Activities

METHOD: Observation.

SKILL: Child can demonstrate a knowledge of math concepts and skills during naturalistic and informal activities.

MATERIALS: Math Center (three-dimensional and two-dimensional materials), sand/water/legume pouring table, dramatic play props, unit blocks and accessories, cooking center, math concept books.

PROCEDURE: Develop a recording system and keep a record of behaviors such as the following:
- Chooses to work in the Math Center.
- Selects math concept books to look at.
- Chooses to work in the Cooking Center.
- Selects working with sand, water, or legumes.
- Can give each person one napkin, one glass of juice, and so on.
- Spontaneously counts objects or people.
- While playing, spontaneously separates objects or pictures into logical groups.
- Spontaneously uses comparison words (e.g., This one is *bigger*).
- Chooses to build with blocks.

- Knows the parts of people and objects.
- Demonstrates a knowledge of *first, biggest, heaviest,* and other order concepts.
- Does informal measurement such as identifying hot and cold, a bigger container and a smaller container, and so on.
- Evidences a concept of time (What do we do next? Is it time for lunch?).
- Points out number symbols in the environment.
- Uses the language of math (whether he or she understands the concepts or not).

EVALUATION: Child should show an increase in frequency of these behaviors as the year progresses.

PREOPERATIONAL: LEVEL 6

6A

Preoperational
Ages 5–6

One-to-One Correspondence: Units 8 and 10

METHOD: Interview.

SKILL: Child can place two groups of ten items each in one-to-one correspondence.

MATERIALS: Two groups of objects of different shapes and/or color (such as pennies and cube blocks or red chips and white chips). Have at least ten of each type of object.

PROCEDURE: Place two groups of ten objects in front of the child.

FIND OUT IF THERE IS THE SAME AMOUNT (NUMBER) IN EACH BUNCH (PILE, GROUP, SET). If the child cannot do the task, go back and try it with two groups of five.

EVALUATION: The children should arrange each group so as to match the objects one-to-one or they might count each group to determine equality.

6B

Preoperational
Ages 5–6

Number and Counting, Rote and Rational: Unit 10

METHOD: Interview.

SKILL: Child can rote and rational count.

MATERIALS: Fifty counters (i.e., chips, cube blocks, Unifix Cubes®).

PROCEDURES:

1. **Rote counting.** COUNT FOR ME AS FAR AS YOU CAN. If the child hesitates, say ONE,

TWO, _____ . WHAT'S NEXT?

2. **Rational counting.** Present the child with 20 objects. HOW MANY _____ ARE THERE? COUNT THEM FOR ME.

EVALUATION:

1. **Rote.** By age 5, the child should be able to count to 10 or more; by age 6, to 20 or more. Note if any number names are missed or repeated.

2. **Rational.** Note the degree of accuracy and organization. Does she place the objects to insure that no object is counted more than once or that any object is missed? Note how far she goes without making a mistake. Does she repeat any number names? Skip any? By age 6, she should be able to go beyond 10 objects with accuracy.

6C

Preoperational
Ages 5–6

Shape, Recognition and Reproduction: Units 8 and 10

METHOD: Interview.

SKILL #1: Identify shapes, Task 4E.

SKILL #2: Child can identify shapes in the environment.

MATERIALS: Natural environment.

PROCEDURE: LOOK AROUND THE ROOM. FIND AS MANY SHAPES AS YOU CAN. WHICH THINGS ARE SQUARE SHAPES? CIRCLES? RECTANGLES? TRIANGLES?

EVALUATION: Note how observant the child is. Does she note the obvious shapes, such as windows, doors, and tables? Does she look beyond the obvious? How many shapes and which shapes is she able to find?

SKILL #3: Child will reproduce shapes by copying.

MATERIALS: Shape cards (4E); plain white paper; a choice of pencils, crayons, and markers.

PROCEDURE:

1. COPY THE CIRCLE.
2. COPY THE SQUARE.
3. COPY THE TRIANGLE.

EVALUATION: Note how closely each reproduction resembles its model. Is the circle complete and round? Does the square have four sides and square corners? Does the triangle have three straight sides and pointed corners?

6D

Preoperational
Ages 5–6

Part/Whole, Parts of Sets: Unit 10

METHOD: Interview.

SKILL: Child can divide a set of objects into smaller groups.

MATERIALS: Have three small dolls (real or paper cutouts) and a box of pennies or other small objects.

PROCEDURE: Have the three dolls arranged in a row. I WANT TO GIVE EACH DOLL SOME PENNIES. SHOW ME HOW TO DO IT SO EACH DOLL WILL HAVE THE SAME AMOUNT.

EVALUATION: Note how the child approaches the problem. Does he give each doll one penny at a time in sequence? Does he count out pennies until there are three groups with the same amount? Does he divide the pennies in a random fashion? Does he have a method for finding out if each has the same amount?

6E

**Preoperational
Ages 5–6**

Ordering, Size and Amount: Units 10 and 12

METHOD: Interview.

SKILLS: Child can order 10 objects that vary in one criteria and five sets with amounts from 1 to 5.

MATERIALS:

1. **Size.** Ten objects or cutouts that vary in size, length, height, or width. An example for length is shown below:

—   ——   ———   —   ————————
————————————   —————————
—————————   ——————————   ———————————

2. **Amount.** Five sets of objects consisting of one, two, three, four, and five objects each.

PROCEDURE:

1. **Size.** Place the 10 objects or cutouts in front of the child in a random arrangement. FIND THE (BIGGEST, LONGEST, TALLEST, OR WIDEST). PUT THEM ALL IN A ROW FROM _____ TO _____.

2. **Amount.** Place the five sets in front of the child in a random arrangement. PUT THESE IN ORDER FROM THE SMALLEST BUNCH (GROUP) TO THE LARGEST BUNCH (GROUP).

EVALUATION:

1. **Size.** Preoperational children will usually get the two extremes but may mix up the in-between sizes. Putting 10 in the correct order would be an indication that the child is entering concrete operations.

2. **Amount.** Most 5s can order the five sets. If they order them easily, try some larger amounts.

6F

Measurement; Length, Weight, and Time: Units 10 and 12

METHOD: Interview.

SKILLS: Child can explain the function of a ruler, discriminate larger from heavier, and identify and explain the function of clock.

MATERIALS:
1. **Length.** A foot ruler.
2. **Weight.** A plastic golf ball and a marble or other pair of objects where the larger is the lighter.
3. **Time.** A clock (with a conventional face).

PROCEDURES:
1. Show the child the rules. WHAT IS THIS? WHAT DO WE DO WITH IT? SHOW ME HOW IT IS USED.
2. Give the child the two objects, one in each hand. Ask, WHICH IS BIGGER? WHICH IS HEAVIER? WHY IS THE SMALL _____ HEAVIER?
3. Show the child the clock. WHAT IS THIS? WHY DO WE HAVE IT? TELL ME HOW IT WORKS.

EVALUATION: Note how many details the child can give about each of the measuring instruments. Is she accurate? Can she tell which of the objects is heavier? Can she provide a reason for the lighter being larger and the smaller heavier?

6G

Practical Activities, Money: Unit 12

METHOD: Interview.

SKILL: Child can recognize money and tell which pieces of money will buy more.

MATERIALS:
1. Pictures of coins, bills, and other similar looking items.
2. Selection of pennies, nickels, dimes, and quarters.

PROCEDURE:
1. Show the child the pictures. FIND THE PICTURES OF MONEY. After he has found the pictures of money, ask, WHAT IS THE NAME OF THIS? as you point to each picture of money.
2. Put the coins in front of the child. Ask, WHICH WILL BUY THE MOST? IF YOU HAVE THESE FIVE PENNIES (put five pennies in one pile) AND I WANT TWO CENTS FOR A PIECE OF CANDY, HOW MANY PENNIES WILL YOU HAVE TO GIVE ME FOR THE CANDY?

EVALUATION: Note which picture of money the child can identify. Note if he knows which coins are worth the most. Many young children equate worth and size and thus think a nickel will buy more than a dime.

Check back to 5I, 5J, and 5K, then go on to the next tasks. The following tasks can be presented first between ages 5 and 6 and then repeated as the child's concepts and skills grow and expand.

6H   **Transitional Period**
                                                                                              Ages 5–7

Ordering, Patterning: Unit 12

METHOD: Interview.

SKILLS: Child can copy, extend, and describe patterns made with concrete objects.

MATERIALS: Color cubes, Unifix® Cubes, Teddy Bear Counters, attribute blocks, small toys, or other objects that can be placed in a sequence to develop a pattern.

PROCEDURE:

1. Copy patterns. One at a time, make patterns of various levels of complexity (each letter stands for one type of item such as one color of a color cube, one shape of an attribute block, or one type of toy). For example, A-B-A-B could be red block, green block, red block, green block or big triangle, small triangle, big triangle, small triangle. Using the following series of patterns, tell the child, MAKE A PATTERN JUST LIKE THIS ONE. (If the child hesitates, point to the first item and say, START WITH ONE LIKE THIS):

    a. A-B-A-B

    b. A-A-B-A-A-B

    c. A-B-C-A-B-C

    d. A-A-B-B-C-C-A-A-B-B-C-C

2. Extend patterns. Make patterns as in # 1 but this time say, THIS PATTERN ISN'T FINISHED. MAKE IT LONGER. SHOW ME WHAT COMES NEXT.

3. Describe patterns. Make patterns as in # 1 and # 2 TELL ME ABOUT THESE PATTERNS (WHAT COMES FIRST? NEXT? NEXT?). IF YOU WANTED TO CONTINUE THE PATTERN, WHAT WOULD COME NEXT? NEXT?

4. If the above tasks are easily accomplished, then try some more difficult patterns such as:

    a. A-B-A-C-A-D-A-B-A-C-A-D

    b. A-B-B-C-D-A-B-B-C-D

    c. A-A-B-A-A-C-A-A-D

EVALUATION: Note which types of patterns are easiest for the children. Are they more successful with the easier patterns? With copying? Extending? Describing?

6I

Preoperational/Concrete
Ages 5–7

Sets and Symbols, Match Sets to Symbols: Unit 12

METHOD: Interview.

SKILL: Child can match sets to symbols using sets of amounts zero to ten and numerals from zero to ten.

MATERIALS: 5 × 8 cards with numerals zero to ten, sixty objects (e.g., chips, cube blocks, coins, buttons).

PROCEDURE: Lay out the numeral cards in front of the child. Place the container of objects within easy reach. MAKE A SET FOR EACH NUMERAL. Let the child decide how to organize the materials.

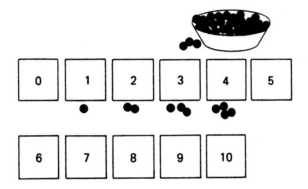

EVALUATION: Note for which numerals the child is able to make sets. Note how the child goes about the task. For example, does she sequence the numerals from zero to ten, does she place the objects in an organized pattern by each numeral, can she recognize some amounts without counting, when she counts, does she do it carefully. Her responses will indicate where instruction should begin.

6J

Preoperational/Concrete
Ages 5–6

Naturalistic and Informal Activities: Units 1–12

METHOD: Observation.

SKILL: Child demonstrates a knowledge of fundamental concepts and skills during naturalistic and informal activities.

MATERIALS: See task 5L.

PROCEDURE: See task 5L. Add the following behaviors to your list:
• Demonstrates an understanding of *more than*, *the same amount*, and *less than* by responding appropriately to questions such as, "Do we have the same number of children as we have chairs?"
• Can match a set to a symbol and a symbol to a set (for example, if the daily attendance total says 22, he can get 22 napkins for snack).

- Can do applied concrete whole number operations (for example, if four children plan to draw and two more children join them, he knows that there are now six children, or if he has three friends and eight cars to play with he figures out that each friend can use two cars).

EVALUATION: Child should show an increase in frequency of these behaviors as the year progresses.

CONCRETE OPERATIONS:
LEVEL 7

The following tasks are all indicators of the child's cognitive developmental level. The child who can accomplish all these tasks should be ready for the primary level instruction described in Section III.

7A

Concrete Operations
Ages 6–7

Conservation of Number: Unit 1

METHOD: Interview.

SKILL: Child can solve the number conservation problem.

MATERIALS: Twenty chips, blocks, or coins, all the same size, shape, and color.

PROCEDURE: Set up a row of nine objects. Then proceed through the following four tasks:

1. MAKE A ROW JUST LIKE THIS ONE (point to yours).

Child □ □ □ □ □ □ □ □ □

Adult □ □ □ □ □ □ □ □ □

DOES ONE ROW HAVE MORE BLOCKS (CHIPS, COINS), OR DO THEY BOTH HAVE THE SAME AMOUNT? HOW DO YOU KNOW? If child agrees to equality, go on to the next tasks.

2. Task 2

NOW WATCH WHAT I DO. (Push yours together.)

Child □ □ □ □ □ □ □ □ □

Adult □□□□□□□□□

DOES ONE ROW HAVE MORE BLOCKS, OR DO THEY BOTH HAVE THE SAME AMOUNT? WHY? (If the child says one row has more, MAKE THEM HAVE THE SAME AMOUNT AGAIN.) (If the child says they have the same amount, tell him, LINE THEM UP LIKE THEY WERE BEFORE I MOVED THEM.) Go on to task 3 and task 4 following the same steps as above.

3. Task 3

Child □□□□□□□□

Adult □□□□ □□□□□

4. Task 4

Child □□□□□□□□□

Adult □□□□□□□□□

EVALUATION: If the child is unable to do Task 1 (one-to-one correspondence), do not proceed any further. He needs to work further on this concept and needs time for development. If he succeeds with Task 1, go on to 2, 3, and 4. Note which of the following categories fit his responses:

Nonconserver 1. Indicates longer rows have more but cannot give a logical reason, (For example, the child may say, "I don't know," "My mother says so," or gives no answer.)

Nonconserver 2. Indicates longer rows have more and gives logical reasons, such as "It's longer," "The long row has more," and the like.

Transitional. Says both rows still have the same amount but has to check by counting or placing in one-to-one correspondence.

Conserver. Completely sure that both rows still have the same amount. May say, "You just moved them."

7B Concrete Operations Ages 6–7

Symbols and Sets, Matching and Writing: Unit 12

METHOD: Interview.

SKILL: Child can match sets to symbols and write symbols.

MATERIALS: Cards with numerals 0 to 20, a supply of counters, paper, and writing implements.

PROCEDURE:
1. Present the child with sets of counters. Start with amounts under 10. If the child can do these, go on to the teens. MATCH THE NUMBERS TO THE SETS.
2. Put the numeral cards and counters away. Give the child a piece of paper and a choice of writing instruments. WRITE AS MANY NUMBERS AS YOU CAN. START WITH ZERO.

EVALUATION: Note how high the child can go in matching sets and symbols and in writing numerals.

7C Concrete Operations Ages 6–7

Multiple Classification: Unit 12

METHOD: Interview.

SKILL: Child can group shapes by more than one criterion.

MATERIALS: Make 36 cardboard shapes.
1. Four squares (one each red, yellow, blue, and green).
2. Four triangles (one each red, yellow, blue, and green).
3. Four circles (one each red, yellow, blue, and green).
4. Make three sets of each in three sizes.

PROCEDURE: Place all the shapes in a random array in front of the child. DIVIDE (SORT, PILE) THESE SHAPES INTO GROUPS, ANY WAY YOU WANT TO. After the child has sorted on one attribute (shape, color, or size) say, NOW DIVIDE (SORT, PILE) THEM ANOTHER WAY. The preoperational child will normally refuse to conceptualize another way of grouping.

EVALUATION: The preoperational child will center on the first sort and will not try another criterion. The concrete operations child will sort by color, shape, and size.

7D Concrete Operations
Ages 6–7

Class Inclusion: Unit 12

METHOD: Interview.

SKILL: Child can perceive that there are classes within classes.

MATERIALS: Make a set of materials using objects, cutouts, or pictures of objects such as the following:
1. Twelve wooden beads of the same size and shape differing only in color (e.g., 4 red and 8 blue)
2. Twelve pictures of flowers: 8 tulips and 4 daisies.
3. Twelve pictures of animals: 8 dogs and 4 cats.

PROCEDURE: Place the objects (pictures) in front of the child in random order. PUT THE (object name) TOGETHER THAT ARE THE SAME. Then after they have grouped into two subcategories ask, ARE THERE MORE (WOODEN BEADS, FLOWERS OR ANIMALS) OR MORE (BLUE BEADS, TULIPS OR DOGS)? Have them compare the overall class or category with the larger subclass.

EVALUATION: The preoperational child will have difficulty conceptualizing parts and wholes of sets at the same time.

CONCRETE OPERATIONS: LEVEL 8

8A Concrete Operations
Ages 6–8

Combining Sets up to Ten

METHOD: Interview.

SKILL: Child can combine sets to form new sets up to ten.

MATERIALS: Twenty counters (cube blocks, Unifix® Cubes, chips): ten of one color and ten of another.

PROCEDURE: Have the child select two groups of counters from each color so that the total is ten or less. PUT THREE YELLOW CUBES OVER HERE AND FIVE BLUE CUBES OVER HERE. Child completes task. NOW TELL ME, IF YOU PUT ALL THE CUBES IN ONE

BUNCH, HOW MAY CUBES DO YOU HAVE ALTOGETHER? HOW DO YOU KNOW? Do this with combinations that add up to one through ten.

EVALUATION: Note if the child is able to make the requested groups with or without counting. Note the method used by the child to decide on the sum:

1. Does he begin with one and count all the blocks?

2. Does he count on? That is, in the example above, does he put his two small groups together and then say, "Three blocks, four, five, six, seven, eight. I have eight now."

3. Does he just say, "Eight, because I know that three plus five is eight"?

8B   **Concrete Operations**
                                                             Ages 6–8

Sets of Ten and Less

METHOD: Interview.

SKILL: Child can subtract sets to make new sets using groups of ten and smaller.

MATERIALS: Twenty counters (cube blocks, Unifix® Cubes, chips): ten of one color and ten of another and a small box or other small container.

PROCEDURE: Pick out a group of ten or fewer counters. I HAVE SEVEN CUBES. I'M GOING TO HIDE SOME IN THE BOX. (Hide three in the box.) NOW, HOW MANY DO I HAVE LEFT? HOW MANY DID I HIDE? If the child cannot answer, give her seven of the other color cubes and ask her to take three away and tell you how many are left. Do this with amounts of ten and less. For the less mature or younger child, start with five and less.

EVALUATION: Note if the child is able to solve the problem without working it out herself. Note whether the child has to count or if she just knows without counting.

8C   **Concrete Operations**
                                                             Ages 6–8

Patterns, Extension in Three Dimensions

METHOD: Interview.

SKILL: Child can extend complex patterns in three dimensions by predicting what will come next.

MATERIALS: Inch or centimeter cubes, Unifix® Cubes, or other counters, that can be stacked.

PROCEDURE: Present the child with various patterns made of stacked counters. Ask the child to describe the pattern and to continue it as far as he can. Stack the blocks as follows one pattern at a time.

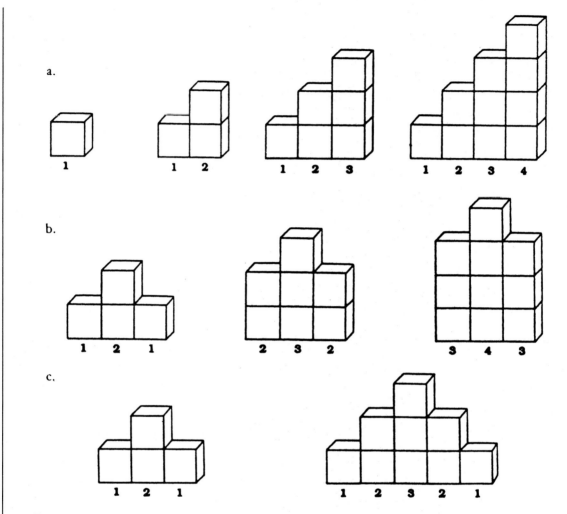

a.

1

1 2

1 2 3

1 2 3 4

b.

1 2 1

2 3 2

3 4 3

c.

1 2 1

1 2 3 2 1

For each pattern ask, TELL ME ABOUT THIS PATTERN. WHAT COMES NEXT? HOW DO YOU KNOW? CONTINUE THE PATTERN FOR ME.

EVALUATION: Note if the child can continue each pattern and state his rationale. Note where the child may need further help and practice.

8D   **Concrete Operations**
                                                                    Ages 7–8

Patterns, Creation: Unit
METHOD: Interview.
SKILL: Child can create patterns using discrete objects.

MATERIALS: Concrete objects such as chips, Unifix Cubes®, or cube blocks.

PROCEDURE: USING YOUR (counters), MAKE YOUR OWN PATTERN AS YOU HAVE DONE WITH PATTERN STARTERS I HAVE GIVEN YOU. When the child is finished, TELL ME ABOUT YOUR PATTERN.

EVALUATION: Note if the child has actually developed a repeated pattern and if she is able to tell you the pattern in words.

8E   **Concrete Operations**
                                                                          Ages 6–8

Equivalent Parts

METHOD: Interview.

SKILL: Child can divide a rectangle into smaller equal parts.

MATERIALS: A supply of paper rectangles of equal size ($8\frac{1}{2}$" $\times$ $2\frac{3}{4}$") in four different colors and a pair of scissors.

PROCEDURE: Show the child a paper rectangle. THIS IS A RECTANGLE. Place two more rectangles (color #2) below the first one. HERE ARE TWO MORE RECTANGLES. ARE ALL THREE THE SAME SIZE? Be sure the child agrees. Let him compare them to be sure. NOW I'M GOING TO FOLD ONE OF THE RECTANGLES (color # 2) SO BOTH PARTS ARE THE SAME. Fold the rectangle. NOW YOU FOLD THIS OTHER ONE. (also color #2) JUST LIKE I DID. Offer assistance if necessary. The three rectangles should look like this:

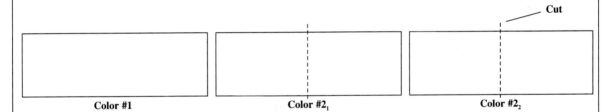

| Color #1 | Color #2₁ | Color #2₂ |

ARE THE PARTS OF (color # 2) RECTANGLE THE SAME SIZE AS THE PARTS OF THIS ONE? (also color #2) SHOW ME HOW YOU KNOW. I'M GOING TO CUT THIS ONE (second color # 2) ON THE FOLD. HOW MANY PARTS DO I HAVE NOW? IF I PUT THEM BACK TOGETHER, WILL THEY BE THE SAME SIZE AS THIS WHOLE RECTANGLE? (color # 1) AS YOUR RECTANGLE? WHAT IS A SPECIAL NAME FOR THIS AMOUNT OF THE WHOLE RECTANGLE? Point to the half. If the response is one-half, go through the procedure again with one-third and one-fourth using colors # 3 and # 4 respectively.

EVALUATION: Note whether the child has to check on the equivalency of the three rectangles. Can he keep in mind that the parts still equal the whole, even when cut into two or more parts? Does he know the terms one-half, one-third, and/or one-fourth?

8F
Concrete Operations
Ages 6–8

One-half of a Group

METHOD: Interview.

SKILL: Child can divide a set of objects into smaller groups when given directions using the term *one-half.*

MATERIALS: Ten counters (cube blocks, chips, Unifix® Cubes, or other concrete objects).

PROCEDURE: Place the counters in front of the child. I HAVE SOME *(name of counters).* DIVIDE THESE SO THAT WE EACH HAVE ONE-HALF OF THE GROUP. If the child completes this task easily, go on to nine counters and ask him to divide the group into thirds and eight counters, then ask him to divide the group into fourths.

EVALUATION: Note the method used by the child. Does he use counting or does he pass the counters out: "One for you and one for me. . . ." Does he really seem to understand the terms one-half, one-fourth, and one-third?

8G
Concrete Operations
Ages 7–8

Place Value, Symbols to Concrete Representations: Unit

METHOD: Interview or small group.

SKILL: Child can translate from written numerals to concrete representations.

MATERIALS: Base 10 blocks or similar material (i.e., Unifix Cubes®, sticks, or straws and rubber bands for bundling); 8 or 10 cards, each with a double-digit number written on it (for example, 38, 72, 45, 83, 27, 96, 51, 50).

PROCEDURE: USING YOUR BASE 10 BLOCKS, MAKE GROUPS FOR EACH NUMERAL. After each group has been constructed, TELL ME HOW YOU KNOW THAT YOU HAVE (number).

EVALUATION: Note if the child constructs the correct amount of 10s and units and can explain accurately how the construction is represented by the numeral.

8H
Concrete Operations

Geometry, Graphs, Charts, and Tables: Unit

See the prerequisite concepts and skills in units 8, 10, and 12, and assessment tasks 3F, 3G, 4E, 5E, and 6C.

REFERENCES

Baroody, A. J. (1988). *Children's mathematical thinking*. New York: Teachers College Press. This book includes many examples of children's common mistakes and misconceptions.

Engelhardt, J. M., Ashlock, R. B., & Wiebe, J. H. (1994). *Helping children understand and use numerals*. Boston: Allyn & Bacon. Chapter 4 contains many diagnostic tasks.

Labinowicz, E. (1985). *Learning from children: New beginnings for teaching numerical thinking*. Menlo Park, CA: Addison-Wesley. Chapter 2 describes the basics of the interview method, Appendix B gives interview hints, and Appendix F provides some starting points for interviews.

Richardson, K. (1984). *Developing number concepts using Unifix Cubes®*. Menlo Park, CA: Addison-Wesley. At the end of each chapter, there is a section on analyzing and assessing children's needs.

See Unit 4 for additional resources.

APPENDIX B Children's Books With Science Concepts

CONTENTS*

*Numbers indicating relevant units follow each entry

FUNDAMENTAL CONCEPTS

One-to-One Correspondence

Gag, W. (1941). *Nothing at all*. New York: Coward-McCann. Ages 3–5; **8, 10**.

Slobodkina, E. (1976). *Caps for sale*. New York: Scholastic. Ages 3–6; **8**.

The three bears. (1973). New York: Golden Press. Ages 2–5; **8, 10**.

The Three Billy Goats Gruff. (1968). New York: Grosset & Dunlap. Ages 2–5; **8**.

Number Sense and Counting

Many of the books listed in this section include ordinal numbers. Most also include number symbols.

Aker, S. (1990). *What comes in 2's, 3's, and 4's?* New York: Simon & Schuster. Ages 4–6; **8**.

Allen, R. (1968). *Numbers: A first counting book*. New York: Platt & Munk. Ages 3–7; **8**.

Anno, M. (1982). *Anno's counting house*. New York: Philomel. Ages 4–7; **8**.

Anno, M. (1986). *Anno's counting book*. New York: Harper-Collins. Ages 4–6; **8**.

Bang, M. (1983). *Ten, nine, eight*. New York: Greenwillow. Ages 3–5; **8**.

Becker, J. (1973). *Seven little rabbits*. New York: Scholastic. Ages 3–6; **8, 12**.

Blumenthal, N. (1989). *Count-a-saurus*. New York: Four Winds Press. Ages 3–6; **8**.

Boynton, S. (1978). *Hippos go berserk*. Chicago, IL: Recycled Paper Press. Ages 3–6; **8, 12**.

Budney, B. (1962). *A cat can't count*. New York: Lothrop. Ages 5–8; **8**.

Carle, E. (1969). *The very hungry caterpillar*. Mountain View, CA: Collins and World. Ages 3–5; **8, 10, 12**.

Carle, E. (1971). *1, 2, 3 to the zoo*. Mountain View, CA: Collins and World. Ages 3–5; **8**.

Carle, E. (1971). *The rooster who set out to see the world*. New York: Franklin Watts. Ages 3–5; **8**.

Carle, E. (1972). *The very long train: A folding book*. New York: Crowell. Ages 3–5; **8, 10**.

Carter, D. A. (1988). *How many bugs in a box?* New York: Simon & Schuster. Ages 3–6; **8**.

Cleveland, D. (1978). *April rabbits*. New York: Scholastic. Ages 3–5; **8, 10**.

Craig, H. (1983). *The little mouse 123*. New York: Little Simon. Ages 3–5; **8**.

Crews, D. (1985). *Ten black dots, revised*. New York; Greenwillow. Ages 4–6; **8**.

Crowther, R. (1981). *The most amazing hide and seek counting book*. New York: Viking. Ages 3–6; **8**.

Cutler, D. S. (1991). *One hundred monkeys*. New York: Simon & Schuster. Ages 3–6; **8**.

Davis, B. S. (1972). *Forest hotel—A counting story*. Racine, WI: Western Publishing. Ages 3–6; **8**.

Dodd, L. (1978). *The nickle nackle tree*. New York: Macmillan. Ages 3–6; **8, 10**.

Duke, K. (1985). *Seven froggies went to school*. New York: Dutton. Ages 2–6; **8**.

Dunbar, J. (1990). *Ten little mice*. San Diego, CA: HBJ. Ages 3–6; **8**.

Eichenberg, F. (1955). *Dancing in the moon*. New York: Harcourt, Brace. Ages 3–5; **8, 12**.

Elkin, B. (1968, 1971). *Six foolish fishermen*. New York: Scholastic. Ages 3–6; **8, 13**

Ernst, L. C. (1986). *Up to ten and down again*. New York: Lothrop, Lee, & Shepard. Ages 2–7; **8**.

Feelings, M. (1976). *Moja means one: Swahili counting book*. New York: Dial. Ages 3–6; **8**.

Friskey, M. (1946). *Chicken little count to ten*. New York: Harcourt, Brace. Ages 3–8; **8, 12**.

Frith, M. (1973). *I'll teach my dog 100 words*. New York: Random House. Ages 3–6; **8**.

Gag, W. (1928, 1956, 1977). *Millions of cats*. New York: Coward-McCann. Ages 3–5; **8**.

Gretz, S. (1969). *Teddy bears 1 to 10*. Chicago: Follett. Ages 3–6; **8**.

Grossman, V. (1991). *Ten little rabbits*. San Francisco: Chronicle Books. Ages 3–6; **8**.

Hamm, D. J. (1991). *How many feet in the bed?* New York: Simon and Schuster. Ages 3–6; **8**.

Hoban, T. (1972). *Count and see*. New York: Macmillan. Ages 2–5; **8**.

Howe, C. (1983). *Counting penguins*. New York: Harper. Ages 3–5; **8, 10, 12**.

Hughes, S. (1985). *When we went to the park*. New York: Lothrop. Ages 1–2; **8**.

Hulme, J. N. (1991). *Sea squares*. Waltham, MA: Little, Brown. Ages 4–6; **8**.

Ipcar, D. (1958). *Ten big farms*. New York: Alfred A. Knopf. Ages 3–5; **8**.

Keats, E. J. (1972). *Over in the meadow*. New York: Scholastic. Ages 3–5; **8**.

Kitamura, S. (1986). *When sheep cannot sleep? The counting book*. New York: Farrar, Straus, & Giroux. Ages 2–5; **8**.

Kulas, J. E. (1978). *Puppy's 1 2 3 book*. Racine, WI: Western Publishing Co. Ages 3–5; **8**.

Leedy, L. (1985). *A number of dragons*. New York: Holiday House. Ages 1–3; **8**.

Mack, S. (1974). *Ten bears in my bed: A goodnight countdown*. New York: Pantheon Books. Ages 2–6; **8**.

Maestro, B. (1977). *Harriet goes to the circus: A number concept book*. New York: Crown. Ages 2–6; **8**.

Matthews, L. (1980). *Bunches and bunches of bunnies*. New York: Scholastic. Ages 2–5; **8**.

Mayer, M., & McDermott, G. (1987). *The Brambleberrys animal book of counting*. Honesdale, PA: Boyds Mill Press. Ages 3–6; **8**.

McMillan, C. (1986). *Counting wild flowers*. New York: Lothrop, Lee, & Shepard. Ages 2–7; **8, 10, 12, 15**.

Miller, J. (1983). *The farm counting book*. Englewood Cliffs, NJ: Prentice-Hall. Ages 3–5; **8, 10, 12**.

Moerbeek, K., & Dijs, C. (1988). *Six brave explorers*. Los Angeles: Price Stern Sloan. Ages 4–6; **8**.

Noll, S. (1984). *Off and counting*. New York: Green Willow. Ages 3–5; **8**.

Parish, P. (1974). *Too many rabbits*. New York: Scholastic. Ages 3–6; **8**.

Pavey, P. (1979). *One dragon's dream*. Scarsdale, NY: Bradbury Press. Ages 3–6; **8**.

Petie, H. (1975). *Billions of bugs*. Englewood Cliffs: NJ: Prentice-Hall. Ages 3–7; **8**.

Pomerantz, C. (1984). *One duck, another duck*. New York: Greenwillow. Ages 3–7; **8**.

Presland, J. (1975). *How many*. Restrop Manor, Purton Wilts, England: Child's Play (International) Ltd. Ages 3–7; **8**.

Samton, S. W. (1991). *Moon to sun*. Honesdale, PA: Boyds Mill Press. **8**.

Samton, S. W. (1991). *On the river*. Honesdale, PA: Boyds Mill Press. Ages 4–6; **8**.

Samton, S. W. (1991). *The world from my window*. Honesdale, PA: Boyds Mill Press. **8**.

Scarry, R. (1975). *Best counting book ever*. New York: Random House. Ages 2–8; **8, 10**.

Schwartz, D. M. (1985). *How much is a million?* New York: Lothrop. Ages 5–9; **8**.

Seuss, Dr. (1938). *The 500 bats of Bartholomew Cubbins*. Eau Claire, WI: Hale and Co. Ages 3–7; **8**.

Seuss, Dr. (1960). *One fish, two fish, red fish, blue fish*. New York: Random House. Ages 3–7; **8, 10**.

Sheppard, J. (1990). *The right number of elephants*. New York: Harper Collins. Ages 4–6; **8**.

Sitomer, M., & Sitomer, H. (1976). *How did numbers begin?* New York: Harper and Row. Ages 4–6; **8**.

Slobodkin, L. (1955). *Millions and millions*. New York: Vanguard. Ages 3–5; **8**.

Steiner, C. (1960). *Ten in a family*. New York: Alfred A. Knopf. Ages 3–5; **8**.

Stoddart, G., & Baker, M. (1982). *One, two number zoo*. London: Hodder & Stoughton. Ages 5–7; **8, 10, 15, 16**.

Sussman, S. (1982). *Hippo thunder*. Niles, IL: Whelman. Ages 2–5; **8, 10, 12**.

Tafuri, N. (1986). *Who's counting?* New York: Greenwillow. Ages 2–5; **8**.

Thompson, S. L. (1980). *One more thing, Dad*. Chicago: Whitman. Ages 3–6; **8**.

Thornhill, J. (1989). *The wildlife 1-2-3: A nature counting book*. New York: Simon & Schuster. Ages 3–6; **8**.

Ungerer, T. (1962). *The three robbers*. New York: Antheum. Ages 3–5; **8**.

Wildsmith, B. (1965). *Brian Wildsmith's 1, 2, 3's*. New York: Franklin Watts. Ages 3–5; **8**.

Zolotow, C. (1955). *One step, two step*. New York: Lothrop, Lee, & Shepard. Ages 2–5; **8**.

Classification

Gordon, M. (1986). *Colors*. Morristown, NJ: Silver-Burdett. Ages 2–6; **8**.

Hill, E. (1982). *What does what?* Los Angeles: Price/Stern/Sloan. Ages 2–4; **8**.

Hoban, T. (1978). *Is it red? Is it yellow? Is it blue?* New York: Greenwillow. Ages 2–5; **8**.

Hughes, S. (1986). *Colors*. New York: Lothrop. Ages 2–4; **8**.

Johnson, J. (1985). *Firefighters A–Z*. New York: Walker. Ages 5–8; **8, 11**.

Wandro, M., & Blank, J. (1981). *My daddy is a nurse*. Reading, MA: Addison-Wesley. Ages 5–8; **8, 11**.

Wildsmith B. (1967). *Brian Wildsmith's wild animals*. New York: Franklin Watts. Ages 3–8; **8, 10, 12, 15**.

Wildsmith, B. (1968). *Brian Wildsmith's fishes*. New York: Franklin Watts. Ages 3–8; **8, 10, 12, 15**.

Winthrop, E. (1986). *Shoes*. New York: Harper & Row. Ages 3–7; **8, 11**.

Comparing

Bourgeois, P., & Clark, B. (1987). *Big Sarah's little boots*. New York: Scholastic. Ages 3–5; **8**.

Brenner, B. (1966). *Mr. Tall and Mr. Small*. Menlo Park, CA: Addison-Wesley. Ages 4–7; **8, 10, 12, 15**.

Broger, A., & Kalow, G. (1977). *Good morning whale*. New York: Macmillan. Ages 3–6; **8, 10, 12, 15**.

Carle, E. (1977). *The grouchy ladybug*. New York: Crowell. Ages 3–5; **8, 10, 12**.

Eastman, P. D. (1973). *Big dog, little dog*. New York: Random House. Ages 3–4; **8, 10, 12**.

Gordon, M. (1986). *Opposites*. Morristown, NJ: Silver-Burdett. Ages 3–5; **8**.

Graham, A., & Wood, W. (1991). *Angus thought he was big*. Hicksville, NY: Macmillan Whole-Language Big Book Program. Ages 3–5; **8**.

Grender, I. (1975). *Playing with shapes and sizes*. New York: Knopf/Pinwheel Books. Ages 3–6; **8**.

Heide, F. P. (1970). *Benjamin Budge and Barnaby Ball*. New York: Scholastic. Ages 3–5; **8**.

Hoban, T. (1972). *Push pull, empty full*. New York: Macmillan. Ages 3–5; **8**.

Horn, A. (1974). *You can be taller*. Boston: Little, Brown. Ages 3–5; **8**.

Hughes, S. (1985). *Bathwater's hot*. New York: Lothrop. Ages 1–2; **8, 10, 12**.

Hughes, S. (1985). *Noises*. New York: Lothrop. Ages 1–2; **8, 10, 12**.

Lewis, J. (1963). *The tortoise and the hare*. Chicago, IL: Whitman. Ages 4–8; **8, 10**.

Lionni, L. (1968). *The biggest house in the world*. New York: Pantheon. Ages 2–6; **8, 10, 12**.

McMillan, B. (1986). *Becca backward, Becca forward*. New York: Lothrop. Ages 3–6; **8**.

Miller, N. (1990). *Emmett's snowball*. New York: Henry Holt. K–3 and above; **8, 10, 12**.

Presland, J. (1975). *Same and different*. Purton Wilts, England: Child's Play (International), Ltd. Ages 4–7; **8**.

Scarry, R. (1976). *Short and tall*. New York: Golden Press. Ages 2–7; **8**.

Scarry, R. (1986). *Big and little: A book of opposites*. Racine, WI: Western. Ages 3–7; **8**.

Shapiro, L. (1978). *Pop-up opposites*. Los Angeles. Price/Stern/Sloan. Ages 3–5; **8**.

Shape

Anno, M. (1991). *Anno's math games III*. New York: Philomel. K–6; **8, 12**.

Budney, B. (1954). *A kiss is round*. New York: Lothrop, Lee, & Shepard. Ages 2–6; **8**.

Carle, E. (1974). *My very first book of shapes*. New York: Crowell. Ages 3–6; **8**.

Ehlert, L. (1990). *Color farm*. New York: Harper-Collins Children's Books. **8, 11, 12**.

Emberley, E. (1961). *A wing on a flea: A book about shapes*. Boston: Little, Brown. Ages 5–8; **8**.

Emberley, E. (1970). *Ed Emberley's drawing book of animals*. Boston: Little, Brown. Ages 6–8; **8**.

Emberley, E. (1972). *Ed Emberley's drawing book: Make a world*. Boston: Little, Brown. Ages 6–8; **8**.

Gordon, M. (1986). *Shapes*. Morristown, NJ: Silver-Burdett. Ages 3–5; **8**.

Hefter, R. (1976). *The strawberry book of shapes*. New York: Weekly Reader Books. Ages 3–7; **8**.

Hoban, T. (1974). *Circles, triangles, and squares*. New York: Macmillan. Ages 5–8.

Hoban, T. (1983). *Round and round and round*. New York: Greenwillow. Ages 3–6; **8**.

Hoban, T. (1986). *Shapes, shapes, shapes*. New York: Greenwillow. Ages 3–7; **8**.

Kessler, E., & Kessler, L. (1966). *Are you square?* Garden City, NY: Doubleday. Ages 5–7; **8**.

Schlein, M. (1952). *Shapes*. Glenview, IL: Scott, Foresman. Ages 2–6; **8**.

Shapes: Circle/Square/Triangle (3 books). (1992). New York: Books for Young Readers. Ages 3–6; **8**.

Sullivan, J. (1963). *Round is a pancake*. New York: Holt, Rinehart, and Winston. Ages 3–5; **8**.

Supraner, R. (1975). *Draw me a square, draw me a triangle, & draw me a circle*. New York: Simon and Schuster/Nutmeg. Ages 3–6; **8**.

Space

Barton, B. (1981). *Building a house*. New York: Greenwillow. Ages 4–7; **8, 10**.

Berenstain, S., & Berenstain, J. (1968). *Inside, outside, upside down*. New York: Random House. Ages 3–7; **8**.

Brown, M. (1949). *Two little trains*. New York: Scott, Foresman. Ages 2–4; **8**.

Carle, E. (1972). *The secret birthday message*. New York: Crowell. Ages 3–7; **8**.

Dunrea, O. (1985). *Fergus and the bridey*. New York: Holiday. Ages 4–7; **8**.

Hill, E. (1980). *Where's Spot?* New York: Putnam's Sons. Ages 2–4; **8**.

Lionni, L. (1983). *Where?* New York: Pantheon. Ages 2–3; **8**.

Maestro, B., & Maestro, G. (1976). *Where is my friend?* New York: Crown. Ages 2–4; **8**.

Martin, B., Jr. (1971). *Going up, going down*. New York: Holt, Rinehart, & Winston. Ages 6–8; **8**.

Russo, M. (1986). *The line up book*. New York: Greenwillow. Ages 3–5; **8**.

Weimer, T. E. (1993). *Space songs for children*. Pittsburgh, PA: Pearce-Evetts. Ages 5–7; **8**.

Parts and Wholes

Dubov, C. S. (1986). *Alexsandra, where are your toes?* New York: St. Martin's Press. Ages 1 1/2–3; **8, 10, 12**.

Dubov, C. S. (1986). *Alexsandra, where is your nose?* New York: St. Martin's Press. Ages 1 1/2–3; **8, 10, 12**.

Le Tord, B. (1985). *Good wood bear*. New York: Bradbury. Ages 4–7; **8**.

Mathews, L. (1979). *Gator pie*. New York: Scholastic. Ages 4–7; **8, 12**

Language

Bemelmans, L. (1969). *Madeline*. New York: Viking. Ages 4–7.

Duvoisin, R. (1974). *Petunia takes a trip*. New York: Knopf/Pinwheel. Ages 4–7.

Hoff, S. (1959). *Julius*. New York: Harper & Row. Ages 4–7.

Shelby, A. (1990). *We keep a store*. New York: Orchard Books. All ages. **8, 11**.

APPLICATION OF FUNDAMENTAL CONCEPTS

Ordering and Patterning

Asbjörsen, P. C., & Moe, J. E. (1957). *The Three Billy Goats Gruff*. New York: Harcourt, Brace, Jovanovich. Ages 2–5; **10**.

Bishop, C. H., & Wiese, K. (1938). *The five Chinese brothers*. New York: Coward, McCann, & Geoghegan. Ages 5–8; **10**.

Brett, J. (1987). *Goldilocks and the three bears*. New York: Dodd, Mead. Ages 3–5; **10**.

Clements, A. (1992). *Mother Earth's counting book*. New York: Simon & Schuster. Ages 5 and up; **10, 12**.

Hoban, T. (1992). *Look up, look down*. New York: Greenwillow. Ages 5–8; **10, 12**.

Ipcar, C. (1972). *The biggest fish in the sea*. New York: Viking. Ages 3–6; **10, 12, 14**.

Macauly, D. (1987). *Why the chicken crossed the road*. Boston: Houghton-Mifflin. Ages 4–8; **10**.

Maestro, B., & Maestro, G. (1977). *Harriet goes to the circus*. New York: Crown. Ages 5–8; **10, 12, 14**.

Mahy, M. (1987). *17 kings and 42 elephants*. New York: Dial. Ages 2–6; **8, 10, 12, 14**.

Martin, B., Jr. (1963). *One, two, three, four*. New York: Holt, Rinehart, and Winston. Ages 5–7; **8, 10**.

Martin, B., Jr. (1970). *Monday, Monday, I like Monday*. New York: Holt, Rinehart, and Winston. Ages 5–8; **10, 12**.

Measurement: Volume, Weight, and Length

Allen, P. (1983). *Who sank the boat?* New York: Coward. Ages 3–5; **10**.

Anderson, L. C. (1983). *The wonderful shrinking shirt*. Niles, IL: Whitman. Ages 3–5; **10**.

Bennett, V. (1975). *My measure it book*. New York: Grosset & Dunlap. Ages 3–5; **10**.

Charles, D. (1977). *Fat, fat calico cat*. Chicago: Children's Press. Ages 3–6; **10, 17**.

Grender, I. (1975). *Measuring things*. New York: Knopf/Pantheon Pinwheel. Ages 4–6; **10**.

Linn, C. (1970). *Estimation*. New York: Crowell. Ages 8–9; **10, 13**.

Lionni, L. (1960). *Inch by inch*. New York: Astor-Honor. Ages 3–5; **10, 12**.

McMillan, B. (1987). *Step by step*. New York: Lothrop. Ages 3–6; **10**.

Myller, R. (1972). *How big is a foot?* New York: Atheneum. Ages 6–8; **10**.

Parkinson, K. (1986). *The enormous turnip*. Niles, IL: Whitman. Ages 4–7; **10, 14**.

Russo, M. (1986). *The lineup book*. New York: Greenwillow. Ages 2–4; **10, 12**.

Schlein, M. (1954). *Heavy is a hippopotamus*. New York: Scott. Ages 3–6; **10, 12**.

Scrivastava, J. J. (1980). *Spaces, shapes, and sizes*. New York: Crowell. Ages 5–8; **10, 12**.

Shapp, M., & Shapp, C. (1975). *Let's find out about what's light and what's heavy*. New York: Franklin Watts. Ages 6–8; **10**.

Väes, A. (1985). *The wild hamster*. Boston: Little, Brown. Ages 5–8; **10, 12, 14**.

Ward, L. (1952). *The biggest bear*. Boston: Houghton-Mifflin. Ages 3–5; **10**.

Zion, G. (1959). *The plant sitter*. New York: Harper & Row. Ages 3–6; **10**.

Measurement: Time

Aiken, C. (1966). *Tom, Sue, and the clock*. New York: Collier Books. Ages 5–8; **10**.

Bancroft, H., & Van Gelde, R. G. (1963). *Animals in winter*. New York: Scholastic. Ages 3–6; **10**.

Barrett, J. (1976). *Benjamin's 365 birthdays*. New York: Atheneum. Ages 3–6; **10**.

Berenstain, S., & Berenstain, J. (1973). *The bear's almanac*. New York: Random House. Ages 3–6; **10**.

Bonne, R. (1961). *I know an old lady*. New York: Scholastic. Ages 3–5; **10**.

Brenner, B. (1984). *The snow parade*. New York: Crown. Ages 4–7; **10**.

Brown, M. W. (1947). *Goodnight moon*. New York: Harper & Row. Ages 3–6; **10**.

Brown, M. (1984). *Arthur's Christmas*. Boston: Little, Brown. Ages 6–8; **10**.

Brown, M. W. (1950). *A child's goodnight book*. New York: W. R. Scott. Ages 3–6; **10**.

Carle, E. (1977). *The very hungry caterpillar*. New York: Collins & World. Ages 3–5; **10, 12**.

Castle, C. (1985). *The hare and the tortoise*. New York: Dial. Ages 5–8; **10**.

Chalmers, M. (1988). *Easter parade*. New York: Harper. Ages 3–6; **10**.

DeArmand, F. U. (1963). *A very, very special day*. New York: Parents Magazine Press. Ages 3–6; **10**.

DePaola, T. (1986). *Merry Christmas, Strega Nona*. San Diego, CA: Harcourt, Brace. Ages 3–6; **10**.

Duvoisin, R. (1956). *The house of four seasons*. New York: Lothrop, Lee, & Shepard. Ages 3–6; **10**.

Flournoy, V. (1978). *The best time of day*. New York: Random House. Ages 3–5; **10**.

Flournoy, V. (1985). *Patchwork quilt*. New York: Dial. Ages 4–8; **10**.

Gibbons, G. (1983). *Thanksgiving day*. New York: Holiday House. Ages 4–8; **10**.

Hall, B. (1973). *What ever happens to baby animals?* New York: Golden Press. Ages 2–5; **10**.

Hauge, C., & Hauge, M. (1974). *Gingerbread man*. New York: Golden Press. Ages 2–5; **10**.

Hayes, S. (1986). *Happy Christmas Gemma*. New York: Lothrop. Ages 2–5; **10**.

Hooper, M. (1985). *Seven eggs*. New York: Harper & Row. Ages 3–5; **8, 10**.

Kelleritti, H. (1985). *Henry's Fourth of July*. New York: Greenwillow. Ages 3–6; **10**.

Krementz, J. (1986). *Zachary goes to the zoo*. New York: Random House. Ages 2–8; **10, 12, 14**.

Kraus, R. (1972). *Milton the early riser*. New York: Prentice-Hall. Ages 2–5; **10**.

Leslie, S. (1977). *Seasons*. New York: Platt & Munk. Ages 2–5; **10**.

Lester, A. (1986). *Clive eats alligators*. Boston: Houghton-Mifflin. Ages 3–6; **10, 12**.

McCully, E. A. (1985). *First snow*. New York: Warner. Ages 3–5; **10, 12**.

Miles, B. (1973). *A day of autumn*. New York: Random House. Ages 3–5; **10**.

Ormerodi, J. (1981). *Sunshine*. New York: Lothrop, Lee, & Shepard. Ages 2–6; **10**.

Pearson, S. (1988). *My favorite time of year*. New York: Harper & Row. Ages 3–7; **10, 15**.

Porter Productions. (1975). *My tell time book*. New York: Grosset & Dunlap. Ages 5–7; **10**.

Prelutsky, J. (1984). *It's snowing! It's snowing!* New York: Greenwillow. Ages 4–7; **10, 12, 17**.

Provensen, A., & Provensen, M. (1976). *A book of seasons*. New York: Random House. Ages 3–5; **10**.

Robison, A. (1973). *Pamela Jane's week*. Racine, WI: Whitman Books, Western Publishing. Ages 2–5; **10**.

Rockwell, A. (1985). *First comes spring*. New York: Crowell. Ages 2–6; **10, 12, 14**.

Rutland, J. (1976). *Time*. New York: Grosset & Dunlap. Ages 2–7; **10**.

Scarry, R. (1976). *All day long*. New York: Golden Press. Ages 3–6; **10**.

Schlein, M. (1955). *It's about time*. New York: Young Scott. Ages 3–7; **10**.

Schwerin, D. (1984). *The tomorrow book*. New York: Pantheon. Ages 3–6; **10**.

Stein, S. B. (1985). *Mouse*. San Diego, CA: Harcourt, Brace, Jovanovich. Ages 4–8; **10, 12, 15**.

Todd, K. (1982). *Snow*. Reading, MA: Addison-Wesley. Ages 3–8; **10, 12, 17**.

Tudor, T. (1957). *Around the year*. New York: Henry Z. Walck. Ages 3–5; **10**.

Tudor, T. (1977). *A time to keep: The Tasha Tudor book of holidays*. New York: Rand McNally. Ages 3–6; **10**.

Vincent, G. (1984). *Merry Christmas, Ernest & Celestine*. New York: Greenwillow. Ages 4–8; **10**.

Wolff, A. (1984). *A year of birds*. New York: Dodd, Mead. Ages 3–6; **10, 12**.

Zolotow, C. (1984). *I know an old lady*. New York: Greenwillow. Ages 4–8; **10, 12**.

Practical Activities/Integration

Cohn, J. M., & Elliott, D. L. (1992). *Recycling for math*. Berkeley, CA: Educational Materials Associates. For teachers of kindergarten and up; **11**.

Shelby, A. (1990). *We keep a store*. New York: Orchard Books. All ages. **8, 11**.

Money

Asch, F. (1976). *Good lemonade*. Ontario, Canada: Nelson, Foster, & Scott. Ages 6–8;

Brenner, B. (1963). *The five pennies*. New York: Random House. Ages 6–7; **11**.

Credle, E. (1969). *Little pest Pico*. Ontario, Canada: Nelson, Foster, & Scott. Ages 6–8;

Hoban, L. (1981). *Arthur's funny money*. New York: Harper & Row. Ages 4–7; **11**.

Kirn, A. (1969). *Two pesos for Catalina*. New York: Scholastic. Ages 6–8; **11**.

Martin, B., Jr. (1963). *Ten pennies for candy*. New York: Holt, Rinehart, and Winston. Ages 5–7; **11**.

Rockwell, A. (1984). *Our garage sale*. New York: Greenwillow. Ages 3–5; **11**.

Food (see also Unit 11)

Brown, M. (1947). *Stone soup*. New York: Charles Scribner's. Ages 3–5; **11, 17**.

Carle, E. (1970). *Pancakes, pancakes*. New York: Knopf. Ages 3–5; **11**.

Ehlert, L. (1987). *Growing vegetable soup*. San Diego, CA: Harcourt Brace Jovanovich. Ages 3–6; **11, 17**.

Hoban, R. (1964). *Bread and jam for Frances*. New York: Scholastic. Ages 3–7; **11, 17**.

McCloskey, R. (1948). *Blueberries for Sal*. New York: Viking. Ages 3–6; **11, 17**.

Norquist, S. (1985). *Pancake pie*. New York: Morrow. Ages 4–8; **11, 17**.

Sendak, M. (1962). *Chicken soup with rice*. New York: Harper & Row. Ages 3–5; **11, 17**.

Sendak, M. (1970). *In the night kitchen*. New York: Harper & Row. Ages 4–6; **11, 17**.

Seymour, P. (1981). *Food*. Los Angeles: Intervisual Communications. Ages 2–5; **11**.

Thayer, J. (1961). *The blueberry pie elf*. Edinburgh, Scotland: Oliver & Boyd. Ages 4–7; **11, 17**.

Cookbooks (see also Unit 11)
Can be adapted to all ages

Ault, R. (1974). *Kids are natural cooks*. Boston: Houghton-Mifflin. **11, 18**.

Better Homes and Gardens new junior cookbook. (1979). Des Moines, IA: Meredith. **11, 17**.

Blanchet, F., & Kaup, D. (1979). *What to do with an egg*. Woodbury, NY: Barrons Educational Series, Inc. **11, 17**.

Cooking is fun. (1970). New York: Dell. **11, 17**.

Kementz, J. (1985). *The fun of cooking*. New York: Knopf. **11, 17**.

Sesame Street cookbook. (1978). New York: Platt & Munk, **11, 17**.

Walt Disney's Mickey Mouse cookbook. (1975). New York: Golden Press. **11, 17**.

Williamson, S., & Williamson, Z. (1992). *Kids' cook! Fabulous food for the whole family*. Charlotte, VT: Williamson Publishing Co. **11, 17**.

SYMBOLS AND HIGHER-LEVEL ACTIVITIES

Sets and Symbols

Alain (Bruslein, A). (1964). *One, two, three going to sea*. New York: Scholastic. Ages 5–7; **12**.

Anno, M. (1977). *Anno's counting book*. New York: Crowell. Ages 5–7; **12**.

Balet, J. B. (1959). *The five Rollatinis*. Philadelphia: Lippincott. Ages 4–7; **12**.

Brown, M. (1976). *One, two, three an animal counting book*. New York: Atlantic Monthly Press. Ages 5–7; **12, 14**.

The count's number parade. (1973); *The count's poem*. (1978). Racine, WI: Western Publishing. Ages 3–6; **12**.

Daly, E. (1974). *1 is red*. Racine WI: Western Publishing. Ages 4–7; **12**.

Duvoisin, R. (1955). *Two lonely ducks*. New York: Knopf. Ages 4–7; **10, 12, 14**.

Duvoisin, R. (1955). *1000 Christmas beards*. New York: Knopf. Ages 3–7; **12**.

Federico, H. (1963). *The golden happy book of numbers*. New York: Golden Press. Ages 3–7; **12**.

Francoise (Seignobosc, F.) (1951). *Jean-Marie counts her sheep*. New York: Charles Scribner's Sons. Ages 3–6; **12**.

Friskey, M. (1940). *Seven diving ducks*. New York: McKay. Ages 4–6; **12**.

Garne, S. T. (1992). *One white sail*. New York: Green Tiger Press. Ages 5–8; **12**.

Hoban, T. (1987). *Letters & 99 cents*. New York: Greenwillow. Ages 4–8; **12**.

Keats, E. J. (1971). *Over in the meadow*. New York: Scholastic. Ages 3–5; **12**.

Kherdian, D., & Hogrogian, N. (1990). *The cat's midsummer jamboree*. New York: Philomel. Ages 5–8; **12**.

LeSeig, T. (1974). *Whacky Wednesday*. New York: Random House. Ages 5–8; **12**.

McNutt, D. (1979). *There was an old lady who lived in a 1*. Palo Alto, CA: Creative Publications. Ages 4–6; **8, 12**.

Numbers: Match-up flip book. (1984). St Paul, MN: Trend. Ages 4–8; **12**.

Thaler, M. (1991). *Seven little hippos*. Old Tappan, NJ: Simon & Schuster. Ages 5–8; **12**.

CONCEPTS AND ACTIVITIES FOR THE PRIMARY GRADES

As already noted, many of the books listed are appropriate for preprimary and primary children. Many books that are read-along books for the younger children become books for individual reading for older children. A few additional titles are included here.

Abisch, R. (1968). *Do you know what time it is?* Englewood Cliffs, N.J.: Prentice-Hall. Ages 6–8.

Allen, J. (1975). *Mary Alice, Operator No. 9*. New York: Scholastic. Ages 6–8.

Anderson, L. (1971). *Two hundred rabbits*. New York: Penguin Books. Ages 7–9.

Belov, R. (1971). *Money, money, money*. New York: Scholastic. Ages 6–8.

Dennis, J. R. (1971). *Fractions are parts of things*. New York: Crowell. Ages 7–8.

Friskey, M. (1963). *Mystery of the farmer's three fives*. Chicago: Children's Press. Ages 6–8.

Hawkins, C. (1984). *Take away monsters*. New York: Putnam's Sons. Ages 3–5.

Martin, B., Jr. (1964). *Delight in number*. New York: Holt, Rinehart, & Winston. Ages 6–8.

_____. 1963. *Five is five*. New York: Holt, Rinehart, & Winston. Ages 6–8.

_____. 1964. *Four threes are twelve*. New York: Holt, Rinehart, & Winston. Ages 6–8.

_____. 1964. *If you can count to ten*. New York: Holt, Rinehart, & Winston. Ages 6–8.

_____. 1971. *Number patterns make sense*. New York: Holt, Rinehart, & Winston. Ages 8–9.

Schertle, A. (1987). *Jeremy Bean's St. Patrick's Day*. New York: Morrow. Ages 5–8.

Schleim, M. (1972). *Moon months and sun days*. Reading MA: Young Scott. Ages 6–8.

BOOKS THAT SUPPORT SCIENCE INVESTIGATIONS

Life Science

Animals

Arnold, C. (1987). *Kangaroo/Koala*. New York: Morrow. Ages 7–10; **14**.

Arnosky, J. (1986). *Deer at the brook*. New York: Lothrop. Ages 1–6; **10, 12, 14**.

Arnosky, J. (1987). *Raccoons and ripe corn*. New York: Lothrop. Ages 3–6; **10, 12, 14**.

Banks, M. (1990). *Animals of the night*. New York: Scribner. Ages 4–6; **10, 12, 14**.

Berger, M. (1983). *Why I cough, sneeze, shiver, hiccup, and yawn*. New York: Crowell. Ages 5–8; **10, 12, 14**.

Bond, F. (1987). *Wake up, Vladimir*. New York: Harper & Row. Ages 3–5; **10, 12**.

Cole, J. (1984). *How you were born*. New York: Morrow. Ages 4–8; **10, 12, 14**.

Cole, S. (1985). *When the tide is low*. New York: Lothrop. Ages 3–9; **10, 12, 14**.

Cowcher, H. (1991). *Tigress*. New York: Garrar. Ages 4–8; **10, 12, 14**.

Crow, S. L. (1985). *Penguins and polar bears*. Washington, DC: National Geographic. All ages; **10, 12, 14**.

Ehlert, L. (1990). *Feathers for lunch*. San Diego, CA: Harcourt Brace and Company. Ages 4–7; **8, 10, 12, 14**.

Fischer-Nagel, H., & Fischer-Nagel, A. (1986). *Inside the burrow: The life of the golden hamster*. Minneapolis, MN: Carolrhoda. Ages 7–10; **14**.

Flack, M. (1930). *Angus and the ducks*. New York: Doubleday. Ages 3–6; **10, 12, 14**.

Flack, M. (1933). *The story about Ping*. New York: Viking. [(1977). Penguin]. Ages 4–6; **10, 12, 14**.

Flack, M. (1937). *The restless robin*. New York: Houghton Mifflin. Ages 4–6; **10, 12, 14**.

Fleming, D. (1993). *In the small, small pond*. New York: Henry Holt. Ages 4–8; **10, 12, 14**.

Fowler, A. (1992). *It's best to leave a snake alone*. Chicago: Children's Press. **10, 12, 14**.

Freeman, D. (1968). *Corduroy*. New York: Viking. [(1976). Penguin]. Ages 3–6; **10, 12, 14**.

George, L. (1987). *William and Boomer*. New York: Greenwillow. Ages 3–7; **10, 12, 14**.

Gill, P. (1990). *Birds*. New York: Eagle Books. Ages 4–8; **10, 12, 14**.

Girard, L. W. (1983). *You were born on your very first birthday*. Niles, IL: Whitman. Ages 3–8; **10, 12, 14**.

Hirschi, R. (1991). *Loon lake*. New York: Cobblehill. Ages 4–8; **10, 12, 14**.

Hoban, T. (1985). *A children's zoo*. New York: Greenwillow. Ages 3–6; **10, 12**.

James, S. (1991). *Dear Mr. Blueberry*. New York: McElderry. Ages 3–8; **8, 10, 12, 14, 16**.

Johnson, S. A. (1982). *Inside an egg*. Minneapolis, MN: Lerner Publications. **10, 12, 14**.

Johnston, G., & Cutchins, J. (1991). *Slippery babies: Young frogs, toads, and salamanders*. New York: Morrow. Ages 5–8; **10, 12, 14**.

King, T. (1983). *The moving animal book*. New York: Putnam. Ages 3–5; **10, 12**.

Koelling, C. (1978). *Whose house is this?* Los Angeles: Price/Stern/Sloan. Ages 3–5; **10, 12**.

Kramer, S. P. (1986). *Getting oxygen: What to do if you're cell 22*. New York: Crowell. Ages 4–8; **10, 12, 14, 17**.

Krementz, J. (1986). *Holly's farm animals*. New York: Random House. Ages 3–8; **10, 12, 14**.

Lionni, L. (1963). *Swimmy*. New York: Pantheon. Ages 3–6; **10, 12, 14**.

McCloskey, R. (1941). *Make way for ducklings*. New York: Viking. [(1976). Penguin]. Ages 4–6; **10, 12, 14**.

McFarland, C. (1990). *Cows in the parlor: A visit to a dairy farm*. New York: Atheneum. Ages 5–8; **10, 12, 14**.

McGrath, S. (1985). *Your world of pets*. Washington, DC: National Geographic Society. Ages 5–10; **14**.

Mellonie, B., & Ingpen, R. (1983). *Lifetimes*. New York: Bantam Books. Ages 4–6; **10, 12**.

National Geographic Society (Ed.). (1985). *Books for young explorers—Set XII*. Washington, DC: Editor. Ages 3–8; **10, 12, 14**.

Nicholson, D. (1987). *Wild boars*. Minneapolis, MN: Carolrhoda. Ages 6–10; **14**.

Nockels, D. (1981). *Animal acrobats*. New York: Dial. Ages 4–6; **10, 12, 14**.

Oppenheim, J. (1986). *Have you seen birds?* New York: Scholastic. Ages 4–7; **10, 12, 14, 20**.

Paladino, C. (1991). *Pomona: The birth of a penguin*. New York: Watts. Ages 5–8; **10, 12, 14**.

Patent, D. H. (1987). *All about whales*. New York: Holiday House. Ages 6–9; **14**.

Potter, B. (1902). *The tale of Peter Rabbit*. New York: Warne. Ages 4–6; **10, 12, 14**.

Powzyk, J. (1985). *Wallaby Creek*. New York: Lothrop. Ages 6–9; **14**.

Rankin, C. (1985). *How life begins: A look at birth and care in the animal world*. New York: Putnam. Ages 7–11; **14**.

Roy, R. (1982). *What has ten legs and eats cornflakes? A pet book*. New York: Clarion/Houghton. Ages 5–8; **14**.

Savage, S. (1992). *Making tracks*. New York: Lodestar. Ages 4–8; **10, 12, 14**.

Seymour, P. (1985). *Animals in disguise*. New York: Macmillan. Ages 4–6; **10, 12, 14**.

Sheldon, D. (1991). *The whales' song*. New York: Dial. Ages 4–8; **10, 12, 14**.

Stanley, C. (1991). *Busy, busy squirrels*. New York: Cobblehill. Ages 4–8; **10, 12, 14**.

Sussman, S., & Sussman, R. J. (1987). *Lies (people believe) about animals*. Niles, IL: Whitman. Ages 7–12; **14**.

Tarrant, G. (1983). *Frogs*. New York: Putnam. Ages 4–6; **10, 12, 14**.

Watson, J. W. (1958). *Birds*. New York: Golden Press. Ages 3–5; **10, 12**.

Weller, F. (1991). *I wonder if I'll see a whale*. New York: Philomel. Ages 4–8; **10, 12, 14**.

Wildsmith, B. (1983). *The owl and the woodpecker*. New York: Oxford University Press. Ages 4–7; **10, 12, 14, 20**.

Yamashita, K. (1993). *Paws, wings, and hooves*. Minneapolis, MN: Lerner. Ages 6–8; **12, 14**.

Bugs, Spiders, and Bees

Berenstain, S., & Berenstain, J. (1962). *The big honey hunt*. New York: Random House. Ages 3–8; **10, 12, 14**.

Carle, E. (1969). *The very hungry caterpillar*. New York: Philomel. Ages 3–6; **10, 12, 14**.

Carle, E. (1977). *The grouchy ladybug*. New York: Crowell. Ages 3–6; **10, 12, 14**.

Carle, E. (1981). *The honeybee and the robber*. New York: Philomel. Ages 3–6; **10, 12, 14**.

Carle, E. (1984). *The very busy spider*. New York: Philomel. Ages 3–6; **10, 12, 14**.

Clay, P., & Clay, H. (1984). *Ants*. London: A & C Black. **10, 12, 14**.

Dallinger, J. *Spiders*. Minneapolis, MN: Lerner Publications. **10, 12, 14**.

Fischer-Nagel, H., & Fischer-Nagel, A. (1986). *Life of the ladybug*. Minneapolis, MN: Carolrhoda. Ages 7–10; **14**.

Fisher, A. (1986). *When it comes to bugs*. New York: Harper & Row. Ages 4–8; **10, 12, 14**.

Fleming, D. (1991). *In the tall, tall grass*. New York: Henry Holt. Ages 4–8; **10, 12, 13, 14**.

Guiberson, B. (1991). *Cactus hotel*. New York: Holt. Ages 4–8; **10, 12, 14, 16**.

Hooker, Y. (1981). *The little green caterpillar*. New York: Grosset & Dunlap. Ages 3–6; **10, 12, 14**.

Hooker, Y. (1984). *The little red ant*. New York: Grosset & Dunlap. Ages 3–6; **10, 12, 14**.

McNulty, F. (1986). *The lady and the spider*. New York: Harper & Row. Ages 5–8; **14**.

Overbeck, C. (1982). *Ants*. Minneapolis, MN: Lerner. **10, 12, 14, 20**.

Palotta, J. (1992). *The icky bug counting book*. Watertown, MA: Charlesbridge Publishing. Ages 4–8; **8, 10, 12, 13, 14**.

Parker, N. W. (1987). *Bugs*. New York: Greenwillow. Ages 8–10; **14**.

Seymour, P. (1984). *Insects: A close-up look*. New York: Macmillan. Ages 3–6; **10, 12, 14**.

Selsam, M. E., & Goor, R. (1981). *Backyard insects*. New York: Fourwinds. Ages 4–8; **10, 12, 14**.

Tarrant, G. (1983). *Butterflies*. New York: Putnam. Ages 3–6; **10, 12, 14**.

Tarrant, G. (1984). *Honeybees*. New York: Putnam. Ages 3–6; **10, 12, 14**.

Yabuuchi, M. (1983). *Animals sleeping*. New York: Philomel. Ages 5–8; **10, 12, 14**.

Yabuuchi, M. (1985). *Whose footprints*. New York: Philomel. Ages 3–4; **10, 12, 14**.

Plants

Bash, B. (1990). *Desert giant: The world of the saguaro cactus*. Boston: Little, Brown. Ages 5–8. **10, 12, 14, 16**.

Ehlert, L. (1991). *Red leaf, yellow leaf.* San Diego, CA: Harcourt Brace and Company. Ages 4–8. **10, 12, 14, 16**.

Florian, D. (1991). *Vegetable garden.* New York: Harcourt Brace. Ages 3–5; **8, 10, 12, 14, 17**.

Gibbons, G. (1984). *The seasons of Arnold's apple tree.* San Diego, CA: Harcourt Brace. Ages 3–9; **10, 12, 14**.

Gibbons, G. (1991). *From seed to plant.* New York: Holiday House. Ages 5–8; **10, 12, 14**.

Krauss, R. (1945). *The carrot seed.* New York: Harper & Row. Ages 3–5; **10, 12**.

Hindley, J. (1990). *The tree.* New York: Clarkson Potter. Ages 6–12; **12, 14, 16**.

Hirschi, R. (1991). *Fall.* New York: Cobblehill. Ages 4–8; **10, 12, 14, 16**.

Hiscock, B. (1991). *The big tree.* New York: Atheneum. Ages 5–12; **10, 12, 14, 16**.

Lauber, P. (1988). *Seeds: Pop, stick, glide.* New York: Crown. Ages 6–8; **12, 14**.

Mitgutsch, A. (1986). *From wood to paper.* Minneapolis, MN: Carolrhoda. Ages 4–7; **10, 12, 14**.

Oechsli, H., & Oechsli, K. (1985). *In my garden: A child's gardening book.* New York: Macmillan. Ages 5–9; **10, 12, 14**.

Romanova, N. (1985). *Once there was a tree.* New York: Dial. Ages 3–9; **10, 12, 14**.

Schnieper, C. (1987). *An apple tree through the year.* Minneapolis, MN: Carolrhoda. Ages 7–10; **14**.

Schweitzer, I. (1982). *Hilda's restful chair.* New York: Atheneum. Ages 3–6; **10, 12, 14**.

Silverstein, S. (1964). *The giving tree.* New York: Harper & Row. Ages 3–8; **10, 12, 14**.

Watts, B. (1990). *Tomato.* Morristown, NJ: Silver Burdett & Ginn. Ages 5–8. **10, 12, 14**.

Physical Science

Ardley, N. (1991). *The science book of air.* New York: Harcourt Brace and Company. Ages 6–8; **10, 12, 15**.

Ardrizzone, E. (1960). *Johnny the clock maker.* New York: Walck. Ages 3–5; **10, 12**.

Brandt, K. (1985). *Sound.* Mahwah, NJ: Troll Associates. Ages 3–5; **10, 12**.

Brown, R. (1991). *The world that Jack built.* New York: Dutton. Ages 4–6; **10, 12, 15**.

Burton, V. L. (1939). *Mike Mulligan and his steam shovel.* Boston: Houghton Mifflin. Ages 3–5; **10, 12**.

Bushey, J. (1985). *Monster trucks and other giant machines on wheels.* Minneapolis, MN: Carolrhoda. Ages 5–9; **10, 12, 15**.

Cobb, V. (1983). *Gobs of goo.* Philadelphia: Lippincott. Ages 6–8; **15**.

Cole, J. (1983). *Cars and how they go.* New York: Crowell. Ages 7–11; **15**.

Crampton, G. (1986). *Scuffy the tugboat.* New York: Western. Ages 3–5; **10, 12**.

Crews, D. (1981). *Light.* New York: Greenwillow. Ages 3–7; **10, 12, 15**.

Fowler, R. (1986). *Mr. Little's noisy boat.* New York: Grosset & Dunlap. Ages 0–9; **10, 12, 15**.

Gabb, M. (1980). *The question and answer books: Everyday science.* Minneapolis, MN: Lerner. All ages; **10, 12, 15**.

Gibbons, G. (1982). *The tool book.* New York: Holiday House. Ages 3–5; **10, 12**.

Gibbons, G. (1983). *New road!* New York: Crowell. Ages 5–8; **15**.

Hulme, J. (1991). *Sea squares.* New York: Hyperion. Ages 4–8; **10, 12, 14, 15**.

Iveson-Iveson, J. (1986). *Your nose and ears.* New York: The Bookwright Press. Ages 3–6; **10, 12, 15, 18**.

Isadora, R. (1985). *I touch.* New York: Greenwillow Books. Ages 0–2; **10, 18**.

Koningsburg, E. I. (1991). *Samuel Todd's book of great inventions.* New York: Atheneum. Ages 4–7; **10, 12, 15**.

Macaulay, D. (1988). *The way things work.* Boston: Houghton Mifflin. Ages 8–adult; **15**.

McNaught, H. (1978). *The truck book.* New York: Random House. Ages 3–5; **10, 12**.

Murata, Michinori. (1993). *Science is all around you: Water and light.* Minneapolis, MN: Lerner. Ages 6–8; **12, 15, 16**.

Piper, W. (1984). *The little engine that could.* New York: Putnam. Ages 3–5; **10, 12**.

Pluckrose, H. (1986). *Think about hearing.* New York: Franklin Watts. Ages 4–8; **10, 12, 15, 18**.

Robbins, K. (1991). *Bridges.* New York: Dial. Ages 5–12; **10, 12, 15**.

Rockwell, A. (1986). *Things that go.* New York: Dutton. Ages 3–5; **10, 12**.

Scarry, R. (1986). *Splish-Splash sounds.* Racine, WI: Western Publishing, Inc. Ages 3–7; **10, 12, 15**.

Simon, S. (1985). *Soap bubble magic.* New York: Lothrop. Ages 6–9; **15**.

Taylor, K. (1992). *Flying start science series: Water; light; action; structure.* New York: John Wiley & Sons. Ages 3–9; **8, 10, 15, 16**.

Wyler, R. (1986). *Science fun with toy boats and planes.* New York: Julian Messner. Ages 5–9; **15**.

Earth and Space Science

Aliki. (1990). *Fossils tell of long ago.* New York: Harper-Collins. Ages 5–8; **10, 12, 16**.

Arnold, C. (1987). *Trapped in tar: Fossils from the Ice Age.* New York: Clarion. Ages 7–10; **16**.

Barton, B. (1990). *Bones, bones, dinosaur bones.* New York: Harper-Collins. Ages 5–7; **10, 12, 16**.

Bauer, C. F. (1987). *Midnight snowman.* New York: Atheneum. Ages 4–7; **10, 12, 16**.

Brandt, K. (1985). *Air.* Mahwah, NJ: Troll Associates. Ages 3–6; **10, 12, 16**.

Branley, F. M. (1982). *Water for the world.* New York: Crowell. Ages 7–11; **16**.

Branley, F. M. (1983). *Rain and hail.* New York: Crowell. Ages 5–7; **16**.

Branley, F. M. (1985). *Flash, crash, rumble, and roll.* New York: Crowell. Ages 5–7; **16**.

Branley, F. M. (1985). *Volcanoes.* New York: Crowell. Ages 6–8; **16**.

Branley, F. M. (1986). *Air is all around us.* New York: Crowell. Ages 3–6; **10, 12, 16**.

Branley, F. M. (1986). *Journey into a black hole.* New York: Crowell. Ages 8–10; **16**.

Branley, F. M. (1987). *The moon seems to change/The planets in our solar system/Rockets and satellites.* New York: Crowell. Ages 5–8; **16**.

Carrick, C. (1983). *Patrick's dinosaurs.* New York: Clarion. Ages 4–8; **10, 14, 15, 16**.

Caveney, S., & Giesen, R. (1977). *Where am I? rev. ed.* Minneapolis, MN: Lerner Publications. Ages 5–8; **16**.

Cole, J. (1987). *Evolution.* New York: Crowell. Ages 5–8; **14, 16**.

Cole, J. (1987). *The magic school bus inside the earth.* New York: Scholastic. **10, 12, 16**.

Elting, M. (1984). *Dinosaurs and other prehistoric creatures.* New York: Macmillan. Ages 4 and up; **10, 12, 16**.

Gibbons, G. (1987). *Weather forecasting.* New York: Macmillan. Ages 5–8; **10, 12, 16**.

Hoban, T. (1990). *Shadows and reflections.* New York: Greenwillow. Ages 4–8; **12, 16**.

Kandoian, E. (1990). *Under the sun.* New York: Putnam. Ages 4–6; **10, 12, 16**.

Keats, E. J. (1981). *Regards to the man in the moon.* New York: Four Winds. Ages 3–6; **10, 12, 16**.

Knowlton, J. (1985). *Maps and globes.* New York: Harper & Row. Ages 5–8; **16**.

Lewison, W. (1990). *Mud.* New York: Random House. Ages 5–8; **10, 12, 16**.

Livingston, M. (1992). *Light and shadow.* New York: Holiday House. Ages 4–7; **10, 12, 15, 16**.

Lye, K. (1987). *Deserts.* Morristown, NJ: Silver Burdett. Ages 8–14; **16**.

Maki, C. (1993). *Snowflakes, sugar, and salt.* New York: Lerner. Ages 6–8; **10, 12, 15, 16**.

Malnig, A. (1985). *Where the waves break: Life at the edge of the sea.* Minneapolis, MN: Carolrhoda. Ages 7–10; **16**.

Markle, S. (1987). *Digging deeper.* New York: Lothrop. Ages 8–12; **16**.

McMillan, B. (1990). *One sun: A book of terse verse*. New York: Holiday House. Ages 5–8; **10, 12, 16**.

Most, B. (1991). *A dinosaur named after me*. San Diego, CA: Harcourt Brace and Company. Ages 4–8; **10, 12, 16**.

Otto, C. (1992). *That sky, that rain*. New York: Harper. Ages 4–7; **10, 12, 16**.

Parmall, P. (1991). *The rock*. New York: Macmillan. Ages 5–8; **10, 12, 16**.

Ressmeyer, R. (1992). *Astronaut to zodiac*. New York: Crown. Ages 5–12; **12, 16**.

Ride, S., & Oakie, S. (1986). *To space and back*. New York: Lothrop. Ages 8–12; **16**.

Rocks and minerals. (1988). London: Natural History Museum. Ages 7–12; **16**.

Sattle, H. R. (1985). *Pterosaurs: The flying reptiles*. New York: Lathrop. Ages 5–10; **16**.

Schlein, M. (1991). *Discovering dinosaur babies*. New York: Four Winds. Ages 6–9; **12, 16**.

Schmid, E. (1990). *The water's journey*. New York: North-South Books. Ages 6–8; **12, 16**.

Simon, S. (1985). *Jupiter*. New York: Morrow. Ages 5–9; **16**.

Souza, D. (1992). *Powerful waves*. Minneapolis, MN: Carolrhoda. Ages 6–12; **12, 16**.

Szilagyi, M. (1985). *Thunderstorms*. New York: Bradbury. Ages 3–9; **10, 12, 16**.

Wade, H. (1977). *Sand*. Milwaukee: Raintree. Ages 4–8; **10, 12, 16**.

Weimer, T. E. (1993). *Space songs for children*. Pittsburgh, PA: Pearce-Evetts. Ages 5–8; **10, 12**.

Environmental Science: Ecology, Nature, and Conservation

Allen, M. (1991). *Changes*. New York: Macmillan. Ages 4–7; **10, 12, 14, 16**.

Arnosky, A. (1991). *The empty lot*. Boston: Little, Brown. Ages 4–8; **10, 12, 14, 16**.

Bash, B. (1990). *Urban roosts: Where birds nest in the city*. Boston: Little, Brown. Ages 6–12; **12, 14, 16**.

Bruchac, J. (1992). *Native American animal stories*. Golden, CO: Fulcrum Publishing. Ages 5–8; **10, 12, 16**.

Cherry, L. (1990). *The great kapok tree: A tale of the Amazon rain forest*. New York: Gulliver. Ages 6–12; **10, 14, 16**.

George, W. (1991). *Fishing at Long Pond*. New York: Greenwillow. Ages 4–8; **10, 12, 14, 16**.

Greene, C. (1991). *The old ladies who liked cats*. New York: Harper-Collins. Ages 5–8; **10, 12, 14, 16**.

Hines, A. (1991). *Remember the butterflies*. New York: Dutton. Ages 4–7; **8, 10, 12, 14, 16**.

Kuhn, D. (1990). *More than just a vegetable garden*. New York: Silver Press. Ages 6–8; **12, 14, 16, 17**.

Leslie, C. (1991). *Nature all year long*. New York: Greenwillow. Ages 6–8; **12, 14, 16**.

Levine, S., & Grafton, A. (1992). *Projects for a healthy planet*. New York: Wiley. Ages 6–12; **12, 14, 16**.

Locker, T. (1991). *The land of the gray wolf*. New York: Dial. Ages 4–8; **10, 12, 14, 16**.

Norsgaard, E. J. (1990). *Nature's great balancing act: In our own backyard*. New York: Cobblehill. Ages 7–12; **12, 14, 16**.

Parnall, P. (1990). *Woodpile*. New York: Macmillan. Ages 5–8; **10, 12, 14, 16**.

Sackett, E. (1991). *Danger on the African grassland*. Boston: Little, Brown. Ages 5–8; **10, 12, 14, 16**.

Siebert, D. (1991). *Sierra*. New York: Harper-Collins. Ages 5–8; **10, 12, 14, 16**.

Stock, C. (1991). *When the woods hum*. New York: Morrow. Ages 4–8; **8, 10, 14, 16**.

Taylor, K., & Burton, J. (1993). *Forest life*. New York: Dorling Kindersley. Ages 7–12; **14, 15, 16**.

Tresselt, A. (1992). *The gift of the tree*. New York: Lothrop, Lee & Shepard. Ages 5–8; **10, 12, 14, 16**.

Health Science

Aliki. (1990). *My feet*. New York: Harper-Collins. Ages 4–6; **10, 12, 17**.

Bayle, L. (1987). *Picture books for preschool nutrition education: A selected annotated bibliography*. Lexington, MA: Author. **10, 12, 17**.

Brown, M. (1947). *Stone soup*. New York: Charles Scribner's Sons. Ages 3–6; **10, 12, 17**.

Brandenburg, A. (1976). *Corn is maize: The gift of the Indians*. New York: Crowell. Ages 3–5; **10, 11, 12, 17**.

Carle, E. (1970). *Pancakes, pancakes*. New York: Knopf. Ages 3–5; **10, 11, 12, 17**.

Cole, J. (1989). *The magic school bus: Inside the human body*. New York: Scholastic. Ages 6–8; **10, 12, 17**.

Ontario Science Center. (1987). *Foodworks*. Reading, PA: Addison-Wesley. Ages 8–12; **17**.

Pomerantz, C. (1984). *Whiff, whiff, nibble, and chew*. New York: Greenwillow. Ages 4–8; **10, 12, 15**.

Rice, J. (1989). *Those mean nasty downright disgusting but... Invisible germs*. Minneapolis, MN: Toys 'n Things Press. **10, 12, 17**.

Sekido, I. (1993). *Science all around you: Fruits, roots, and fungi*. Minneapolis, MN: Ages 6–8; **10, 14, 16, 17**.

Sendak, M (1962). *Children soup with rice*. New York: Harper & Row. Ages 3–5; **10, 11, 12**.

Sendak, M. (1970). *In the night kitchen*. New York: Harper & Row. Ages 3–5; **10, 12**.

Shaw, D. (1983). *Germs!* New York: Holiday House. Ages 8–12; **17**.

Skeleton. (1988). London: Natural History Museum. Ages 7–12; **17**.

Suhr, M. (1992). *I'm alive series: How I breathe; I am growing; I can move; When I eat*. Minneapolis, MN: Carolrhoda. Ages 4–6; **10, 12, 17**.

CHILDREN'S PERIODICALS THAT EMPHASIZE SCIENCE CONCEPTS

Chickadee: The Canadian Magazine for Children. Young Naturalist Foundation, 56 the Esplanade, Suite 304, Toronto, Ontario, Canada M5E 1A7. Ages 3–9.

Child Life. P.O. Box 10681, Des Moines, IA 50381. Ages 7–9.

Children's Playmate Magazine. Children's Better Health Institute, 1100 Waterway Blvd., P.O. Box 567, Indianapolis, IN 46206. Ages 4–8.

Koala Club News. Zoological Society of San Diego, Inc., P.O. Box 551, San Diego, CA 92212. Ages 6–15.

National Geographic News. P.O. Box 2330, Washington, DC 20009. Ages 5–12.

Ranger Rick's Nature Magazine. National Wildlife Federation, 1412 16th Street, NW, Washington, DC 20036. Ages 5–11.

Scienceland, Inc. 501 5th Avenue, Suite 2102, New York, NY 10017. Ages 3–12.

Science Weekly. P.O. Box 70154, Washington, DC 20088. Ages 4–12.

Scholastic Let's Find Out. Scholastic Magazines, 1290 Wall Street West, Lyndhurst, NJ 07071. Age 5.

Sesame Street. Children's Television Workshop, P.O. Box 2896, Boulder, CO 80322. Ages 3–8.

3 2 1 Contact. P.O. Box 2933, Boulder, CO 80322. Ages 6–14.

Your Big Back Yard. National Wildlife Federation, 1412 16th Street, NW, Washington, DC 20036. Ages 3–5.

SOFTWARE PUBLISHERS USED IN THIS TEXT

Advanced Ideas
2902 San Pablo Avenue
Berkeley, CA 94702

American Guidance Service
Publishers' Building
P.O. Box 99
Circle Pines, MN 55014

Broderbund Software
17 Paul Drive
San Rafael, CA 94903-2101

CBS Software, CBS, Inc.
One Fawcett Place
Greenwich, CT 06836

Counterpoint Software, Inc.
4005 West 65th Street
Minneapolis, MN 55435

Davidson
6069 Grovecreek Place, #12
Rancho Palos Verdes, CA 90274

D.C. Heath and Company
125 Spring Street
Lexington, MA 02173

DLM
1 DLM Park, P.O. Box 5000
Allen, TX 75002

Edu-Ware Services, Inc.
P.O. Box 22222
Agoura, CA 91301

Edutek Corporation
P.O. Box 2560
Palo Alto, CA 94702

Energy Center
Sonoma State University
Rohnert Park, CA 94928

Harper and Row
Keystone Industrial Park
Scranton, PA 18512

Hayden Software Company
600 Suffolk Street
Lowell, MA 01853

Lawrence Hall of Science
University of California
Berkeley, CA 94720

Lawrence Productions
1800 South 36th Street
Galesburg, MI 49053-9687

Learning Company
4370 Alpine Rd.
Portola Valley, CA 94015

Learning Well
200 South Service Road
Roslyn Heights, NY 11577

MECC
3490 Lexington Avenue North
St. Paul, MN 55126

Midwest Software
Box 214
Farmington, MI 48024

Milliken Publishing Company
1100 Research Boulevard
St. Louis, MO 63132-0579

Mindscape, Inc.
3444 Dundee Road
Northbrook, IL 60062

OL-Opportunities for Learning
20417 Nordhoff Street
Department KSP
Chatsworth, CA 91311

Optical Data Corporation
30 Technology Drive
Warren, NJ 07060

Orange Cherry Media Software
7 Delano Drive
Bedford Hills, NY 10507

Panda/Learning Technologies
4255 LBJ Freeway, #131
Dallas, TX 75244

Pelican Software
768 Farmington Avenue
Farmington, CT 06032

Polarware
1055 Paramount Parkway, Suite A
Batavia, IL 60510

Random House
201 East 50th Street
New York, NY 10022

Reader's Digest Software
Microcomputer Software Division
Pleasantville, NY 10570

Scholastic, Inc.
730 Broadway
New York, NY 1003

Scott, Foresman, & Company
1900 East Lake Avenue
Glenview, IL 60025

Sierra On-Line, Inc.
Sierra On-Line Building
Coarsegold, CA 93614

Spinnaker
1 Kendall Square
Cambridge, MA 02139

Springboard Software, Inc.
7807 Creekbridge Circle
Minneapolis, MN 55435

Stone and Associates
7910 Ivanhoe Avenue, STE139
La Jolla, CA 92037

Sunburst Communications
39 Washington Avenue
Pleasantville, NY 10570

Troll Associates
100 Corporate Drive
Mahwah, NJ 07430

Ventura Educational Systems
3440 Brokenhill Street
Newbury Park, CA 91320

Waterford Institute
1480 East 9400 South
Sandy, UT 84092

Weekly Reader Family Software
Xerox Education Publications
Middletown, CT 06457

Wings for Learning
1600 Green Hills Road
P.O. Box 660002
Scotts Valley, CA 95067-0002

APPENDIX C

Code of Practice on Use of Animals in Schools

This code of practice is recommended by the National Science Teachers Association for use throughout the United States by elementary, middle/junior high, and high school teachers and students. It applies to educational projects conducted and lessons taught, involving live organisms in schools or in school-related activities such as science fairs, science clubs, and science competitions.

The purpose of these guidelines is to enrich education by encouraging students to observe living organisms and to learn proper respect for life. The study of living organisms is essential for an understanding of living processes. This study must be coupled with the observance of humane animal care and treatment.

I. CARE AND RESPONSIBILITY FOR ANIMALS IN THE CLASSROOM

A. A teacher must have a clear understanding of and a strong commitment to the responsible care of living animals before making any decision to use live animals for educational study. Preparation for the use of live animals should include acquisition of knowledge on care appropriate to the species being used including housing, food, exercise, and the appropriate placement of the animals at the conclusion of the study.

B. Teachers should try to assure that living animals entering the classroom are healthy and free of transmissible disease or other problems that may endanger human health. Not all species are appropriate. Wild animals are not appropriate because they may carry parasites or serious diseases.

C. Maintaining good health and providing optimal care based on an understanding of the life habits of each species used is of primary importance. Animal quarters shall be spacious, shall avoid overcrowding, and shall be sanitary. Handling shall be gentle. Food shall be appropriate to the animal's normal diet and of sufficient quantity and balance to maintain a good standard of nutrition at all times. No animal shall be allowed less than the optimum maintenance level of nutrition. Clean drinking water shall always be available. Adequate provision for care shall be made at all times including vacation times.

D. All aspects of animal care and treatment shall be supervised by a qualified ADULT WHO IS KNOWLEDGEABLE ABOUT RESEARCH METHODS, BIOLOGY, CARE, AND HUSBANDRY OF THE SPECIES BEING STUDIED.

E. Supervisors and students should be familiar with *literature on care and handling* of living organisms. Practical training in these techniques is encouraged.

F. Adequate plans should be made to *control possible unwanted breedings* of the species during the project period.

G. Appropriate plans should be made for future care of animals at the conclusion of the study.

H. As a general rule, laboratory-bred animals should not be released into the wild as they may disturb the natural ecology of the environment.

I. On rare occasions it may be necessary to sacrifice an animal for educational purposes. This shall be done only in a manner accepted and approved by the American Veterinary Association, by a person experienced in these techniques, and at the discretion of the teacher. It should not be done in the presence of immature or young students who may be upset by witnessing such a procedure. Maximum efforts should be made to study as many biological principles as possible from a single animal.

J. The procurement, care, and use of animals must comply with existing local, state, and federal regulations.

II. EXPERIMENTAL STUDIES OF ANIMALS IN THE CLASSROOM

A. When biological procedures involving living organisms are called for, every effort should be made to use plants or invertebrate animals when possible.

B. No experimental procedure shall be attempted on mammals, birds, reptiles, amphibians, or fish that causes the animal unnecessary pain or discomfort.

C. It is recommended that preserved vertebrate specimens be used for dissections.

D. Students shall not perform dissection surgery on vertebrate animals except under direct supervision of a qualified biomedical scientist or trained adult supervisor.

E. *Experimental procedures* including the use of pathogens, ionizing radiation, toxic chemicals, and chemicals producing birth defects must be under the supervision of a biomedical scientist or an adult trained in the specific techniques. Such procedures should be done in appropriate laboratory facilities that adhere to safety guidelines.

F. *Behavior studies should use only reward* (such as providing food) and not punishment in training programs. When food is used as a reward, it should not be withheld for more than 12 hours.

G. If embryos are subjected to invasive or potentially damaging manipulation, the embryo must be destroyed prior to hatching. If normal embryos are hatched, provisions must be made for their care and maintenance.

III. RESEARCH INVESTIGATIONS INVOLVING VERTEBRATE ANIMALS

The National Science Teachers Association recognizes that an exceptionally talented student may wish to conduct research in the biological or medical sciences and endorses procedures for student research as follows:

A. Protocols of extracurricular projects involving animals should be reviewed in advance of the start of the work by a qualified adult supervisor.

B. Preferably, extracurricular projects should be carried out in an approved area of the school or research facility.

C. The project should be carried out with the utmost regard for the humane care and treatment of the animals involved in the project.

—Adopted by the NSTA Board of Directors in July 1985.

(Reprinted from Hampton, C.H., Hampton, C.D., & Kammer, D.C. (1988) Classroom creature culture. Wahington D.C.: National Science Teachers Association, 1742 Conneticut Avenue, NW, Washington, D.C., 20009)

HOW TO CARE FOR LIVING THINGS

Food and Water	Rabbits	Guinea Pigs	Hamsters	Mice	Rats
Daily					
pellets or grain	rabbit pellets: keep dish half full	corn, wheat, or oats	large dog pellets: one or two canary seeds or oats		
green or leafy vegetables, lettuce, cabbage, and celery tops or	keep dish half full 4–5 leaves	2 leaves	1½ tablespoon 1 leaf	2 teaspoons ⅛–¼ leaf	3–4 teaspoons ¼ leaf
grass, plantain, lambs' quarters, clover, alfalfa or	2 handfuls	1 handful	½ handful	—	—
hay, if water is also given carrots	2 medium	1 medium			
Twice a week					
apple (medium)	½ apple	¼ apple	⅛ apple	½ core and seeds	1 core
iodized salt (if not contained in pellets)	or salt block	sprinkle over lettuce or greens			
corn, canned or fresh, once or twice a week	½ ear	¼ ear	1 tablespoon ⅓ ear	¼ tablespoon or end of ear	½ tablespoo.. or end of ear
water	should always be available		necessary only if lettuce or greens are not provided		

Food and Water	Water Turtles	Land Turtles	Small Turtles		
Daily					
worms or night crawlers or	1 or 2	1 or 2	¼ inch of tiny earthworm		
tubifex or blood worms and/or			enough to cover ½ area of a dime		
raw chopped beef or meat and fish-flavored dog or cat food	½ teaspoon	½ teaspoon			
fresh fruit and vegetables		¼ leaf lettuce or 6–10 berries or 1–2 slices peach, apple, tomato, melon or 1 tablespoon corn, peas, beans			
dry ant eggs, insects, or other commercial turtle food			1 small pinch		
water	always available at room temperature; should be ample for swimming and submersion				
	¾ of container	large enough for shell	half to ¾ of container		

Food and Water Plants (for Fish)	**Goldfish**	**Guppies**
Daily		
dry commercial food	1 small pinch	1 very small pinch; medium size food for adults; fine size food for babies
Twice a week		
shrimp—dry—or another kind of dry fish food	4 shrimp pellets or 1 small pinch	dry shrimp food or other dry food: 1 very small pinch
Two or three times a week		
tubifex worms	enough to cover ½ area of a dime	enough to cover ⅛ area of a dime
Add enough "conditioned" water to keep tank at required level	allow one gallon per inch of fish; add water of same temperature as that in tank—at least 65°F	all ¼–½ gallon per adult fish; add water of same temperature as that in tank—70°–80°F
Plants:		
cabomba, anarcharis, etc.	should always be available	

	Newts	**Frogs**
Daily		
small earthworms or mealworms	1–2 worms	2–3 worms
or		
tubifex worms	enough to cover ½ area of a dime	enough to cover ¾ area of a dime
or		
raw chopped beef	enough to cover a dime	enough to cover a dime
water	should always be available at same temperature as that in tank or at room temperature	

(Reprinted from Science and Children *(1965) with permission from the National Science Teachers Association, 1742 Connecticut Avenue, Washington, D.C. 20009, Pratt, G.K. "How to . . . care for living things in the classroom.")*

Note: Page number in **bold type** refer to non-text materials.